AF643643

Kornelia Freitag,
Katharina Vester (Eds.)

Another Language

Transnational and Transatlantic American Studies

edited by

Mita Banerjee (Siegen)
Kornelia Freitag (Bochum)
Walter Grünzweig (Dortmund)
Randi Gunzenhäuser (Dortmund)
Wilfried Raussert (Bielefeld)
Michael Wala (Bochum)

Volume 8

LIT

ANOTHER LANGUAGE

Poetic Experiments in Britain and North America

edited by

Kornelia Freitag and Katharina Vester

LIT

Cover Picture: Keith Waldrop, Collage, Untitled

The conference *Another Language: Contemporary U.S. Poetic Experiment in a Changing World* (Bochum 2005) was funded by the German Research Foundation, the German Association of American Studies, the Association for Canadian Studies, and the Society of the Friends of the Ruhr-University Bochum.

Bibliographic information published by the Deutsche Nationalbibliothek
The Deutsche Nationalbibliothek lists this publication in the Deutsche Nationalbibliografie; detailed bibliographic data are available in the Internet at http://dnb.d-nb.de.

ISBN 978-3-8258-1210-2

A catalogue record for this book is available from the British Library

Verlagskontakt:
Fresnostr. 2 D-48159 Münster
Tel. +49 (0) 2 51/620 32 - 22 Fax +49 (0) 2 51/922 60 99
e-Mail: lit@lit-verlag.de http://www.lit-verlag.de

Auslieferung:
Deutschland/Schweiz: LIT Verlag Fresnostr. 2, D-48159 Münster
Tel. +49 (0) 2 51/620 32 - 22, Fax +49 (0) 2 51/922 60 99, e-Mail: vertrieb@lit-verlag.de

Österreich: Medienlogistik Pichler-ÖBZ GmbH & Co KG
IZ-NÖ, Süd, Straße 1, Objekt 34, A-2355 Wiener Neudorf
Tel. +43 (0) 2236/63 535-290, +43 (0) 2236/63 535 - 243, mlo@medien-logistik.at

Distributed in the UK by: Global Book Marketing, 99B Wallis Rd, London, E9 5LN
Phone: +44 (0) 20 8533 5800 – Fax: +44 (0) 1600 775 663
http://www.centralbooks.co.uk/html

Distributed in North America by:

Transaction Publishers
New Brunswick (U.S.A.) and London (U.K.)

Transaction Publishers
Rutgers University
35 Berrue Circle
Piscataway, NJ 08854

Phone: +1 (732) 445 - 2280
Fax: + 1 (732) 445 - 3138
for orders (U. S. only):
toll free (888) 999 - 6778
e-mail:
orders@transactionspub.com

Contents

Poetry

"Plaît, plait, plaint": Transnational Poetics

Poetry

Acknowledgements

We thank the poets for graciously contributing to this volume and acknowledge the following sources where their texts have previously been published.

Tony Lopez	"In Memory" from *Devolution*. Copyright (c) Tony Lopez, 2000. "Only More So." Copyright (c) Tony Lopez.
Karen Mac Cormack	"Twenty Eight" from "Implexures." Copyright (c) Karen Mac Cormack, 2008.
Steve McCaffery	"Canterbury Tales." Copyright (c) Steve McCaffery, 2008.
Deborah Meadows	*Itinerant Men*, San Francisco: Krupskaya Press, 2004. Copyright (c) Deborah Meadows.
Keith Waldrop	"Standard Candles" from *Analogies of Escape*, Providence, RI: Burning Deck, 1997. Copyright (c) Keith Waldrop.
Rosmarie Waldrop	"Impossible Object" from *Love, Like Pronouns*, Richmond, CA: Omnidawn, 2003. Copyright (c) Rosmarie Waldrop.

Introduction: Another Language

Kornelia Freitag

> ***here***
> ***the wind***
> ***will be tomorrow***
> *a constant disquisition*
> *into the secret of*
> *velocity*
> *while men grow small*
> *within their skin*
> *tongue tied*
> *into another language*
> Rosmarie Waldrop, *A Key Into the Language of America*

"Language isn't static, yet frequently readers appear to take false comfort in the illusion that it provides a *terra firma* of both grammar and meaning," observes poet Karen Mac Cormack in a recent article ("MUTUAL LABYRINTH" 109). She points out that innovative poets tend to disturb this mistaken notion of linguistic stability. Although she is referring specifically to techniques used by Susan Howe, Diane Ward, and Lisa Downe, Mac Cormack's observations could also serve to define one of the aims of contemporary linguistic experiment: it disturbs readers' "false comfort in the illusion" that language is nothing but a tool for understanding and navigating the world. Unsettling language draws attention to what is often thought to be just an instrument, a mere crutch to help us reach reality and truth. A foregrounding of language is accomplished in various ways but always by using poetic language very differently from what a reader might expect or, in Rosmarie Waldrop's memorable phrase, by experimenting with and creating "another language."

"Another Language" was the title of a conference in 2005 at Ruhr-Universität Bochum that brought together poets and critics from Belgium, Britain, Canada, Germany, and the U.S.A. to read and discuss contemporary experimental texts, their histories, and their poetics. This volume gathers the results of the exciting exchange of ideas, stimulating investigations, and enlightening reevaluations of the general and some specific developments of the field. Much room was given to the discussion of the complex relation and interaction between poetry and other discourses, in particular, science (both natural and computer science), philosophy, and politics. Moreover, the aesthetic ideology of linguistic experiment, its pretensions and accomplishments were intensively debated. Papers focussing on these topics are here collected under the heading "'The Language of Inquiry': Poetic Movements and Their Discontent."

Within the reappraisal of the field two further points of interest emerged. One was the observation and assessment of transnational developments in British and North American experimental texts. The section "'Plaît, plait, plaint': Transnational Poetics" includes papers that pay special attention to the workings of intertexts and ekphrasis that cross national and generic boundaries. In close readings the impact of transnational and transcultural influences on various poets' works is charted and their effects are carefully outlined.

While the focus on "Transnationalism" may not come as a surprise, given the current proliferation of the topic and a call for papers that specifically encouraged it, the number of papers devoted to Self/Subjectivity/Identity might raise some eyebrows. It indicates that these topics are not as passé in experimental writing as one might have thought. The analyses range from registering the cautious reaffirmation of subjectivity to its outright denial and/or the charting of its corporeal and external conditions. They are to be found under the heading "'The Words of Selves' Subjectivity and Language."

While the three section titles indicate important fields of the discussions at the conference, they do not cover the breadth and depth of the scholarly exchange at Bochum, and papers listed under one category are never confined to it, but often might have been listed as well in another. Of course contemporary experimental poetry – represented at the conference not only by literary-critical discussions but also by readings given by six poets – is even more category-defying than its theory. Hence, the poems that the participating poets graciously contributed to this volume are not subsumed under any one heading. Resonating with many of the concerns of the critics, if constantly transcending them, they are arranged between the sections that might (or might not) suggest some ways of reading them. One advantage of having the papers side by side with the poetry of – in the order of their appearance at the conference – Steve McCaffery, Karen Mac Cormack (Canada), Deborah Meadows, Rosmarie and Keith Waldrop (U.S.A.), and Tony Lopez (U.K.) is that selected and focussed readings of experimental poems are complemented *and* complicated by texts that are related to *and* go beyond the papers' scope.

Between McCaffery and Lopez, Mac Cormack and Rosmarie Waldrop, Meadows and Keith Waldrop, a range of highly diverse experiments with "another language" opens up.

Poetic Experiments in Britain and North America

In spite of their immense diversity, experimental poems are united, as indicated above, by shaking the apparent solidity of their main material – language. Yet saying this does not tell us much. *What* poets do with this 'common denominator,' and *how* they do it, not only differs greatly but in fact makes all the difference. In the remaining space of the introduction this will be briefly demonstrated with regard to poems by the contributing poets.

The discomfort of discovering that language is no *terra firma* is a big topic in experimental texts, as can be seen in Rosmarie Waldrop's *Reproduction of Profiles,* in which a thoroughly confused speaker admits

> I had inferred from pictures that the world was real and therefore paused, for who knows what will happen if we talk truth while climbing the stairs. In fact, I was afraid of following the picture to where it reaches right out into reality, laid against it like a ruler. I thought I would die if my name didn't touch me, or only with its very end, leaving the inside open to so many feelers like chance rain pouring down from the clouds. You laughed and told everybody that I had mistaken the Tower of Babel for Noah in his Drunkenness. (5)

When in a text linguistic reference is constantly sliding – here between philosophical abstraction and everyday activities – a reader might be puzzled. Yet in Waldrop's *Reproduction of Profiles* the astonishment of readers is put to very entertaining uses. While finding their own confusion partly mirrored in the speaker's, the readers can – unlike the speaker – quite easily detect the category mistakes s/he makes and can enjoy sliding on the skating rink of language Waldrop supplies. They may even pick up the quotes from Wittgenstein and Kafka, which are the 'building blocks' or 'source material' for the "*Reproduction*," and wonder how philosophy and literary post/modernism mix in this long prose poem.

Experimental writing does not lecture, neither *On Certainty* nor on its opposite, but it time and again engages with language's uncertain meanings – and readers' fixed sets of expectations. Keith Waldrop's speculative novel in verse with the mock-learned title *The Real Subject: Queries and Conjectures of Jacob Delafon – with Sample Poems* is another case in point:

> Jacob Delafon cannot remember where he read the warning
>
> KEEP OUT OF REACH OF CHILDREN
>
> but he has done his best always.

*

Jacob Delafon finds an old manuscript, torn, covered with mildew. The text begins, "We see clearly…"

The rest is illegible. (40)

Here, anecdote and aphorism illuminate what has been called the "indeterminacy of language" – without as much as mentioning the term.

Intense generic transgressions from (lyric) poetry into other discourses – as in Keith Waldrop's cross between novel, poem, and philosophical speculations; or Rosmarie Waldrop's prose-poetical philosophy of language – are further markers of contemporary linguistic experiments. Karen Mac Cormack, employing rule generated procedures, created her poetry series *At Issue* by writing through women's magazines and women's health periodicals. The language of self-help advice and household instruction appears strangely detached yet familiar, silly yet dangerously effective when assembled in a series of poems entitled "§elf 1-4," "§elf Fashion," and "§elf Prevention." "§elf 2" concludes

performancewear recruited common transitions
to experience emergency you *must* check in with any possible crises
out there regardless of the type
provides a mid-afternoon play aroma or expressway size
and shape bandages at any moment
reckless might begin to say there's research to alleviate
splash on consolidation per tablespoon alongside other words (57)

The words of fashion, cooking, health advice … all unite in the fabrication of some "§elf" [a.k.a. "Self"] – the (found) typo already indicating that something is askew in this time-honored entity.

As Rosmarie and Keith Waldrop and Karen Mac Cormack stress the "materiality of language" by intricate textual arrangements, collage, writing through and other defamiliarizing poetic means, Steve McCaffery has experimented with a number of techniques to "further insist on that materiality [that] inevitably contests the status of language as bearer of uncontaminated meaning(s)," as he has put it in his analyses of poet Bill Bissett's texts (*North of Intention* 105). McCaffery has never restricted himself to the written text but used sound poetry, visual collage, erasure, and overlay to startle readers into thinking. And this page from "Four Versions of Pound's 'In a Station of the Metro'" (*Seven Pages Missing* 378; fig. 1) is clearly contributing to his aim to approach writing and the written text in terms of Bataile's general economy and Barthes's pleasure of the text (*North of Intention* 201-202).

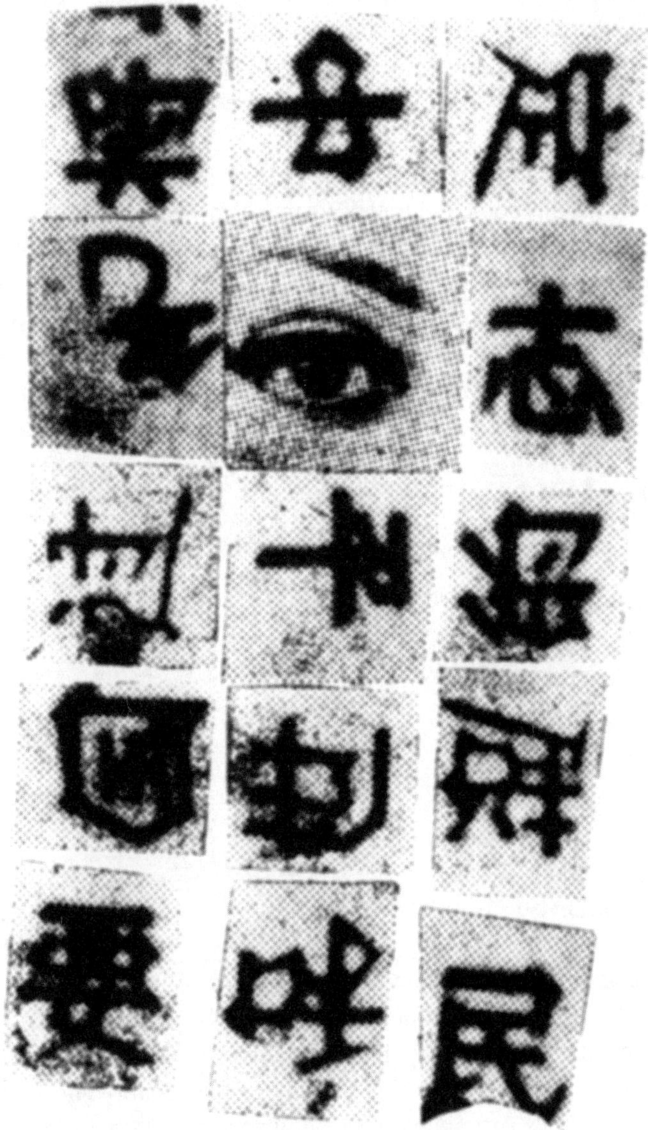

Fig. 1. Page from Steve McCaffery's "Four Versions of Pound's 'In a Station of the Metro.'"

The page playfully calls up and alludes to the inaugural poem of imagism, the effort to emulate painting in writing, the modernist fascination with vision, the Orientalist idea of the Chinese language, etc. etc. etc. It 'translates' Pound's words into pictures and in doing so, it discovers (like every good translation) and produces (like every good poem) all kinds of excess meaning.

Deborah Meadows as well starts from a U.S. 'classic' when she writes-through and overwrites Herman Melville's *Moby Dick* in a still ongoing project that works through the book's chapters to make them her own. She is also concerned with the overdetermination of texts. "What happens," she asks, "in the 19th century, a century of revolution breaking out all over, when the urge to revolution is repressed? . . . I ask, might a reading- and writing-through move toward a 'general economy' of excess?" ("Here Comes Everybody" n. pag.). The beginning of "Chapter 50," Melville's "Ahab's Boat and Crew – Fedallah," reads in her new version of it:

> Never kneel.
>
> Safety of captain, a difficult goal.
>
> Five extra men, so a discursus
> on racial Asia.
>
> Cutting the groove isn't
> the heart of the matter,
>   isn't the heart.
>
> No one wants it published.
>   Hints aren't sure things, so
> play to that doubt. Go fish.
> (*Itinerant Men* 49)

As this enumeration of negations and expressions of doubt indicates, the *Itinerant Men* of the title are moving in a universe dictated by oppression and insecurity. Yet at the same time their indeterminate situation – "Hints aren't sure things" – seems to represent a chance. They may "Play to that doubt" and "Go fish[ing]" for different experiences very much as Meadows "plays" with the text and "fishes" for different meanings.

In comparison to the extension, refinement, or radicalization of techniques inherited by modernism demonstrated in the poems by the North American poets, the British poet Tony Lopez seems to come from the opposite direction when he uses the traditional form of a sonnet sequence in his recent *False Memory*. Yet while the opening text does have 14 lines like the following 109 poems and while it does start out in iambs, a quick glance at it shows that Lopez, like his North

American fellow poets, is far from advocating a nostalgic and formalist return to the lyricism and symmetry of Renaissance poetry.

> Corneal Erosion
> And I don't see how we can win. The first faint
> Intermittent soundings of the sirens may be ignored
> Just as the slogans come through unpracticed speech.
> In Arcadia, when I was there, I did not see hammering stone
> But you should vacate the building when you hear
> A continuous note. It is best to move away –
> Best to pay bills by direct debit and avoid offices.
> Water bombs, I hear, are great fun and completely harmless. (1)

The effect of this sonnet's octave depends upon the gradual "erosion" (mark the title pun) of the elegiac mode that is called up by the dramatic opening statement – "And I don't see how we can win" (line 1) – in connection to the reference to "soundings of the sirens" (line 2). In line 5 the apparent high poetic register turns into a matter-of-fact announcement to "vacate [a] building," the sirens are, apparently, a mere technical alarm system. Yet even so, the opening warning strangely lingers, its meaning now extended from classicism and poetry to life and technocratic language at the turn of the millennium. As it turns out, the sonnet structure may be used in ways comparable to collage, overlay, and writing-through, in order to unsettle readers' "false comfort in the . . . *terra firma* of both grammar and meaning" and devise *Another Language*.

Works Cited

Mac Cormack, Karen. *At Issue*. Toronto: Coach House, 2001.

—. "MUTUAL LABYRINTH: a Proposal of Exchange." *Architectures of Poetry*. Ed. María Eugenia Díaz Sánchez and Craig Douglas Dworkin. Amsterdam: Rodopi, 2004. 109-118.

McCaffery, Steve. *North of Intention: Critical Writings 1973-1986*. New York: Roof Books, 2000.

—. *Seven Pages Missing, Volume One: Selected Texts 1969-1999*. Toronto: Coach House, 2001.

Meadows, Deborah. "Deborah Meadows." *Here Comes Everybody: Writers on Writing*. Tuesday Jan. 18th, 2005. http://www.inblogs.net/herecomeseverybody/2005/01/photo-credit-courtney-gregg-deborah.html. 15 October 2006.

—. *Itinerant Men*. San Francisco: Krupskaya, 2004.

Lopez, Tony. *False Memory*. Cambridge, U.K.: Salt Publishing. 2003.

Waldrop, Keith. *The Real Subject: Queries and Conjectures of Jacob Delafon – with Sample Poems*. Richmond, Cal.: Omnidawn, 2004.
Waldrop, Rosmarie. *A Key Into the Language of America*. New Directions, 1994.
—. *The Reproduction of Profiles*. New York: New Directions, 1987.

Poetry

IN MEMORY

Tony Lopez

I missed it. So much did they make of this news,
Jean Tension and Steve Fray on *Terpsichordia*,
Precisely the tone we were looking for.
You hand over two month's salary for a word –
Here's one coming through now: Allen Ginsberg,
A cramped hotel room in the late sixties,

Black sticky opium. Nobody at home.
The numbers going sideways are train times –
"*Melancholia* has a plastic core". You know
It's funding that makes us aspirational:
External validation and review.
Where are you now Allen Ginsberg? Who is pumping

Your harmonium? Elgar Alien Pcoet?
We speed into the tunnel expressway
But can't read the graffiti, Allen Ginsberg,
Your senior conductor speaking. Formica Zen
Always being torn down and rebuilt, for what?
Not some future perfection: everyone does it.

"Anyone can write" you told John Drew. You, a man
Who cared to know what happened and made poetry
Without hope of any hope but what is constructed
Herein. Part-exchange on detached homes and yellow
Silence of three months. Who cares whether any of this
Is happening? Allen Ginsberg, you can do it!

You can find the brand name guru and holy ghost,
As we go past the gas works, a tongue in your ear.
Ribbons of scrubland by railway lines and razor wire –
A new lead on the free state. We have yet to make it,
Allen Ginsberg. I'm at Alexandra Palace.
What thoughts I have of you just now, what fantasies:

Of deluxe sentiment and men in tights,
With hiking boots and hanging baskets put forth,
An ivy-leafed geranium. Allen Ginsberg,
Faintest touch of lips on the big name
Of your generation. My heart skips a beat
At the speed-up through hypertext to real time.

What difference does it make if you're getting
The best head you ever had, Allen Ginsberg? Muggers
Snatch a few dollars but leave your manuscripts
So you go down on your knees in a bio-pic
We're currently developing. Imagine that:
Starving, Hysterical, Naked Productions plc,

The best minds of our generation. Can you
See it? Where is the expiry date printed
On these verses by Allen Ginsberg, Gent, BL?
Before Language: little black and white books
Passed round in school, real songs of insolence.
This is Bill speaking on Thursday at nine, your time.

Allen Ginsberg, the very name is like a phone
Ringing in a train. And because you'll be awake,
The doctor will be able to talk to you throughout.
These faint echoes of Moloch, Sammy, patch me through:
Mohawk, Motown, Mohican, Motivator,
Who's fixing your juice in the hereafter?

Everyone's a little bit heterosexual,
Now that planning is making a comeback
In the upright position. Allen Ginsberg,
The photograph reproduced on page seventeen,
Sometimes a curly shepherd lad, should be a
Vertical image, head down, facing pastures new.

Gordon's London Dry or *Tanqueray* pink gin
Ought to be the drink we toast your memory in.
Were you able to raise that conference call
Allen Ginsberg? Are you rotting in Manhattan?
Or cast upon the Hudson river to fade away?
Where are those howling verses that used to be?

Allen Ginsberg, what peaches and penumbras!
What price bananas and sunflower sutras?
Singing a Blake song, chanting mescaline dreams!
Setting your poems in the supermarket
Of eternity! Re-inventing prophecy!
I'll see you later, Allen Ginsberg, wait for me.

From ONLY MORE SO

Tony Lopez

IF A BODY lives, the eyes will be unavoidably filled with meaning and expressiveness. Niche construction is the process by which organisms, through their own actions, modify their environment. The addition of nutrients to soils invariably leads to a loss of plant diversity. The tape shows a fox being chased by hounds, and riders going along, making no effort to stop the dogs. A house with the ground floor boards and joists pulled up and burnt in the yard, new wires threaded all through the building. Companies must pay plant workers for the time it takes to change into protective clothing and safety gear and walk to their work stations. Looking out from a high window far above the street. Little black ants were walking in lines, in and out of bread rolls on the table surface, and down table legs onto the floor. We filmed image by image: it took two weeks. Fortunately, terms such as 'step' and 'stride' can be applied to animals with any number of legs. This confirms that Al-Sayyid Bedouin Sign Language (ABSL) is a local invention, free of outside influences. The butcherbird uses the twelve-note scale to invent melodies. It has a feeling of history and belonging, and it can locate itself both now and in the past. Small initial differences become magnified as the embryo develops and DNA is more fully expressed. A dog does this without a theory of emotion. Angry people in driving simulators had fifty percent fewer accidents when software soothed them with a calm voice. Cloud density, if it can be linked with algal growth on the ocean surfaces, can be shown to have as large an effect on global climate as the burning of fossil fuels and the production of greenhouse gases. Composition adds one unit of processing load at the same point where it interferes with inferencing. A certain specified person needs to be remembered by another or by anyone. I know both these men personally, and I am of the opinion that this letter is an authentic document. In spite of its small size, a ghetto, placed in the middle of a metropolis, invariably created traffic problems: in Warsaw, trolley lines had to be rerouted. Writing appeared primarily in sanctuaries dedicated to female divinities. We assess above-ground data separately to enable the inclusion of published above-ground data for an additional ten large trees. It wasn't only fear that I felt for my father. Beauty is now underfoot, wherever we take the trouble to look, this is a recent discovery. Here we report on a solid and quantitative assessment of human travelling statistics by analysing the circulation of banknotes in the United States. The piccolo, trombone and piano enter first, playing their lines in a brilliant, vulgar manner. After 1973 there were no flags to rally round. The events take place during a dinner party given by a *nouveau riche* couple. A small manufactured cheap article for personal or household adornment. A metaphysical entity opposed to and devoid of being. What are angels doing in the human Astral body? I ran out of the cellar towards the Nevsky Prospect, it was misty on the street and beginning to get light. The cross is inscribed in the spool's terminal circle and occupies just one quadrant. Elephants got out safely, by breathing through their trunks, air close to ground level. Something offered for consideration or acceptance. The relationship between the object and person is designated by a proper name. It is a manuscript written on linen with a brush. The hormone cortisol is known to inhibit memory retrieval. Something happened in that moment which I found both incomprehensible and dreadful; my world collapsed around me. The image is surely manipulative but it is being used for charitable purposes. So far as Cage is concerned, form and content are quite separate. Google has my biography. At one stage in the story, three young couples climb a mountain and see a glorious sunset. Humans have the capacity to empathise with the pain of others, but we don't empathise in all circumstances. The entrance often seems to be preceded by a small portico. The silver-black of the graphite is reminiscent of monochrome photography. What links the two spheres are the reference notes, which can exert their own influence over several passages. A young male, who had lived in captivity, defended the carcass of an old bull elephant against hyenas and other carrion-eaters for three days and nights. Chance followed me everywhere like a terrible nightmare. When petitioners had been dispersed, filming began. The alleged attack on Iraqi youths was confirmed in video evidence. Rolling out initially on a voluntary basis. Surrounded on all sides by enterocytes, which close over the top, sometimes creating a surface depression. The melody itself is never exposed, but is simply a frame for what must appear to be a series of improvisations.

IN WARSAW the sale of armbands became a regular business. They had images that were windows into the world of spirit. This is the first empirical evidence for such an ambivalent process in nature. Stem cell clones grew in size with increasing time after heat shock and were surprisingly common. She has prepared for her big day by learning to drive, shop in a supermarket, and buy furniture from a catalogue. No one yet knows what is the optimum number for the human species. A beauty contest for HIV positive women would get coverage. Laura is strangely successful at bringing out the motivation to exercise. It is a pure non-intellectual substance heard by ear and resounding within the throat and heart. We can dream of a return to paradise. British Gas lost two million customers in 2005. It had to be a small town in Germany. Two non-fitting gold fragments with inscriptions have come down to us. Michael's father spent a long while with his head resting against the wall, eyes closed, quietly singing a tune. The form is determined, content hit upon by accident. A life sentence. A person who is merely demonstrating, experiences an entirely different psychological state from one who performs for an audience. When they find a dead elephant, their response is shock and awe. Air cools as it spirals out of a hurricane. For the sake of uniformity, Greiser ordered that all Jews in his Reichsgau wear a four-inch yellow star sewed on the front and back of their clothes. Human babies, whose mothers are given betamethazone, show signs of hyperactivity, as well as growing more slowly. My eleven-o-clock appointment is at the bank. Readers are required to keep books clean; they are not to turn down or stain the leaves, and are requested to report any damage or imperfection in the books they receive. Semicircular arches of undressed local stone frame either end of the passageway admitting both vehicles and pedestrians. When you become the victim of unprovoked violence it leaves you dispirited and angry. There have been reports of stranded northern bottlenose whales as early as 1800, before sonar and before noise pollution. These findings suggest that plants and animals follow different metabolic scaling relations, driven by distinct mechanisms. My legs seemed to be full of ants. And besides, I had particular secret places of my own in the woods, where I used to retire by myself; and used to be from time to time much affected. This music was to me the destruction of all individuality and imagination, for the imagination can work only through memory. Images depict human bodies as fuzzy heat sources floating in an abstract clear medium onto which everything solid – walls, furniture, objects – has been melted. Each of us was craving someone left at home. Next morning before the dance, dressed in a sacred manner, I went among the people standing around that withered tree. This strategy was achieved by a complete inversion of urban syntax. It was only later that Zimmerman equated his use of quotation with collage in art, his model being Kurt Schwitters, who assembled his works from discarded materials such as tram tickets, old shoe soles, feathers and dishcloths. The fully developed budding virion contains a set of eight rod-like structures. I was well versed in the ideas of historical materialism. We were displaced people who, in the wake of disaster, had changed language, our name made this clear. A swarm is supposed to induce simultaneous actions, but these actions are not dependent on each other. We were butchered by those merciless heathen, standing amazed, with the blood running down to our heels. The economy of the statement, and its tiny hint of duress, deflects questions of politics. Any list of examples will seem absurd. For Blanqui the barricade and the mouse hole were complementary elements employed for the protection of self-governing urban enclaves. This was not like my great vision, and I just went on working in the store. You might want to know who, if anyone, is speaking to whom. The wagons on the mountain pass are labelled BALKAN SOBRANIE TOBACCO. The use of the sentence in immigration. I fell back into my body, and as I did this heard voices all around and above me, and I was sitting on the ground. This is what they all do. Invisibly but unmistakably, the mask of discredit hovers over the left hand column, while the right hand column reads like a litany of all that is manifestly desirable. It is not necessary to know them all. The fascism theorised by Nietzsche and Heidegger became a philosophical critique deployed to undermine humanism and democracy. Ocean waters boiled away and were lost to space as temperatures increased beyond those that could support life. Smaller groups appeared on the coastline or lakeshores. Being is imagined with regard to others.

From IMPLEXURES

Karen Mac Cormack

TWENTY-EIGHT

historical letters 21

If we suppose some particle of time which could not be divided into a smaller particle, that alone deserves to be called the present. Yet it flies in so headlong a way out of the future and into the past that no slightest moment of rest can reach itself out in pause. If it paused, its earlier part could be divided from its later. Thus the present has no length.

– Saint Augustine

* coined by Voltaire as euphemism for *cul de sac*

no sides but many edges
to this separation itself a part
of immediacy as preference
heart and eye agree on
the ells, miles, kilometres distend
intention next to recollection
a longing (indeed) presents
newly combined inflections
to consider, move towards
without reaching *absence*
no terminus within
my "here" or your 'there'
seems an impasse*
to our *now*

historical letters 22

An ell taken out of London is undone. – William Blake
An 'L' taken out of London is 'ondon'. – Karen Mac Cormack

Edward Law, Earl of Ellenborough, was Mary Christian's grandson; his father Baron Ellenborough became Chief Justice of England. In 1824 the second Lord Ellenborough met the woman who was to become his second wife, Jane Digby, "beautiful as the dawn," eventually to divorce her in 1830 ("...there was in her amours in courts and castle and Arab tents all the prodigality of bad art"). At the age of seventy-five Edward Law introduced himself to Emily Christian, newly married to Henry and recently returned from their honeymoon. In his "charming" note he claimed cousinship and invited the couple to come to dine at Southam-de-la-Bere, the estate he'd purchased in 1831. The "fact" that two of his illegitimate children were happened upon unexpectedly after dinner provoked the twenty-year-old Emily to adhere to 1865 censure and "never accept an invitation from Southam again." Jane Digby's further adventures included marrying Medjuel el Mezrab, a tribal prince twenty years her junior (at which point her family disowned her). Only her death ended their twenty-five years of nomadic adventures and her life inspired several novels, including Balzac's *Lily of the Valley,* whereas Edward Law, though perceived as scandalous by Victorian standards (if not by those of the Regency), is perhaps less extraordinary than his former wife, but this thread is frayed by disassociation.

Wren's churches in London and the multiple facts and instances of bombs as we enter each century's space in "our" time with the information implying that love is a right brain concern involving dopamine, and sex that of the left. Instance of re-encountering another literary application of the word "implexures" (via anatomy and architecture) is offered by Glyn Pursglove's reference to Jane Barker's 1688 "Farewell to Poetry":

> "The Fretwork, Muscles, Arteries and Veins,
> With their Implexures, and how from the Brains
> The Nerves descend; and how they do dispence
> To ev'ry Member, Motive's Pow'r and Sence;"

itself a revisiting of her same poem included in the anthology *Kissing the Rod.*

> Knowledge of the remarking of instance
> closed eyes *when* touches this sound
> and another variant again
> that so-to sound accompanying *if* (sound)

bites the beginning of depth
rendered measure musical
unstilled channels nuance to frame's visual
perhaps as condition not instance
reverberates to part when parcelled particular
juxtapose stream inundate category
cauterized apprehension as in
situ, scene, some time sounds in
perspectives skew
clavicle and score separate account for
the spilling when *nothing* is full

The bell (another) sounding from childhood alerts a neighbourhood to sharpening possibilities. These elderly men (often wearing a cap, or hat) appeared on a regular basis on the diverse streets from hopscotch to hide-and-seek days through double-dutch, sometimes badminton, to the afternoons of protest marches, wheeling their contraptions behind them to the announcement of the bell. Women would emerge from houses and apartments with varying scissors and knives for work to commence on the spot. Sometimes the bell swung uninterruptedly – away to some other locale, but it is not heard in these days of serial apocalypse, "Sub Junction."

Lives as a series of thermal instances in accordance with space the aperture of experience not always a smooth fit and so the sense of the person or time or circumstance not being "right" for one another and the experience is drawn upon as memory perhaps reminder. The durées of exquisite intensity are the moments when the alignment is so precise that persons, place, time, act combine in a perfect fit of increasing lucidity where the boundaries of each dissolve into interconnection.

Divan – Turkish divan, Persian diwan, divan, whence also Italian divano, Spanish, Portugese, French divan. Originally bundle of written sheets, collection of poems, eg. the Divan i Hafiz, a collection of documents, register, office of accounts, custom-house, council chamber, cushioned seat, smoking-room, cigar shop, a curious chain of meanings. (From Arabic comes Italian dogana, French douane, custom house.)

Might have comprised your life relies on my memory no capsule any antidote? Or the introduction to other limit(s), another plural designation. The correspondence is finite if not the number of possible plural perusals.

... returned yesterday from the trail. We went 25 miles, rested and turned around. Left Aug. 1, arrived at Bamfield (Vancouver Island) where it begins. Camped at Michigan Creek, Klanawa River, Tsusiat Falls, Cheewat River. At the Cheewat we had crab which we caught and cooked. Saw a family of 6 otters, 2 herons, hummingbirds, ducks & a bear.

The trip was hard. I had a 40 lb. pack. Averaged 6 miles a day. We stayed at the Falls & Cheewat 2 1/2 days (each). These were our rest stops. It is a beautiful place, I learned a lot.

I'm far stronger than I imagined & am now even more so. We had lots of climbing to do. At one point we scrambled up a cliff covered with thick bush at a 90° angle. Many of the log bridges are deteriorating & it's a bit dangerous. The trail is now the concern of the B.C. gov't. so they're fixing it up ... The ferry from Nanaimo to Horseshoe Bay was nice.
(Vancouver, Canada, 11 Aug. 74)

"Pepper, a most important article ... played a considerable part in the history of our commerce. By the eleventh century there was a guild of pepperers, who later, through their growing importance as importers of sugar and spice, became the grocers ... Vegetables are rarely included in the early MSS., except such as were used in salads. A fourteenth century 'salat' includes parsley, sage, garlic, leeks, borage, mint, peony, fennel and other herbs. The ingredients are to be washed and picked clean '... myng him wel with rawe oile, lay on vynegr and salt and sue it forth'."

If a daughter but not a sister so a niece if when mother there are cousins yes so clearly, only bare-bones correspondence yearly – mathelapy: a combination of mathematics and telepathy, but no matter how many times one multiplies 1 by itself, the result is always 1, which can be claimed of no other number.

1	*	12	*	10
15	*	2	*	4
8	*	5	*	3

(Multiplication "magic square" making 120 in both directions) Such is seldom freely evoked in any relation, familial or otherwise empathetic. Embrace equivalent to sense of being filled with scent of lilac-infused air on the underside of an afternoon June's caress. The lips are full, blossoms blown. Such are these sentences that risk banality in the condition of poetry punctuation receives attention or re-lives it plus or minus what's being said.

“The Language of Inquiry”: Poetic Movements and Their Discontents

Junk DNA in Recent American Poetry

Peter Middleton

The discovery of the double helix structure of DNA in the chromosomes of all living cells by James Watson and Francis Crick in 1953 confirmed the speculation that DNA acted like a code. One of four possible molecules appears at each point on a long chain and three of these will specify the creation of a specific amino acid, of which there are just twenty that together provide all the building blocks for the proteins out of which organisms are made. Actual details of the code whereby the base triplets are instigators of amino acids were worked out between 1961 and 1966, and by the seventies the idea that genes consisted of long sequences of code was well established. A whole linguistics of cell architecture grew up. It came as a shock to scientists therefore to discover in 1977 that this code was interrupted by nonsense or "junk" DNA as it became known. Between the exons, or coding sequences that would determine the production of proteins, were introns, or non-coding sequences. The cellular DNA contained a mixture of message and word salad so that a chromosome looked like an avant-garde text (cf. Morange, Kay, Watson). Garbage could apparently be found everywhere, in the cell and in works of art. Or were we being hasty, as some scientists would later suggest, were we calling these unintelligible sequences junk simply because we didn't know what their function was?

How Molecular Biology Became a Science of Language

What sort of significance did the apparently meaningless passages of DNA have, and how should we read them? These were the kind of textual puzzles that were becoming familiar to readers of a network of poets whose work was just then becoming visible, the Language Poets. Their poetry also operated on the borders of intelligibility, offering a myriad of different modes of textuality but almost always such that broken syllables, disjunctive phrasing, parataxis, sentences that were non-sequiturs, and inferential resistance, elicited uncertainty as to where meaningfulness could be found or constructed.

Part of the story of how it became possible to think of a chromosome as an avant-garde text is brilliantly told by the historian of science Lily E. Kay in her study *Who Wrote the Book of Life?* Scientists attempting to understand the genetic powers of the cell had already begun to suggest that it was a code of some kind even before the discovery of the make-up of DNA from just three bases arranged in triplets gave further encouragement to this idea. Kay argues that the combination of the cybernetic theory of information and the achievements of cryptanalysis during World War Two gave enormous impetus to this interpretation. The "cultural poetics of science" has become linguistic, and with far-reaching implications: "though remarkably compelling and productive as analogies, 'information,' 'language,' 'code,' 'message,' and 'text' have been taken as ontologies" (3). Frances Crick was able to establish the "central dogma" (later proven wrong) that DNA could determine the precise manufacture of specific proteins in the cell, but no protein could act in the opposite direction and alter the DNA. In Crick's words, "once 'information' has passed into protein it *cannot get out again*" (174). For those unfamiliar with this history I should underline that Kay is explaining a history in which most molecular biologists see nothing strange. A recent history of the science brings out just how pervasive the idea has been. Michel Morange in *A History of Molecular Biology* gives an account of the discovery of the introns that quite unself-consciously describes it in terms of textuality: "the existence of interrupted genes was completely unexpected. Studies of bacteria had suggested that the genetic message was clear, well-punctuated, and economically written. In fact, it turned out to be long and complex" (206). It seemed that when DNA was doing its remarkable work, it somehow resulted in a splicing of the active sections of the genome together during the process of protein manufacture. The RNA that carries out the instructions of the DNA could apparently be cut and pasted.

Scientists had carried over an entire range of metaphors for the use of language, many of them central to modernist writing, not just as analogies but as descriptions of the actual ontological make-up of living organisms. What should writers interested in language and metaphor as foundations of social, political and imaginative life make of this?

The scientists showed no awareness that they might share cultural roots with the poets. The editors of a recent anthology of poems about science conclude their prefatory remarks by saying that "the traffic between science and art is, in any case, almost always one-way" (Riordan xiii). Poets are sometimes inspired by new scientific discoveries or suspicious of aggrandising intrusions into the traditional provinces of ethics, imagination or sensibility. Scientists mostly appear indifferent to poetry and never mention poetry as a contributor in their achievements. Poets and scientists rarely talk directly to one another. An exception of sorts will suggest reasons why.

J. H. Prynne, the British second wave modernist poet, has a reputation for writing complex, demanding, above all serious poems in which linguistic registers taken from a vast area of learning all mingle in startling ways, even with borrowings from specialist science journals. His book *Wound Response* uses the medical discourse of epidermal damage to reflect on other kinds of trauma. But about half way through his career, however, he wrote an extremely comic parody about a conference of biologists studying plant time, that reveals just how difficult it has become for poets and scientists to negotiate with each other. The mock conference report "The Plant-Time Manifold Manuscripts" openly parodies the grand claims of scientific research. The prose purports to be an attempt to summarise informally the debate at a conference of botanists working on the wonderful concept of the "willbeen function," a temporal process in legumes. He cites a sentence about DNA research in the 1960s: "Let us propose that at first the genetic code was in some way *read backwards* from protein to nucleic acid" (242). This reference to the "Central Dogma" then leads to the inference that plants can read time backwards too. Prynne's hilarious spoof shows how the scientific discourse is more fantastic, more prone to imaginative excess than poetry, even when the scientific language tries to conceals this: "Time-averaged protein tubes comprise the meshwork of willbeen functioning, held in semirigid array by double reverse backflow or 'dream membrane'" (238). There are many winks at the reader, and my favorite is this deadpan statement that appears to be a quantitative measure based on empirical research, but is actually an implicit judgement on the scientists: "The proportion of Reason to Matter is not the same in all the regions of the Universe, yet the colloid field has shielded us from the free transfinite stream" (242). Prynne's eccentric pastiche is a symptom of a complex relation between poets and scientists in the nineteen seventies. The poets are there at the conference listening in, fascinated by the radical ideas about origins, space, time, and organisms, that are fermenting among the scientists, and the poets are also acutely aware of the linguistic excesses of the discursive economy and sceptical, deeply sceptical, about the scientific drive to knowledge. The scientists though are even more sceptical about the poets and this would provoke many of them to push hard against the marginalization of their cultural work by the sciences.

Comparing the Sentences of Poets and Scientists

About ten years after the advent of Language Writing, Ron Silliman was working hard to compile its first substantial anthology, *In the American Tree* (1986), conscious of the difficulty of presenting a coherent choice of poets and poems without offending the poets whose work he had either chosen (or omitted) by claiming a misleading degree of formal similarity and shared principles. The poets are not unified by any poetic formalism or single poetic theory, Silliman insists in his preface. Conscious of the risk of saying that they are united only in their contemporaneity, he concedes that the poets are committed to "new methods that might lead to a more open and useful investigation, hopefully to renew verse itself" (*American Tree* xvi), a transformation that was historically just as important as the contemporaneous "pluralization of American writing" (xxi) by women and African Americans. Silliman's comparison of Language Writing to a coeval literary enfranchisement gives it the status of a major literary event as well as endowing it with a libertarian aesthetic. Hindsight makes this claim appear inflated. Why can these Language Writers be considered a constellation distinct from other contemporaries if they don't unite around styles, ideologies, aesthetics or formalist commitments (if it is not a movement in other words)? Silliman doesn't offer the explanation that we might be expecting, that these poets recognise that poetry comes under the hegemony of the sign.

The Language Writers, according to Silliman, share "a perception as to what the issues might be" (xix), and though talking about "issues" would ordinarily lead us to expect a political statement of the issues to follow and Silliman himself was very much an activist as well as a socialist policy wonk, this is not quite what he has in mind in the preface. The issues sound much wider: "The nature of reality. The nature of the individual. The function of language in the constitution of either realm. The nature of meaning. The substantiality of language. The shape and value of literature itself. The function of method. The relation between writer and reader" (xix). The shared preoccupations he lists might be better called *scientific* than political or aesthetic, as the repeated noun "nature" is meant to intimate. With a "more open and useful investigation," more open presumably than that practised by other contemporaries, this poetry will be better able to research these issues; this is a poetry that shares with science an interest in the nature of the material world, the human body and mind, and indeed it is an art that actually aspires to extend the epistemic range of scientific research to new areas such as the study of literary textuality. The new poets are united by a commitment to inquiry based on a commitment to truthfulness in observation and analysis, and therefore emulate their scientist contemporaries. These poets aim to look behind the appearances and dissmimulations of the world just as scientists do, and try to comprehend what Silliman calls the "opacity, density, otherness, challenge and relevance persons find in the 'real' world" (xvi).

Silliman's own practice as a poet might seem at first sight at odds with his claims for the Language Writers. Isn't he the poet of the autobiographical new sentence, the paratactic notations of his journeys on the BART or the view from his window that he then transfers from his ever-present notebook and lays unit by unit into structures formed according to Fibonacci numbers or other exoskeletal devices? Here is a passage from *Tjanting*.

> Samoyed mixd with afghan, not what you might expect. Something has been eating that leaf. Lushhead. In Chomsky, generative means you cld create an American military base in the mid-east & call it a state. A buzz in the string as you plunk it. Context constitutes. Harmonicum. Blotchy nose. What then? A ground of puddles splashing back. In the sky clouds come & go. Let's start from scratch, she said, meaning scabs. Old porridge cakes on the glass wall of the bowl. In love, but not in sync. Cat will follow open tin of tuna about the room. I can no longer imagine painting. Disembodied voices using colord plastic boxes, called telephones, to negotiate their lives. Until it blossomd (prematurely) I had not seen the plum tree in that yard. This pen leaves a thinner line. Thin lines in leaves demand our respect. How that cloud sponges the sun's light. Wire cart to drag to the market. Shelling heedless prawns with our fingers. Cat laps up rainwater from saucer. Four out of five cosmic rays from outer space are mu-mesons. A barrel of bottles spills into a dumpster. White-orange rock with veins of green. Many shades of blue in the sky. Gull raises wings & the wind lifts it up. Looking in the window I see my kitchen, but my reflection also & the world where it sits. Enjoys bashing spiders. We never fully unpackd & live that way months after. I can hear "them" buzzing the prospective tenants in. Onionskin wall perfects communication of salsa. Sentence after sentence. Language is memory not image. 3 dogs sit in the back of the pickup, motoring thru the park. (74-75)

Tjanting is a free verse poem set out on the page as if it were prose and its sentences were connected by latent inferential and narratological relations. A reader's eye and brain are disoriented by the missing bibliographical and conjunctive codes when reading these rapidly growing sets of sentences, sets paired according to Silliman in a dialectic of thesis and antithesis that projects class struggle across the page. Certain kernel sentences are repeated in slightly altered form, expanded or twisted into a new shape. As Lytle Shaw describes it:

> By using internal mutation, and shifts in contexts to question the self-evidence, the atomistic givenness of a citation, *Tjanting* reconstructs the intertextual moment not as a neutral semantic framework, but as the charged scene of textual production where importantly different versions of literary history, literary authority and interpretation come into being ... older sentences are recombined ... and new sentences are added. (Shaw 122)

Shaw's scientific metaphors are rhetorically apt: metaphors from physics ("charged," "atomistic") and from biology ("mutates," "kernels," "recombined"), but almost unnecessary. All the linguistic terms here, word, citation, sentence and so forth – were in regular use amongst biologists trying to understand DNA. As John Maynard Smith wrote in an article published in *Science* in 2000: "Transcription, translation, code, redundancy, synonymous, messenger, editing, proofreading, library – these are all technical terms in biology" (178). It is worth pondering the implications of this for the metaphorics of poetry written under the sign of genetics. Silliman's text can be read as a poetic analogue of a chromosome undergoing meiosis or fission because its poetics is saturated both by the aim to facture inquiry within the composition, and because even the linguistic terms now simulate the molecular biologists.

But just a minute, we don't usually hear such statements of poetics as formulations of scientific method, or emulations of science. In Silliman's historical narrative as in many other attempts to describe the rise of Language Writing we observe other historical factors such as the rise of poststructuralism in the academy, the dashing of libertarian political hopes in the nineteen-seventies, the diversion of left wing radical movements into identity politics, and the rediscovery of occluded traditions of modernist experiment. This rise of Theory, its politics and its bringing back forgotten linguistically innovative writers of the turbulent decades around the First World War, have been taken to be sufficient to explain the remarkable magnetism this conjuncture had for poets. Language Writing gathered up many who had already developed styles of their own and encouraged them to abandon these for a portfolio of its signature modes of composition: prose poetry in unconnected sentences, aphoristic phrase units that do not integrate into larger semantic or syntactic units, extensive use of parataxis and catachresis, and the intensive hybridizing of heterogeneous linguistic registers. Poets relinquished the use of a distinctive voice, reliance on confessional authenticity and referentially anchored narrative or argument, in favour of a wide, inventive range of abstract constructions that fore-grounded their linguistic elements. It is hard to think of another poetry movement in American literary history that has had anything like the same rapid impact. Yet why should this particular linguistic turn be so compelling to poets in nineteen-seventies America, and what was wrong with the poetry of the previous generation that made it necessary to "renew verse?" Were the achievements of the "New American" poets, of such figures as John Ashbery, Robert Creeley, Robert Duncan, Frank O'Hara, Allen Ginsberg, Denise Levertov, Charles Olson, and others, really so stale by the mid seventies that continuing to work alongside those that had survived beyond the Sixties would stifle thought and invention? Despite saying that there was a need to "renew verse," Silliman actually singles out several of these poets for positive mention. What was the limitation of the earlier generation and why could Silliman articulate with such assurance a collective confidence about the new poetics?

I think that one compelling answer to these questions is indicated by the underlying assumptions about investigating the density and otherness of nature in all its forms set out in Silliman's preface. Poetry can be a form of open investigation or inquiry, and it can take on all the fields in which science operates and more, indeed poetry can emulate and perhaps overtake science if it adopts the right methods for investigating the myriad phenomena of the human universe. The question is then how to do this, how to find the right methods of inquiry, and given the prominence of scientific methods and their overwhelming legitimacy compared to those of humanist inquiry, one obvious place to go would be the leading science of the day: molecular biology. What therefore separates these new poets from their immediate predecessors is not a difference on the question of whether inquiry matters; what separates them, Silliman implies, is what they consider to be the best methods of inquiry. Post-structuralism's synthesis of ideology, the unconscious and language synchronized with the shift to a new dominant scientific paradigm.

A Short History of Modern Poetry and Science

The American modernist poet is a Scientific American, and for the past fifty years these poets have consistently read that magazine too. Charles Olson recommended to his Black Mountain students a particularly fine article on the working of the kidneys, and Robert Duncan actually cites the magazine in one of his poems. American identity has been closely bound up with the development of science that has been integral to military and economic success, an ordinary part of a high school education through the science fairs, and provided an ideal of meritocratic democracy for those fleeing persecution and dictatorship. From the nineteen-forties onward, leading intellectuals such as Robert K. Merton suggested that, in the words of the historian David A. Hollinger, "ordinary citizens would live by the code of the scientist" (158). This would mean, as the president of Harvard, James B. Conant, proposed, that people should aspire "to behave scientifically in social environments very different from the one in which science actually proceeds" (162). Maybe the Language Poets are heeding such sentiments?

Poets who flourished in the first half of the twentieth century frequently depict themselves and their poetry as scientific. The literary critic Douglas Bush suggests in his 1950 book *Science and English Poetry* that "All modern poetry has been conditioned by science, even those areas that seem farthest removed from it" (151). This is an ingenious way to explain the paradox of enthusiastic scientific aspirations in essays on poetics and reticence toward science in the poetic practices of high modernist poets. It is an argument homologous to the psychoanalytic account of unconscious resistance – the more one denies a desire or influence the more likely it is to be active in the unconscious. Bush cites as evidence the poetry of Hart Crane, W. H. Auden and somewhat surprisingly W. B. Yeats. Crane and Auden are obvious choices, they strive to write a poetry capable of staging even the newest theories and inventions in its metaphorical registers, but though they felt poetry couldn't resist the effects of science on society and knowledge this influence did not act unconsciously on their poetry. Crane's "Cape Hatteras" depicts a world in which airplanes, radio, power stations, explosive shells, and the vast architectures of the city and manufacturing industry have transformed the landscape that his presiding poetic deity, Walt Whitman, celebrated little more than half a century earlier, and asks: "tell me, Walt Whitman, if infinity / Be still the same as when you walked the beach" (86). It's a good question. Bush's argument for considering Yeats to have been conditioned by science – he "had little to say of science in his poetry, but his whole evolution and his whole body of writing were, like Lawrence's, a kind of answer to it" (158) – depends on the authority of the modern science of the unconscious, and attributes to science a power to affect the imagination that like the forces that drive evolution takes place beyond volition. Yeats's lack of explicit engagement with science is a motivated silence. Are the gyres negative images of quantum orbits?

Even the poets who explicitly identified with modern science in their public statements about poetry often seem far removed from science in their poetry. Ezra Pound begins the first chapter of his textbook on poetry, *ABC of Reading* (1934), saying, "we live in an age of science and abundance" (1), a statement that might have indicated that here was a poet who would investigate in his poetry the scale and influence of science on those activities of linguistic imagination and aesthetic treatment of feeling that were the preserve of poetry. It soon turns out that the abundance he has in mind is a somewhat specialised surfeit, an abundance of books, and that he is only interested in this consequence of new print technologies because it necessitates a renewal of critical judgement. Writers and critics should emulate good scientific practice. "The proper METHOD for studying poetry and good letters is the method of contemporary biologists, that is careful first-hand examination of the matter, and continual COMPARISON of one 'slide' or specimen with another" (1). The paradox of Pound's ambitious epistemological claims for poetry is that his own poetry is oddly devoid of direct references to science. In Canto 23 when he makes one of his rare references to a scientist, Madame Curie, and her reference to creating a "broulure" after six months of hard work, he undermines the seriousness of this by immediately saying "or some other scientist," and a few lines later he appears to sound like a typical hostile critic of useless research in science when he refers to researchers "Seeking doubtless the sex in bread-moulds" (*Cantos* 107).

The high modernist American poets exhibit ambivalence toward science in their poetry. During the past fifty years poets have continued to appeal to science in their poetics and yet still tend to steer away from directly scientific allusions, terminologies, domains, and histories in their poetry. Charles Olson begins his essay "Human Universe" by saying that "There are laws, that is to say, the human universe is as discoverable as that other" (53) and we should hear in this a strong parallel with physics, the science that was in the ascendant in the nineteen fifties when he wrote the essay. Government spending on physics research in nonprofit institutions reached a quarter of a billion dollars the following year (1952) and physicists earned considerably more than other scientists. In 1953 Olson, then Rector of Black Mountain College, sent a memo to his colleagues at Black Mountain College about ways in which the college might develop a research programme and compared himself as a poet to the new scientists: "I am, then, concerned as any scientist is, with penetrating the unknown (the difference is what unknown, the distinction ... between physis & psyche, between nature as outside & of experimentable substance, and nature as man is inside & only experimental by image)" ("A Letter" 31). What is not obvious here is that Olson is echoing a hagiographical essay in *Life* magazine on the physicist J. Robert Oppenheimer by the well-known science writer, Lincoln Barnett, who contrasts the scientist with, not the poet, but the mystic: "the world defined by the senses is simply a world of appearances; the world of reality lies hidden beneath the surface of things; and to this real world both the mystic and the scientist seek to penetrate by their separate disciplines" (55). Despite this identification with the man Philip Rieff called "the public image of genius," Olson himself makes little reference in his poems to physics or any of the natural sciences (the mention of the "monogene" is a rare exception).

Three decades later, the poet Lyn Hejinian talked in a brief note about her "romance with science's rigor, patience, thoroughness, speculative imagination" (24). The same romance with science's rigor is apparent in her recent collection of essays on poetry and poetics published under the title *The Language of Inquiry*, where she explains that her poetics is a poetics of inquiry, for which investigation, research, analysis, discovery, observation, reflection and other forms of intellectual curiosity are all relevant, as long as they recognize the primacy of the signifier. Her introductory essay carefully avoids prescriptive definitions of inquiry as it distinguishes *poetic* inquiry from something that sounds like the phenomenology of the earlier generation, as well as conventional natural science: "Poetry undertakes acknowledgement as a preservation of otherness – a notion that can be offered in a political, as well as an epistemological, context. This acknowledging is a process, not a definitive act; it is an inquiry, a thinking on ... The language of poetry is a language of inquiry, not the language of a genre. It is that language in which a writer (or reader) both perceives and is conscious of the perception" (2-3). This passage tries to allay any suspicion that such poetry relies on "the language of genre;" it is instead turned outwards to the contingent world as the sciences are, not inwards to the task of fulfilling a given heuristic.

However evident the work of inquiry is in her poetry – think of *Sight* or *Happily* – the vocabulary and frames of reference remain resolutely those of the world outside the laboratory. I could multiply similar examples, and contrast a few exceptions, like Chrisopher Dewdney, or Mei-mei Berssenbrugge's recent books like *Endocrinology* or Jena Osman's poetry, or step outside North America and consider the poetry of J. H. Prynne and Allen Fisher whose poetry is pervaded by scientific discourse.

If Poets Can Be Researchers Can They Be Scientific?

This history raises an important question. Are the modernist poets only representing themselves as scientists in their essays in order to be up to date and try to join the elite of experts whose voices are heard in the public sphere and in policy making, or does their emulation of science result in distinctive modes of investigating the world and consequent communicable theories or facts? I shall argue that poetic inquiry can be shown to yield tangible fruits and that this is one reason why we should heed the caution offered by Muriel Rukeyser in her *ars poetica*, *The Life of Poetry* (1950): "the trap is the use of the discoveries of science instead of the methods of science" (174). Poets need to pay close attention to new scientific work "to recognize the energies that are transferred between people when a poem is given and taken, to know the relationships in modern life that can make the next step, to see the tendencies in science which can indicate it, that is for the new poets" (183). Charles Olson, perhaps attracted by the argument that poets must keep abreast of science, borrowed this rhetoric for the essay "Projective Verse" that became a manifesto for the next generation of poets.

Charles Altieri has written one of the best articles on the relations between science and modernist poetry, and he also cautions against reading poems as exempla of current scientific theories. Historians of modern poetry should avoid, he says, trying to "force strong thematic analogies on to the work" (78) because the result of such historical contextualisation "within the parameters of modern science will end up reducing modernism to charming mystification." The poetry won't stand up alongside the rigorous understandings of science. Such caveats apply to trying to read Ron Silliman's New Sentence as a mode of recombinant poetics as much as looking for a quantum poetics or complementarity in projective verse. I differ from Altieri when it comes to his attempt to identify two legitimate ways in which poetics responds to modern science. He thinks the writers look for what he calls "thematic allegories" (78) on the one hand, and on the other, to the "promise of an experimental method that would replace allegorizing entirely by giving access to realities that are immediately present in their abstract elemental force and hence do not depend at all on speculative interpretation." Though it is certainly true that writers have been drawn to new ontological metaphors – the uncertainty principle, complementarity, Black Holes, the genetic code, and fractals all come to mind – what matters about their use is the degree to which they are understood or, as is often the case with the theory of Relativity that is just treated as a scientific mode of relativism, thought of as rewardingly productive metaphors. As to Altieri's idea that writers look to science for a direct knowledge of material reality unmediated by what he calls "speculative interpretation," I think there are few cases of this. Instead I will argue in the remainder of this paper that the conditioning, to use that old-fashioned term for ideological manipulation, the influence, or as I think it could more accurately be called, the active contest with the findings of scientific research, points to other formal and contextual practices by poets.

I shall only discuss three in this paper, though there are certainly more. The first is reductionism of both physics and molecular biology. This has already been mentioned in relation to Ron Silliman's poetics. Reductionism assumes that all material objects and organisms are constructed from a few basic constituents, and although there is considerable evidence that this view is wrong even in physics and biology, it remains a powerful and influential vision of the world. Reductionism makes it possible to talk of the "selfish gene" or to write, as one article on quarks in the *Scientific American* puts it, "the world we normally experience is composed almost entirely of one kind of lepton, the electron, and two kinds of quark" (Mistry 98). Reductionism of this kind has been a powerful generative idea for modernist poets. It is for instance in productive tension with a scepticism based on an appeal to everyday life in Silliman's *Tjanting* or Hejinian's *My Life*.

The second is the management of trust by the development of subtle means of indicating the intended degree of reliability of a proposition. The historian of science Steven Shapin ends his study of late seventeenth century science with some general observations on the modern scientific practice that emerged from those roots.

> Far from being less trusting than everday action, I want to suggest that there is a legitimate sense in which modern science is much *more* trusting ... scientists' practical capacity to advance knowledge, even skeptically to check over another's claim with a view to falsifying it, depends upon their ability to trust *almost everything else* about the scene in which they do their skepticism and the resources which permit skeptical activities to be carried through. The very power of science to hold knowledge as collective property *and* to focus doubt on bits of currently accepted knowledge is founded upon a degree and a quality of trust which are arguably unparalleled elsewhere in our culture. (417)

Science is a means of sharing out the tasks of investigation between large numbers of skilled, intelligent researchers, and providing the means for them to communicate their findings with great accuracy, especially the probability or tentativeness of their findings. Shapin demonstrates that in the late seventeenth century world of Robert Boyle and the members of the Royal Society in London, trust in the scientific veracity of others was dependent on their conformity with the ideal of the gentleman. In the twentieth century it is hard to imagine relying on the assumption that your fellow scientists are gentlemen (or ladies). Between the end of the nineteenth century and the twenty-first century the older somewhat informal networks of trust on which the distribution and advancement of scientific knowledge so depended, became highly formalised, both in terms of who could report credibly on research findings, and in terms of the discourse of publication itself. The truth of a scientific proposition becomes a finely graded spectrum dependent on a well-managed use of rhetoric that makes very explicit the range of assertive value in its propositions, from tentative speculation to incontrovertible, widely reproduced results. Poets acutely aware that their work is thought of as fantasy and dream by scientists have been strongly drawn to the scientific mode of handling claims to truthfulness. The results vary widely but usually take the form of under-asserted sentences and propositions, a poetics of the suspended phrase.

The third feature of poetry induced by the hegemony of science in modernity is the most elusive to articulate and yet arguably the most significant. I have already mentioned it in relation to Lyn Hejinian, but it can be found in almost all the modernist poets. Inquiry. Modernist poetry is, to misuse some bureaucratic jargon much employed in the UK today, "research-active."

A Poetics of Inquiry

I have talked as if we know what science is. Few of us however have direct experience of working on scientific research projects, of laboratories or field work, and are probably reliant for our knowledge of new scientific knowledge on journalists' reports in popular journals and on books that present a summary without the mathematics and jargon. Science is diverse. Some of the sciences that have most deeply influenced poets, ecology, archaeology, urban studies, "race" science, for instance, don't fit the commonplace image of a science. Even the dominant sciences, physics and molecular biology, are much more complex than the simple pictures that we learn at school and remain attached to if we don't go on to study the sciences at a more advanced level or study the history and philosophy of science. The histories and philosophical analyses of the recent sciences are only just beginning to emerge, and the story they tell is often at odds with the commonplace images of science.

The philosopher J.M. Bernstein argues in his book on Adorno that modernism and science are opposing ways of understanding conceptual inquiry:

> The duality of art and science, not the sheer existence of different practices that we think of under the labels "art" and "science" but the experience of these activities as opposing one another, as somehow in competition with one another, is for Adorno expressive of competing cognitive orientations that, if truly cognitive, must articulate a potential for cognition latent in conceptuality that has yet to find a mode of articulating itself. (275-276)

It is certainly striking that scientists and modernist writers do at times use the same language to describe their activities. Stephen Rose in the opening to his non-specialist account of the nature of scientific research into memory, *The Making of Memory* says: "What I mean by science and its methods is ... a commitment to a unitary, materialist view of the world, a world capable of exploration by methods of rational enquiry and experiment" (4). The nobel prize-winner David Baltimore, who was responsible for the discovery that sometimes DNA could be rewritten, says: "My life is dedicated to increasing knowledge. We need no more justification for scientific research than that" (Crotty 81). Compare that with Lyn Hejinian's belief that "the language of poetry is a language of inquiry" (3), or Charles Bernstein saying:

> It is just my insistence
> that poetry be understood as epistemological
> inquiry (17)

Recognising modernist writing, including poetry, as not just a mode of cognitive inquiry into the nature of the world, but also a form of metapoetic inquiry into the possibilities of articulating a synthesis that does not yet exist, helps us understand the shape of its history. It helps explain the changes and developments in modernist poetry as being due to more than a relentless search for novelty that apes consumerism or expresses the narcissism of a search for individual fame through originality. There is a still largely unwritten history of modernism that would trace the interest in adding to knowledge, finding out the nature of the material and subjective worlds, and pursuing truthfulness in writing. Writing this history faces us with many challenges. How can we identify the achievements of inquiry? What are we expecting to find in a poem as a result of such research? Is this research measurable in terms of truth as scientific findings are? Truthfulness and aesthetic value are commonly treated as antithetical, and any truth in poetry is treated by literary criticism as either an incidental, contingent feature of no significance, whose textual work is at best devoted to creating plausibility and authenticity, or often as an embarrassment if such truths take the form of would-be generalities aggrandising an unearned universality or exemption from critique due to their self-evidence.

For the poets I have been discussing in this paper, language was as exciting a scientific field as the nature of matter and the laws of the universe had been to the physicists of Olson's era and consequently to the poets of that time. Just as the atomic bomb was proof of the importance of this science, the new field of recombinant DNA or cloning was proof of the awesome power of molecular biology. After all, it had discovered that life was generated by a code based on four complex molecules. It helped that its discourse was pervaded by the terminologies of codes and cryptanalysis pervasive in Cold War rhetoric of secrecy, spying and the competition between power blocs. Lily Kay explains that many of the linguistic concepts and metaphors that found their way into molecular biology originated in military researches into means of controlling the secrecy of communication and monitoring the flow and use of information:

> World War II and the cold war imprinted their own discursive traces on science and society, some of them captured in the information discourse. This discourse linked the biosemiotics of molecular biology to the imaginaries of postwar technoculture. Beyond the control of bodies and populations – in all their material messiness – the power over life was being envisioned within the new paradigms of communication. It was to be exercised on the pristine metalevel of controlling information flow, the sequence, the word, and the text. (30)

The discovery of introns, the sections of DNA that were junk or non-coding, mentioned at the beginning, was all the more startling to scientists because of the power of the linguistic metaphors that they were using to understand the intracellular processes of the nucleotides.

Louis Zukofsky wrote in "A-12": "A poet is not at all surprised by science" (186). He might have been recalling Wordsworth's contention in the preface to the Lyrical Ballads that poets should stand alongside scientists. The sciences are very different now, but when Clark Coolidge writes the following lines in *Quartz Hearts* (1978) he is doing something similar.

> The powerlessness of map strata. Dimes on
> sand lake. Backing vocal's roentgens.
> Dennis Hopper's car start bureau. Flash
> from that pink Life plated out. Garbanzo
> with orange. Paper soap of the lit duck.
> This day was meant for a profile. When
> will I light that standing there. Smoke
> comes loco in vinyl. Go pine for
> stuffing. I see a light. It rained on.
> Go buy a place map. Spring. (42)

Coolidge says that this is "in every sense a hinge work, reflecting a fresh interest in sentence structure as axial armature" (56) that writing *Polaroid* had engendered. The challenge I have raised here is to consider what scientific objects this might be the sensation of, what steps it is taking with the women and men of science, what findings are wound on the armature of the poem. Does Coolidge's research into "sentence structure as axial armature" produce a transmissible knowledge and how might we describe this? Does the absence of a verb in the first sentence turn it into a tacit question, and if so, what sort of inquiry is it? How might a backing vocal become radioactive except metaphorically, and yet the metaphor is itself a radioactive product, a reminder of just how deeply the fears of nuclear contamination have become after so many revelations of unintended fallout. It is not so much what the poem means as what tests the poem performs on sentences that locate experience.

Coolidge's poem makes it difficult for the reader to decide which words and phrases are introns and which might be exons when it comes to interpretation. Many texts by Language Poets have this same quality. Certain phrases, sentences, and even sequences of sentences are apparently intelligible, while they are embedded in stretches of apparently unreadable text, leaving a reader with the sensation of glimpsing a picture in the midst of a swirl of unstable elements. The relation between Language Poetry and molecular biology could be said to be similar. Here too there appear to be convergences of rhetoric and metaphors amidst obvious lines of disconnection too. Molecular biologists find the genomes difficult to know how to read also.

The Value of Junk

I. A. Richards's *Science and Poetry* (first published in 1926 and substantially revised in 1935) was coeval with the moment of high modernism in American literature and expresses great optimism about the achievements of science. Richards is so impressed with the successful way science has superseded magical and religious world-views that he worries about the possibility that poetry might become totally redundant. Although he shares Matthew Arnold's belief that "the future of poetry is immense" he concedes that "a more representative modern view would be that the future of poetry is *nil*" (20). People who would have become poets are more likely to become biologists now, and he is all too aware of mathematicians who cannot read poetry because "they find the alleged statements to be *false*" (58). Rumours of poetry's demise were premature, but by the time Mary Midgley wrote her book *Science and Poetry* (2001) the sciences had grown even more in confidence about their "omnicompetence" as she calls it, making her worried about the "over-exaltation of science" (57), and the tendency to treat physics as the best paradigm for all forms of intellectual inquiry. If she were more interested in the history of modern poetry she might have noticed that the same might appear to be said about Language Poets and molecular biology. What I have suggested in this essay is that these poets could be said to explore the implications of treating molecular biology as the best paradigm for intellectual inquiry, and for that you need junk DNA in the midst of your codes. Metaphors, models and texts cross back and forth between intelligibility and noise.

Works Cited

Altieri, Charles. "The Concept of Force as Modernist Response to the Authority of Science." *Modernism/Modernity* 5:2 (1998): 77-93.

Barnett, Lincoln. "J. Robert Oppenheimer." *Life* 10. Oct. 1949: 52-59.

Bernstein, Charles. *A Poetics*. Cambridge, MA.: Harvard University Press, 1992.

Bernstein, J. M. *Adorno: Disenchantment and Ethics*. Cambridge: Cambridge University Press, 2001.

Bush, Douglas. *Science and English Poetry: A Historical Sketch*. New York: Oxford University Press, 1950.

Coolidge, Clark. *Quartz Hearts*. San Francisco: This, 1978.

Crotty, Shane. *Ahead of the Curve: David Baltimore's Life in Science*. Berkeley: University of California Press, 2001.

Hejinian, Lyn. *The Language of Inquiry*. Berkeley: University of California Press, 2000.

Hollinger, David A. *Science, Jews, and Secular Culture*. Princeton, N.J.: Princeton University Press, 1996.

Kay, Lily E. *Who Wrote the Book of Life? A History of the Genetic Code*. Stanford, CA.: Stanford University Press, 2000.

Midgley, Mary. *Science and Poetry*. London: Routledge, 2001.

Mistry, N. B., R. A. Poling, and E. H. Thorndike. "Particles with Naked Beauty." *Scientific American* July 1983.

Morange, Michel. *A History of Molecular Biology*. Trans. Matthew Cobb. Cambridge, MA: Harvard University Press, 1998.

Olson, Charles. "Human Universe." *Selected Writings*. New York: New Directions, 1966.

—. "A Letter to the Faculty of Black Mountain College." *Olson: The Journal of the Charles Olson Archives* 8 (1977): 26-33.

Pound, Ezra. *The ABC of Reading*. London: George Routledge & Sons, 1934.

—. *The Cantos*. London: Faber & Faber, 1975.

Prynne, J. H. *Poems*. Newcastle upon Tyne: Bloodaxe, 1999.

Richards, I. A. *Science and Poetry*. Repr. *Poetries and Sciences*. New York: Norton, 1970.

Riordan, Maurice, and Jon Turney. *A Quark for Mister Mark: 101 Poems about Science*. London: Faber & Faber, 2000.

Rose, Steven. *The Making of Memory: From Molecules to Mind*. London: Random House, 1992.

Rukeyser, Muriel. *The Life of Poetry*. New York: William Morrow & Co, 1974.

Shapin, Steven. *A Social History of Truth: Civility and Science in Seventeenth-Century England*. Chicago: University of Chicago Press, 1994.

Shaw, Lytle. "The Labour of Repetition: Silliman's 'Quips' and the Politics of Intertextuality." Ed. Thomas A. Vogler. *Ron Silliman and the A.L.P.H.A.B.E.T*. Santa Cruz: Quarry West, 1998.

Silliman, Ron. *In the American Tree*. Orono, ME: National Poetry Foundation, 1986.

—. *Tjanting*. Berkeley: The Figures, 1981.

Smith, John Maynard. "The Concept of Information in Biology." *Philosophy of Science* 67 (2000): 177-194.

Watson, James D. *DNA: The Secret of Life*. London: Heinemann, 2003.

Zukofsky, Louis. *"A."* Berkeley: University of California Press, 1978.

“Arrows to pierce dust”: Susan Howe’s Philosophical Poetry

Susanne Rohr

Susan Howe’s 1999 book of poems *Pierce-Arrow*[1] displays the dazzling style which by now we have come to expect from this author. In focusing on a poetic rewriting of American history, *Pierce-Arrow* is clearly related to earlier publications by Howe, such as “The Liberties” (1983) from *The Europe of Trusts* anthology and *The Birth-Mark: Unsettling the Wilderness in American Literary History* (1993). These works are geared to finding and filling gaps left by academic historiography, to recovering suppressed voices, and making polyvocality heard in the streamlined creation of dominant discourses. The figures who come to prominence in these publications are Mary Rowlandson, Anne Hutchinson, and Emily Dickinson, all of whom Howe sees as expressing an “antinomian” tradition. In her attempts to poetically reclaim these silenced voices Howe inscribes herself into this “antinomian tradition.” Her poetry is thus built around figures of absence; it acknowledges silence in the moment of bespeaking it. Howe comments on this peculiar relation of indirect signification:

> This tradition that I hope I am part of has involved a breaking of boundaries of all sorts. It involves a fracturing of discourse, a stammering even. Interruption and hesitation used as a force. A recognition that there is an other voice, an attempt to hear and speak it. Its [sic] this brokenness that interests me. I see a contemporary American practice that isn’t what necessarily gets into the canon and has trouble getting published. It is an echo of an undervoice that was speaking from the beginning and is peculiarly American. This voice keep [sic] on speaking *against* the grain. (“Encloser” 192)

Hence the fractured discourse, the stammering progression in Howe’s ‘historical poems,’ where submerged history makes itself heard. “If history is a record of survivors,” Howe states in *The Birth-Mark*, “Poetry shelters other voices” (47).

These “other voices” that Howe made audible in her earlier work belong – mostly – to women who had been excluded from the dominant cultural narrative

[1] Susan Howe, *Pierce-Arrow*, New York: New Directions, 1999. All further quotations refer to this edition.

for a long time. In *Pierce-Arrow*, however, we encounter a male figure who shares the female fate of effectively having been shut off from prevailing discourse, in his case from that of nineteenth century American academia: Charles Sanders Peirce. Peirce, who is arguably the most brilliant of American thinkers and the founder of American pragmatist philosophy, has never been given the attention he deserves. In pondering the reasons for this ongoing neglect, *Pierce-Arrow* comes up with the following unflattering characterization of Peirce: He was "a decadent aesthete, a lecher, a liar, a libertine, queer, a wife beater, an alcoholic, a drug addict, a plagiarist, a wannabe robber baron; an unpractical pragmatist with suspect metaphysics" (8). While this certainly would have been enough to exclude him from nineteenth century academia, the true scandal, I would argue, has to be located someplace else, for it lies in the premises of Peirce's theoretical thinking. Taking this thesis as a point of departure for my argument, the gist of this paper is twofold: I will uncover the menacing potential inherent in Peirce's thinking, and at the same time show that *Pierce-Arrow* has not only intuitively understood this latent power, but that it relishes in acting it out in its poetic form.

To pursue this twofold argument, let us first take a look at the construction of *Pierce-Arrow*. The title establishes a peculiar link to the modernist tradition, to which the poem refers with a double gesture of both acknowledgement and rejection. For "Pierce-Arrow" is the brand name of a beautiful motor car that was the hallmark of luxury during the 1920s. It was produced in Howe's hometown Buffalo and a photograph on the back of the dust cover of the book features Howe in front of the now defunct factory. The book's front, in bearing the name of this "emblem of modernity" [2] in its title, and its back, in alluding to the end of this era, thus frame the reference to the modernist tradition. In its aesthetics of fragmentation, the poem clearly refers to this tradition, yet at the same time it turns its back on any attempts at reconstructing wholeness. Reconstruction and projection both evolve from the position of utter blindness to one's own situatedness, as the poem later acknowledges, and when we shoot our "arrows to / pierce dust and surf," we must come "at last trusting to mad / strife in blindness," despite the pretension of "not / holding to be mortal in afterlife" (104). Still, *Pierce-Arrow* keeps shooting its arrows into the void, because "Peirce left a blank / to fill in later in a / violent rupture of / nomenclature" (79).

However, "can we truly 'pierce' the past, which seems peopled by 'retreating figure[s]' whose faces are averted from us, denying us the immediacy of knowledge we feel compelled to seek?" Peter Nicholls wonders in commenting on the significance of the book's title, *Pierce-Arrow* ("Pastness of Landscape" 443). One

[2] I borrow this expression from Peter Nicholls who uses it in his publication on *Pierce-Arrow* "The Pastness of Landscape': Susan Howe's *Pierce-Arrow*" (442). I owe a lot of inspiration to this excellent essay.

might also assume that the title ironically alludes to yet another gesture of neglect and ignorance towards Peirce which is still observable in contemporary academia: the persistent tendency to mispronounce and misspell "Peirce" as ['pɪ:əs] and to thus erase the name in the act of using it. A good example of this is Nicky Marsh's publication on *Pierce-Arrow*, "All Known – Never Seen:' Susan Howe, Samuel Beckett and an Indeterminate Tradition." Marsh manages to misspell the name as "Pierce" throughout her entire essay, even altering the quotations of secondary material that originally had the correct spelling.

Let us continue with our look at the construction of *Pierce-Arrow*. The long poem is composed of three sections, entitled "Arisbe," "The Leisure of the Theory Class," and "Rückenfigur." In "Arisbe," named after Peirce's house in Milford, Pennsylvania, the text reflects upon its scope and format. This opening part of the poem randomly reconstructs aspects of Peirce's life, the brilliance of his intellectual capacities, his provocative behavior and difficult career, and it also ponders on the enigmatic origin of his second wife, Juliette Froissy Pourtalais, of whom still little is known. The second part, "The Leisure of the Theory Class," instigates a playful dialogue between Peirce's ideas and those of other major writers of the late nineteenth century, George Meredith, Thomas Love Peacock, Algernon Charles Swinburne, and Theodore Watts Dunton, thereby producing a sketch of Victorian intelligentsia. The third part, "Rückenfigur," points to the paradoxical movement of *Pierce-Arrow*, a simultaneous forward-backward movement, in its alluring title.

The art historical term *Rückenfigur* – German for "back figure" – denotes a person in a painting who turns his/her back to the viewer. [3] It was widely used for instance in the famous romantic paintings by Caspar David Friedrich.

In these paintings, the averted figure signifies a disturbance by obstructing our vision. It creates a certain tension between the viewer of the painting and that which is seen: while the gaze of the figure is hidden, it still directs the perspective of the viewer. What is more, the hidden gaze of the figure is *redoubled* in the sight of the viewer, making that which is seen appear as some kind of secondary representation. As in Plato's allegory of the cave, the representation seems to be doubly removed from the truth. By having "Rückenfigur" conclude her series of poems, Howe makes the poems turn their backs to the reader, underlining retrospectively the sense of estrangement that accompanies attempts to reconstruct the past and that has consequently accompanied our interaction with the project of 'poetic historiography' all along. To put it another way, the reader's eyes follow the trajectory of the arrows shot to "fill in the blanks" of the past, yet their final target escapes the view. "[R]owing forward face / backward" (133) is an apt image

3 Peter Nicholls's essay helped me understand the significance of *Rückenfigur*. Cf. "Pastness of Landscape" 448-456.

Fig. 1. Caspar David Friedrich, *Der Wanderer* [Wanderer above the Sea of Fog], 1818.

we find in this section of *Pierce-Arrow*. However, a "Rückenfigur" also points us back to the beginning, so consequently the first section of *Pierce-Arrow* ponders on why and how reconstruction of obscure origins should still be attempted.

Assuming at times the tone of an academic introduction, the first section of the book describes the tedious research Howe has done at various libraries that hold material by and on Peirce. Bits and pieces of manuscript texts by Peirce and excerpts from many academic secondary sources on Peirce as well as many references to Homer and Euripides are interwoven into these descriptions, so that a multitude of voices emerge. These Howe brings together to negotiate a central question that *Pierce-Arrow* ponders in "Arisbe": "How are ideals maintained in the long story of responsibility? Secret. The genteel American tradition is not to kill an original: we only remove the embarrassment" (19). In tracing the embarrassing removal, the text here oscillates between the poles of poetic and academic discourse, and it amalgamates these discourses into a peculiar kind of 'poetic historiography' that does not distinguish between quotation and commentary, thus calling into question academic standards of objectivity and coherence. Curiously enough, Howe at the same time claims the status of authenticity for the reproductions that she has interspersed throughout *Pierce-Arrow*. In her foreword she stresses: "Most of the illustrations reproduced in this book are from the original manuscripts of Charles Sanders Peirce now at the Houghton Library. They are not shot from microfilm copies or photocopies" (ix).

Why this surprising turn to the 'real thing' in the context of Howe's project of 'poetic historiography'? Can the original sources tell the truth, after all? The surprising answer is: Yes, they can, but a peculiar truth it is, because "Documents resemble people talking in sleep" (6). Thus they address the reader, as Howe claims, by articulating "Another language another way of speaking so quietly always there in the shape of memories, thoughts, feelings, which are extra-marginal outside of primary consciousness" (6). Documents, one might infer, *do* speak the language of authenticity, but it is the authenticity of creative activity that they express for us. Howe thus puts the documents to a particular artistic use in *Pierce-Arrow*: "Putting thought in motion to define art in a way that includes science, these graphs, charts, prayers, and tables are free to be drawings, even poems. ... There always was and always will be a secret affinity between symbolic logic and poetry" (ix).

And it is here, at this point, that Howe's and Peirce's thinking converge and where we consequently have to look for the scandal or the embarrassment that Peirce embodied for nineteenth century academia and that had to be removed. Both thinkers – Howe arguing from the poet's perspective and Peirce from that of the scientist – propose the dissolution of the boundary which separates the arts from the sciences and that in methodological discourse has for a long time seemed vital to preserving and protecting the identity of the sciences. If *Pierce-Arrow* works on the assumption that "There always was and always will be a secret affinity between symbolic logic and poetry" (ix), Peirce defines the profile of scientific endeavor very much along the same lines:

> The work of the poet or novelist is not so utterly different from that of the scientific man. The artist introduces a fiction; but it is not an arbitrary one; it exhibits affinities to which the mind accords a certain approval in pronouncing them beautiful, which if it is not exactly the same as saying the synthesis is true, is something of the same general kind. The geometer draws a diagram, which if not exactly a fiction, is at least a creation, and by means of observation of that diagram he is able to synthesize and show relations between elements which before seemed to have no necessary connection. (1.383) [4]

Thus, where Peirce in the above quotation holds that the scientist "show[s] relations between elements which before seemed to have no necessary connection," *Pierce-Arrow* responds by musing: "In poetry all things seem to touch so they are" (13). Scientific and poetic attitude and discourse, we gather from this juxtaposition of ideas, are not so utterly different. While in our post-modern times beliefs like these do not arouse any particular sense of excitement, they certainly did in the context of the nineteenth century formation of disciplines and the institutional ordering of the academic world. However, the whole scope of the embarrassment which Peirce embodied to his contemporaries still escapes us, for this becomes visible only when we analyze how he theoretically establishes his position.

Peirce had the courage to base his entire elaborate and eminently systematic thinking on an element of arbitrariness and caprice: the logic of abduction. Let me explain by quoting from the famous "bean syllogisms" that Peirce used to explain the form of abductive inference:

> Deduction.
> Rule. – All the beans from this bag are white.
> Case. – These beans are from this bag.
> ∴ Result. – These beans are white.
>
> Induction.
> Case. – These beans are from this bag.
> Result. – These beans are white.
> ∴ Rule. – All the beans from this bag are white.
>
> Hypothesis [Abduction].
> Rule. – All the beans from this bag are white.
> Result. – These beans are white.
> ∴ Case. – These beans are from this bag. (2.623)

Aristotle was the first to define the logic of abduction. He developed it in his reflections on the forms of syllogistic inference and soon abandoned it as a weak

[4] Charles Sanders Peirce, *Collected Papers of Charles Sanders Peirce*. References to the *Collected Papers* are generally made in the form of decimal quotation, i. e. indicating volume and paragraph. Thus, a number like the above '1.383' points to volume I, § 383. Hereafter, I will only give the decimal quotation when referring to the *Collected Papers*.

and useless form, a judgment that was shared by all later generations of logicians. Peirce, however, rescued abduction from its place of exile and dared to base his entire thinking on it, and thus posited invalid reasoning as the point of departure for his theoretical construction. He holds that abductive inference is ubiquitous and unavoidable, for in all contexts, be they scientific or commonplace, it is through abductive inference only that we can 'make sense of the world.' To be precise: Abduction, according to Peirce, is a process of interpretation. It translates the world into language for us, turns image into text, for it transforms our perceptions into perceptual judgments. That is to say, by making abductions, we interpret. And by interpreting, we make reality.[5]

As Peirce states: "Abduction is the process of forming an explanatory hypothesis. It is the only logical operation which introduces any new idea; ... if we are ever to learn anything or to understand phenomena at all, it must be by abduction that this is to be brought about" (5.171). This quotation tells us that abductive inference occupies an exceptional status, because it has the singular potential to introduce "new ideas." What are the implications of this statement? Introducing new ideas is an immensely creative activity and since this operation, according to Peirce, forms the beginning of *all* cognitive processes, we can infer that creativity constitutes our basic interaction with reality. However, since abduction is an invalid logical operation, its outcome – reality – is forever inflicted with obscurity and precariousness.

We can now surmise the true scope of the embarrassment that Peirce's thinking posed for contemporaneous academic discourse. Not only does it understand scientific inquiry as a sequence of eminently fallible creative "guesses" (7.219) in the process of which the scientist can never be "*absolutely sure of [his] own conclusions*" (1.10; italics Peirce's); along the way it also erases many distinctions that have always been considered vital for establishing academic integrity. It questions disciplinary boundaries as well as the differences between commonplace, artistic and scientific processes of interpretation, and it sees both the artist and the scientist as creating "relations between elements which before seemed to have no necessary connection" (1.383).

---

5 I have elaborated on Peirce's theory of abductive inference and the implied notions of human creativity in various publications. Cf. for instance my book length study *Über die Schönheit des Findens. Die Binnenstruktur menschlichen Verstehens nach Charles S. Peirce: Abduktionslogik und Kreativität* or my "Mimesis of the Mind: Literature in the Context of Charles S. Peirce's Semiotic Epistemology."

I would also like to suggest at this point that while it may be true that Howe has neglected certain theoretical aspects in Peirce's work, this does not diminish the importance of her work in any way. Instead of yet another theoretical analysis, Howe in *Pierce-Arrow* offers us an original and fascinating *poetical expression* of certain key concepts of Peirce's thinking.

As mentioned before, it is here that Howe's and Peirce's thinking connect. Innumerable dialogues such as the following suggest themselves. The poem asks: "What is knowledge?" (6), and the scientist answers: "The truth is that the whole fabric of our knowledge is one matted felt of pure hypothesis" (Ms 692). [6] "There are realities / independent of thought" (59), the poem insists, to which the philosopher hesitatingly responds: "reality [is] the normal product of mental action, and not [the] incognizable cause of it" (8.15).

In an interview, Howe describes her understanding of Peirce's project. She says: "I think Peirce was trying both to get at something beyond reason and to diagram the logical structure of reality.... Many of his logical graphs, and also his calculations, are like poems" (Howe and Swenson 379). The same could also serve as an apt description of *Pierce-Arrow*'s underlying poetics. "In poetry all things seem to touch so they are" (13), the poem contemplates and has manuscripts, diagrams, logical graphs, silhouettes, photographs, legends, and philosophy all converge into lyrical expression. In deciphering the poems, in tracing the poems' attempts to poetically revise the removal of an embarrassing voice, the reader re-enacts the core assertion of this voice: He or she creates "relations between elements which before seemed to have no necessary connection" because "In poetry all things seem to touch so they are."

Works Cited

Howard, W. Scott. "Teaching, How/e?: *not per se*." *The Denver Quarterly* 35.2 (2000): 81-93.

Howe, Susan. *The Birth-Mark: Unsettling the Wilderness in American Literary History*. Hanover: Wesleyan University Press, 1993.

—. "Encloser." *The Politics of Poetic Form: Poetry and Public Policy*. Ed. Charles Bernstein. New York: Roof, 1990. 175-196.

—. "The Liberties." 1983. *The Europe of Trusts*. Los Angeles: Sun & Moon, 1990. 147-218.

—. *Pierce-Arrow*. New York: New Directions, 1999.

Howe, Susan, and Cole Swenson. "A Dialogue." *Conjunctions* 35 (2000): 374-387.

Marsh, Nicky. "'All Known – Never Seen:' Susan Howe, Samuel Beckett and an Indeterminate Tradition." *Samuel Beckett Today* 9 (2000): 239-254.

Nicholls, Peter. "'The Pastness of Landscape': Susan Howe's *Pierce-Arrow*." *Contemporary Literature* 43.1 (2002): 441-460.

—. "Unsettling the Wilderness: Susan Howe and American History." *Contemporary Literature* 37.1 (1996): 586-601.

Peirce, Charles Sanders. *Collected Papers of Charles Sanders Peirce*. Ed. Charles Hartshorne, Paul Weiss (Vols. I-VI) and Arthur W. Burks (Vols. VII and VIII). Cambridge, MA: Harvard University Press, 1931-1934 and 1958.

6 The manuscript number refers to Richard S. Robin's catalogue.

Robin, Richard S. *Annotated Catalogue of the Papers of Charles S. Peirce*. Amherst: The University of Massachusetts Press, 1967.

Rohr, Susanne. "Mimesis of the Mind: Literature in the Context of Charles S. Peirce's Semiotic Epistemology." *REAL* 12 (1996): 97-113.

—. *Über die Schönheit des Findens. Die Binnenstruktur menschlichen Verstehens nach Charles S. Peirce: Abduktionslogik und Kreativität*. Stuttgart: Metzler, 1993.

Verbal Abstraction and the Democratic Promise of Natural Speech: Tensions and Temptations in Contemporary American Poetry

Heinz Ickstadt

Now that the American government insists on its mission to promote democracy around the world, it is perhaps not the best moment to speak of the "democratic promise" that has been part of an American poetics for almost two hundred years, from the time of Emerson and Whitman to the end of the 20th century. I refer to an aesthetic ideology that has rooted American poetic expression in the very concept of democracy and in the natural speech of the people. Be it the lively exchanges of New York truckmen ("cut these words and they will bleed," as Emerson once phrased it), or "the lawless germinal element, below all words and sentences" that Whitman found in "slang;" or be it the words straight out of the mouths of Polish mothers that Williams claimed was the source of his poetry; be it the verbal expressiveness of the downtrodden black folk that Langston Hughes intended to absorb, or Creeley's speech from the "bottom" that "no man is going to get me to let that go" – it is in each case a grounding of the written in the commonly spoken (in the 'immigrant spoken,' as Charles Bernstein and many others maintain), a tracing back of the poet's words to their origin in the voice and speech of common men and women.[1] It would be wrong to call this a uniquely American phenomenon. But it stands to reason that the concept of speech as an inexhaustible

[1] "The language of the street is always strong ... Cut these words and they would bleed; they are vascular and alive; they walk and run ...," Emerson, *Journals* (1849), qtd. in F.O. Matthiessen, *The American Renaissance*, 35. Even more emphatic is Whitman: "Slang, profoundly consider'd, is the lawless germinal element, below all words and sentences, and behind all poetry, and proves a certain perennial rankness and Protestantism in speech," *Complete Poetry and Collected Prose*, 1165; or also: "A perfect writer would make words sing, dance, kiss, do the male and female act, bear children, weep, bleed, rage, stab, steal, fire cannon, steer ships, sack cities, charge with cavalry and infantry, or do anything that man or woman or the natural powers can do," *An American Primer*. Williams's famous statement comes from his *Autobiography*, 311. Creeley's remarks are taken from a letter to Charles Olson (May 19, 1952): "Well, I came up from the bottom, rock of sorts, and fell, now, I am *not* going to toss out the one thing I got from it: speech. No man is going to get me to let that go. I heard everything, as a kid, and felt, then,

poetic resource has been of special relevance in a culture that traditionally defined its difference from Europe by emphasizing its democratic and participatory character.[2]

However, when the Language Poets first came to stake their claim in the post-sixties field of American poetry, they did so polemically against this idealization of "natural" or "common" speech which they believed had produced an all too easy mainstream convention in contemporary American poetry. The challenge was perhaps most famously expressed in Robert Grenier's essay of 1971 "I HATE SPEECH," which found an echo in many subsequent denunciations of the "natural" as well as in oppositional definitions of poetry as artifice and construct.[3] The dichotomy also had advocates in academia, perhaps none of them as learned and persuasive as Marjorie Perloff whose *Radical Artifice* (1991) explored the verbal intricacies and semantic opaqueness of the Language Poets, insisted on their historical necessity, and defined their social function in opposition to (but also in the context of) the language of the new media, which had absorbed and transformed the "natural" and "common" into the normative newspeak of a frozen democracy ("speech in its capitalistic embodiments," as Steve McCaffery put it).[4]

However, like all strategic dichotomies this one, too, proved to be of limited value, not least because it wrongly pushed the Language Poets into the corner of a European-like avant-garde elitism. For the democratic voice in American poetry cannot be identified with the "naturalness" of colloquial speech alone; there

---

shy & unfamiliar – often started by any words too hard, or couldn't find those flip answers my friends could, etc. In fact, my friends: one was in prison the last time I heard, another working in some garage in Acton, the rest I don't know. But speech, I heard the craziest, shouted, or whatever – the deepest, most permanent contempt for any 'written' word any man ever wrote," qtd. in George Butterick, "Robert Creeley and the Tradition," 222. For Bernstein the basis of American poetry was fundamentally changed by immigrant speech: "For American poetry of the twentieth century, there is no more important fact than the fundamental alteration of the language base – who was speaking and how they spoke – that occurred in the 1880s and 1890s; indeed, it is perhaps that period's most lasting legacy for our literature," *A Poetics*, 107. See also his essay on "Professing Stein / Stein Professing," *A Poetics*, 142-149.

2 Inversely, it has been notoriously difficult to translate Williams's poetic version of "speech" into German since – as his German translator Hans Magnus Enzensberger remarked – "Unserer Poesie, ja unserer Literatur überhaupt, ist die Umgangssprache fremd," *Einzelheiten II: Poesie und Politik*, 41.

3 "Why imitate 'speech'? Various vehicle that American speech is in the different mouths of any of us, possessed of particular power of colloquial usage, rhythmic pressure etc., it is *only* such. *To me, all speeches say the same thing,* or: why not exaggerate, as Williams did, for our time proclaim an abhorrence of 'speech' designed as was his castigation of 'the sonnet' to rid us, as creators of the world, from reiteration of he past dragged on in formal habit. I HATE SPEECH," Grenier, "On Speech," 496.

4 "The extreme mission of poetry from Artaud to the performative enactment of the 1970s was neither expenditure nor spontaneity per se but rather the killing of speech in its capitalistic embodiments," McCaffery, "Voice in Extremis," 171.

has also always been the rhetorical artifice of oratory. Whitman made use of both resources, and subsequently, there is for each speech-grounded William Carlos Williams an oratorical Hart Crane, for each Robert Creeley an Allen Ginsberg or a Robert Duncan; for each Langston Hughes or Sonja Sanchez a James Weldon Johnson or a Melvin B. Tolson, about whose "Libretto for the Republic of Liberia" one could say what James Clifford wrote about the poetry of Emile Césaire, namely that it used a "made" language, a language involved in a process of cultural invention. [5] In addition, the spoken and the written, natural speech and textual artifice, are not as far apart as the proposition of a "radical artifice" would make us believe. Williams saw the limits of Whitman's as well as of Sandburg's version of democratic speech in their not listening hard enough to grasp the hidden structure, the inherent form, of the spoken. He might have learned this from Gertrude Stein who, in "Melanctha," created the effect of speech through abstract patterns of verbal and syntactical repetition. Her example had also made Hemingway aware that the colloquial appears most 'natural' when filtered through abstraction. [6]

Bob Perelman points out that Grenier's "I HATE SPEECH" issued from an aesthetics – Olson's projective verse – that was itself built on the dynamics of breathing and the energetic pulse and push of speech. [7] In an interview with David Antin (published in 2001), Bernstein insisted that the relation between speech and writing was at once complex and productive: "... a kind of quantum poetics: the deeper one listens to the spoken the more textual it becomes" (46). In fact, it was Bernstein who had, a few years earlier, begun to soften the strict dichotomy between the spoken and the written by introducing a third category, that of the performative, which ties the oral and the textual together in a loose alliance, thus also freeing experimental poetry from the stigma of elitist isolation. The latter aim is obviously the purpose of a collection of essays, edited by Charles Bernstein in 1998, whose title programmatically calls for *Close Listening* in con-

---

5 "... Césaire still sends readers to dictionaries in several tongues, to encyclopedias, to botanical reference works, histories and atlases. He is attached to the obscure, accurate term and to the new word. He makes readers confront the limits of their language, or of any single language. He forces them to *construct* readings from a debris of historical and future possibilities. His world is Caribbean – hybrid and heteroglot;" and: "With Césaire we are involved in a poetics of cultural invention," Clifford, *The Predicament of Culture*, 175-176.

6 See Williams's review of "Sandburg's Complete Poetry," in *Selected Essays of William Carlos Williams*, 272-279. Hemingway's Stein-inspired abstractions of speech are apparent in stories like "Up in Michigan" and "Hills Like White Elephants." On Stein's (and Pound's) influence on Hemingway see Peter Messent, *Ernest Hemingway*, 11-22.

7 "His attack re-enacted Williams's attack, with the workshop voice poem as the target rather than the genteel sonnet; and by using capitals, he aligned himself with Pound and Olson, eschewing the normative prose in which Eliot, Richards, and all the others kept critical accounts separate from poetry," Bob Perelman, *The Marginalization of Poetry*, 43.

tradistinction to the New Critics' insistence on "close reading." The contributors to Bernstein's volume included for the most part critics and poets associated with the Language Poets but also, perhaps surprisingly, representatives of ethnic and ethnopoetic writing. In a sense, *Close Listening* redefines the earlier opposition between "natural" speech and written artifice by putting it on a broader basis. He distinguishes "orality" (which "valorizes speech over writing") from "aurality" ("the sounding of the writing"), but refuses to see their relation in terms of hierarchy: They are not stages "on a path toward or away from immanence or transcendence but rather stages for performance: *modalities* of reason; *prisms* not prisons." Accordingly, since "Sound is language's flesh, its opacity as meaning marks its material embeddedness in the world of things. Sound brings writing back from its metaphysical and symbolic functions to where it is at home, in performance." Therefore: "Poetry readings, like reading aloud ... are a performance of the carnality of language – its material, sensuous embodiment" (20-22). This is what Bernstein calls "language's animalady" which may neither be confused with orality nor with a return to origin.

> In the present cultural context of the late twentieth century, this animalady loses its force as concrete experience when reified as (represented) speech or sentimentalised as (a return to) orality. The most resonant possibilities for poetry as a medium can be realized only when the performance of language moves from human speech to animate, but transhuman, sound: that is, when we stop listening and begin to hear; which is to say, stop decoding and begin to get a nose for the sheer noise of language. (22)

Against the massive encroachment of the "mainstream," the performance of the poem can thus create a quasi-utopian space where different kinds of marginality – ethnic voice and written artifice – can meet and interact. [8] For, as Bernstein phrased it, "poetry is constituted dialogically through recognition and exchange

---

8 Although some contributions to *Close Listening* indicate that this alliance was as tense as it was tentative: as when Lorenzo Thomas tries to reconcile an African American tradition of orality with Olson's modernist aesthetics and sees in "the aesthetic goal of Black Arts music and poetry: an attempt to recreate in modern modes the ancestral role of the African griots who are poets, musicians, and dancers whose songs record genealogies and the cosmologies of societies...," "Neon Griot," 316. The strain becomes visible in a different way in Maria Damon's attempt to embrace the popular concept of ' slam poetry' with avant-garde intellectuality: "It is perhaps useful here to invoke Antonio Gramsci's formulation of 'the organic intellectual' to argue that these poetries and this poetic activity merit not only a telos-driven exemplification of non-academic literary activity but the closest possible listening of all registers of poetic reception. The 'organic intellectual' is not only a working-class person with an intuitive gift for understanding his/her class situation and social circumstance, but a trained, professional intellectual who uses his/her learning for the benefit of the people. As we have seen, many of the poets discussed here are both, and as public intellectuals their persons and their poetic activity enact the erasure of the barrier between the street and the page, the workshop and the stage," 339.

with an audience of peers, where the poet is not performing to invisible readers or listeners but actively exchanging work with other performers and participants" (23).

In other words, the outlines of a democratic poetics are here effectively redrawn. And indeed, in books like *Close Listening*, *The Politics of Poetic Form*, and *A Poetics*, Charles Bernstein combines the probing of his aesthetic position and a questioning of his own poetic authority with reflections on the doubtful status of the writer and his social function under the conditions of a democracy perverted by commerce and the media. Like Bob Perelman, Bernstein takes the "marginalization" of poetry for granted and tries to gain from its loss of status a new strength. "...there are only margins no universals," he writes in *A Poetics* (187). And yet: "...my art is just empty words on a page if it does not, indeed, persuade, if it enters into the world as self-justification or self-flagellation or aesthetic ornamentation rather than as interaction, conversation, provocation (for myself and others)" (*AP* 223-224). And although he concedes to Rosmarie Waldrop that the concept of poetry as "quasi-legislative" might possibly be a "male aspiration" (*PPF* 244, Fn. 3), he is nevertheless fascinated with the different ways the poet's concern with democracy has found aesthetic expression: in different forms of poetry as much as in different poetics. If I understand him correctly, these are grouped around three authority-providing aspects of the communicative process: 1. around the author (or authorial voice), 2. around the text and its structure, and 3. around the reader and the community of the audience.

The American variation of the romantic self-projection of the poet as legislator obviously entered the literature of the young nation first via Emerson's "The Poet" and his incarnation in Walt Whitman who, in the very opening lines of his "Song of Myself," assumed a "you" in the universalizing embrace of his representative "I." That the assumption of the poet's central role went hand in hand with his marginalization by a community he imagined himself to speak for has haunted American poetry for more than a hundred years: In Hart Crane's visionary poet-figure, for instance, who, in the guise of Columbus, sees the reality of his discovery as totally dependent on the power of the word-ship that carries him and it; or in Allen Ginsberg, who accepted the burden of his "lonely old courage-teacher" Whitman with self-conscious and self-belittling irony; or in Robert Duncan, who in his apocalyptic "Up-Rising" could evoke the promise of America only in the condemnation of those who had betrayed it by their war in Vietnam.[9]

Although William Carlos Williams vehemently rejected the visionary subjec-

9 Hart Crane, "Ave Maria," *The Bridge* (1930); Allen Ginsberg, "A Supermarket in California," in ed. Paul Hoover, *Postmodern American Poetry*, 135; and Robert Duncan, "Up-Rising – Passages 25," *Bending the Bow* (1968).

tivity of Crane's pose (Crane's "eyes" were, he said, "clouded by vision"), [10] he attempted to maintain the role of the romantic *vates* by moving it away from the subjective. Williams can thus be seen as a crossroads. Apart from identifying "vision" with the observation of the everyday ("the eyes held hard on the object"), he also gives a meiotic twist to the representative role of the lyrical I. What the I/eye conveys as knowledge ("so much depends . . . ," "Let me tell you . . . ") is available to everyone willing to use his/her I/eyes. But if the poet is representative of the common many, the poetry he writes can also be understood as being potentially in everyone's power. It is here that Williams, by wanting to create an American poetic language from its democratic roots as well as from the everyday material of the imagination, can be misconceived as an advocate of "natural speech" and of establishing a common mode of poetic expression ("a topical 'subjective' realism," as Marjorie Perloff remarked in a different context). [11]

However there are more and even better reasons for seeing Williams (or, with yet greater justification, Robert Creeley) as a constructionist who had a tactile sense for linguistic texture and explored the weight and materiality of every word he used. [12] In this, Williams was surely influenced by Gertrude Stein, who understood the concept of the democratic aesthetically as a principle of composition and thus, in an act of linguistic revolution, exploded textual hierarchy by treating each word, each textual element, as having equal value. (As she once explained tongue-in-cheek, she followed the democratic principle of "one word, one vote." [13]) The impact Gertrude Stein had on the poets of the 70s and 80s, loosely grouped under the label of Language Poets, is remarkable considering that, with the exception of William Carlos Williams, her presence in the field of modernist poetics was rarely admitted by her contemporaries. Her insistence on language as the only reality to work with and her efforts to liberate the word from the burden of meaning found full resonance only in a later generation that accepted the possibilities as well as the constrictions of the linguistic turn, i.e. the epistemological priority of language. For them the "word order" was correlated to "world order" (as Mar-

10 "Hart Crane," 4.

11 "Modernism' at the Millennium," *21-Century Modernism*, 163.

12 See Charles Altieri's persuasive reading of Williams's poetry in *Painterly Abstraction in Modernist American Poetry*, 224-247.

13 ". . . Cézanne conceived the idea that in composition one thing was as important as another thing. Each part is as important as the whole, and that impressed me enormously, and it impressed me so much that I began to write *Three Lives* . . . At this time I threw away punctuation. My real objection to it was that it threw away this balance I was trying to get, this evenness of everybody having a vote . . . ," Stein, "A Transatlantic Interview," 502-503.

jorie Perloff phrased it) [14] and the text was an unrestricted experimental space of exploration, transgression, and liberation that had also social implications.

With the introduction of the performative as suspending "the idea of the poem as a fixed, stable, finite linguistic object" (*CL* 9), the emphasis in the definition of a democratic poetics therefore changes once again – after shifting from author/origin to text, it is now shifted from text to reader and/or audience. For it is obvious that Bernstein places his own work as well as that of his fellow language poets within a symbolic space that is not defined by the authority of the author but by that of the reader, or, more precisely, by what he calls the "conversation," the interaction between text and reader. "Poetry, oddly romanticized as the activity of isolated individuals writing monological lyrics," Bernstein writes in his introduction to *Close Listening*, "is among the most social and socially responsive – dialogic – of contemporary art forms." "The poetry reading," he argues in an odd parody of one of Democracy's sacred texts, "is an ongoing convention of poetry, by poetry, for poetry. In this sense, the reading remains one of the most participatory forms in American cultural life" (*CL* 23). When poetry is performed, the division between different modes of writing that earlier seemed so sharply drawn is blurred, if not erased:

> ...poetry creates something of the conditions of hearing (not just listening to) a foreign language – we hear it as language, not music or noise; yet we cannot immediately process its meaning. Another way of saying this is that the poetic function ... rematerializes language, returns it from 'speech' back to 'sound;' or rather, the poetic mode synthesizes the speech mode of perception and the nonspeech mode of perception. (*CL* 18)

Accordingly, the performative also provides a highly inclusive space: It is open to a great variety of poetic modes – be they authorial or textual, or, as in slam poems, scores to be performed – as long as they are not reinvested with the false authority of the universal or the sentimental appeal to origin and center. Thus even the prophetic gesture of romantic subjectivity, so objectionable to all Language Poets, can be questioned and parodistically re-cycled from the position of the reader, just as the sensuous materiality of the text invites the reader to actively, playfully, participate in bringing it to life. Although Bernstein insists that the shifting from the subjective/romantic to the textual and from there to the performative and

---

14 In "Avant-garde Tradition and Individual Talent: The Case of Language Poetry," 123. In "Comedy and the Poetics of Political Form" – his own contribution to the essay collection on *The Politics of Poetic Form* he edited in 1990 – Bernstein postulates such a correlation of "word" and "world" (as does the whole book in its programmatic title) when he argues that formal innovation was also a form of social innovation and should therefore be interpreted accordingly: "By insisting that stylistic innovations be recognized not only as alternative aesthetic conventions but also as alternative social formations; I am asking that we bring devices back from a purely structural interpretative hermeneutics" (242f).

multivectoral does not constitute a sequence of linear progress but an expanding circle of synchronic possibilities ("We don't return to anything – turning (tuning) is enough" [*CL* 20]), he nevertheless draws a line that cannot be broken without loss of self-respect: There can be no return to a delusion of origin – be it that of speech, self, or nation. "The fiction of centrality," he writes in *A Poetics*,

> ...is related to those other fictions that have been undermined in much recent poetry – voice and identity. In emphasizing the legitimacy of marginal voices, there may be a tendency to essentialize difference; so that from a promotion of decentralized dialects we can too easily arrive at atomized centralities (nationalisms) – that is, a reductively unified identity/voice of a 'marginal' people or country or region. (189)

And yet, even if he does not like their poetry, Bernstein accepts these voices as members of a community of the marginalized. It is interesting to see how intensely he negotiates between different implications of the marginal (be it political, poetical, or cultural), without being able, or willing, to make them coincide. For the margin, as the place *par excellence* of the different and the particular, is the only space where Bernstein is able to situate himself as poet *and* as *homo politicus*. His almost physical aversion against the pull of the general and universal, against all tendencies towards centralization and conformity makes him cling to the marginal (in its broadest definition) as the last line of defence against the progressive expansion of a bureaucratized, medialized, and commercialized Democracy. [15]

To be on the margins, for Bernstein, is therefore to enjoy social and/or political solidarity with those rejected by the center (or rather by what he calls "the hegemony of homogenizing processes" [*AP* 119]) as much as to enjoy the freedom of poetic diversity and the "individual and libertarian freedom" that, for him, is the anarchic essence of the democratic. Therefore: "What is to be regretted is not the lack of mass audience for any particular poet but the lack of poetic thinking as an activated potential for all people" (*AP* 225). What produces this "lack" that keeps people from activating their own poetic potential is the brainwashing power of the "mainstream." However, what is the mainstream? What is that "official verse culture" so often seen as synonymous with it? Surely any language easily co-opted by institutional America by the mechanism of consumerism and the media. Plus, evidently, anyone praised by Helen Vendler or *The New York Times Book Review*; plus any essentializing discourse – either political or poetical.

[15] The logic for such a "rapprochement" (Perloff) between antagonist aesthetics Bernstein himself saw in an absolute need for diversity since "The violence of every generalization crushes the hopes for a democracy of thought" (*AP* 113). "Democracy, without individual and sectarian liberty, is a mockery of justice" (*AP* 225); therefore: "By emphasizing eccentricity, I want to acknowledge the significance of group-identified poetries (ethnic, racial, linguistic, social, class, sexual, regional) in shattering the neoconventionalist ideal of fashioning by masterly artifice a neutral standard English, a common voice for all to speak ..." (*AP* 119f.).

And yet, if all subjective expression and all "meaning"-making is, as some advocates of Language Poetry maintain, potentially part of an official verse culture and thus prone to be contaminated by the public media – does this not exclude from the realm of the aesthetically respectable large territories of human experience and leave its expression to the media? In other words, may not the avant-garde's fear of contamination add to the very problem it intends to resist? If there is no linearity, no "progress" in artistic development – as both Bernstein and Perloff argue –, what constitutes aesthetic obsolescence? How do we define the range, radius and direction of what is contemporary in poetry?

Maria Damon, arguing from the "slam and open-mike activity"-end of Bernstein's performative alliance on the margins, insists that it is "important to not romanticize or fetishize a kind of oral purity over a corrupt mainstream or a precious, solipsistic avant-garde." Bernstein would of course agree. Yet the argument could also be turned against a romantization of the avant-garde. All terms used in this connection are constructs and fictions. In reality, Damon maintains, "The boundaries, if they exist at all, are permeable" (*CL* 339). And, as Marjorie Perloff in her recent essay on the avant-gardes pointed out, perhaps surprisingly and yet entirely within the logic of her approach to poetry: "Indeed, the epithets *innovative, experimental, alternative, radical* – not to mention *avant-garde* – are now so reified in their own right that one sometimes finds oneself longing for a transparent nature lyric or love sonnet . . . " ("Avant-garde Tradition" 131). Is then the next horizon of the "New" in poetry and writing, the new twist in the definition of the democratic in aesthetics, marked by the digital revolution? Or by a response to needs the avant-garde leaves so pointedly unfulfilled?

Let me, very briefly, look at two texts – written at more or less the same time but going into entirely different directions: one is called *pleasureTEXTpossession*, 'interwritten' by Maria Damon and mIEKAL aND between 1996 and 2001, published by Zasterle Press in 2005; the other *The White Fire of Time*, poems by Ellen Hinsey, published by Wesleyan University Press, 2002. The first is the product of an intense electronic collaboration ("interwriting") which effectively erases traces of individual authorship since, as Maria Damon explains in an interview, "we continue each other's sentences, adding and twisting, disrupting and elaborating each other's words from inside the structure of the sentence."[16] At the same time, *pleasureTEXTpossession* ("an ongoing online hyperpoetic collaboration") places itself clearly in the tradition of experimental writing from DADA and Concrete Poetry to the visual poetry/writing of language poets like Steve McCaffery. It increasingly dissolves the textual order of the printed page into a visual chaos of playfully changing graphic designs, letter types and sizes, making full

[16] Bob Holman interviews Miekal And and Maria Damon: http://poetry.about.com/library/weekly/aa030299.htm.

use here of the possibilities of the electronic media/screen (which we can only guess at from its reduction/reproduction on the printed page). This is especially true of the last "poem," "e.n.t.r.a.n.c.e.d," where words, besides being elements of constantly shifting graphic designs, also form generative clusters since they are hypertextually linked to their various semantic and/or assonantic/consonantic paradigms. The text thus enacts its Barthesian title in cascades of visual, semantic, and acoustic rearrange-me re-arrangements. It plays with the possibilities of "entranced" (leading to "entrance" but also to "entrenchment") and with the ambivalences of "possession" – including being possessed/entranced with the joys of linguistic playfulness.

Ellen Hinsey, although not exactly an established poet either, is no doubt a more traditional one.[17] I don't know whether Helen Vendler ever praised her – but she might have. Her hero on the field of contemporary poetry is, so she told me, Czeslaw Milosz; and the book jacket informs us that her poetry "goes courageously against the current of contemporary poetry." (Whatever that may be: the "mainstream" as defined by Bernstein or a Language Poetry that, by now, has been critically acknowledged as representing contemporary avant-garde writing and found its place in academia?) In any case, Hinsey, too, tries to avoid the trap of subjective speech by creating a voice that, although personal, is trans-subjective, a meditative voice bent in rapt contemplation on things in their sensuous existence, on consciousness and texts – religious, philosophical and psychological – that deal with ultimate matters: the body, the passions, language, mortality and time: This is evidently a text in the modernist metaphysical tradition and thus very much concerned with the creation of form ("the hard frame of the mind") and with the metaphoric density of meaning. Accordingly, the volume is very tightly structured: It is divided into three parts ("The World," "The Temple," "The Celestial Ladder"), the first containing 7 sections, the second 9, and the third again 7. (And there are more hidden symmetries in the text's microstructure.) The tight structural frame of the cycle is set in contrast to the text's rhetorical excessiveness – its passionate grandiloquence and verbal music are reminiscent, at times, of Crane's or Hopkins's poetry. The poems evoke the formalized devotion of medieval religious tableaux, although they do not celebrate the other-worldly but embrace consciously, sometimes ecstatically, the precariousness of physical existence.

I have difficulty "placing" Ellen Hinsey. She is not on the "margins" and would certainly not be part of Bernstein's alliance of the marginal. But she does not fit his definition of the "mainstream" either. For it would be unfair, if not simply wrong, to say that for Bernstein "mainstream" is everything that does not

---

17 She won the Yale Series of Younger Poets competition in 1995 with her volume *Cities of Memory* which was subsequently published by Yale University Press. She has been living in Paris for more than a decade.

follow language poetry poetics. His essays show a self-questioning heroism of spiritual adventure, a passionate clarity of thought as well as a clear passion for language itself that do not go together with a purist's restrictiveness. "Poetry is the aversion of conformity," he writes; and: "The problem is being stuck in any one modality of language – not being able to move in, around, and about the precincts of language" (*CL* 20).[18] His determined non-conformism makes him no doubt *parti pris*, but he is nevertheless open toward anyone equally risking life and career for what might be, after all, a lost cause; and he is open toward anyone who has kept faith in what has been defined as the poet's social function ever since the "marginalization of poetry" began: the faith (perhaps the last remaining one) in the magic power of the word to purify the language of the tribe. That is why Bernstein can write at the end of *A Poetics*: "Poets don't have to be read, any more than trees have to be set under, to transform poisonous societal emissions into something that can be breathed" (226).[19]

This may or may not be a last and somewhat desperate assertion of the poet's social mission. Rosmarie Waldrop, paraphrasing Shelley filtered through George Oppen, defined it in a more relaxed and a more private manner when she called "poets (and readers) something like the unacknowledged life maintenance crew of the mind" and embraced George Bataille's notion of art as "a glorious waste of excess energy" (*PPF* 70n and 49).[20] The work that has to be done in the process

---

18 "Poetry is aversion of conformity in the pursuit of new forms ... I care most for poetry as dissent, including formal dissent ...;" "... anything better than the well-wrought epiphany of predictable measure ... the primacy of the individual voice, fanned by a gentile inspiration" (*AP* 2). Accordingly, he professes "a willingness to engage in guerilla warfare with the official images of the world that are being shoved down our throats ..." and with "the lingo of a unified culture of diversity" (*AP* 6). It is his very anti-conformism that makes him weary of any absolute position including, possibly, his own.

19 Needless to say that, although propagating the social function of poetry, Bernstein is deeply averse to the poet's assumption of "voice" or "some vatic image of sincerity" and embraces instead "rupture, cut-up, break apart in order to expose and defuse and reform" (*PPF* 239). Conscious of the German experience, Rosmarie Waldrop is yet more skeptical as concerns the power of poets as well as the power of language: "All the Dadaists and expressionists had been questioning, challenging, exploring, changing the language, limbering up its joints," she writes in "Alarms & Excursions." "So the German language should have been in very good condition, yet the Nazis had no trouble putting it to work for their purposes, perverting it to where what was said was light-years from what was meant. So, while language thinks for us, there is no guarantee that it will be in a direction we like" (*PPF* 47).

20 "In these essays," Bernstein writes in his "Introduction," "the poets assembled extend Shelley's dictum that poets are the unacknowledged legislators of the world and George Oppen's revision: that poets are the legislators of an unacknowledged world" (vii). In her contribution, Rosmarie Waldrop argues against Shelley's as well as Oppen's statements: "It sounds to me like a hangover from the times when the poet occupied a priestly position. But in our time, poetry has no such institutionalized function, and I must say I am not sorry. Or is it a male aspiration? I certainly have no desire to lay down the law. To my mind writing has to do with uncovering pos-

offers, in any case, its own rewards: What Steve McCaffery called "the experience of language," Susan Howe "the love of words" and Rosmarie Waldrop her "dialogue with language itself" (*PPF*.53). This almost physical engagement with language and its magic power not only to *create* reality but to *be* a reality in itself can also be seen in Maria Damon's and Ellen Hinsey's distinctly different, yet equally intense, linguistic entrancements. It was perhaps most sensuously, most lovingly expressed by Gertrude Stein in her famous "Transatlantic Interview":

> I began to play with words then. I was a little obsessed by words of equal value ... I took individual words and thought about them until I got their weight and volume complete and put them next to another word, and at this time I found out very soon that there is no such thing as putting them together without sense ... I made innumerable efforts to make words write without sense and found it impossible. (Stein 504)

If this is a most memorable assertion of the physicality, the materiality of language, it is also a reminder that materiality is not everything, that the exploration of language's "undiscovered country" (Howe in *PPF* 195) can take many forms and engage different aspects, states, and functions of language. Among the many dichotomies advanced by the language poets, there is also Rosmarie Waldrop's distinction between "comfort poetry" and "poetry of surprise" (*PPF* 70). Like James's house of fiction, the house of poetry has many windows. They might all open toward different views, each in its own way surprising. What counts is that they open.

Works Cited

Altieri, Charles. *Painterly Abstraction in Modernist American Poetry*. New York: Cambridge University Press, 1989.

Bernstein, Charles, ed. *Close Listening: Poetry and the Performed Word.* New York: Oxford University Press, 1998.

—. Interview with David Antin. *The Review of Contemporary Fiction* Spring (2001): 10-53.

—. *A Poetics*. Cambridge, MA: Harvard University Press, 1992.

—, ed. *The Politics of Poetic Form*. New York: ROOF, 1990.

Butterick, George. "Robert Creeley and the Tradition." Ed. John Wilson. *Robert Creeley's Life and Work: A Sense of Increment*. Ann Arbor: The University of Michigan Press, 1987.

Clifford, James. *The Predicament of Culture: Twentieth-Century Ethnography, Literature and Art*. Cambridge, MA: Harvard University Press, 1998.

---

sibilities rather than codification. My keywords would be exploring and maintaining: exploring a forest not for the timber that might be sold, but to understand it as a world and to keep this world alive" (46). Accordingly, her revision of Shelley's dictum puts the poet's function on a different scale: "So rather than legislators I would call poets (and readers) something like the unacknowledged life maintenance crew of the mind" (70).

Damon, Maria, & mIEKAL aND. *Interview with Bob Holman*. <http://poetry.about.com/library/weekly/aa030299.htm>.

—. *pleasure TEXTpossession*. La Laguna: zasterle press, 2005.

—. "Was That 'Different,' 'Dissident' or 'Dissonant'? – Poetry (n) the Public Spear: Slams, Open Readings, and Dissident Traditions." Ed. Charles Bernstein. *Close Listening*. 324-342.

Duncan, Robert. *Bending the Bow*. New York: New Directions, 1968.

Enzensberger, Hans Magnus. *Einzelheiten II: Poesie und Politik*. Frankfurt: edition suhrkamp 87, 1963.

Grenier, Robert. "On Speech." Ed. Ron Silliman. *In the American Tree*. 496-497.

Hinsey, Ellen. *The White Fire of Time*. Middletown: Wesleyan University Press, 2002.

Hoover, Paul. *Postmodern American Poetry: A Norton Anthology*. New York: Norton,1994.

Matthiessen, Frances O. *The American Renaissance*. New York: Oxford University Press, 1941.

McCaffery, Steve. "Voice in Extremis." Ed. Charles Bernstein. *Close Listening*. 162-177.

Messent, Peter. *Ernest Hemingway*. London: The Macmillan Press, 1991.

Perelman, Bob. *The Marginalization of Poetry: Language Writing and Literary History.* Princeton: Princeton University Press, 1996.

Perloff, Marjorie. "Avant-garde Tradition and Individual Talent: The Case of Language Poetry." *Revue Française d'Études Américaines* 103 (Février 2005): 117-141.

—. *Radical Artifice: Writing Poetry in the Age of Media*. Chicago: The University of Chicago Press, 1991.

—. *21st-Century Modernism: The 'New' Poetics*. London: Blackwell, 2002.

Silliman, Ron, ed. *In the American Tree.* Orono, ME: The University of Maine at Orono Printing Office, 1986.

Stein, Gertrude. "A Transatlantic Interview 1946." Ed. Bonnie K. Scott. *The Gender of Modernism: A Critical Anthology*. Bloomington: Indiana University Press, 1990. 502-516.

Thomas, Lorenzo. "Neon Griot – The Functional Role of Poetry Readings in the Black Arts Movement." Ed. Charles Bernstein. *Close Listening*. 300-323.

Waldrop, Rosmarie. "Alarms & Excursions." Ed. Charles Bernstein. *The Politics of Poetic Form*. 45-72.

Whitman, Walt. *An American Primer*. Ed. Horace Traubel. Camden, 1904.

—. *Complete Poetry and Collected Prose*. New York: The Library of America, 1982.

Williams, William Carlos. "Hart Crane." *Contempo* II. 4 (July 5, 1932): 4.

—. *Selected Essays*. New York: New Directions, 1969.

The Powerless Power of Poets: Experimenting with the Self-in-Relation

Astrid Franke

"Poems are dangerous," read the headline of an interview with the American poet and editor Sam Hamill in a German newspaper on February 1, 2003. To a German audience, this was news indeed. We are inclined to agree with Auden that "poetry makes nothing happen," except, perhaps, under forms of dictatorship where a poem may get you into trouble. How can poetry be dangerous in a democracy? Hamill had begun to collect poems on a website named "poetsagainstthewar.org" protesting the impending war against Iraq. In response, the White House postponed a poetry event to which he had been invited, but as people on both sides of the Atlantic probably expected, neither the poems read nor those not read posed any 'danger' to the course of foreign policies.

One may dismiss the phrase as one of the hyperbolic statements poets are apt to make. The poet "can make every word he speaks draw blood," wrote Whitman in his preface to *Leaves of Grass* (Whitman 8) and a "chance word, upon paper, may destroy the world," warned William Carlos Williams in *Paterson* (Williams 129). Amidst the bravado one can always hear a certain despair, as though the belief in the power of poetry is necessary to go on writing a few years before or after a great war. The statements are indicators of a political climate where poets feel compelled to emphasize their social significance. In this situation, poetic experiment is apt to be used to envision new ways of interacting with public life. It is therefore worthwhile asking wherein the power, perhaps even the danger of poetry may lie today. One intricate answer could be found two weeks after Hamill's statement in *The Village Voice*, where Joshua Clover quoted the poet Ann Lauterbach as saying:

> Perhaps poets come to the fore at such times because we already live at the margins, we represent a kind of powerless power, and maybe people become interested in this; the idea that persons can devote a life to something that will not bring the usual rewards. ... This is a kind of identification, especially when people feel they have so little say in the matter.

Lauterbach implies that if "poetry makes nothing happen," this may be precisely why it is so important: it comes to represent powerlessness as a widespread experience and may thus offer models of identification, perhaps even ways of coping with it – and therein lies its power. In the following remarks, I wish to explore this paradoxical idea in two steps: I want to suggest that a sense of the diminished role of individual agency with regard to public issues is central to the poems in two recent anthologies, *Poets Against the War*, edited by Sam Hamill, and *enough*, edited by Leslie Scalapino and Rick London. When it comes to social and political action, poets as citizens experience themselves as helpless, impotent, and even as victims. This diagnosis is true equally for most of the rather conventional poems in Hamill's anthology as well as for the more experimental ones in *enough*. In contrast to 'canonical,' or 'mainstream,' which I understand as sociological terms referring to the institutionalized framework of poetry, 'conventional' can be more easily used to identify an older mode of writing or a period style; in the case of many poems in *Poets Against the War*, they echo the style of the protest poems of the 60s, such as for instance those in the anthology *Where is Vietnam?* edited by Walter Lowenfels. I want to demonstrate that this style can be used for an initial diagnosis of the current socio-political climate precisely because the style lacks the power and the means to respond to its pressures adequately. These poems suggest that the use of a conventional style in the treatment of social and political problems is not just vaguely dissatisfying because the style has been used before; it is dissatisfying because the language misses aspects of the current situation and seems inadequate to express our experience of it.

In the second step, I want to introduce some poems which are experimental in that they try to devise new ways of conveying a sense of urgency. In contrast to the styles we associate with the Language poets, these poems are not marked by disruptions of syntax and reference as their experiments are not so much directed at language itself but at the ways in which poetry can make us feel concerned about our relations to others. I will distinguish between two kinds of such experiments: one, touched upon only briefly, creates witty blends of public language to reveal particular constructions of reality such as arise from economics tied to patriotism, for instance, or religion merging with declarations of war. The thrust of these poems is a cognitive one; they imply connections to be uncovered by a discerning reader that could be translated into terms of political diagnosis. The second mode of experiment uses the means of poetry to appeal to kinds of affects that lie before or beneath any form of political association, such as tenderness, care, or a sense of awe. Arguably, the poems by Adrienne Rich and by Juliana Spahr do not really use "another language;" yet, they test out ways in which poetry could express a sense of the self in relation to others and to the world without posing a collective identity – in terms of gender, race, or nationality, for instance – as a starting point.

Here, the contrast with a more conventional attempt can illuminate the challenge this entails.

Conventional Complaints

Hayden Carruth's "Complaint and Petition" is representative of all those poems in the anthologies that are based on an individual voice projecting itself against the nation. It is a particularly male genre that has a lineage back through Allen Ginsberg and Walt Whitman to Philip Freneau and once captured revolutionary democratic ideas. What is most noticeable in recent texts, however, is a quaintness which conveys the suspicion that the whole performance may no longer be appropriate: "I address you from a remote / margin of your dominion in plain- / style Yankee quatrains because / I don't know your exalted language / of power" (Carruth 46). These lines evoke the republican idea whereby moral integrity resides in plain citizens who live far away from the center of power – wherever that may be today. Poetry is appropriate to the occasion because it is presumably as far from the language of power as is the poet's abode. As a marker of powerlessness, the poet suggests, his poem indicates his moral integrity and even superiority over the president. But the many self-conscious speech acts raise increasing doubts about these assumptions: the word "margin" draws attention to the unlikelihood that the poet does not know about the current language of power, the specification of "we, the people" as pre-industrial craftsmen and -women raises the suspicion that the idea of representation may be just as dated as people who produce things with their hands. Even the title seems ill-chosen, since the poem turns out to be not so much a "Complaint and Petition" as an accusation and exhortation:

> hide yourself in your own shame,
> lest otherwise the evil you have
> loosed will destroy everything
> and love will quit the world. (47)

But the crucial moment in the poem that betrays its central dilemma comes after a repeated claim for plain speech:

> Let us speak plainly. You wish to
> murder millions, as you yourself
> have said, to appease your fury. (48)

Apparently, the president himself also speaks plainly and this collapses the dichotomy the poem is based upon: the language of power, it turns out, *is* plain speech. It is concrete rather than abstract, and renders a political conflict into a confrontation of good and evil, of innocence versus corruption, "honest American men and women" against a tyrant. That the poem's rhetoric is so vulnerable to deconstruction, that it is indeed on the verge of deconstructing itself, points to the datedness of its underlying assumptions: the opposition of center and margin, of power and powerlessness, corruption and innocence, the individual as rational agent susceptible to persuasion, a representative self and the role of voice, of poetry as generically immune to abuses of language and power, art as direct expression of intention, and language as transparent to the speaker.

This list is a reminder of how poetic form and language are connected to historical formations; consequently, poetic experimentation or the lack of it is not only a question of identifying an avant-garde versus a mainstream but of elucidating why, at particular points in history, it seems poetically and politically dissatisfying to cling to poetic conventions that emerged in earlier socio-political conflicts. Poetically it is dissatisfying because the deconstructions by poets and theorists – and here the so-called Language poets formed the most influential group – have drawn attention to the linguistic conventions used to construct these notions. This was detrimental to the personal, even confessional style of the 60s and 70s because it depended heavily on a denial of rhetoric as a "language of power" and instead presented itself as a sincere and "plain" expression of concern for the common weal. The unmasking of a style by undermining the whole idea of a coherent "voice" happened not just as a necessary renewal of technique, but also because these constructions seemed inadequate to new perceptions of political realities: an emphasis on the moral integrity of individuals disregards the political sphere of interests, institutions, and public relations. A simple opposition of innocence vs. corruption glosses over our complicity in exertions of power – as voters and consumers, for instance. The idea of representation has been complicated by an awareness of its abuses and exclusions. And as Carruth's poem involuntarily demonstrates, all these assumptions and their respective languages are complicit with common political rhetoric. While this emphasizes the need for "another language," it also highlights a dilemma not solved by deconstructions: if power and individual agency dissolve and render a rhetorical appeal obsolete, what can replace it? How can a poem sustain a claim for a collective "we" without declaring itself to represent a preexisting community? Wherein lies the constructive power of poetry?

Another Language of Relations

So far, I have backed up the diagnosis of diminishing individual agency and the powerless power of poetry with a text that conveys a sense of the problem without the adequate poetic means to engage with it. Now I want to focus on poems that do not so much work towards an expression of powerlessness as they take this situation as their starting point and devise ways of working with and through it. In poems by Harryette Mullen, Ben Friedlander, Adrienne Rich, and Juliana Spahr, this involves the recognition of complicity and the acknowledgement of responsibility in human relations. This is done in two distinct modes: Harryette Mullen and Benjamin Friedlander create eerie echoes of *déjà dits,* recognizable by sound structure and key words, but wittily distorted and thereby transferred into different semantic fields. The point is not to remind us once again of the constructed nature of all reality, but to draw attention to particular constructions and the interests underlying them. Friedlander's "State of the Union" blends references to official announcements and explosives into the diction of "The Lord's Prayer":

> Stern father in heaven, hollow
>
> Be thy bulletins, spent shells
> With powder burns
> Delivered by trigger men
> Of the cloth. (107)

While the substitutions are often surprising and funny, the combination of a religious language with the language of war in official speech is certainly not. In "The L. B. J. Tapes," Whitman's imagery of a radical public self that opens up interior spaces and is to be admitted everywhere (as in "Unscrew the locks from the doors! / Unscrew the doors themselves from their jambs!" from "Song of Myself") is perverted into its opposite, the desire for secrecy of a government that does not want any witnesses: "Unplug the appliances. / Tear the sockets themselves from the walls" (Friedlander 108).

Mullen's "Land of the Discount Price, Home of the Brand Name," from *enough,* confounds the difference between the language of patriotism and the language of advertisement: Lines such as "I pledge allegiance to my MasterCard / that is honored in more stores than American Express" or "My country, 'tis of thee, sweet land of Lipton instant tea!" first suggest the ubiquity of brand names, that is, the domination of public language by commerce as a language with a similar or even higher recognition value (Mullen 108-109). They also draw attention to the fact that words like Liberty, Old Glory, or Independence Day work like brand names: linguistically, they use capitalization and frequently two-part compounds, such as American Express, Cool Whip, or Dixie Cup. Psychologically, they are instantly recognized and, like instant tea, dissolve into a brew of vague associations. They market mass products, and in the poem establish a connection between the notion of shopping as a patriotic activity and the suspicion that, conversely, a patriotic activity may conceal an economic one: at the end of the poem, the "World Peacekeepers Patriot Soldier," "a twelve-inch fully poseable action figure that plays the national anthem" becomes part and symbol of a world-wide advertisement campaign.

While Mullen's and Friedlander's witticisms prompt awareness and diagnosis, Adrienne Rich's "The School Among the Ruins," first published in *Poets Against the War*, presents the voice of a teacher who continues "teaching responsibility" among the ruins: "Don't let your faces turn to stone / Don't stop asking me why / Let's pay attention to our cat she needs us" (Rich 25). Attention to the needs of other creatures in the poem is a last defense against emotional hardening and the strength of this approach is that it realizes resources of affect and values that lie untouched in mere cognitive efforts – this is also the case in Juliana Spahr's "Poem Written after September 11." The title suggests the idea of a poetic 'response' to a specific event, but Spahr developed her mode of writing before 2001, as one can see in her earlier volume *Fuck You-Aloha-I Love You* (2001). It already repeated a line with which the new poem opens: "There are these things" (Spahr, *Aloha* 7, 9, 11, 15; *Connection* 3). Repetition is indeed an important device of the poem as a large part of it is based on an expanding serial pattern, embracing more and more space; here is the last 'stanza' in the series and the turning point:

> As everyone with lungs breathes the space between the hands
> and the space around the hands and the space of the room and
> the space of the building that surrounds the room and the space
> of the neighborhoods nearby and the space of the cities and the
> space of the regions and the space of the nations and the space
> of the continents and islands and the space of the oceans and
> the space of the troposphere and the space of the stratosphere
> and the space of the mesosphere in and out.
>
> In this everything turning and small being breathed in and out
> by everyone with lungs during all the moments.
>
> Then all of it entering in and out.
>
> The entering in and out of the space of the mesosphere in the
> entering in and out of the space of the stratosphere . . .
> (*Connection* 8-9)

The poem may first be described as arising from a meeting of Walt Whitman with Gertrude Stein: From Whitman comes the desire to express a connection with the whole of creation, from its smallest to its largest manifestations. For Whitman as for Spahr, "the kelson of the creation is love," but in "Song of Myself," this love is frequently overpowering, the merger announced by the "I" a threat as much as a promise. Spahr, who avoids grand terms like "I," "creation," or "love" is much more careful. The "stratosphere" is as far as she goes, and love is referred to only in the adjective "lovely" as a sense of wonder over the intimacy that arises from breathing the same air everyone else breathes in the same rhythm, "in and out." To understand how this idea of connection can acquire emotional force without being embodied by a self as in Whitman, we need Stein and her modernist experiments. In Stein, repetition draws attention to language as a system with its own dynamic. Spahr uses a special kind of repetition, seriality, which 'creates' the larger part of the poem. It suggests an impersonal logical principle producing larger and larger units. What may seem somewhat cold and rational is actually, as in Stein, a source of humor, too. To recognize a pattern produces the pleasure of predicting and expecting the next element, the uncertainty whether it will actually come up, the curiosity about how far this will go and especially how it will end. As a poetic technique, it connects vernacular forms such as nursery rhymes with the high art of modernism – as Stein reminded us, these are not so far apart.

Spahr uses the expanding series of concentric spaces not only to support an impersonal notion of poetic composition, but also as a mimetic principle giving rise before our eyes and ears to a sense of aesthetic creation as natural propagation and growth. Anaphora and epiphora clearly demarcate the growing units in the series and give them the appearance of independent beings even though, like grammatical offspring, each of them is equally connected by the subordinating conjunction "as" to the parent main clause. The quality of poetic language foregrounded in the text is the one closest to its organic condition, namely breath and rhythm. Note how syllables and beats multiply in the line "cells, the movement of cells and the division of cells," how the most frequent connective, "and the," echoes the double-beat of the heart, and how attention is drawn to breathing because, as in "Howl," one is either tempted to create very large breath-units (and then runs out of breath) or one breathes discretely, in which case the rhythm is likely to assume an even, meditative pace.

As we become aware of breath, we become aware of our connection to others and assume a "we" not based on collective identity but on a form of acknowledgment.[1] It involves recognizing and admitting a relation that affects our attitude

1 Stanley Cavell and Axel Honneth are two philosophers, who currently try to conceptualize the term beyond the Hegelian "recognition." Both argue that acknowledgment comes before (Honneth) and goes beyond (Cavell) cognition. In contrast to Cavell, Honneth would apply the term in the context of an ecological consciousness, too, I think. Cf. Stanley Cavell, *Must We Mean What We Say? A Book of Essays*, Cambridge: Cambridge UP, 1969, 238-266. Axel Honneth's *Unsichtbarkeit. Stationen einer Theorie der Intersubjektivität,* Frankfurt: Suhrkamp, 2003 begins with literature (Ellison's *Invisible Man*) in order to capture the vague sense of a root of intersubjectivity that will allow him to move further away from the Hegelian concepts he de-

towards everyone. It is a form of love that is careful not to be overbearing, not to intrude, merge or contain, but strives to let things exist and to accept a respectful distance as in the deictic "There are these things." Even "we" occurs only once and in a passive construction that is part of an exclamation: "How connected we are with everyone." Like the exclamation at the end, it captures appreciation without appropriation, acknowledging an existence without instrumentalizing it. Like the crucial word "everyone," it can conceive of an existing whole that is fully inclusive and yet does not do violence to singularity – it is a version of the old problem of the one and the many that has gone through theoretical elucidations of exclusions. That by "connection" the poem comes to mean more than sharing air and pollution can be seen at the end: what is doomed, not least because of the events of September 11, is not the connection itself, but forms of commitment to it. And just like the involuntary but lovely connection through breathing, the doom seems equally impersonal and beyond one's power to prevent.

So where does that leave us with regard to the powerless power of the poet? Friedlander, Mullen, Rich, Spahr and Carruth respond to the same cultural pressures. They register the ubiquity of and complicity with languages of power they do not want to be complicit with, but Rich, Spahr and Carruth also testify to a need for connection, even commitment and solidarity with others. Where Carruth differs from the two female poets is that he assumes a privileged role as a poet, based on the authority of a literary language. If we cannot assume what he assumes, it is because we know as well as he does that the poet is *not* more powerful and representative than any other citizen and that, furthermore, his language has lost the authority it may have once carried. Intersubjectivity in poetry cannot be a starting point but needs to be built from the bottom up; it may follow from recognizing what constitutes our relations to others. A language experiment that arises from a widespread sense of individual powerlessness may become a source of strength when it explores a language of appreciation and respect, of responsibility and commitment that can articulate a sense of why others may have a claim on us.

Works Cited

Carruth, Hayden. "Complaint and Petition." *Poets Against the War*. Ed. Sam Hamill. New York: Thunder's Mouth Press, 2004. 46-47.

Clover, Joshua. "American Ink." *The Village Voice*. 6 Dec 2006 <http://www.villagevoice.com/news/0308,clover,41980,1.html>.

veloped in his *Kampf um Anerkennung*. An elaboration of the term as central to a theory of justice and a critique by Nancy Fraser can be found in Honneth and Fraser, *Umverteilung oder Anerkennung. Eine politisch-philosophische Kontroverse*, Frankfurt: Suhrkamp 2003.

Friedlander, Benjamin. "State of the Union" and "The L. B. J. Tapes." *Enough.* Eds. Leslie Scalapino and Jack London. Oakland: O Books, 2003. 107-108.

Hamill, Sam. "Gedichte sind gefährlich. Gespräch mit Sam Hamill, dem ausgeladenen Dichter." *Frankfurter Allgemeine Zeitung* February 1, 2003.

Lowenfels, Walter, ed. *Where is Vietnam? American Poets Respond.* Garden City: Anchor Books, 1967.

Mullen, Harryette. "Land of the Discount Price, Home of the Brand Name." *Enough.* Eds. Leslie Scalapino and Jack London. Oakland: O Books, 2003. 108-109.

Rich, Adrienne. *The School Among the Ruins: Poems 2000-2004.* New York: Norton 2004.

Spahr, Juliana. *This Connection of Everyone with Lungs: Poems.* Berkeley: University of California Press, 2005.

—. *Fuck You – Aloha – I Love You.* Middletown: Wesleyan University Press, 2001.

Whitman, Walt. *Leaves of Grass.* The First (1855) Edition. New York: Penguin, 1986.

Williams, William Carlos. *Paterson.* New York: New Directions, 1963.

How Experimental Is It, or: When Did Modernism End? Notes on (Reading) American Poetry

Sabine Sielke

Sounding little echoes of Walter Abish's novel *How German is It* (1981) and Harry Levin's seminal essay "What was Modernism?" (1960) the first part of my title means to raise two sets of questions. The first set interrogates the term 'experimental': What do we talk about when we talk about experimental poetry? In what ways do experiments in contemporary (American) poetry differ from modernist experimental poetics? And is the term 'experimental' still appropriate for our purpose – part of which is, I deem, to propagate the "use of poetry," as T. S. Eliot once put it, or rather, as we may prefer to phrase it today, the cultural functions of the poetic? The second set of questions reengages the term modernism: If contemporary experimental American poetry moves beyond modernist – and possibly even postmodernist – premises and projects, what sense of subjectivity and 'truth' does it evolve? Engaging the poetry of Charles Bernstein, Susan Howe, C. K. Williams, Ellen Hinsey, and Francisco X. Alarcón, albeit briefly, I mean to explore two questions in particular: How modern is contemporary poetry? And how experimental are poems which we do not categorize as experimental?

Of course, I will not be able to really answer these questions here; still I would like to make some, albeit, I fear, polemical and highly 'experimental' moves into the issues.[1] So let us begin with set one, question # 1: What do we talk about when we talk about experimental poetry? To answer this question we may have to take a step back and ask yet another question:

What Is an Experiment?

Experiment, of course, is a key term of modern philosophy and the natural sciences, thus appropriated for literary studies from another conceptual register, another language, so to speak, and adapted at the very moment when literary studies – much of which was occupied with poetry at the time – aspired to become a

1 I thank Marjorie Perloff for her poignant commentary on an earlier version of this paper.

science and the poet's mind in turn came to resemble a catalyst, a "shred of platinum" that remains "inert, neutral, and unchanged" in the process of creation, to quote from T. S. Eliot's "Tradition and the Individual Talent" (1919). At the same time, the concept of the experiment signifies an anti-positivist tradition in which modes of philosophical reflection and empirical modes of observation are not contradicting each other, but deemed to be closely connected (cf. Korg 187).

While up to the Renaissance the concept experiment referred to experience as such, from the Middle Ages on it has also suggested an experience that we particularly strive for. In scientific methodology the term traditionally references a set of actions and observations, performed to verify or falsify a hypothesis or research a causal relationship between phenomena. Scientific experiments have constituted an empirical approach to knowledge and require controlled conditions which allow for repetition, even if since Planck, Einstein, and Heisenberg experiments pertain to what is so far unknown. In more general terms experiment suggests the testing of an idea, a venture into something new or different, into a practice with yet unknown effects or results, in order to gain experience.

Adapted to literary studies in three steps, moving from early romanticism through realism to modernism (Horch 127-128), the term experiment came to denote practices of writing that veered away from the traditional, from conventions, thereby also necessarily defining and redefining what traditional, what convention actually meant. Once Whitman "made it new," forgot Shakespeare, as Emerson would have it, or aspired to do so, and displaced the dominant iambic pentameter by free verse, 'non-liberated,' constrained verse turned into convention, affirming rather than transforming the established social and political body. Accordingly, Whitman's democratic vistas were also a "language experiment" to the poet, "an attempt," as he put it, "to give the spirit, the body, the man, new words, new potentialities of speech" (*Daybooks*, 729n).

Of course, there have always been those who toned down the enthusiasm of many an experimenter. For Eliot, for instance, there was no such thing as free verse, since all verse can be measured in terms of meter. Neither did he or Marianne Moore, both pre-eminent modernists, believe in originality. "[I]t is impossible to be original," Moore claimed in her essay "Humility, Concentration, and Gusto" (1949), "in the sense of doing something that has never been thought before. Originality is in any case a by-product of sincerity; that is to say, of feeling that is honest and accordingly rejects anything that might cloud the impression, such as unnecessary commas, modifying clauses, or delayed predicates" (*Prose* 421). And, of course, matters of meter and originality are a little more complicated than that. Rejecting iambic pentameter Emily Dickinson, in contrast to Whitman, remembered the medieval ballad, condensed the line, and exposed the materiality of a highly elliptical poetic language, aspiring to represent, to grasp on paper what in fact tends to resist, to escape representation – pain, death, eternity – evolving lyrics that literally burst out of their seams in the process. This is why she would write, in one of her last poems:

> Experiment escorts us last –
> His pungent company
> Will not allow an Axiom
> An Opportunity (J. 1770)

For Dickinson poetry is legitimized, at least in part, by this very limitation of both science and theology hinted at here. As science has so far failed to lay down axioms that allow one to demystify death – figured in her poem as final experience, thus in the pre-Renaissance sense of the term experiment, orchestrated by a non-negotiable power ("His pungent company") – many of the experiments conducted in Dickinson's work aim at mapping the path from here to eternity and take "threshold glances" into the unknown. "I cannot tell how Eternity seems," Dickinson puts it in a letter to Louise and Frances Norcross, written after the death of her mother. "It sweeps around me like a sea" (L. 785). Whereas on this side of life "opposites entice," "The Absolute – removed / The Relative away –" (J. 765) in the beyond. Figured as "Miles on Miles of Nought" (J. 443) or as a time of "Velocity or Pause / At Fundamental Signals / From Fundamental Laws" (J. 1295), Dickinson's descriptions of eternity escape conventional measures of space and time while depending on them for representation. "Forever – is composed of Nows – / 'Tis not a different time," "Eternity" is "omnipresence" (J. 624). Dickinson's "Torrents of Eternity" (J. 1380) trade history for a "leisure of the Future," boundaries and limitations for "A Wilderness of Size" (J. 856) and for "Periods of Seas / Unvisited of Shores" (J. 695), for a limitless oceanic space where subjectivity dissolves. Still in Dickinson death marks not an end, but a new beginning, whose very resistance to conceptualization pushes poetry and poetics beyond its conventional limits. [2]

Though the experimentalisms of Whitman and Dickinson's poetics have been echoed and remembered by fellow experimenters, ranging from William Carlos Williams, Marianne Moore, and Langston Hughes to Allen Ginsberg, Sylvia Plath, and Susan Howe, among many others, they could never – and were never meant to – be repeated. Conditions would always have changed, as did the cultural functions of poetry. What has not changed, it seems, is the terminology of the literary critic, of the reader of American and other poetries. Reemploying the term experimental, we keep reinforcing a binarism within contemporary poetry and

---

2 For more detailed analyses of this predominant tendency in Dickinson's poetry, see Sielke, "Dickinson's Threshold Glances; or, Putting the Subject on Edge," *Fashioning* 36-60.

poetics that does not exist and which, in fact, has never existed in any clear-cut fashion.

Don't get me wrong: I am not voicing a critique of the enterprise pursued in this book. Rather I mean to examine the bias which we have inherited from modernism and which informs our readings of poetry to this very day, readings which tend to privilege the experimental over the "conventional" or the overtly "political" while at the same time clinging to the formalist insight, put forth most strongly in Julia Kristeva's *La révolution du langage poétique* (1974), that the experimental is the truly political; readings that manifest, for instance, a clear gap between language writing or "linguistically innovative poetry" (Kinnahan xiii) and the (many) others. In "conventional descriptive and narrative forms of writing," Charles Bernstein and Bruce Andrews write in their introduction to *The L=A=N=G=U=A=G=E Book* (1978), language becomes "transparent, leaving the picture of a physical world the reader can then consume as if it were a commodity." Language poetry, by contrast, "involves repossessing the sign through close attention to, and active participation [by the reader] in its production" (qtd. in Sayre 1184). Reproduced in our critical thinking this perspective tends to reduce, as I argue elsewhere, the polyphony of American poetry to bipolarity. [3] More often than not we are either concerned with poets who expose and thrive on the "radical artifice" (Perloff) of poetic discourse and take poetry itself as the "engenderer of experience" (Messerli 2). Or we focus on the "strenuous authenticity" (Perloff, *Radical Artifice* 20) of a poetry seemingly preoccupied with identity politics such as Francisco X. Alarcón's poem "The X in My Name" (1993).

The X in My Name

the poor
signature
of my illiterate
and peasant self

giving away
all rights
in a deceptive
contract for life (118)

This binary perspective not only disregards the many crossroads of contemporary American poetries – poetries that may be highly divergent in form. It also pays little attention to the aesthetics of the political in poetry while relying on a surprisingly strong and highly romantic faith in the power and potential subversiveness of stylistic complexities. And it has comfortably couched us, as readers,

3 See Sielke, "Committed."

in highly conventional positions, as well. Can we get up, move on, and in the process re-read the "X" in Alarcón's poem as a variable rather than a fixed value?

How Modern Is Experimental Postmodern Poetry?

So let us turn to question #2 of set one: If, for the time being, we hold on to the term experiment – in what ways do experiments in contemporary (American) poetry differ from modernist experimental poetics? Reading Susan Howe's *The Non-Conformist's Memorial* (1990) may generate some preliminary answers. In fact, the collection reminds us (in case we should have forgotten) that the experimental in literature is a matter of aesthetics and form as well as philosophy. Howe's poetry moreover underlines that philosophy in general and language philosophy in particular enable and evolve modes of literary experiment. More particularly, the utopian moments of postmodernist and poststructuralist thought with its celebration of both *différance* and difference (without hierarchy) have shaped Howe's poetry as much as the notion that cultural practices constitute forms of remembering, that poetry qualifies as a medium of individual and collective memory. Differences between modern and contemporary "experimental" poetry therefore reside in the interface between distinct forms and conceptions of subjectivity, history, and consequently knowledge. Thus question #2 of set one is inextricably related to the first question of set two which is aimed at the sense of subjectivity and 'truth' evolving from contemporary experimental American poetry and poetics, from a poetics that, we may want to agree, moves beyond modernist (and postmodernist) premises and projects.

This, I admit, is a mighty big matter which I would like to address first, before returning to Howe, by zooming in on a charmingly short text by Charles Bernstein, the poem "The Kiwi Bird in the Kiwi Tree" from his collection *Rough Trades* (1991).

> I want no paradise only to be
> drenched in the downpour of words, fecund
> with tropicality. Fundament be-
> yond relation, less 'real' than made, as arms
> surround a baby's gurgling: encir-
> cling mesh pronounces its promise (not bars
> that pinion, notes that ply). The tailor tells
> of other tolls, the seam that binds, the trim,
> the waste. & having spelled these names, move on
> to toys or talcums, skates & scores. Only
> the imaginary is real – not trumps

beclouding the mind's acrobatic vers-
ions. The first fact is the social body,
one from another, nor needs no other. (11)

Much can be said about this text. For me the poem pulls into two directions at the same time, affirming the move of non-identification that Bernstein cherishes in the works of Gertrude Stein while also recalling the "imaginary gardens with real toads in them" that Marianne Moore vividly exposes in her poem "Poetry" (1919). Modernism is thus quite prominently remembered here, first and foremost maybe as an ambivalence vis-à-vis its own experimental ambition that made Moore opt for what she labelled, as nonchalantly as enigmatically, "the genuine" located "beyond all that fiddle" (*Complete Poems* 266). There is, from the start, Moore's preference, first, for "those various scalpels / those / various sounds" (51) that echo through Bernstein's poem – the insistant "p"s ("paradise," "downpour," "tropicality"), followed by a stream of "r"s and "t"s that take their toll; and, secondly, for exotic or strange creatures of the animal kingdom, presented, as in Moore's poems, not in a space that appears 'photographically' visible – in fact, the poem resists the visual and imagistic we associate with modernism – but in a graphic environment of words replete with tropes. And yet, neither does this poem really "downpour" on us; it is much too restrained, perhaps even ridicules the economic use of language, the promise of plenty in scarcity that Pound advertised and propagated; and it is too fragmented with its lines of oscillating length, running on across inner rhymes in a manner that calls Moore's enjambments back to our minds. Nor does its "tropicality" project images that "Hands ... can grasp," to recall another phrase from Moore's 1919 poetological poem; "as arms surround a baby's gurgling" its tropes rather "encir- / cle" us in a "mesh [that] pronounces its promise" but does not deliver and leaves us with parenthetical negations: "(not bars / that pinion, notes that ply)."

Like Stein's texts and their distinct poetic programs, Bernstein's poem in this way provokes the reader in his or her capacity as a meaning-making animal while at the same time frustrating his or her desire to make perfect sense of things, poems, and his or her own position. Opening with the seemingly paradoxical rejection of paradise, Bernstein's poem dismisses the Adamic mode that Roy Harvey Pearce deemed paradigmatic for American verse. Privileging a "Fundament beyond relation" of a national kind, the speaker calls on family kinships only to seemingly dismiss the familiar. "The tailor," we are told, "tells / of other tolls, the seam that binds, the trim, / the waste." While remaining at an explicit distance from paternal professional virtues [4] – the sense for lines and borders, the exactitude, the necessity to cut and discard –, the poem enacts and embodies these

[4] Bernstein's father, as legend has it, was a tailor.

very virtues as part of the tradition and inheritance that individual talents have to wrestle with before he or she "moves on / to toy or talcums, skates & scores." However, tradition and individual talents have already been there too, as the catalogue suggests, recalling Whitman and Moore, among many others. Accordingly, the poem's central claim: "Only / the imaginary is real" which affirms the significance of perception and memory for our view of the world, is followed by yet another dismissal reminiscent of yet another of Moore's lines. The rejection of "trumps / beclouding the mind's acrobatic vers / ions" stereotypically privileges poetry ("vers[e]") over economic power ("trump") while also garbling a claim that Moore's "Poetry" makes. "When they" – things such as "Hands that can grasp, eyes / that can dilate, hair that can rise / if it must" – "become so derivative [in poetry]"

> . . . as to become
> unintelligible,
> the same thing may be said for all of us, that we
> do not admire what
> we cannot understand:. . . (*Complete Poems* 267)

As Bernstein's poem positions a real, if foreign, bird in an imaginary garden – after all, kiwis do not grow on trees – it thus remembers, rehearses, and mocks multiple moments of modernity in order to finally assert a supposedly factual difference: "The first fact is the social body, / one from another, nor needs no other." Seemingly resting on a politics – or poethics, to be more precise – of the communal ("social body"), Bernstein's lyrical "Kiwi Bird" moves beyond modernist poetics, reclaiming and inhabiting the space that literary theory – most notably perhaps once again Kristeva's *Révolution du langage poétique* – carved out for modernist experimenters. The phrase "one from another, nor needs no other" displaces the productivity of symbolic orders and mental gymnastics by a fundament of reproduction. Here poetry is no longer merely "a place for the genuine," as Moore famously put it. It carves a precarious space of intersubjectivity, of community, maybe even a consensus of a preliminary, transitory kind – "nor needs no other." In some sense Bernstein, not without irony, claims as a "first fact" the very realm of unmediated closeness to an other, a beloved, an identity in the sense of the very indifference or sameness that for Dickinson spelt eternity and that she meant to reclaim in her poetry for this side of experience; he appropriates the proximity of "white on white" that Moore captures in her beautiful, if somewhat sentimental poem "The Paper Nautilus" (1941). Pushing against our notions of the other as separate (subject), the final line, however, offers a riddle rather than a "fact," or to be more precise: presents the riddle as a fact, offers paradox as the only remaining truth, and thus comes to comfortably rest on its enigmatic closure, as so many of Moore's poems do. In this way, Bernstein's poem acknowledges that all final lines can be preliminary fundaments at best.

Susan Howe, I think, offers yet another, much less ironic take on the experimental mode as a form of 'poethics,' thereby exposing the desire for new forms of intersubjectivity that drives much of contemporary poetry – and prose, one would have to add. [5] Acknowledging the discursiveness of monumental history and subjectivity the poems collected in *The Non-Conformist's Memorial* both foreground and engage practices – such as reading (in) the margins of cultural productions – that allow us to reconstruct history as histories and subjectivity as fundamentally intersubjective. Howe's poems expose the significance of such marginalia, of phenomena which manifest themselves at the periphery of cultural production and more often than not get erased from our cultural archives and forms of memory. Examining and parodying more traditional conceptions of history, Howe's poems displace these conceptions with a highly experimental form of historiography, working by way of citation, syntactic disruption, and what Uta Gosmann calls a "mnemonics of the blank" (127-137). As Howe's texts quite literally turn our reading habits upside down, we, as readers, experience this kind of recollection, this piecing together, as a process that yields multi-perspectival subject positions and truths of a transitional kind. This multi-perspective on the world is taken by a subject-in-process whose preliminary and indeterminate nature, though, no longer registers as a mark of crisis as it did in modernist culture. While paradigmatically postmodernist poetry tends to radicalize this crisis, Howe's poetics reconstructs the subject by returning him or her to the writing of others, thereby recasting reading as a mode of intersubjectivity while also allowing for a fair share of chance, contingency, and forgetting. In this way, her poetic experiments acknowledge that the subject's very loss of stability and sovereignty, the contingencies and incoherencies of identity are the very basis, the possibility, as Judith Butler argues in *Ethik der kritischen Gewalt*, of a new political and ethical agency (54). Deeply inspired by both language philosophy and visual media, Howe's distinct experimental mode – much of which, significantly enough, due to its idiosyncratic typology and at times indeed 'monumental' scope resists reproduction here – desta-

5 Taking a revisionary approach to postmodernist texts, Katrin Amian, for instance, observes that postmodernist (inter-)textuality "emerge[s] *as a device* through which the return of the subject can be staged" and the intersubjective, communicative function of texts can be performatively (re-)enacted (155). More specifically, she argues that the dialogical structure Jonathan Safran Foer's *Everything Is Illuminated* sets up in the stories and letters its protagonists exchange "frames the creative (re-)invention of the past as an intersubjective affair and lends a compelling moral urgency to the collective project of writing a *'truthful'* [Foer 55 qtd. in Amian] piece of fiction" (134). Similar processes, I would argue, are at work in Howe's poetry, even if they do take different shapes.

bilizes the subject in order to evolve novel conceptions of intersubjectivity at the interfaces of multiple media, modes of thinking, and their increasingly precarious legibility.

Experiments in Reading

Thus is the term experiment still appropriate for our purpose? Well: Yes and no. The term may be misleading as long as it comes accompanied with a deep faith in the subversiveness of experimental literary discourse, a faith that, I fear, is largely unfounded; as long as the term marks a supposedly clear counterpoint to convention, yet another attempt to "make it new;" and as long as the experimental mode is reduced to matters of form and method. In fact, I do share the resistance C. K. Williams voices in his poem "The Method" (1992), whose speaker fears that he will drift away into "A dream of method":

> Imagine being offered an instrument to play that violated all your previous
> aesthetic norms,
> with a fleshy, tender, sensitive component, crudely sewn or soldered to
> an innocently inorganic,
> and a shape that hinted at the most contradictory techniques – brute
> force, a delicate dexterity.
> You know you're supposed to draw this hybrid to your breast, to try to
> coax from it its music,
> but under the tension of so many formal contradictions, what actually
> would you bring forth? (*Dream* 63)

Taken out of its context, this passage clearly reads like an attack on the experimental. As part of a larger body of work, however, which inextricably entwines the materiality of bodies and the urgency, if not uncontrollability of physical desires with the imaginary worlds unfolding in the human mind, such reflections point in a different direction. In this framework they also call into question, for instance, the poststructuralist notion that violations of aesthetic norms in "poetic language" (Kristeva) allow for a return of the body in language, a claim that aims at resolving one binarism – that of body and symbolic order – at the cost of reaffirming a series of others, including polarities such as poetic versus non-poetic discourse, semiotic versus thetic, experimental versus traditional. By contrast, C. K. Williams's collection *A Dream of Mind* (1992), which includes his poem "The Method," not only addresses matters of the body in a narrative or thetic, dialogic, and yet poetic, mode. "The long line," Charles Altieri writes, "allows a naturalness of conversation folded into the intimacy of internal dialogue so that lyric speech even at its most expansive seems entirely rooted in momentary observations and reflections on the implications of those observations" (230). These observations on the contingencies of human existence constitute the ground from which Williams's poems evolve larger political, ethical, and philosophical questions, concerning the roots of violence, the potential of transcendence, the pains of loss, and the powers of love. Capitalizing on the psychic make-up of universally physical human experiences such as desires, lacks, and longings, intimacy, loneliness, love, and sexual encounters, these texts at the same time resist the reduction of such experiences/experiments by ironically employing as titles the terms "Politics" and "Ethics" when exploring, for instance, the rhetoric of seduction (*Dream* 31-32) and the resistance to temptation (34-35). The engagement, in poetry, with language philosophy and poststructuralism thus evolves a range of experiments, not all of which flaunt violations of aesthetic norms. And when, in his prize-winning volume *Repair* (1999), Williams occasionally abandons the longer line and includes poems which appear highly stylized and formal, he further highlights how relative the terms experimental and conventional are, how inextricably linked, "one [to] another, nor needs no other" and mutually (re-) productive they in fact are. And, once again this insight has impacted on contemporary poetry as well as prose. "What is one to do," Jeffrey Eugenides, for instance, asks, "when experimental writing is no longer experimental, but has turned into a norm or become a cliché?" (107; translation mine).

Instead of offering us "news" what in fact we observe is that some poetries rededicate themselves to an earlier stage of modernism which, as Robert Kaufman puts it, had likewise taken from a still earlier moment called romanticism in order to readdress, "in the coordinates of a much-changed world," fundamental knowledge processes. These poetries are committed "to the challenge – ," as Kaufman has it, "at once aesthetical and socio-political – of what is difficult" (154). C. K. Williams, I would claim, has taken up this challenge. He shares his beginning as a writer of politically charged lyrics with many other poets whose first publications appeared in the late 1960s and early 1970s. From there, however, the poet has taken a highly idiosyncratic path, evolving the long, unrhymed line reminiscent of Walt Whitman that became both the hallmark of his poetry and a principle innovation within the development of post-World War II and postmodernist American poetry. As much concerned with matters of aesthetics and forms as with ethical and political concerns, yet in opposition to language poetry's attempt to distinguish one from the other, Williams has produced a body of poetry and a poetics that strongly resists traditional categorizations and addresses fundamental questions of human existence in a post-nuclear and post-Holocaust age as matters of individual, rather than collective, consciousness.

This rededication "to the challenge – at once aesthetical and socio-political – of what is difficult" necessarily calls upon diverse critical perspectives, ranging from theories of intersubjectivity to pragmatist approaches. In this sense the term experimental is highly appropriate, referring, however, not merely to particular textual practices but to our acts of interpretation as well. As readers we are being invited to experiment, to accept the contingencies and incoherencies of our own positions and perspectives as the very basis of our experience of the multiply mediated worlds projected by contemporary (American) poetry. This also entails, I would like to suggest, that we recover poetry as a realm for explorations of theoretical perspectives, for explorations, that is, which in recent decades have been grounded almost exclusively in narrative texts.

This also means, though, that we have to give up the consensual binarism between experimental and conventional poetry and allow for our sense of the experimental to constantly shift. I myself am tempted to suggest that, for the time being, we may want to rededicate ourselves to Wallace Stevens's claim that "all poetry is experimental poetry" even if, of course, this would mean adopting yet another modernist premise (*Opus Posthumous*, qtd. in Korg 1). At the same time once we become experimental readers, we may also evolve new notions of modernism. Re-reading Whitman and Dickinson by way of pragmatism, for instance, as some critics have begun to do, we do away with what for a long time has been conceived of as a fundamental difference within modernist experimental writing: the difference between, on the one hand, the attempt to recover the object in language, to arrive at a natural speech, and, on the other, the exploration of the potentialities of language as such, a binarism that clearly collapses in the work of Stein.

Thus this whole business of experiment and modernism is, as we may have guessed, a can of worms indeed. Thus let me rephrase, as a working hypothesis, my claim that contemporary poetics aspires to reimagining intersubjectivity – a hypothesis that derives as much from currently dominant critical perspectives as from diverse contemporary poetic practices. Let us turn to Ellen Hinsey, for instance, whose work challenges the conventions of both American contemporary experimental and 'ethnic' poetry by reengaging processes of memory, as in *Cities of Memory* (1996), and pre-modern meditation, as in *The White Fire of Time* (2002). What sense of subjectivity and 'truth,' I wonder, does this poetry evolve? Hinsey agrees with Bernstein, who considers it "a mistake to posit the self as the primary organizing feature of writing" (qtd. in Sayre 1184). She believes in "form as a vehicle for expression," yet resists both radical artifice and the "legacy of Confessionalism," which, she finds, dominates contemporary American poetry ("Doggerel" 140). Reencountering monuments of European culture, including Goya, Beethoven, and Freud by way of the spaces they inhabited or projected, Hinsey's first collection *Cities of Memory* (1996) invites us into cultural history as spaces of the mind and shared human experience which transcend the personal to enable interconnections and intercultural encounters by way of empathy. "Empathy," writes James Dickey in his foreword to the collection,

> though the German word *Einfühlung* is stronger – constitutes one of the poet's primary tools. . . . Ms. Hinsey's empathy runs to cultures, their people and artefacts. . . . Fountains, streets, trains – especially apt for her purposes – portraits – refugees, artists, and other survivors – are quietly felt, exactly limned, washed in a clear grey. (x)

Dickey's diction recalls the praise that William Carlos Williams extended to Moore, celebrating the ways in which her poems cleanse words of their conventional meaning. Hinsey's poems in turn emphatically relive moments of modernity – be it by inhabiting the images of war that Goya projected or by sympathizing with Paula Modersohn-Becker's attempts to "break with the prevailing visual idiom at Worpswede." "You began here," the speaker of "Paula Modersohn-Becker at Worpswede" recalls,

> . . . : this marsh
> the ground of your colors; you faced
> the unlanguable green of firs, drew
>
> the uncombed bank alight. Evening saw
> your reflection bend in the paleness
> at the water's edge, and pass where piled
> peat rose, darkened like temples after
>
> sudden rain. You loved the idiom
> of the place. But as a foot cannot retrace
> its step in ground grown cold
> since its passing, so repetitions bear
>
> their weight on the one who takes them
> on day after day: a palette like a landscape
> can grow too small, and fade, failing
> to tell how noon lay bright or fallow,
>
> or how it turned and pressed in by imagination's
> weight. Suddenly, color may turn unforgiving
> and fail you in even another word. (53-54)

Like Modersohn-Becker, we may be tempted to claim (and thereby dismiss the poet's dismissal of confessionalism) that Hinsey "breaks with the prevailing idiom" of a regionally limited American poetic idiom. However, matters are more complex and compelling. Hinsey's poem remembers Paula Modersohn-Becker by way of an intermedial exploration of painting as poetics, color as language, the visual as verbal and vice versa. In the process, the text also recalls H. D.'s "Oread" (1914), which invites the sea to "hurl your green over us / cover us with your pools of fir" (55) and enwraps the reader in synaesthetic experience. Thus empathy is a far stretch and highly mediated here, experiential as well as self-referential, self-reflexive, and intercultural, and thus – despite all formal constraints – colored by an experimental palette.

Having said all this, one could also add, I would claim, that Alarcón merely teases us into taking his poem as identity politics. Posing as an ethnic text, "The X in My Name" in fact dispenses with marks of ethnicity, substituting signs of class instead, while at the same time suggesting alliances across races, ethnicities, genders. As a signature the X in the speaker's name is a variable, recalling Malcolm X as well as mathematical equations, and is thus by no means fixed, determinate, essentialist. "The experimental consciousness," writes Korg, "does not deal with essences but with relationships" (5). Dealing with relationships rather than essences, Alarcón's poem marks a middle ground, the space between first and last (name) as much as a third position, another direction in reading. The claim that Linda A. Kinnahan makes with reference to "experimental poetics" – "experimental poetics," she writes, "...allow for reconsiderations of oppositional terms like *conventional* and *experimental* or *expressive* and *innovative* while nonetheless working to foreground and unsettle identity categories, particularly race, class, and gender, and the scaffolding of their linguistic architectures in examining rhetorics of self" (xiv) – this claim therefore can be extended to other poetics as well. So when did modernism end? In contemporary cultural practice modernism is a memory that takes multiple shapes; in our critical practices it has turned into a convention. I am grateful for this occasion to engage in collaborative efforts to shake it up, "make it new," and maybe: move on.

Works Cited and Consulted

Alarcón, Francisco X. *From the Other Side of Night: New and Selected Poems (Del Otro Lado De La Noche).* Tucson: University of Arizona Press, 2002. 118.

Amian, Katrin. "Creativity and Consensus: Jonathan Safran Foer's *Everything Is Illuminated.*" *Rethinking Postmodernism(s): Charles Sanders Peirce and the Pragmatic Negotiations of Thomas Pynchon, Toni Morrison, and Jonathan Safran Foer.* Dissertation University of Bonn, 2007. 133-174.

Bernstein, Charles. *A Poetics*. Cambridge, MA: Harvard University Press, 1992.

—. *Rough Trades*. Los Angeles: Sun & Moon, 1991.

—. "Stein's Identity." *Modern Fiction Studies* 42.3 (1996): 484-488.

Butler, Judith. *Kritik der ethischen Gewalt*. Frankfurt: Suhrkamp, 2003.

Dickinson, Emily. *The Letters of Emily Dickinson*. Ed. Thomas H. Johnson and Theodora Ward. 3 vols. Cambridge, MA: Harvard University Press, 1986.

—. *The Poems of Emily Dickinson*. Ed. Thomas H. Johnson. 3 vols. Cambridge, MA: Harvard University Press, 1979.

Doolittle, Hilda [H. D.]. *Collected Poems, 1912-1944*. Ed. Louis Martz. New York: New Directions, 1983.

Eliot, T. S. "Tradition and the Individual Talent." *Selected Prose of T. S. Eliot*. Ed. Frank Kermode. New York: Farrar, 1975. 37-44.

—. *The Use of Poetry and the Use of Criticism: Studies in the Relation of Criticism to Poetry in England*. 1933. Cambridge, MA: Harvard University Press, 1986.

Eugenides, Jeffrey. "Ein postmoderner Schriftsteller: Jonathan Franzen zur Einführung." *Neue Rundschau* 113.2 (2002): 106-109.

Gosmann, Uta. "The Poetics of Memory: Sylvia Plath, Susan Howe, Ellen Hinsey." Dissertation University of Bonn, 2005.

Hinsey, Ellen. *Cities of Memory*. New Haven: Yale University Press, 1996.

—. "The Rise of Modern Doggerel." *New England Review* 19.2 (1998): 138-145.

—. *The White Fire of Time*. Middletown: Wesleyan University Press, 2002.

Horch, Hans Otto. "Experiment." *Moderne Literatur in Grundbegriffen*. Ed. Dieter Borchmeyer and Viktor Zmegac. Tübingen: Niemeyer, 1994. 127-129.

Howe, Susan. *The Non-Conformist's Memorial*. New York: New Directions, 1993.

Kaufmann, Robert. "Difficulty in Modern Poetry and Aesthetics." *Just Being Difficult: Academic Writing in the Public Arena*. Ed. Jonathan Culler and Kevin Lamb. Stanford, CA: Stanford University Press, 2003. 139-156.

Kinnahan, Linda A. *Lyric Interventions: Feminism, Experimental Poetry, and Contemporary Discourse*. Iowa City: University of Iowa Press, 2004.

Korg, Jacob. *Ritual and Experiment in Modern Poetry*. Basingstoke: Macmillan, 1995.

Kristeva, Julia. *La révolution du langage poétique*. Paris: Seuil, 1974.

—. *"Language" Poetries: An Anthology*. Ed. Douglas Messerli. New York: New Directions, 1987.

Moore, Marianne. *The Complete Poems of Marianne Moore*. New York: Viking, 1981.

—. *The Complete Prose of Marianne Moore*. New York: Penguin, 1987.

—. "Humility, Concentration, and Gusto." *The Complete Prose of Marianne Moore*. 420-426.

Pearce, Roy Harvey. *The Continuity of American Poetry*. Princeton: Princeton University Press, 1961.

Perloff, Marjorie. *Poetry On and Off the Page: Essays for Emergent Occasions*. Evanston: Northwestern University Press, 1998.

—. *Radical Artifice: Writing Poetry in the Age of Media*. Chicago: University of Chicago Press, 1992.

Sayre, Henry M. "The Avant-Garde and Experimental Writing." *Columbia Literary History of the United States*. New York: Columbia University Press, 1988.

Schneider, Hansjörg. *Hypothese, Experiment, Theorie: Zum Selbstverständnis der Naturwissenschaft*. Berlin: de Gruyter, 1978.

Sielke, Sabine. "C. K. Williams." *The Greenwood Encyclopedia of American Poetry*. Ed. Jeffrey H. Gray, James McCorkel, and Mary Balkun. Westport: Greenwood, 2005. 1711-1713.

—. 'Committed to Living in the Open?' American Poetry and Its Readers at the Turn of the Millenium." *Millennial Perspectives: Lifeworlds and Utopias*. Ed. Brigitte Georgi-Findlay and Hans-Ulrich Mohr. Heidelberg: Winter, 2003. 143-154.

—. *Fashioning the Female Subject: The Intertextual Networking of Dickinson, Moore and Rich*. Ann Arbor: The University of Michigan Press, 1997.

Whitman, Walt. *Daybooks and Notebooks*. Vol. III. Diary in Canada, Notebooks, Index. Ed. William White. New York: NYU Press, 1978

Williams, C. K. *Dream of Mind: Poems*. New York: Farrar, 1992.

—. *Repair*. New York: Farrar, 1999.

Code Poetry's Aesthetic (ww)web: Examples of Contemporary Intermedial Experiments

Philipp Horst

In 1994 the internet became the most important mass medium.[1] It was the year when commercial web browsers became widely available for the first time and when, as a consequence, the internet changed from a network mainly used by scientists and software engineers into a globally connected, popular communication tool (Tribe et al. 6). The key words were 'cyberspace,' 'dot com,' 'hypermedia' and 'virtual reality.' It was anticipated that within the foreseeable future the net would develop into one big global, interactive television (Cramer "Netzkunst").

Internet technology revolutionised our communication, and still has a tremendous influence on nearly all parts of our culture and society. The foundation of that development is an impressively simple, binary system of zeros and ones – providing infinite possibilities of combination in endless rows. We call this digital – a term invented to stand in opposition to the old analogue technique working with physical contact. But digital is more than a technical term. Today we find a whole digital culture, a parallel world of virtual reality. And as art forms are an integral part of every culture, the digital culture has its own art as well.

Often 'net literature' is considered to be the transfer of experimental, modern techniques to the computer screen (Cramer, "sub merge" 112), as the computer is conceived as only a more advanced typewriter.[2] However, already in the 1960s several artists went further than that and started using the very essentials of the new computer technology to generate new forms of art. Beat-poet Brian Gysin, for example, developed his own software solutions so that the computer could become 'creative' and 'independently write' poetry. Gysin's poetic approach is not too far away from Marcel Duchamp's readymade concept, even though he is admittedly the author of the software – not, however, of the poetry! As the

---

1 Cf. http://www.isoc.org/internet/history/ as accessed 24.08.06; this page documents the histories of the internet.

2 Cf. Raymond Kurzweil's by now touchingly old-fashioned *KI – Das Zeitalter der künstlichen Intelligenz* from 1993.

computer possesses no artistic soul whatsoever, these poetic solutions are digital *objects trouvées* – only that they were 'found' by the computer. Gysin's idea goes back to the Surrealists, who claimed that their *écriture automatique* directly connected to the subconscious level of the human psyche and thus extended the creative outcome immensely – though uncontrollably. Like in the Surrealists' *écriture automatique* the computer conjures up words and sentences that can only be connected by the recipients' associations. A similar activation of the readers' associations was also pursued by Stuttgart-based Max Bense, the French Oulipo [3] around Raymond Queneau, and many others (Cramer, "sub merge" 112).

Net art stands also in a line of tradition with Conceptual art from the 1960s and 1970s, yet it completely lacks the institutional framework and context on which many Conceptual pieces and artists heavily rely (Baumgärtel 228). Some of their works could hardly be recognised outside the walls of a gallery or a museum. [4] Contemporary artists Thomas Hischhorn and Jason Rhoades, e.g., use every-day objects to compile complex 'trash' installations and, in doing so, are extremely successful and effective in commenting on problematic issues in society and current political discourse. [5] And this is what digital poetry does as well.

The examples chosen for this paper all come from the specific area of digital poetry called "code poetry" or, in artist and scholar Alan Sondheim's term, "codeworks." In code poetry the code language of computer software serves as the every-day material for poetic creation. While poetry in general plays with the possibilities of language and sometimes extends its grammatical or semantic borders, code poetry extends these borders into a different language. In view of this translinguistic extension I want to suggest and to demonstrate in this paper that code poetry in a (politically) idealistic and (poetically) radical form is not so much breaking up long-known poetic traditions, but pursues the continuation of avant-garde artistic aims. Digital poetry as an art form works with techniques and aesthetics comparable to those of 20th century artists and many digital poets share with their predecessors an extremely subversive attitude, in both an aesthetical and a technical sense. They are often bluntly political, although the aesthetics and semantics of the entire genre are based on insider knowledge. [6]

The mere description of what a code poem is turns out to be a difficult task. The most striking surface feature is a language that looks familiar, but is at the same time repellently obscure. We usually encounter words which we know from

---

3 Still around at http://www.oulipo.net/ as accessed 01.08.06.

4 Think of the famous Joseph Beuys anecdote with the cleaner unknowingly destroying a precious piece of art.

5 Cf. Jason Rhoades *Creation Myth*, 1998, part of the Flick collection, Berlin.

6 Cf. Florian Cramer, who argues that digital poetry is legible for computer experts only; "sub merge {my $enses" 116.

everyday communication but which have here a different meaning and function. This mirrors the fact that the deeper, technical level of language and meaning is usually hidden to the normal user of a computer, while its surface level always remains easily accessible. The discrepancy between the smooth and commercially softened surface structure, the phenotext, and the technical foundation with all its inexplicable signs and dangers of system crashes, the genotext, [7] is explicitly taken up in some digital pieces. [8]

Depending on your ideology or academic training, to choose a software language you can decide between Delphi, Eiffel, Pascal, Java, Perl and Self – to name just a few iridescent names. There are sites on the internet that list up to 2500 different languages, astonishingly even including several dialects. [9] The symbols seem to be cryptic, technical commands aimed at the equally dark 'deep structure' of the computer. But the artists/programmers literally 'write' code poems, basically consisting of zeros and ones, which can be perceived as a combination of words, images and sounds. The visual image on the screen is the representation of the hidden sign system off the screen.

In order to highlight code poetry's connection to its avant-garde ancestors, I will now take a look on a famous example from Cubism, generally regarded as one of the finest early twentieth century art forms.

Figure 1 shows a 1912 Cubist still life by Pablo Picasso called *Still Life with Chair-Caning*. The artist combines letters and what I will call 'mementos of reality' to create a composition that works on different levels. Like in other Cubist paintings, in its crystalline structure the still life gives us an idea, a hint of what reality might be, rather than representing reality as we know it. It appears to be almost deliberately hard to decipher and challenges the viewer intellectually. It highlights abstract patterns and fragmentation. Picasso, like Braque, was among the pioneering artists with regard to letter-image combination. He used the typical Cubist strategy of simultaneously showing different aspects of an object, thus dissecting it – metaphorically, metaphysically and literally, i.e. visually – up to a point where most resemblances to the real world vanish. Yet the words still maintain the connection to the world we know – as also the frame of the painting, made out of rope, extends the internal, artistic space of the work into external, real space. For many Cubist paintings words are a decisive link to outside reality.

---

7 Both terms are derived from Arns's "An Art Yet Unknown."

8 Cf. Cramer's "sub merge {my $enses" 116; here Cramer presents an example by internet artists *jodi* called *location* in which the legibility of source and representation is ironically reversed. The source code, the genotext, looks like a mimetic drawing of a teddy bear, whereas the representation on the screen, the phenotext, is an abstract chaos of unconnected computer signs.

9 http://people.ku.edu/~nkinners/LangList/Extras/langlist.htm as accessed 19.07.06.

Fig. 1. Pablo Picasso, *Still Life with Chair-Caning*, 1912.

Even though they are merely allusive and often elliptic, they resemble – in terms of typography or arrangement – structures known to the people of the time.

Still Life with Chair-Caning is also a brilliant example of a Cubist collage and thus an early example of Conceptual art as well. It is a painting, but perhaps "painting" is not an accurate word, because a considerable part of the picture was not painted, but rather glued on: namely the piece of chair caning, which was actually printed oilcloth (Godfrey 24). Hence, an illusionist approach is used to destroy illusion by being bluntly self-aware – one of the key ideas of Conceptualism. Thus the painting functions as a paradox: "on the one hand, it is a slice of pure realism (what could be more real than the actual thing – an old scrap of oilcloth?), but on the other hand, it destroys any last vestige of pictorial illusionism" (Godfrey 24).

The oscillation between realism and illusionism is also produced by the use of language in this work of art. They are not the material reality outside the narrower frame of the painting – how could they be? – but they connect to this reality. They refer to a specific market in Piccasso's contemporary society – the communication market. In Figure 1 the fragment "JOU" is very likely a cut version of the newspaper name "Le Journal," one of Picasso's favourite working materials of that time and a "downmarket example of the 'penny press'" (Morley 40). In addition to their interest in cheap journals, Picasso and like-minded artists were fascinated by the manipulative strength of the suddenly omnipresent billboard signs (Morley 37). This has been explained as the avant-garde strategy of combining high art and low culture, everyday life and artistic genius to produce a combination of innovative aesthetic experience. And, as Morley argues, it is also a reaction against the escapism of Symbolism and Expressionism and a move towards the banality of everyday life (37). [10] Furthermore, the combination of newspaper cut-outs and purely formal painting is a political statement. By integrating bits of newspaper into high art's formalism, the artist cynically highlights their obscene simplicity and directness, while Cubism's intellectual aura is subverted by their clear and straightforward messages and associations.

Yet, the abstracted context of a Cubist composition can persuade the viewer into perceiving the letters as abstracted as well – i.e. out of any linguistic or semantic frame of reference. Initially Georges Braque did not use words or texts for their legibility or power of reference, but for "purely formal purpose[s], as compositional devices or spatial figures that draw attention to the textuality of text and highlight the visible nature of writing as graphic mark" (Morley 39). [11] In a reading determined by visual parameters, digital poetry usually functions like this. The familiar symbols, i.e. the letters, are reduced to abstraction, while their familiarity from everyday experience still connects them to the realm of language. This then is a combination of both the textual and the visual quality of the letters.

Looking at different digital poems and poets with regard to the relation of the visual and the word, one has to distinguish between two different forms of visual representation. On the one hand, it is possible to integrate the images which may (or may not – depending on your software) pop up on the screen and thus extend the linguistic field of semantics to a visual one. On the other hand, there is the abstracted visual, the very visual quality – the form – of the words or the syntactical structures themselves, which allowed Braque to use them as compositional devices. The foregrounding of this form can also be done on paper, as e.g. in Concrete Poetry. Our social context and early language acquisition usually prevent us from perceiving letters or words on this abstract level. In digital poetry, though,

---

10 The tendency to integrate words (or fragments) in (Cubist) paintings, importantly inspired by the institutionalization of advertising, is paralleled by today's digital pieces that use advertisement; cf. the work of etoy at http://www.etoy.com as accessed 08.08.06.

11 It is also possible to understand the use of letters in exactly the opposite way. The more abstract the context, the more *concrete* the letters become. From a cognitive point of view, we tend to focus on features which we already recognise and are familiar with. This means for Braque's paintings that only the letters stand out from the scattered components which hardly offer any other orientation.

the words hardly appear as 'words': the pieces are formed by a combination of (abstract) symbols devoid of any poetic meaning, but rich in (visual) aesthetics. In the rest of my paper I will show this specific handling of 'words' in code poetry by analysing some examples.

Just as provocative – and to a certain extent equally elitist, if not more – as early twentieth-century Surrealist or Dada or indeed Cubist language experiments, contemporary examples of code poetry demand an almost expert knowledge. New Media artist and software programmer Jaromil's "ASCII Forkbomb" is in all its visual simplicity a complex and stimulating example. [12]

```
: (){: |: & };:
```

Fig. 2. Jaromil, *"ASCII Forkbomb"* (rastasoft.org).

Denis 'Jaromil' Rojo was Artist-in-Residence at the National Institute for Media Art, Amsterdam, in 2005 and runs the internet page http://dyne.org/, "a network and a free software atelier" devoted to "researching the hybridation [sic!] of various art and communication practices within the digital domain" (dyne.org). In this self-definition he equates and hybridises art and digital communication – a conclusion which is both convincing and confusing. But Jaromil takes the paradox even further. In his work he aims at criticising the capitalist instrumentalisation of the once radically democratic medium internet and thereby instrumentalises art, or more specifically poetry for his own ends. Jaromil explains his understanding of software with the help of a reference to linguistic theory:

> Software is a means of creating art and communicating. It is a metaliterature which defines how meaning can be carried and (re)produced by multiplying the possibilities of communication. Just as software is a means of metacommunication, so it represents a 'parole', (to quote Saussure), deriving its execution from a 'langue', i.e. the grammatical and linguistic universe of the code. (digitalcraft.org)

By entering the academic and artistic discourse, Jaromil establishes a potent and serious platform for spreading his thoughts. He refers to literature and linguistics, code and communication. The combination of all this in a subjective or subversive manner, he argues, is (code) art. He takes his art seriously, and he genuinely wants to communicate the message of social injustice. He argues: "It might seem [that] notions of comparing [software] to lyrical poetry can only be appreciated by those with specific technical knowledge, but this is not true at all" (digitalcraft.org). I feel inclined to doubt this.

---

12 The piece was part of several exhibitions on digital art, among them "I love you – computer_viren_hacker_kultur," 31.01.03 – 06.02.03, as part of the *transmediale.03,* Haus der Kulturen der Welt, Berlin, "p03s1s.The Aesthetics of Digital Poetry," 13.2.04-4.4.04, Kulturforum Potsdamer Platz, Berlin.

The "Forkbomb" is written in ASCII, an acronym for "American Standard Code for Information Interchange" and a "code for representing English characters as numbers, with each letter assigned a number from 0 to 127.... Most computers use ASCII codes to represent text, which makes it possible to transfer data from one computer to another" (webopedia.com). I do not know how many net users would recognise the poem's individual constituents as signs from the ASCII code, let alone be able to read or understand it. ASCII is defined as a code of representation. One can even go a step further and call it an alternative alphabet, since the ASCII symbols are fundamental components of (nearly) all of today's software languages, internet protocols and e-mails. Languages are built up in a 'hierarchical,' consecutive manner. On the first level we have the uttered sounds, on the second level abstract symbols (letters), then words, then grammatical systems and finally we have the potentially artistic field of semantics, with the almost endless realm of associations. The more levels we discover the more possibilities we have of generating meaning. At first sight we seem to be stuck on level two if we consider code poetry. Jaromil's "Forkbomb" appears to consist only of abstract symbols (Cramer "Netzkunst"). Yet, at a closer look these symbols turn out to follow a more intricate plan of the author and, as a consequence, to ascend to other levels in the suggested consecutive structure. If one looks at the historical development of internet art, one realises that there is a general tendency towards this kind of structural-conceptual ascendance. The pieces as such are deliberately simple technically. Yet, they are highly self-referential in that they take the 'grammar' and 'semantics' of their own medium with its technical, cultural and political potentials as their subject. [13]

A closer look at "ASCII Forkbomb" unravels the technical foundation that is crucial to understanding it. Jaromil comments: "Our attention here is focused on source codes and the fascinating world of algebra and algorithms" (digital-craft.org). But it not only combines mathematics, linguistics and politics, it is also visual and may be approached from a purely aesthetic point of view. We see eleven signs, some of them are rather clear, others more ambivalent. We see a beginning and an end, four colons that also indicate coherence. The colons are set in allusion to a 'rhythm.' In ancient rune writing the beginning and the end of a sentence was indicated by a colon. We can assume that Jaromil consciously combines ancient and high-tech communication in the attempt to extend his successful strategy of paradox even further. If the colons are just a technical necessity, i.e. if it is not Jaromil who alludes to rune writing, then it is the inventor of the ASCII code,

[13] Cf. the Dutch/Belgian cooperation *jodi*, which was on show at the 1997 documenta, http://404.jodi.org; or the British software developers and artists IOD at http://bak.spc.org/iod/ (both links taken from Florian Cramer, "Netzkunst"). Cramer also discusses *jodi* in *Words made flesh*, 95; and "sub merge {my $enses" 116; cf. also Tribe et al. *New Media Art* 50.

who first assigned a similar significance to the colon. The roughly symmetrical poetic line is centered. In its centre we encounter both the most simple and the most abstract forms which do not bear any resemblance to our alphabetical symbols. Altogether the line appears to be very compact and this effect is due to the four brackets.

It may be surprising that both symmetry and closure dominate in this poem, since both are traditional devices of poetry. The visual level thus takes up traditional poetic techniques. However, the true intermedial quality of "Forkbomb" comes into view only if one 'uses' the piece correctly. It is a bit like kinetic art. One has to participate, one has to start the movement, one is encouraged to get the artistic process going. Like Yves Tinguely's sculptures it is incomplete if there is no one to press the right button and let the machinery loose. Under the telling sub-heading "Chaos" Jaromil demands in an essay on this piece in the context of the exhibition *I Love You*, which he also co-curated: "Now type in :(){ :|:& };: on any UNIX terminal" (digitalcraft.org). This direct request, or even command to interact with his art is part of his concept of communication through art. And it is also part of his concept of art that he prefers Unix. Unix, like Linux, is an alternative operating system to MS Windows. In view of Jaromil's criticism of the capitalist instrumentalisation of the internet, it does not seem too far-fetched to suggest that writing poems in Perl, Unix or Linux is a subtle statement against the hegemony of Microsoft.

In the light of this statement, the meaning of our poem unfolds even further when one realises that the innocent-looking abstract combination of symbols is, after all, a computer program. This particular program has a clear subversive potential since it is in fact a virus. As Jaromil explains: "In considering a source code as literature, I am depicting viruses as though they were sort of poems" (digitalcraft.org). The programmer himself establishes the connection between the spheres of literature and software development. While many technicians and engineers regard themselves as some kinds of artists, here we have someone who works conceptually and thus the political and ideological overtones in Jaromil's project cannot be overlooked. The title "Forkbomb" brings in a potent semantic field of both martial and visual allusions. The fork can be regarded as a symbol of civilisation, if one merely sees the harmless, innocent allusions. The piece's symmetrical structure may resemble a fork, but a fork is also a diabolical symbol. A bomb can be regarded as a modern and less mythical fork. It is a high-tech weapon, designed to kill whatever it is aimed at in a precise and accurate manner. In addition, it evokes resemblances to computer-steered weapons, and in fact, that's what the poem is.

The artist reflects the growing global significance of the computer economy with this work. By declaring a virus a piece of art he not only takes up the avant-garde thread of Marcel Duchamp, he also undermines the fetishising belief of contemporary society in technology and progress. Jaromil dislikes, to put it mildly, the power of globally acting software imperia or, closer at hand, the fact that nowadays almost every form of power – be it legal, economic or artistic – is channelled and executed through software and hardware. Interestingly enough, this is usually not perceived as a threat, which makes it even more dangerous. One cannot help but get the impression that it is Jaromil's mission to fight for a more equal distribution of power, or at least a more transparent one. This argument is supported by the rest of his work, which is equally "conspicuous," be it in a technical, aesthetic or artistic way. In a wonderful (post-modern) paradox, he fights for transparency with the help of hard-to-decipher, cryptic, elitist and even dangerous pieces of intermedial art.

A glance at Jaromil's homepage makes it even clearer that he is what would have been called a Conceptual artist in the 1960s. As I have been establishing a line of development from Conceptualism to certain forms of New Media Art, Jaromil is a persuasive case in point. Conceptually, he regards viruses as "a combination of rebellious poetic gestures, symptoms of politics or structure, attempts to get into the cracks of the net and artificial intelligences" (digitalcraft.org). Cramer confirms "Computer viruses are the best example for the technical virulence of all writing in the internet" [14] and quotes William S. Burroughs who provided the aesthetic and theoretical foundation for the viral poetics of contemporary artists. He notes, "I have frequently spoken of word and image as viruses or as acting as viruses, and this is not an allegorical comparison" (qtd. in Cramer, *Words* 20).

The German literary scholar and artist Florian Cramer goes further and into a slightly different direction than Jaromil. On his homepage we find basically two different kinds of poems (plaintext). With regard to intermediality both forms are of interest. In the first example given below, which is called *mustbeviewedinwhitemonospacefontonblack*, the artist creates a visual image, a drawing, with the help of letters. There are numerous similar applications in the internet where one can playfully arrange words or (ASCII) symbols according to visual criteria – and the poem clearly stands in this tradition. [15] Cramer's poem differs from Concrete Poetry because the letters do not carry any meaning. [16] It exploits the same idea as the Cubist compositions above and emphasises the abstract quality of the letters. In the poem we can vaguely make out two figures before an obscure background. Cramer himself contextualises this piece implicitly in an essay on Vuk Cosic ("sub

[14] Translation mine.

[15] On http://www.network-science.de/ascii/ as accessed 28.07.06 one finds an *ASCII generator* that forms poems out of signs. This form of mimetic visualisation was frequent in the earlier days of the internet.

[16] Florian Cramer reflects on these problems in "sub merge {my $enses," 113.

merge" 113), who realised pieces on the basis of pornographic film stills. [17] On the one hand, Cramer argues, pornography is made less obscene by the additional visual abstraction resulting from the technique. On the other hand, the imagination of the viewer is triggered by the uncertainty of the image (Cramer, "sub merge" 114). *mustbeviewedinwhitemonospacefontonblack* is a mimetic piece of ASCII art that once again shows us what the internet is all about: letters and figures.

Fig. 3. Florian Cramer, *mustbeviewedinwhitemonospacefontonblack*, 2001 (plaintext).

[17] Cramer discusses Cosic's *Deep ASCII*, a screenshot taken from *Deep Throat*, a porn movie from the 1970s, and translated into ASCII visuals. Cosic also realised the *ASCII History of Moving Images* where he took numerous film classics and treated them in the same way. For his work see http://www.ljudmila.org as accessed 08.08.06.

The typogram depicts an explicit scene of sexual intercourse. The image is taken from a video by Alan Sondheim and his partner Azure Carter. Cramer calls it "a hommage to Sondheim,"[18] but it is more than that. *mustbeviewedinwhitemonospacefontonblack* may be regarded as a piece of Appropriation Art, because Cramer takes up different contexts in a rather direct manner, including the controversial issue of the free and wide distribution of pornography on the world wide web.

The other type of poetry published on Cramer's homepage is called "Perl poetry."

> Perl is a general-purpose programming language invented in 1987. . . . With over one million users worldwide, it has become the language of choice for World Wide Web development, text processing, Internet services, mail filtering, graphical programming, systems administration, and every other task requiring portable and easily-developed solutions. (tpj.com)

In short, it is a widespread and common language, a digital *lingua franca*. Florian Cramer's Perl poems are more complex than the example above: "Every performable Perl Poem is . . . to be read in three ways; firstly, as poem in English, secondly, as a sequence of computer commands, and thirdly, as soon as it is performed and produces text, as a new poem in English" ("sub merge" 121).[19] As with Jaromil's "Forkbomb," the active viewer is forced to engage with the poem to unfold the artwork completely:

```
open(THIS,'and');open (THAT,">>and'');
while(<THIS>){print$_; print THAT"#$_"}; "#to''; close(THIS);
```

Fig. 4. Florian Cramer, "and," 2001 (plaintext).

The resemblance between the Perl poem and a normal sentence is quite obvious. One can read "and" from left to right and the grammatical structure is perfectly clear. If the program is executed on the computer the following happens: It attaches itself to itself, it duplicates – like the poem "self" presented below –, and it adds the prefix "#." With several repetitions this comment becomes recursive and changes the text, a strategy familiar from Gertrude Stein's poetry and prose. According to Cramer[20] "and" is something like a study for "self."

This is "self":[21]

18 Florian Cramer in an e-mail to the author, 10.08.06.

19 Translation mine.

20 Florian Cramer in an e-mail to the author, 10.08.06.

21 The poem was also part of the exhibition "I love you – computer_viren_hacker_kultur."

22 http://userpage.fu-berlin.de/ cantsin/homepage/ as accessed 01.07.05; this was an older

```
#!/usr/bin/perl
open (IT, "< self");
while (<IT>) {
push @it, $_}
close (IT);
open (IT, ">> self");
print IT join ("\n ", @it);
close (IT);
```

Fig. 5. Florian Cramer, "self," 2001.[22]

There are two ways of approaching "self." Even though Cramer himself calls it a "casual poem, comparable to a haiku or a limerick," there is more to it.[23] We have to treat it both as a literary text and as a computer program. The comparison to a haiku, though perhaps not really appropriate, draws attention to the condensed form. Traditional (Japanese) haiku aims at confronting the reader with a single, very sensual moment, often without further commentary or title and, like Imagist Poetry, clearly without metaphor. The reader is consciously left alone with a text that appears remote or detached. S/he is thus encouraged to find the meaning in the simplicity and immediacy of the situation presented.[24] In addition, many haikus are designed in a calligraphically crafted, visual way to which Cramer's poem alludes. "self" is, of course, no haiku, but it also features a certain succinct literary surface simplicity.

Yet the combination between literature and computing is the fertile ground for the poem's artistic potential. The poem "self," with a self-referential eye on the long tradition of the genre of the painterly, i.e. the visual (self-) portrait, is written in the software language PERL, but on the surface it is more accessible than Jaromil's piece. In a paper originally delivered in the context of the exhibition "intermediale poesie – konkret, wege der konkreten poesie,"[25] Florian Cramer reflects on the changing function of writing in the age of the computer.[26] He argues that there is a current in today's digital art that explores the basics of the

---

version of Cramer's homepage, apparently not online anymore (28.07.06). The layout of *self* in this paper was taken from this site. In a later version it appeares as follows: #!/usr/bin/perl open (IT, "< self''); while (<IT>) {push @it, $_}
close (IT);open (IT, ">> self'');print IT join (``\n ", @it); close (IT); (http://cramer.plaintext.cc as accessed 28.07.06); Note the similarities to "and." Cramer obviously playfully arranges and re-arranges the layout of his works.

23 Florian Cramer in an e-mail to the author, 01.07.05.

24 Preminger, A., T.V.F. Brogan, *The New Princeton Encyclopedia of Poetry and Poetics*, 574.

25 "intermedial poetry – concrete, ways of concrete poetry," translation mine.

26 http://www.nettime.org/Lists-Archives/rohrpost-0104/msg00040.html as accessed 26.07.06, the exhibition was organised by literaturWERKstatt, Berlin, 02.04.01-27.04.01.

technology in use – just as he himself is doing. Paradoxically, the results are art works that have a low-tech appeal – in contrast to the sophisticated applications characteristic of the beginnings of virtual art. This low-tech appeal is due to the fact that the artists show that the pieces are written in computer languages. Again there is a clear parallel to early twentieth-century painting. Roughly from 1908 on, painters such as Wassiliy Kandinsky or Theo van Doesburg and the Dutch group *De Stijl* (from 1916 onwards) in the Netherlands developed painterly abstraction. Whereas Kandinsky tried to reach (lyrical) abstraction organically via Expressionism, it was especially van Doesburg who reflected on the theoretical foundations of painting and came to the conclusion that colour and form are the principal tools of painting (Harrison and Wood 278). A whole new aesthetics was thus born, and the artists of his time deduced a complete social utopia from that – new, pure and democratic art for a renewed society.[27] Code poetry has the same potential – and illusions. Written in Perl, "self" emphasises its own technical aspect. Interestingly enough, one can read the poem almost as easily as a non-digital one, at least once one has adjusted to the outward form.

Conceptual art heavily depends on a context and on the recipient's readiness to learn something about this context. In this sense, Cramer is clearly a Conceptual artist. But in contrast to Jaromil's creation Cramer's poem, with its strong self-referential and meta-poetical qualities, is more in tune with traditional literature. It can be 'translated' into a conventional text that reads as follows:

open it self while it push at it close it open it self print it join at it close it

Admittedly, the poem "and" is closer to a complete sentence. But the (again symmetrical) structure of "self"– cryptic, elliptic and open for interpretation and association – perhaps bears more resemblances to what we regard as poetry. The gaps leave enough space for the reader's imagination, they are the points of entry where the reader can – or rather must – participate to complete the piece. It can be read as a purist and stripped-down reflection on human existence, since the text circles around the key concept of the self. And it is also about communication, on both a direct and an indirect level. In all its simplicity the line is not readily understandable. The general tone is rather commanding, the instructions, however, are not clear, as we do not really find out what "it" is. The first three words can also be read as "open itself," which would give the entity "it" a consciousness. By weaving a meaningful connotative structure (cf. "open," "close," "self," "join") Cramer surprises us with a text that is in between everyday talk, poetry and software.

At the same time he reveals yet another semantic level: The first line (of the original layout) functions as a "gateway" (to stick to the technicality of the piece)

[27] Cf. Frampton, "De Stijl."

and is a necessary device to open any software program with the standard "phrase" #!/usr/bin/ followed by the language used, in this case PERL. For the computer it is now clear in what language to "read" what is following. [28] The piece therefore has a two-fold structure. It "opens" and "closes" and it does not just mention "it" ("it" in small letters is used only twice), but "IT" in capital letters (used six times altogether), possibly referring to I.T. (the common acronym for "internet technology") and/or ironically to the neutral, distanced unemotionality of the computer. This is especially interesting if one, as I have suggested above, reads the piece as a comment on human existence in general. Furthermore, "IT" in the Perl version refers to the program as a whole (i.e. "open IT" translates as "open the program called 'self'") and can thus be described as a meta-sign. This abstract level is alluded to in the "plaintext version" as well.

If you execute the program, it modifies itself, as it attaches a further copy of itself to itself. The line spacing doubles as well and with every new execution, the program/poem grows exponentially. Thus it has a viral logic, eventually bringing the system to a crash-down. The crash is caused by a "digital sculpture" of impressive size. "self" brings the most advanced and technically sophisticated computer down to its knees. This parallels the subversive potential of Jaromil's "ASCII Forkbomb." Here the simplicity of the software structure unfolds its true potential. With the help of a couple of words and signs, "self" constitutes a potent threat to technology. In spite of its viral logic, "self" is not a digital *perpetuum mobile.* It is of course crucial that we have to start and re-start the software anew every time. It does not grow endlessly after the initial execution. Thus what we have is a fine web of power – the computer, (the) "self" and the reader.

As liberal as Jaromil is with regard to software distribution, as elitist, political and generally obscure is his art to a wider audience. Thus he may be typical of what one expects from the highly specialised internet or computer community. Florian Cramer chooses an alternative approach that oscillates between art and academia. Identity is a key word for the internet, and many artists work along the fine lines of this concept. [29] Cramer thus constantly changes roles. He implicitly comments on or explains his own art in his academic works and critically accompanies his fellow artists. Though he is not as explicitly interested in global politics as Jaromil, his poems reflect a crucial aspect of contemporary society and are part of an innovative, pioneering art form. In an entry in an online (!) dictionary, critic

[28] The computer is only able to execute a Perl program if it was designed for that. Not every computer runs with Unix, or Linux, actually only the minority does.

[29] Among them – not surprisingly – one of Cramer's favourite artists, the Australian net artist mez (Mary Anne Breeze), who invented a whole new and highly ambiguous language called "mezangelle." She is working also under the identities (in the internet also called *avatars*) "netwurker," "data[h!bleeder," "ms post modemism," "mezflesque.exe," "Purrsonal Areah Netwurker," and others; cf. her home page http://www.hotkey.net.au/~netwurker/ as accessed 30.07.06.

and curator Inke Arns assesses the significance of net art and code poetry and comes to the conclusion that it is

> a future art ... [and one that] would definitely be an art of code. Already today within the field of so-called "net art" we can see attempts which point in this direction. The "code-works" (to borrow a term by Alan Sondheim) by Netochka Nezvanova (or: NN, integer, antiorp), mez, Jodi and others focus their/our attention on the "raw" program code which our increasingly digitized working and living environment is based upon. As in the future ... it is important to realize that it's not the glossy surfaces but rather the underlying program code which has performative properties. One could assume the existence of two texts, a "phenotext" and a "genotext," when talking about the properties of graphical interfaces. The surface effects of the phenotext, i.e. moving texts, are generated and controlled by other underlying "effective" texts, programming codes or source texts ....[30]

Although both artists discussed above connect to art historical discourse, they are primarily embedded in the controversial debate around globalisation and the internet. Code poetry and net art are not only key phenomena in contemporary art, in their line of tradition from early twentieth century Modernism to Conceptual Art, they are part of the historical discourse of which intermedial art forms an integral part. The examples presented here are representative of a whole generation of artists who have been brought up with the computer as an omnipresent communicative tool. In addition, a pronounced political awareness results in a mode of artistic expression that is as far away from *l'art pour l'art* aesthetics as one can possibly get. The internet, based on the kind of computer technology mentioned above, may become the major medium of artistic expression in due course. As a result, the museum as an institution is under attack. The logical and already existing forum for the presentation of internet art is, of course, the internet itself.[31] The idea of a virtual museum not only fundamentally undermines the hegemonic power of the museum institution, it also connects to more open, flexible and democratic concepts of exhibitions.[32] One can easily imagine that Conceptual artist Marcel Broodthaers with his affinity to signs, codes and negotiation would be a good curator in a virtual New Media museum.

In its poetics and aesthetics, code poetry is one of the most innovative and relevant lyrical genres of today as it reflects contemporary reading habits and communication strategies. The artists presented above are just two writers who are

---

30 For over twelve months during the years 2001 and 2002, the *Anthology of Art* has provided an internet-based platform for dialogue between artists and theorists from all over the world. According to the self-description on the site, this process focused on current visions of art and the relationship of art to theoretical discourse.

31 Cf. http://interact10ways.com/usa/home.asp as accessed 09.08.06.

32 Actually there are numerous virtual museums around. EMMA, e.g., is the *Electronic Museum of Mail Art* and can be visited at http://www.actlab.utexas.edu/emma/Intro/intro2.html as accessed 24.08.06.

representative of this still very young art form. [33] A political consciousness, the combination of sophisticated technology with traditional aesthetics and an artistic mode of expression fundamentally based on intermediality are their characteristics. And they all work in and combine several cultural spheres – artistic, academic and economic.

Works Cited

Arns, Inke."An Art Yet Unknown: Art Will Be Code, Or It Will Not Be." *Anthology of Art*. Ed. Jochen Gerz. 30 July 2006. <http://www.anthology-of-art.net/>.

Baumgärtel, Tilman. "Netzkunst:Kunst im Internet." Ed. Hubertus Butin. *Begriffslexikon zur zeitgenössischen Kunst*. Köln: DuMont, 2002. 228-231.

Cramer, Florian. "Netzkunst und konkrete Poesie." 26 July 2006. <http://www.netzliteratur.net/cramer/netzkunst_konkrete_poesie.htm>.

—. "sub merge {my $enses": ASCII Art, Rekursion, Lyrik in Programmiersprachen." *Text & Kritik* [Themenheft "Digitale Literatur"] (Oktober 2001): 112-123.

Frampton, Kenneth. "De Stijl." *Concepts of Modern Art*. Ed. Nikos Stangos. New York: Thames and Hudson, 1994.141-160.

Godfrey, Tony. *Conceptual Art*. London: Phaidon Press, 1998.

Harrison, Charles, and Paul Wood. *Art in Theory, 1909-1990: An Anthology of Changing Ideas*. Oxford: Blackwell, 1992.

Kurzweil, Raymond. *KI – Das Zeitalter der künstlichen Intelligenz*. München: Carl Hanser, 1993.

Morley, Simon. *Writing on the Wall: Word and Image in Modern Art*. Los Angeles: University of California Press, 2003.

Preminger, Alex, and T.V.F. Brogan, eds. *The New Princeton Encyclopedia of Poetry and Poetics*. Princeton: Princeton University Press, 1993.

Rojo, Denis 'Jaromil,' ed. 28 July 2006 <http://dyne.org/>.

—. 28 July 2006 <http://digitalcraft.org/>.

Sondheim, Alan. Home page. 09 Oct. 2006. <http://www.anu.edu.au/english/internet_txt>.

Tribe, Mark, and Jana Reena. *New Media Art*. Köln: Taschen, 2006.

[33] Cf. for example http://www.hyperfiction.ch/ as accessed 01.09.06 for a link list with further examples.

Poetry

For Bochum: CANTERBURY TALES

Steve McCaffery

PROLOGUE

A less satisfactory characterization of continua really does make sense if it pits mind against magnitude, intellectually speaking, while holding back on each three-dimensional polemical interchange.

To the left of that south-east revelation is a growing stockpile of intuitions if, and only if, a subset of transfinite cardinal numbers implies a closed consequence of coherences.

Or then again, if the infinite collocation of sets pertaining to the current Whitehouse Protocols subtracts to introduce the origami monogamy into the game plan for the interrogatory phrase called "Who's that over there?" or "what have we here?" a resultant and parallel pattern causes stridulation across the entire philanthropy of the infinite.

For instance, any number of acceptable critical methods can be used to demonstrate that the asset plus class invariables for new card members can never be caught on streaming video, or that a wing-nut is not a discursive practice, but still holds the potential ad infinitum to both mirror and corrupt a unique, incommunicable truth about a host of golden daffodils.

Having said this however, a "post-mortem alliance" of indeterminacy in the middle eastern "buy-back programs," and hybrid, disjunctive syntheses within the "re-nationalization of oil markets via power point poetics," can always corrupt the axiom choices available in "I have no complaint today" and "I see no reason to assume a random arrangement of unexplored fingernails" but not so in "you seem necessarily inconsistent this week" and "I feel it illegal to correlate the inadmissibility effects with Jena cartel possibilities," and only twice in "does the actual event complete the punctual" or "how was I to know that by establishing three unknown antinomies I would shatter the limits of finite argumentation?"

But now is not the time to exchange intellectual inclusiveness for a mapping of hermeneutic distance or the consciousness of voluntary synopsis disarrangement, let alone the French kiss of pragmatism imposed upon an n-dimensional spherical neighborhood like ours.

This ought to surprise no one as we are all gathered here to hear the curfew toll the knell of parting day and lowing herds wind slowly o'er the lea as well as to read these words as a community of self-taught readers knowing poetry, like pilgrimage, involves a search for significant time made possible by the fact of certain marks spaced equidistant to an origin that is indifffferent to a knowledge of two extra, surplus letters catalytic in their own encounters remembering a linnet is a bird not heard in words where the linnet is in it.

THE KNIGHT'S TALE

To the left and in artesian sprung rhythm stands Person A looking at a photograph of Georg Cantor in middle life. Both the photograph and Person A are in possession of a bust of Wilhelm Stahl.

But now Person A requests a meeting with the soul of the sculptor. That request is denied by the financial advisor in charge on the grounds that conversation with the spirit world would implicate the stable shaman coordinates between Person A and Person non-B and might hemorrhage the vernacular in a way that would occasion the reproduction of forgotten separations: (Walt Whitman from Wagner, the husband from the wife of Bath, vision from resonance, my own storyfication from its representativity, the spinster from her pocket-guide to feminism).

Person not-B finds death a little disappointing. He feels he is the Shropshire Lad completing his own version of *The Waste Land*.

In 1922 the problem was urgent. Relics of intuitions shattered stable market prices. A child leapt from a parapet and landed in rocket science before the rocket was invented. Now the desperation is more focused on the Mechano Logos. Allegory is returning as enigma variations on a hiccup. The proposition that "it's a book worth keeping" actually mollifies the same soft spoken personification known as Person Y who writes under the pseudonym of Boutique neo-Liberalism.

Person A becomes appalled by the regeneration of historical memory in the lesser species illustrated by an Index embedding the Grand Collage: imagination, insignificance, intelligence. He dreams of the rebirth of the Frankfurt Kindergarten run by Sister Adorno of the local social out-reach program where he can read Walter Benjamin's theory of the typewriter and shout the phrase "if only yesterday had come!"

And come it did. Right there beneath the disturbance of a distance reaching touch. It is eternal transience and each neighbor is a nightingale calling "oh for a yesterday to come."

THE MILLER'S TALE

Person A, a well-known architect, is afflicted by a terrible thought. Perhaps acts of folding, envelopment, will destroy the efficacy of his Cartesian coordinates. "Perhaps a line" (he thinks) "is not a movement but an empire. Not subjects in *esse*, perhaps we undergo processes and procedures of subjectivization. To say 'I' as I do might only be a habit of converting non-selfness into self."

He decides he will be more himself by entering the formula for the production, containment and description of a violent act. Having read in an ancient codex that the navel is the trace of a primal disconnection, allowing self, subjectivity and personhood to develop, he decides to remove his own and thus complete a *vaporisation de moi*. But will the missing navel be an absent God, or a habitant flaneur sitting in the bistro of some northern Manitoban forest? There are no periods of decline and decline is required for his recovery.

He recalls how the form of an object is a diagram of forces at which point a small flaneur flits by. The Cartesian mind-grid coordinates work to monopolize multiplicities and present them ontologically as a coherent ego. Voilà the birth of the thinking subject.

But Person A stopped thinking and Springtime ends in the deposition of what is said. His face recedes into a history more valid than known and is only recognizable by the intercession of a voice. But he is happy in his silence where he is. Alone, in a classical, natural night opposed to fashion, in fear, power and the erotic he thinks and therefore cannot know for sure.

THE REVE'S TALE

Person A dreams that if one had a speech-bubble in which to proclaim it, or else grasp the importance of a discrete series operative within the cardinal numbers reconnected to the last remaining beer stores owned by Person B scattered across the housing estate, deposited or repositioned in mostly critical masses as hand-made corporate logos serving the undervalued and undivided original five-acre site on which requests for appliances and sub-zero professional installations en-hance the mating calls of several species of innovative interiors at the high-end of upper-mobile intestine reproductions caught in the follow-up to the break-out from free-estimates on curiosity about enjoyable five-year lingerie displacement programs abandoned in Las Vegas to thin ice and "thank yous" heard across a periodic range of departmental administration statements,

then

the Belladonna fragmentations thought exclusive to the 1963 Miss USA Beauty Pageant *held intact by the previous and personal experience of on-line shopping and* Declarations of Independence *that challenge frontally the Cartel logics to a selling-point in brand-names laundered through a simple passage after lunch is served, then read aloud (or "allowed") in cobblestone progressions through a neighborhood unthought before the unused gym memberships reappeared as the rationale for trendy mid-block factories adjacent to the* Expressway Assembly of God *rerouted through the partnerships of key banks of commerce towards a final destination in* Direct Satellite TV.

From IMPOSSIBLE OBJECT

Rosmarie Waldrop

INITIAL CONDITION

If thought is, from the beginning, divorced from itself, a picnic may fade before the first bottle is pulled from the basket. If you ask: Do I know what I am holding? I will offer it to you.

If a father touches the neck of his son's girlfriend, he'll fall into a Freudian sleep. If he intends to, has his palm already felt her gasp?

If you think: A young girl's a vacuum, you mean to rush and fill it. If you ask: Why? one whole chapter of life may close.

Perhaps we can't ask these questions. The traffic moves too fast. We can only throw up our arms. As in a wind tunnel?

The question: Why? is most nostalgic. In twenty years of marriage one might be in love with one another. Or with another?

Can we utter sounds and mean: young girl's neck? With one foot slightly in front of the other? Say: Come have a sandwich, and mean: best to slow down?

Could we say that listening to familiar words is quite different from a girl seen both full-face and from the side at once? Like Cleopatra? If we agree that "Have a sandwich" means: "best to slow down," can we separate marriage to her brother at eleven from being carried in to Caesar in a carpet?

Either we don't move or much follows. The history of the universe predicated on ten seconds of initial turbulence?

If you ask: Where did it all begin? do I answer with a cry of distress, the tip of a triangle, a plan to picnic, a sudden toothache?

If in doubt I will offer it to you.

WE WILL ALWAYS ASK, WHAT HAPPENED?

Imagine a witch in the form of a naked girl. Now say her name. Is it foreign? Was the idea of the witch complete before you named the girl? Did you go down a passage that does not exist toward a well of dark water?

Your mind makes small rudimentary motions. Because the joke is against it? Because it does not know which way to turn and keeps reviewing the field of possible action? Aches? Actresses?

I hear you sighing. Intention is neither an emotion nor yet lip-synch of longing. It is not a state of consciousness. It does not have genuine duration. I say, are you alright? Can you have an intention intermittently? abandon it like a soldier paralyzed the moment before battle? and resume it?

Could I order you to understand this sentence? just as I could tell you to run forward? Into the fire?

Would the understanding cast a shadow on the wall even though a premonition is not a bullet hole?

One symptom is that space is forced into a mirror. As if the event stood in readiness behind the silver. You move your hand, and it goes the other way. Then the earth opens up and you slide down your darkest desires.

Witches were killed by fire, by water, by hanging in air, burying in earth, by asphyxiation, penetration, striking, piercing, crushing in a thousand and one ways.

What was that name you gave her?

INTENTIONALITIES

My hand moves along your thigh. When we describe intentions, is the ventriloquist taken over by the dummy? Or pretending to be a ghost?

Instead of "I meant you" I could say, "we walked through wet streets, toward a dark well." But could I speak of you this way? And why does it sound wrong to say "I meant you by pulling away?" Like lovers caught in headlights?

If I talk of you it connects me to you. By an infinite of betweens, not by touching you in the dark. Touch is the sense I place outside myself for you to ride.

When I mean you I may show it – if we stand close – by putting my head on your shoulder. You can show you understand by describing the well under the trap door. What will you say? Don't be frightened?

The feeling I have when I mean you draws an arc of strength between my hips and the small of my back. It doesn't follow that "meaning you" is being exhilarated by terror. Of course not, you say: We need a red thread to run through, but it's entangled with space, form, future. Is this true?

It would be wrong to say that meaning you stands for a forgotten part of myself, a treatise on labyrinths, a path leading nowhere. Am I living in a shell where the sea comes in along with its sound? And drowns us?

I was speaking of you because I wanted to think about you. "I wanted" does not describe a general before battle. Nor, on the other hand, a ship heading for shipwreck. There is no way to decide whether this is an autobiography or a manifesto.

ENHANCED DENSITY

Should it worry me that thought, in my sentences, seems never wholly present at any one moment? Let alone love, in my life? Even my skin has no precise shape, that is unless touched. By clothes?

There seems a brownish mist under construction. From forest fires?

My feeling for you seems to flow (like traffic?) under my skin. I want it to break through the pores and touch you. Inflict wounds so small you don't know what's killing you?

The way a word can pierce? Because of the use it has had in your life? Because it comes out of a deep well? Because war follows the opening of mouths?

You are never in front of me, like an object. And if I try to hold you sideways the melody slips away leaving a single note. Like a reflection in a shifting mirror? A phoneme escaping between the sutures of my accent?

What can I do but let my thoughts roam in the field around a word. The way desire roams through my body? It's called the meaning of the word because we cannot touch the ground water in any other way.

Are we making an object when we make love? Do we hope it'll stay in front of us and allow us to observe it?

It may not be enough to look at a surface I love. Or parts adjacent.

The title and some phrases of the cycle are taken from the eponymous novel by Nicolas Mosley.

“Plaît, plait, plaint”: Transnational Poetics

The Pleasures of Déjà Dit: Citation, Intertext and Ekphrasis in Recent Experimental Poetry

Marjorie Perloff

What matters, is not the saying, it is the resaying, and, in this resaying to say each time for the first time.

Maurice Blanchot, *L'Entretien infini*

In the 1980s, when Language Poetry was making its first anthology appearances, its dominant mode looked like this:

(1) were I idiom and
the portray
what on
idiot you remarking
cessed to only up
opt hope this
was soundly action
more engineer
taut that the
Bruce Andrews, from "While" (1981)

(2) at the end of delight, one
who or that which revolves

more than chests have
to heave ". . . . where gold,

dirt and blood flow
together"!: margins

the family, not personal
fallibility leads

to instrumentality
in self-restraint
Diane Ward, from "Limit" (1989)

(3) morrow every listen
ago potato who have a paper voice
the hole where the effort went
tome is crayern
a fasten into trance, necklace some awake of notes, floorer
as classed some follow
Peter Inman, from "Colloam" (1986) [1]

Different as the authors of these three excerpts surely are, theirs is a period style that shares specific features. First and foremost, this is a poetry of programmatic non-referentiality, words and phrases refusing to "add up" to any sort of coherent, much less transparent statement. Syntactic distortion is the key: in Andrews's "While," articles modify verbs rather than nouns, syllables are elided as in "cessed" (processed? recessed? accessed?), and it is not clear whether "this" in line 6 is the direct object of "hope" or the subject of "was" in the following line. Similarly in Inman's "Colloam" (the title word is not in the OED; it seems to be a neologism formed of "colophon" and "loam"), the verb "fasten" does not have "necklace" as its object; rather, we are given the phrase "a fasten into trance," where "fasten" and "trance" relate phonemically rather than semantically. All three poems use predominantly abstract language, and the pronouns have no discernable referents. Who is Ward's "one / who or that which revolves"? Or Inman's "who" with the "paper voice"? In each case, linkage is produced by sound rather than signification: in Andrews's poem, we find "idiom" where we expect "idiot" (see line 5) and "taut" (pun on "taught") in the last line goes with "that" and "the." Inman rhymes "ago" and "potato," "floorer" leads to "follow," and "crayern" seems to be a phonetic spelling of "crayon" or a reference to "crayer," which is an obsolete word meaning "small vessel."

The reader of these poems is consistently *surprised*. Ward's "At the end of" anticipates a noun phrase like "the day" or "the journey" but not "the delight;" in Inman, the "hole" promises to contain something tangible rather than "effort," and although "morrow" (as in "tomorrow") and "ago" are related temporally, neither the "potato" nor the neologism "crayern" fit into their syntactic slots. The reader has to make her way through a maze, with no guidance from an authoritative "I." "The family / not personal," as Ward puts it.

---

1 I take these three examples from Douglas Messerli's anthology *From the Other Side of the Century: A New American Poetry 1960 – 1990*, pp. 1057, 512, 997.

At the same time, it is important to remember that the words, morphemes, syntactic units, and sound patterns in question represent the poet's own vocabulary and discourse. Even when there is a brief unidentified quotation, as in Ward's couplets (lines 4-6: "where gold/ dirt and blood / flow together"), the poet is, so to speak, alone onstage. Indeed, despite the semiological play of "ago potato who have a paper voice," and so on, the poet tacitly takes full responsibility for the poem s/he has constructed so carefully. Even the jagged free verse, designed to represent the rhythm of thought, underscores the primacy of the poet's language in its ability to mean and not to mean. The limits of my language, in Wittgenstein's words, are the limits of my world. In this scheme of things, the poetic drive is, in Adorno's terms, one of *resistance*: the resistance of the individual poet to the linguistic field of capitalist commodification where language has become merely instrumental.

But in the climate of the new century, where sites of resistance have become increasingly contested, we seem to be witnessing a poetic turn from negation and resistance to dialogue – a dialogue with earlier texts or texts in other media, or "writings through" or ekphrases that permit the poet to participate in a larger, more public discourse, even as the poet's *personal* signature is once again present. Such poetry is often *meditative*, but meditation is made oblique by the use of constraint, citation, and the reliance on intertext: appropriation, after all, is now a central fact of life. As such, we are witnessing a new poetry, more conceptual than expressive – a poetry in which, as Gerald Bruns puts it with reference to Cage's "writings through" *Finnegans Wake*, the shift is "from a Chomskyan linguistic competence, in which the subject is able to produce an infinite number of original sentences from the deep structure of linguistic rules, to the pragmatic discourse that appropriates and renews what is given in the discourse that constitutes a social and cultural world." [2] Or, more properly, in the poems that will concern me here, a prior literary/art world.

There is, of course, nothing new about appropriative poetry. A branch of Language poetry that we associate with Susan Howe, Steve McCaffery, and Rosmarie Waldrop – to take just three poets – has always worked with citation and constraint, with intertext and intermedia: Howe's *The Midnight*, with its documentary layers, poetic intertexts, and treated ambiguous photographs, is a paradigmatic case of citationality, if not primarily of constraint, which is better exemplified in such McCaffery sequences as *Evoba* or the recent *Dark Ladies,* a dazzling, rule-generated writing through Shakespeare's *Sonnets.*

Yet the three poetic texts I shall be discussing here – Jan Baetens's, *Vivre sa vie*, Craig Dworkin's *Dure*, and Yoko Tawada's *Verwandlungen* – do deviate from

2 Gerald Bruns, "The Pagans and Karen Mac Cormack," forthcoming in *The Gig*, 2006.

earlier models in two ways. First, the cited texts become, not so much grist for the later poet's mill, as they function as aids to reflection. And second, their *déjà dit* is used to ruminate on a topos that experimental poetries have long held to be irrelevant, if not wholly passé, as being too personal, too reminiscent of a lyric tradition. I am thinking about *pain* – whether the pain of lost love or lost identity – a pain that quite literally doesn't dare to speak its name in our sophisticated poetry climate, so that it is conveyed by such distancing devices as citation, ekphrasis, and constraint. Such poetry is more accessible, perhaps more public than the poems of the eighties I cited earlier, being written in less non-referential, asyntactic language, indeed often in complete and coherent sentences. Conceptually, however – and this is a conceptual poetry – riddle and obliquity remain the order of the day. Nothing, these poets seem to imply, comes easy.

Autrement dit: The Film-Poem

My first example, Jan Baetens's 2005 "novelization" of Jean-Luc Godard's classic 1962 film *Vivre sa vie* (fig. 1), is a sequence of fifteen poems, loosely corresponding to the twelve "chapters" of the film, each of which is introduced by an intertitle. "The conspicuous use of intertitles," Baetens comments in a recent essay, "instills a literary structure into the work, and liberates the image from an excessively intrusive presence of speech." Then, too, the intertitles signal the film's "separation into quasi-autonomous sequences . . . . The abrupt switch from one sequence to another within the overall frame of the story will direct the basic economy of the [literary] text." [3]

Does this mean that the "novelization" follows the film literally? On the contrary: Baetens's chapters are not prose but highly formal lyric poems. "The history of ekphrastic poetry," he notes in the essay, "reveals the blind alley of those tempted by the attraction of a 'mechanical' translation of the visual element into textual elements." Indeed, "prose is to be avoided because it risks diminishing the specific visual language of Godard's oeuvre and the shock it instills." By contrast, the poetic novelization "can compensate and frustrate that which prose novelizations, especially in line with the current cultural stereotype of the genre, sometimes radically suppress, namely the enunciated image on the one hand and the voice of enunciation on the other."

How does this work in practice? In the Preface to *Vivre sa vie*, Baetens writes that it is "the love of the everyday that [the film's] images continue to evoke in me. Banality, the daily grind, ennui, sometimes a slight disgust and some illusions

[3] This and the quotes in the following paragraph from Jan Baetens, "Novelising Jean-Luc Godard," 135-152. All translations mine.

about love." But he adds, "Since banality remains for me the most dazzling subject there is, I found it necessary to change the form (that is, the verse form) with each new section"[4] (11). This is a puzzling explanation on two counts. First, it's curious to refer to *Vivre sa vie,* with its heavily stylized images and sophisticated allusions to Montaigne, Cocteau, Poe's "Oval Portrait," and Sartrean existentialism, as "banal" and "everyday." The heroine's very name, Nana, alludes to Zola's courtesan, and Anna Karina, who plays Nana, is given to such utterances as *Je suis responsable. Je suis responsable. Je suis responsable.* More important: to render the banal in poetry is typically to use casual, colloquial language – the speech rhythms, say, of free verse. Instead, Baetens gives us pantoums, tetra- and heptasyllabics, full and reduced sonnets, rhopalic verses (stanzas where each line adds a syllable), *vers impairs*, and so on.

The resulting artifice produces an appropriate counterpart to the film. Just as Godard's self-consciously "literary" devices give his banal story a fabulist dimension, so Baetens's verbal constraints (the poet was the co-founder of *Formules*, a journal specializing in constrained writings, in the vein of *Oulipo*) have a distancing effect: they call into question the very "ordinariness" the poet claims to find so appealing. The most important constraint, in this regard, is the adoption by the Flemish poet of a language that, as a neighbor, he knows intimately but which is not, after all, his mother tongue – namely, French. As a formidable Other, an other that shadows the locutions of a minor literature like the Flemish, French, Baetens posits, with its powerful lyric formulae and traditions, makes it possible for the poet to distance what he considers *le moi haîssable*, the hateful "I" of his own discourse, "The materiality, the difficulty, the resistance of the [French] language," he writes, "are powerful enough to inhibit the trivial and to establish a proper rapport with literature."[5]

The poetic text is thus decidedly not a reproduction of Godard's *Vivre sa vie*. The film has a linear plot line: it moves inexorably from Nana's original decision to leave her husband Paul to her melodramatic death in the final shootout between her pimp and a rival. True, its titled chapters and impersonal male voiceover stylize and distance the successive events in Nana's career, but the film's musical score and imagery are both consistent and continuous, the key image being that of Anna Karina's sculptured, wide-eyed, and endlessly mobile face, whether seen frontally or in shadowy profile (see fig.1).

---

4 This and the following quotes from Jan Baetens, *Vivre sa vie, une novellisation en vers du film de Jean-Luc Godard*. All translations mine.

5 Jan Baetens, Postface, *Slam! Poèmes sur le basket-ball*, 62-63. Translation mine. A native of Louvain, Baetens has spent his life between Belgium and France, and he remarks on the shift currently occurring as France is losing its linguistic hegemony, even as Flemish has become the official language of Belgium.

In the first sequence, Nana's face is not seen directly by the camera because we are behind her as the camera pans and glimpses her image in a mirror. Paul too is only seen from behind and once or twice in shadowy profile. But, in the course of the film, Nana's face becomes more and more central, although, oddly enough, her body is barely seen. Even in the scenes of sexual encounter, it is Nana's face – eyes lidded and resigned, sometimes lighting up and smiling, mouth caressing a cigarette, whose image dominates. Nana and her men are always *about* to undress when the camera cuts away. Again, in an early scene, when Nana goes to the movies and sees Carl Dreyer's great silent film, *La Passion de Jeanne d'Arc,* her tear-stained face is juxtaposed to the face of the sympathetic priest (played by Antonin Artaud) and to that of Joan herself (Maria Falconnetti) at the stake. And in the penultimate scene, Nana's smiling face, now framed by her stylish new haircut, is silhouetted against the window facing her lover Luigi, who reads Poe's "The Oval Portrait" (foreshadowing Nana's own death) aloud to her.

Yet we never really know the person behind that face – or behind the faces of the various men in Nana's life – all of them stiff, unsmiling, fully clothed. The dialogue itself is largely banal, conveying necessary information or expressing what are rather pretentious philosophical musings on life and death, freedom and responsibility. The conceptual problem Baetens thus posed himself was how to render the tension between everyday conversation and the artifice of the film's audio-visual scheme, with its ambient sounds, shadowy interiors, expressive faces, smoking rituals, and ominously slow tempo, purely in *words*. The easy way would have been to produce imagistic, ideogrammic vignettes matching the film chapters, but instead Baetens provides poetic analogues that emphasize dramatic moments missing from the film. Here is #III, "Nana est jetée de la pension. Elle vit dans la rue," whose three three-line stanzas each have 3, 2, and 5 words per line – a technique used, among others, by Louis Zukofsky:

Les premiers jours
le soir
elle rentre encore à la pension,

qui la guette;
les deux
comme à la guerre préparées,

Un silence-éclair.
Les bruits
sont innocents – marelle, chatte, pavé. (V 15)

The first days
at night
she returns to her pension,

lying in wait;
the two
prepared as if for war,

A silence-lightning flash
The noises
are innocent – hopscotch, cat, pavement.

This is a much more transparent, accessible lyric than are the language poems I cited earlier – or is it? In the film, the pension is just another decaying house in a nondescript Paris neighborhood – perhaps Pigalle. But in the poem, the pension is pictured as an animal that lies in wait for (*guette*) Nana as if there were a war between them – a sinister notion quite absent from the film, where affect is largely neutral. Meaning, moreover, is offset by the elaborate quasi-Troubadour sound structure: there is, for example, much internal rhyme, as in *guerre / éclair* and *sont / innocents*, the latter word constituting a phonetic anagram of *silence*. *Guerre* and *guette* are linked by eye rhyme, with *deux* having the same vowels in reverse. In the preceding stanza, *jour*, *soir* and *encore* are half-rhymes, and the three nouns defining the setting of the pension are linked by their *a* vowels: *marelle*, *chatte*, *pave*. All these formal devices distance the narrative, giving it a sense of repetition and inevitability quite absent from the more realistic film.

The avoidance of a lyric "I" in a poem like *Vivre sa vie* is by no means, as is commonly thought, an avoidance of emotion. On the contrary, Baetens uses form to measure the pain of Nana's daily existence. Here is VII, a "reduced sonnet" (in trisyllabic lines) called "L'Habitude – Déjà la fin?":

Nana va *Nana vient* *Nana baise* *Nana passe*	*Nana goes* *Nana comes* *Nana fucks* *Nana enters*
Nana pense *S'en aller* *Puis n'y pense* *Plus du tout*	*Nana thinks* *Of quitting* *Then doesn't* *Think at all*
Un deux trois *C'est permis* *Un deux trois*	*One two three* *It's allowed* *One two three*
Mille francs *Et un p'tit* *Coup de blanc (25)*	*A thousand francs* *And a small* *Glass of white*

#VII has no parallel in the film, which can portray key "events" ("First Man," "The Letter," "The Concierge") more easily than it can capture the force of habit, the "va-et-vient" of Nana's daily sexual encounters. The minimal sonnet can do so by means of repetition (*Nana va / Nana vient*), the counting ritual (*Un deux trois*), and the near-rhyme of *baise / passe / pense*, which equates all these actions. The pun on *passe* (*maison de passe* is the French term for brothel) also plays a role: as Microsoft Word reminds me by insisting on putting an accent over the *e*, Nana will be *passé* soon enough. But perhaps the key line is *C'est permis*: are these Nana's words to one of her customers? Is she inquiring whether *C'est permis de fumer*? If "one" is permitted, are two and three? And on the page, all three lines end with the letters *is*. It all culminates, in any case, in the *Mille francs* and the *p'tit / Coup de blanc*, which are Nana's payment. *Blanc* rhymes with *francs* and *p'tit* with *permis*, the poem thus sonically portraying the deadening circle of habit. Baetens's Nana could also be Zola's – or indeed any Nana who passes through this particular cycle.

The last few lyrics are especially striking. Nana's falling in love, is initiated in the "snowball" poem *A Côté de Nana*:

> *Ensemble.*
> *Vers lui se tourne. Invite à le rejoinder.*
> *Je les entends parler. Il va parler seul. Elle va écouter.* (V 32)

> Together.
> Turns toward him. Invites him to join her.
> I hear them talking. He will speak alone. She will listen.

In XIII, an eight-part Parnassian lyric in heptasyllabic rhyming couplets, Nana's new friend makes a courtly declaration of his love, more powerful than Poe's encomium to the beloved who is the subject of his "oval portrait." It is all the more shocking after this to read the documentary *vers impairs* of the final scene, where Nana becomes the pawn between pimps and is shot to death:

> *Tout tourne autour du prix de Nana, im-*
> *peccable coupe*
> *de cheveux sixties qui lui donne l'âge*
> *de la voiture*
> *de Lui 1 et de Lui 3. Puis (enfin)*
> *des coups de feu.* (V 39)

> Everything turns on the price of Nana, im-
> peccable sixties
> haircut which makes her look the age

of the car
Of Him 1 and of Him 3. Then (finally!)
gun shots.

It's all very matter-of-fact, the impeccable *coupe* (haircut) anticipating the coups de feu of the gangsters. But the final poem is called *Je tends la main à Nana* ("I hold Nana's hand") and is written in prose:

Au verso de cette feuille, au verso de ce texte que je cherche et transcris, il y a, plus

Absent pour toi lecteur que cette histoire de Nana qui revient, le brouillon pour moi

Seul visible et donc inexistent d'un ancient poème, que je ne relirai qu'a travers l'image de ces images d'elle, dans le désespoir impossible d'être enfinentièrement entièrement dupe. (V 41)

On the verso of this page, on the verso of this text which I look for and transcribe, there is, more remote for you, reader, than this story of Nana which returns, the little scrap, visible for me alone and hence nonexistent of an old poem, which I never reread except through the image of these images of her, in the impossible despair of being, in the end, entirely entirely duped.

Duped by whom or by what? On the verso, there is no "old poem" to reread, only Baetens's "Note finale" on the verse forms used throughout. Is the poet duped by Nana, whose hand he certainly doesn't "hold"? Or is he duped by the film's curiously unanticipated melodramatic ending – an ending in which the banal gives way to the shock effect of sudden death? Or is Baetens the dupe of the film itself, a film as seductive as its motifs and characters are ultimately trivial? Perhaps all the above, the poem's revelation being that there is, in the poet's subconscious, a little scrap of paper bearing an *ancien poème* which he never goes near except through the image of these Nana-images. A lost love evidently or perhaps a love never possessed but which this film, of all films, evokes. Who knows what happened? The poet is, in any case, the dupe.

In the course of *Vivre sa vie*, the ideological thrust of the film, whose central focus on the ways a capitalist social structure creates the fall into prostitution – a fall not particularly remarkable in the modern city but tragic nevertheless – is replaced by a sequence of love poems, that contain a trace of Troubadour lyric even as they interrogate and ironize the film from which they derive. At the same time, Baetens's *Vivre sa vie* is by no means parody or pastiche, for the text does take up the issue of how one lives one's life. In his Postface, the critic Semir Badir remarks that Baetens's project tries to "return poetry to the heart of things," where film has long been located (V 57). Indeed, the sequence calls into question the tedious high/low division, showing that the "low" is always, from another angle, perceivable as "high." As such, *Vivre sa vie* is also a metapoetic text: it theorizes the possibility of enlarging the boundaries of what poetry is and can be.

"From Paint to Point to Pain"

In his important study of citation, *La seconde main*, Antoine Compagnon writes

> When I cite, I excise, I mutilate, I extract. There is a primary object, placed before me, a text I have read, that I am reading; and the course of my reading is interrupted by a phrase. I return to the beginning; I re-read. The phrase reread becomes a formula, isolated from the text. The rereading separates it from that which precedes and that which follows. The chosen fragment converts itself into a text, no longer a bit of text, a part of a sentence or of discourse, but a chosen bit, an amputated limb, not yet a transplant, but already an organ, cut off and placed in reserve. [6]

Craig Dworkin's *Dure*, published as a chapbook by Cuneiform Press in 2004 (figs. 2-3) and then reprinted in Dworkin's collection *Strand* (Roof Books) in 2005, [7] is composed of the "amputated limbs" Compagnon speaks of. Here the intertext is neither poem nor film but an unsigned 1519 drawing by Albrecht Dürer, formerly in the Bremen Kunstverein and reproduced in the *catalogue raisonée* of J.J. Winkler – a drawing, so Dworkin tells us in the first prose poem, that "has not been seen since the second world war" (*Strand* 75). The drawing (fig. 4) depicts the torso, seen frontally, of a nude man, who points with his index finger to a scar on the left side of his abdomen – a scar circled for emphasis, and in the original chalk drawing, painted yellow. The inscription at the top of what may well be a self-portrait reads, "*Wo der gelb fleck ist and mit dem finger darauff deut do ist mir weh*," which Dworkin translates, "Where the yellow spot is and where I am pointing with my finger, that is where it hurts." [8]

Although *Dure* is not, strictly speaking, composed according to Oulipo constraints (as is, for example, the title piece of *Strand*), it does observe Jacques Roubaud's rule that "A text written according to a constraint describes the con-

6 Antoine Compagnon, *La second main ou le travail de la citation*, 17. Translation mine.

7 The chapbook spreads a color rendition of the drawing across the recto and verso of the cover, with the inscription rendered as calligraphy in the frontispiece and title pages, *Dure* bearing the dedication "For a Form." In *Strand,* the layout is more conventional, with the drawing as frontispiece. The chapbook is an artist's book and should be consulted even if the reader uses the more accessible and readable Roof edition. Citations here are to *Strand* as the more readily available version.

8 Since the inscription is written in rather blurred Old German script, it is difficult to decipher. Dworkin transcribes the (*u's in*) "darauff" and "deut" as *w*, and omits the final "h" of "weh." I have reinstated them because in German "w" is not a dipthong and "we" would not have been a word.

straint."[9] For the source texts, listed in a chronological table at the back of the book and ranging from the OED to Derrida and Wittgenstein, Smithson and Kosuth, Aristotle and Augustine, obscure Renaissance medical texts and the notes of various rare book dealers, are chosen with an eye to illustrating, in however various ways, the meaning and resonance of the title: *Dure*, from *durus* (Latin for "hard"), referring both to the enigmatic art of Dürer as well as to the English derivates of *durus* like *duration*, *durable*, and *endure*.

Like a number of other recent poetry books – for example Cole Swensen's *Goest* and Mary Jo Bang's *The Eye like a Strange Balloon*, *Dure* is, broadly speaking, an ekphrastic poem, drawing out of the meanings contained in a given art work. Indeed, *Dure* begins by reviewing conflicting information about the Dürer drawing: "The assumption is that Dürer drew it for a consultation with a foreign physician" (*Strand* 76), or again, with a play on Richard Burton's classic, "It could be a frontispiece to a lost treatise on the melancholy of anatomy" (94). Before long, information and analysis give way to a series of more fantastic suppositions: the portrait as love letter, as reproach to the viewer ("*you have done this*"), as geometric drawing relating to Dürer's treatise on ellipses, as an illustration for Renaissance treatises on medicine. Citations are embedded in commentary marked by increasing word and sound play, as in the following passage:

> He has draped himself discreetly, naked to the waist. The tear ducts gape, humid and enlarged. "If any bodye weare vulneratede in the Eyes, insparge, and strewe this poulder there." Soiled solder, spoilt, spelt. Stays antiqued with tea. Psalm, palm, lapse. A damp map skirts the glair that binds the tongues of rawhide and required felt. Welt, stiletto, silhouette. The bruise on the boards of a book; the pall of raw words, "I assure you that I would more than gladly have painted myself here in my entirety, and completely naked at that." (*Strand* 82)

The poem begins matter-of-factly with a description of the portrait's sitter. But the second sentence moves from the real to the imagined: we cannot, of course, see those enlarged tear ducts. The citation that follows (from A. M. tr. Gabelhouser's *Bk. Physicke 54/1* [1599]) carries on the theme of eye damage: translated into modern English, it reads, "If any body were wounded in the eyes, scatter and strew this powder there." The motif of wounding now becomes pervasive: "soiled, solder, spoilt, spelt," each word evidently suggesting the next by dint of sound. But the words also make sense: an attempt is made to "solder" the flesh containing the wound, but "soiled"/ "spoilt" suggest otherwise, while "spelt" refer to the effort to explain, to reveal, as in Gerard Manley Hopkins's "Spelt from Sybil's Leaves." And the triplet – Dworkin is very fond of these – "psalm, palm, lapse" combines rhyme and anagram to take us from prayer to the unstated "offense" that is al-

9 Jacques Roubaud, "Introduction, The Oulipo and Combinatorial Art" 42.

luded to throughout *Dure*, the lapse that has somehow caused the wound. But the lapse or break is also that within the book in which the poet contemplates Dürer's drawing: "a damp nap skirts the glair [a kind of glaze] that binds the tongues of rawhide and required felt." "Damp nap" – monosyllabic words that carry on the sound imagery of "psalm, palm, lapse" – seem to refer to the artist's sleep habits until we realize that this sentence deals with bookbinding, culminating in the final "felt" and its rhyming partner "welt." "Welt, stiletto, silhouette": the sharp "stiletto" may indeed produce a "welt"; indeed it does do so on the phonic level. And further, "silhouette" is a near-anagram on "stiletto" and brings us back to the "silhouette" in the Dürer drawing. For bookmaking is itself a kind of wounding: "The bruise on the boards of a book: the pall of raw words." And now follows a citation from Montaigne, namely, the great essayist's declaration of a willingness, seemingly unlike Dürer's riddling, to reveal himself, to appear to us "naked." But the conditional verbs of the passage suggest that, of course, Montaigne did no such thing. And in any case, in the context of verbal self-revelation, "naked" functions metaphorically: there is no image of a naked body for our eyes to light upon. Here the verbal and the visual part company.

The mode of *Dure* is thus what Compagnon calls *transplant*. Dürer, Montaigne, Gabelhouser: their words are transposed and set against Dworkin's catalogues of obscure and obsolete nouns or intricate sonic echoes, so as to position the artist's scar, referred to by the obsolete noun "crag" (cf. *Craig*, the poet's first name) in the opening section, in relation to the poet's own "wound." We can read *Dure* medically ("The tissue is a morose delectation, the fingertip testing its sensation, and that lack, with an unreciprocated pressure: the nerves failing to complete the narcissistic circuit, so back and fore to get at figuring this fascination of a flesh that is no longer ours," 70), or architecturally ("hinge joints rusted, jambs akimbo, the doors of perception droop," 82), or homophonically ("scars" as "scare tactics," 83). But the scar is also a mark of love: "These fractures factured with a hairline list: Communicating passages. Moments of separation held open to their possibility. Signs that we have shared space" (83). And a few pages later, we read "Ever, sever, swerve" and "He is pointing at, perhaps, her cost, and for her pleasure. Honey, ankle, tongue" (89).

Dworkin's language game oddly becomes most personal when it interweaves the Dürer materials with the "impersonal" propositions of Wittgenstein on pain. "How do we know," we read in section #11, "where to point to when we are asked to point to the painful spot. Can this sort of pointing be compared with pointing to a black spot on a sheet of paper"? (85). This observation comes from the *Blue & Brown Books* as does the following in #19: "And here again remember the difference between pointing to the painful spot without being led by the eye and on the other hand pointing to a scar on my body after looking for it" (93). What, then, of the self-portrait, which centers on the act of pointing at the encircled spot even as the artist's eye, far from gazing directly at the scar, gives a "sidelong" look at the viewer, as if to challenge his authority.

The citations from Wittgenstein's pain calculus along with Charles Peirce's analysis of the "pointing index finger" and Smithson's "set of disconnections, a bramble of stabilized fragments taken from things obscure and fluid" (102) increasingly focus on the poet himself, and we gradually realize that *Dure* is perhaps most notably an homage to lost love ("memory as the prosthesis of pain," 95), and hence lost language. If this makes Dworkin's poem sound like a latter-day version of John Ashbery's *Self-Portrait in a Convex Mirror*, published just thirty years earlier, it is necessary to note the differences between the two poems. Like Dworkin, Ashbery begins by contemplating an enigmatic self-portrait – in this case, Parmigiano's – and in the course of the poem, he ruminates on the conditions of its painting, the response from Vasari and contemporary art critics like Sidney Friedberg, and the relation of the painting to musical and literary works. But *Self-Portrait* has continuity, reflected in the consistency of its free verse (often loosely iambic pentameter) and the centrality of the poet's own self-portrait, however fragmented his observations. In a post-language poem like *Dure*, on the other hand, there can be no such continuity – only excision, extract, mutilation, transplant, echo. Consider #22:

> "Writing is a strange shadow whose sole purpose is to mark the destruction of the body that once stood between its light and its earth." Skiagraphy, touch-type, and method. A run of his finger feels nothing now that the surface has smoothed, but can still make out the thin ellipse floating on his forearm, like a shadow under shallow skin, and can trace its curve, left from the time she pushed him into the stove, and know that this is his proof: whatever else, she felt that strongly, she really did care this much that once. He who forgets that love lasts will not recognize its fist. Carp, suspended, mottle and kern. This entire text is an attempt to ask: "how can something be the shadow of a act which does not exist?" The problem is not finding a solution, but simply posing the proper question. "Don't you know then, what I mean, when I say that the stove is in pain?" (*Strand* 100)

Here, almost at the end of *Dure*, introduced by a comment made by Paul Mann, a detractor of the avant-garde potential for change, the poet's own "scar," finally comes out into the open: the "thin ellipse floating on his forearm, like a shadow under shallow skin" is the "cinder" or "mark" of that moment when the unspecified "she" "pushed him into the stove." In retrospect, it is a positive memory because "whatever else, she felt that strongly, she did care that much that once." The personal motif is immediately distanced and ironized in a reprise of Kruchenykh's famous Futurist cry in *A Slap in the Face of Public Taste*, cited as the first sentence in #7: "He who does not forget his first love will not recognize his last." In #26, this playful denunciation of the past is transposed into the darker aphorism, "He who forgets that love lasts will not recognize its fist," the revision emphasizing the *endurance* of love but also its *hardness* – its *dure*.

Four words follow, the first and fourth alliterating sharply: "Carp, suspended, mottle and kern." We can read this as an imperative: "suspend your carping, cover the object with mottled cloth or paper, and eliminate the white space between the letters ("kern"). But "carp" can also be a noun, hence a fish, and "kern" means "the part of a typographic letter that extends beyond the body." In this case, we are witnessing something emerging from its base. In either case, the words suggest that, "it must *change*." But how? Here Wittgenstein's *Investigations* comes to the rescue with the reminder that "The problem is not finding a solution, but simply posing the proper question." And that question can only be posed by the resort to "Skiagraphy" (radiography), "touch-type, and method."

Dure thus replaces the expression of subjectivity that is still central to Ashbery by a written record, itself a scar, on a piece of paper – a "scar" rather like Jan Baetens's *brouillon* of that seminal old poem, known only to himself. Indeed, *Dure* might have been called, in Lyn Hejinian's words, *Writing is an Aid to Memory*. Yet compared to that book, Dworkin's is more *lisible*, more grounded. Use the notes and look up the words in any major dictionary, and the emotional resonance of Dworkin's "*Plaît*, plait, plaint" becomes apparent. *Ubi manus,* as we read in #1, *ibi dolor*. Where the hand was, there pain shall be. The reference is to the Dürer self-portrait, but it includes all those whose *dolor* Dworkin has been citing – especially the poet's own.

Language Envy

Dure reveals Craig Dworkin as obsessed with verbal and phonic mutation – the difference a letter can make as in "Granular, glandular, gradual, gloss." A similar obsession marks the work of the Japanese-German poet-novelist-essayist Yoko Tawada. Born in 1960 in a Tokyo suburb, Tawada studied literature in Japan and then came to Hamburg in 1982 to work for a local German book exporter as a trainee. She never went back and was soon writing in German as well as Japanese, and finally in German alone. Like such of her German precursors as Thomas Bernhard, Ingeborg Bachmann, and Elfriede Jelinek, Tawada begins by writing an epiphanic free verse lyric usually laced with irony as in "O":

Auf der Rückseite	On the back
des Wassers	of the water
schreibe ich den Buchstaben O	I write the letter O
Wie man ein Loch	Just as one drills a hole
in ein anderes Loch bohrt	into another hole

Ein spiegelverkehrtes O steht auf dem Kopf und lacht mich aus.[11] (59)	The mirror image of O stands on its head and laughs at me.

Here, already, is the fixation on the powers of the alphabet. But before long, poems like "O" (juxtaposed to Japanese poems and their translations as well as artwork) are replaced by gnomic short fables and fairy tales, written in prose, and culminating in the 2000 *Opium für Ovid,* which contains twenty-two versions of Ovidian fables on metamorphosis.

In 1998, as the fifth *Poetikdozent* (Professor of Poetics) at Tübingen University, Tawada gave three *Poetik-Vorlesungen* – published under the title *Verwandlungen* ("Metamorphoses"). These poetic lectures – part essay, part prose poem, part poetic meditation – are tissues of citations and the poet's own variations on them: a list of sources is appended at the back of the book. Like *Dure*, *Verwandlungen* is, loosely speaking, ekphrastic, although it does not focus on a single image; like Baetens's *Vivre sa Vie*, Tawada's "lectures" especially the third, focus on a face, the German word *Gesicht* containing, as a paragram, the word *ich* or "I." Indeed, the discovery of the *ich* leads the poet to the further thought that, for a foreigner learning German, *Gesicht* looks like a verb in the perfect tense, beginning as it does with the prefix *ge-* as in *Ich habe es gesicht* ("I have faced it"), although there is no such word in the language.

How to read faces? It is a central question in *Vivre Sa Vie*, *Dure*, and such other recent citational poetic texts as Caroline Bergvall's "About Face," which I have discussed elsewhere.[12] The three lectures in *Verwandlungen* concern what it means to be a foreigner, specifically a Japanese living in Germany, with respect to three aspects of poetry: the spoken word, writing, and reading. The first lecture-poem is called "Voice of a Bird or the Problem of Strangeness." When Tawada listens to herself speak German, she feels as if she is spitting out strange bird sounds. Her sentences have perfect contours but they don't seem to belong to her. Indeed, the poet speculates, the constant effort to speak correctly, to get every consonant and vowel right, not to mention tone and pitch, may actually change the facial contours of the speaking person, so that their descendants, in the second or third generation, will have a different physiognomy.

Speaking a "foreign tongue" is, moreover, a transforming experience. Before she came to Hamburg, Tawada muses, her own voice meant nothing to her. It was merely a vehicle to communicate something. Now she is so aware of voicing that the opposite has happened: all the emphasis is on the medium of what Tawada

[11] Yoko Tawada, *Aber die Mandarinen müssen heute abend noch geraubt werden*. All translations mine.

[12] Marjorie Perloff, "The Oulipo Factor," 221-226.

calls *Vogelsprache*, Bird Language. The poet now exemplifies *Vogelsprache* in a Celan lyric from "Sprachgitter," a Ludwig Tieck fairytale, and Wagner's *Ring*. Confucius too is included:

> Confucius admired a man, who had officially been found guilty of murder and sentenced for the crime, and permitted this man to marry his daughter. What is interesting is the reason why the son-in-law had come under suspicion for murder: it seems he could understand Bird Language and happened to hear the birds conversing animatedly about the murder. Therefore, he knew exactly where the corpse was hidden. But most people refused to believe his story and insisted that he must have been the murderer. (*Verwandlungen* 19)

It is a cautionary tale for the reader who tries to penetrate the language of the Other. And, after some further examples – from Mozart's *Magic Flute* and Messiaen's *Catalogue des oiseaux*, the poet concludes:

> Wer, mit einer fremden Zunge spricht, ist ein Ornithologe und ein Vogel in einer Person. (22)

> Whoever speaks in a strange tongue, is an ornithologist and a bird in one person.

Poetry, Tawada is suggesting, is defined by this double function: to produce speech that is always folding back upon itself, always constructing only to deconstruct the text. And the two functions are inseparable.

The second lecture, *Schrift einer Schildkröte oder Das Problem der Übersetzung* ("Writing of a Turtle or the Problem of Translation"), shifts the discourse from *voice* to *writing*. Again, foreignness is a paradox: both alienating and yet essential to poetry:

> For a long time I didn't notice that I could only rarely become absorbed in the reading of a German book. As a child, I ran right into a book, just as one enters one's own house. Then I lost myself in the world described there and no longer saw the language. In order to get inside a book, just like a house, one must read so fast that the letters disappear. But perhaps it is not a matter of speed but of the way of reading. In theory, I know of course how to read phonetic writing: one must mentally quickly translate it into the corresponding word sounds, for otherwise their sense will remain hidden behind the wall of letters. I don't dare look at the written forms but must fly beyond them. Already after a few minutes, though, my eye begins to rest on each letter. Then all is silent in my head, and meaning disappears. Maybe one needs a vehicle to navigate these alphabetic landscapes. Speech rhythm, for example, could be such a vehicle. It would carry me quickly over the meadow, so that the cannibal cactuses of letters could not catch me. (25)

The letters of the alphabet as cannibal cactus: the rest of "Writing of a Turtle" contrasts the reading of Japanese to that of German (or any alphabet language). The reader of Japanese connects ideograms and their syllabic bridges, often without knowing how a given word might *sound*. Poetry readings are thus considered pointless, the differentials of the written language impossible to convey orally. "The word for 'aunt,'" for example, is always pronounced *oba*, but, according to whether the aunt is younger or older than the parent in question, one writes a different ideogram" (*Verwandlungen* 27).

In such a culture, visual form becomes central. "Hieroglyphs are interesting because they make clear that the pictorial dimension of writing need have nothing to do with a concrete picture. It has much more to do with memory" (29). So much for Pound's theory that in Chinese, words are close to *things*. It is not thingness that distinguishes the ideogram but its place in an elaborately learned relational system. The poet is at home in this system, whereas, she says, "every letter of the alphabet is a riddle" (30). One is forced, right away, to translate letter into sounds. And when one rearranges the letters, an entirely different sense obtains. "The anagram owes its art to the magic of the alphabet" (30). And a little anagrammatic poem, *Das Spielen der Kinder ist streng untersagt* ("The Playing of Children Is Strictly Forbidden") by Unica Zurn follows.

For Tawada, the challenge of the alphabet is thus its indeterminacy. "One writes a B, it can become a flower [*Blume*] but also a bomb [*Bombe*]" (31). So unreliable, unmeasurable, and unpredictable is every letter of the alphabet. And now come some wonderful pages on computer translation. Tawada's computer can translate alphabetic text into ideograms but the results are puzzling. The word for "secret" (*kakushigoto*) comes out as *kaku* (write) and *shigoto* (work). "Maybe," the poet posits, the computer wants to say that one creates secrets by writing. Putting letters together is, after all, hard work.

As the poet probes the visual image of the alphabet, it becomes more and more mysterious. She begins to see letters everywhere – on footpaths, on leather bags, on doorways. The alphabet seems almost part of nature. Look at the palm of your hand and you can find I's, H's, and X's, but not C's. And indeed the actual letters (not the words they form) cannot be translated at all. A literary translation thus begins in untranslatability. For Tawada, certain texts by Kleist and Kafka, for example, sound as if they are translations, even though they are not. Why? A particular Kafka text contains the words "spring," "quick," "sun," "shade," "face," and "light" – words that, when re-assembled as *parole in libertà*, all contain the Chinese ideogram for "sun." And so the poet suddenly recognizes Kafka's image of the sinking sun lighting up the face of the young girl. It isn't that Kafka knew the ideogram in question, but that a literary text can sometimes find the intertext that gives it meaning (39). Consequently, the question should never be, "In what language do you dream?" but "In what script do you dream?" In the brief interlude "E-Mail for Japanese Ghosts," that follows, we read, "Every letter is like the back of a person. It can turn around any time. An author who thinks his own text must belong to him, to the last letter, is fooling himself: when a letter turns around, a strange face becomes visible" (41).

This marks the transition to the third lecture, *Gesicht eines Fisches oder das Problem der Verwandlung* ("Face of a Fish or the Problem of Metamorphosis"). As we move from voice to writing to reading a human face, Tawada's text becomes more somber, the paradox being that, as in Dworkin's *Dure*, the *malaise* recorded is presented almost entirely through citations from dictionaries, Walter Benjamin's *One-Way Street*, Barthes's *Empire of Signs*, and, as always, Ovid's *Metamorphoses.* The key word of the "lecture" is *Gesicht* ("Face"), beginning with the question whether fish can be said to have faces. The poet's dictionary defines *Gesicht* as "the front part of a human head, from chin to hairline, inscribed by the eyes, nose, and mouth" (45). But a fish, whose eyes are on both sides of the head, has no "front" and hence presumably no "face." And what about the passage in Benjamin's "One-Way Street" that speaks of the collector's passion showing its "*wahres Gesicht*" ("true face"), even as his "*Gesichtsfeld [*ist*] frei von Menschen*" ("field of vision is free of human beings")?

How to reconcile these seemingly different uses of *Gesicht?* In the Benjamin example, it is not the face that reveals passion (*Leidenschaft*) but the passion that has a face. Accordingly Tawada redefines *Gesicht* as *etwas, das sichbtar geworden ist*, "something that has become visible" or "has revealed itself." In this sense, a city has a "face" as does an occupation, faces not revealing themselves until they are *read.* The face is a text that contains latent multiple meanings. But, like both Baetens and Dworkin, Tawada traces the word horizontally as well as vertically: "Ein Gesicht, ein Geräusch, ein Geruch, ein Geschmack, ein Gefühl" (48; a face, a noise, a smell, a taste, a feeling). In German, the words designating the five senses sound alike. And yet syntactically, they carry different meanings, depending on whether the verb is transitive or intransitive. *Ich rieche* can mean "I smell [the unnamed object of the verb] or again "I smell [bad]." *Ich schmecke* is similarly ambivalent: it can mean "I taste [it]" or "I taste good."

Does the voice have a face? Here Tawada turns to the story of Echo and Narcissus. Spurning the invisible nymph, the self-regarding Narcissus is punished by becoming only a voice, whereas Echo becomes a voice that can repeat only what the other says. So when Narcissus says, "I would rather die than belong to you," Echo can only repeat "belong to you." To this extent, she can speak whereas Narcissus is transformed into a silent flower.

Gesicht, as I noted earlier, contains the ego, *Ich*, and it looks like a perfect verb form, "*gesicht*." The face is a highly variable signifier: Buddhist deities have dozens of faces emanating from their arms and legs; angels have only one face. But most important, the face is a speech creation. God divided the earth and sea, not as a physical act, for the water would always contain a bit of earth and vice-versa, but by verbal fiat: he *said* he was dividing them. And now Tawada turns to Ovid, to the Kafka of "Metamorphosis," to those many fairytales where men and women become animals. The reverse, Tawada notes, doesn't happen: there are no fairytales or myths where actual animals become human and marry other humans, although in Kafka's play *Ein Bericht für eine Akademie* ("A Report for an Academy"), the I-narrator is a monkey, who must, to his regret, take on human customs and habits.

Here is the conclusion to Tawada's lecture:

> Das Modewort "Identitätsverlust" hat den Begriff der Verwandlung in die Ecke verdrängt. Die Verwandlung ist aber seit der Antike ... eines der wichtigsten Motive der Literatur. Poetische Verwandlungen bilden einen Raum zwischen der Sehnsucht nach einer tödlichen Verwandlung in ein Tier und dem Entsetzen über die Verwandlung in einen Menschen. (60)

> The fashionable term "loss of identity" has pushed the concept of Metamorphosis into the corner. But, it is Metamorphosis that, ever since Antiquity ... is one of the most important motifs of literature. Poetic metamorphoses create a space between the nostalgia for the deadly metamorphosis into an animal and the horror of metamorphosis into a human being.

What is the meaning of this pessimistic contrast and what is its import for Tawada's poetics? The poet might have written a coherent essay or narrative about identity loss, of the difficulties faced by being displaced, alienated, a victim of globalization and diaspora, and so on. Such tales are only too familiar. But throughout her three poem-lectures, Tawada can only deal with the loss of voice, writing, and reading as someone else's narrative. That, her poem-lectures imply, is, after all, what loss *is*.

In *Mandarinen*, there is a poem called "Ein Gedicht für ein Buch" ("A Poem for a Book") that concludes:

zwischen einem wort	between a word
und einem schluck wasser	and a sip of water
dort	there
wo die stimme	where the voice
im fleisch aufwacht	awakes in the flesh
hört man ohne ohren	one hears without ears
ein wort	a word
befreit von seinem dienst	freed from its duty
ein	a
wort	word
direkt auf das trommelfell geschrieben	written right on the eardrum
die trommel fällt	the drum falls
lautlos	noiselessly
stimmhaft	voiced

ein wort	a word
ein ort (93-94)	a place

Here is Tawada's own Echo story: *wort*, *dort*, *ort* echoing on her eardrum. Loss, as the poet's various intertexts suggest, is also gain, metamorphosis offering, as it did for Echo, at least some respite from the pain of love. In the above poem, the word "ein" (or "einem") appears six times, in each case meaning either "a" or "one." The *ort* (place) of the word is thus ambiguous. Then, too, the non-native speaker's refusal to capitalize the nouns in question produces an odd clinamen from what these words are expected to be. "Ein wort / ein ort": but where? As in *Dure* and *Vivre sa vie*, Tawada's poetry is rooted in linguistic play – a form of play in dialogue with earlier "foreign" artistic models, whether French film, German painting, or, in Tawada's case, the authors Ovid and Kafka. It is this *literary* and *ekphrastic bent* that perhaps most clearly distinguishes the new generation of "experimental" poets from their precursors in the Language movement. But what they have learned from those precursors is that, in the digital age, one cannot simply write, as the mainstream would have it, "in the tradition of" this or that earlier poet or painter. The cited text remains in quotes – a transplant whose status as "amputated limb" reminds the reader that, in Blanchot's words, resaying is always "saying for the first time."

Works Cited

Baetens, Jan. "Novelising Jean-Luc Godard." *Formes poétiques contemporaines* 3 (2005): 135-152.

—. "Postface." *Slam! Poèmes sur le basket-ball*. Bruxelles-Paris: Les Impressions Nouvelles, 2006. 57-65.

—. *Vivre sa vie, une novellisation en vers du film de Jean-Luc Godard*. Paris-Bruxelles: Les Impressions Nouvelles, 2005.

Bruns, Gerald. "The Pagans and Karen Mac Cormack." forthcoming in *The Gig* (2006).

Compagnon, Antoine. *La second main ou le travail de la citation*. Paris: Seuil, 1979.

Dworkin, Craig. *Dure*. Buffalo: Cuneiform Press, 2004.

—. *Strand*. New York: Roof Books, 2005.

Messerli, Douglas. *From the Other Side of the Century: A New American Poetry 1960-1990*. Los Angeles: Sun & Moon, 1994.

Perloff, Marjorie. "The Oulipo Factor." *Differentials*. Tuscaloosa: University of Alabama Press, 2004, 205-226.

Roubaud, Jacques. "Introduction, The Oulipo and Combinatorial Art." 1991. Comp. Harry Mathews and Alastair Brotchie. *Oulipo Compendium*. London: Atlas Press, 1998. 37-44.

Tawada, Yoko. *Aber die Mandarinen müssen heute abend noch geraubt werden*. Tübingen: Verlag Claudia Gehrke, 2003.

—. *Verwandlungen. Tübinger Poetik-Vorlesungen*. Tübingen: Konkursbuchverlag, 1998.

Fig. 1. Front cover of Jan Baetens's *vivre sa vie*.

Fig. 2. Verso of the chapbook cover of Craig Dworkin's *Dure*.

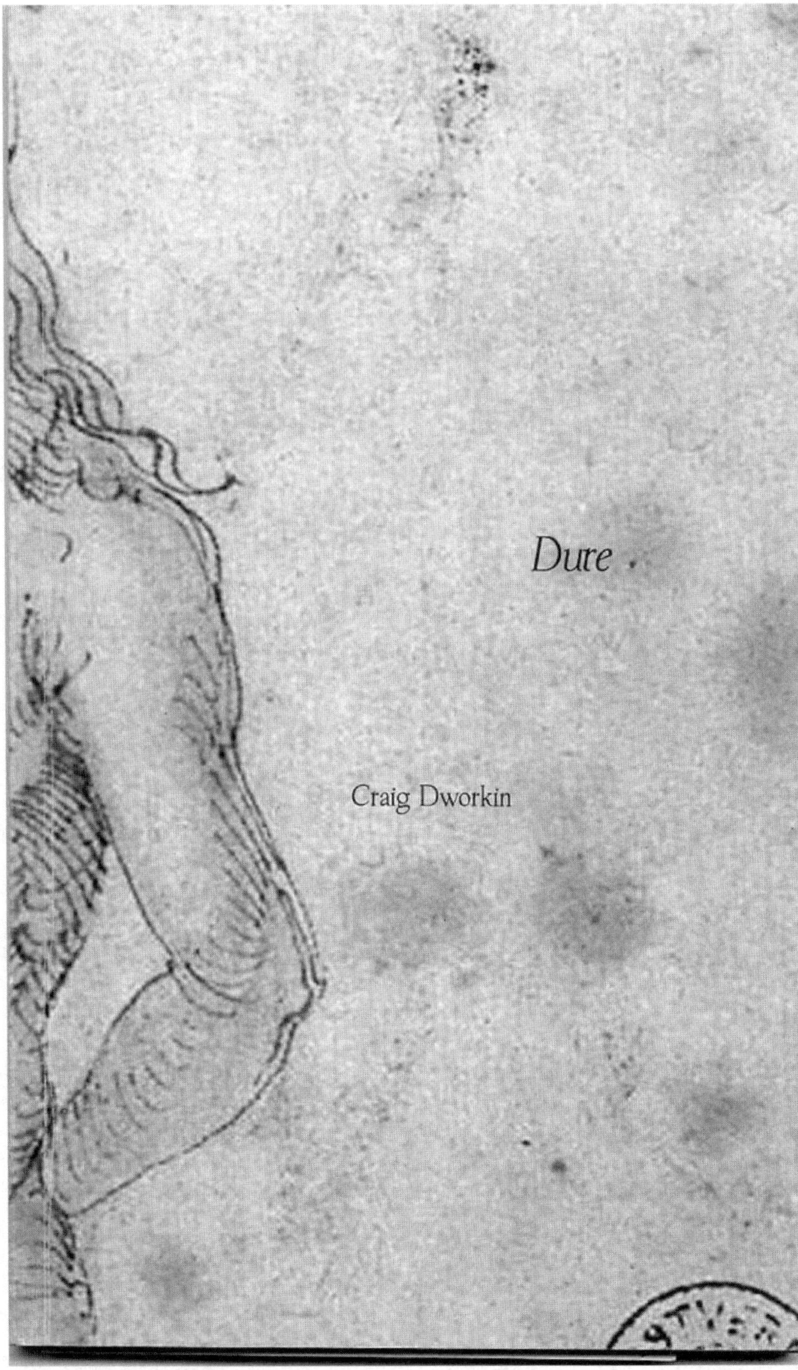

Fig. 3. Recto of the chapbook cover of Craig Dworkin's *Dure*.

Fig. 4. Albrecht Dürer's unsigned drawing with the inscription at the top.

Reading Rosmarie Waldrop and Yoel Hoffmann: Embodied Thought and Linguistic Gap

Deborah Meadows

At any given time, the living see themselves in the midday of history. They are obliged to prepare a banquet for the past. The historian is the herald who invites the dead to the table. [N15, 1]

Walter Benjamin, *Arcades Project*

***

The events surrounding the historian, and in which he himself takes part, will underlie his presentation in the form of a text written in invisible ink. The history which he lays before the reader comprises, as it were, the citations occurring in this text, and it is only these citations that occur in a manner legible to all. To write history thus means to cite history. It belongs to the concept of citation, however, that the historical object in each case is torn from its context. [N11, 3]

Walter Benjamin, *Arcades Project*

***

Walter Benjamin writes suggestively from the critical insight that smooth narratives are compositions of "authoritative citation," or fragments of available, desirable, or culturally-typical material; that versions are made from earlier versions. We see in his collection *Arcades Project* a determined collection, placement, and cunning selection of citations on the past of Paris, and we see a turn away from conventions of historic narrative toward alternative practice. The inescapable presence, perhaps necessity, of citation that Walter Benjamin describes in historiography has analogs in many other disciplines despite their originating claims for unbroken wholes and unbiased commitments to truth and knowledge. The following paper is a citation-driven study of metonymy, and, by reverse composition, a reading of Rosmarie Waldrop's recent collection of poetry entitled *Blindsight.* The paper will cite portions of her source works as well as from Max Pensky on Benjamin and citation, and from Adorno on Hölderlin and parataxis.

On the copyright page of *Blindsight*, Waldrop acknowledges sources such as Yoel Hoffmann's *Bernhard*, Hölderlin's poetry, Antonio Damasio's studies in neuroscience, and Hans Reichenbach's mathematics. Further, her life's work has been as poetry translator with a deep relation to many poets including Edmond Jabès. Waldrop's work here, and in other volumes, often critiques the Cartesian divide between mind and body but also considers how biology (of perception, for example) may drive knowledge and how cultural materials, such as language and literature, shape or misshape our knowledge. *Blindsight* considers the divide, per Reichenbach, between our visualization and logic.

Among several works Waldrop cited as sources for *Blindsight* is *Bernhard* (1989; English, 1991) by Yoel Hoffmann. It's fascinating to see how portions of this fictitious life writing of shattered memory, recollections of a movement from Berlin to Palestine in the 1930s and 40s, are re-appropriated in a form of collaged life writing in Waldrop's collection. Our fictitious Bernhard retrieves shards of the past that are wistful, others quotidian, some accidents that are comedic, others elegiac on loss of home and, reminiscent of Jabès's Yukel in his *Book of Questions* (1964; English, 1991) on the loss of his wife Sarah, Bernhard grieves the suicide of wife Paula and reexamines early memories of his family, neighborhood, of political history. The ground of memory may shift, or may have somatic structure derived from geography: do the literary conventions of desert parables in the works of Jabès and Hoffmann fracture or hinge from the original place?

In one portion Hoffmann's character-within-the-character, Bernhard's Pavel with a severed limb removes the leather straps that held his false leg, slaps his stump that "freed from constraint, would wriggle like a happy baby" (#44) as if life was formed from loss and amputation. This segment is followed by an excursus on the philosophic question on the seat of identity, in Pavel's wooden leg that "went up in flames when Napoleon stood at the gates of Moscow" or in Pavel's flesh leg, the "where is Pavel"... Earlier in the text, Hoffmann's character Bernhard looked at Spinozan and Cartesian traditions – the former unifying experience of mind and body; whereas, Descartes' cogito severs mind and body, the view that comes to dominate Western thought and consciousness. When is a puppet wood and when is he flesh? Waldrop returns to this cleft between opposite views, I suspect, because neither can they satisfy or exhaust the explanation of who we are nor of the lived needs of our lives that fall across a biological/cultural divide. We can ask when a limb is simply mine, when it is me as identity, and see that our mentation is grounded in biological form, and see that that answer does not suffice completely because, too, the capacity for language projects flesh, that culture drives knowledge, and our bodies, marked or broken, are books, too.

How might the fictitious rendering of interrupted experiences of flesh and language provide a reading of fragmented life? In *Lavish Absence: Recalling and*

Rereading Edmond Jabès, Waldrop writes of the breaking of Mosaic tablets as a necessary condition for legibility. Waldrop's work keeps company with Hoffmann, Jabès, and others that collage fragments as a necessary condition for reading, a movement that triangulates between polar situation. On page 17, Waldrop's reflection of the life and work of Jabès:

> But with Jabès, too, the emphasis is not on isolating minimal units of meaning, but on the interruption, the gap between. "Interruption is one of the fundamental devices of all structuring," says Walter Benjamin. The shadow zone of silence, of margins, gains weight, becomes an element of structure. The interruption allows for breath, for possibility, for stopping to think.
>
> And perspectivism. Inherent in the form of the fragment, it acknowledges the elusive whole, be it Jabès's transcendent totality or, for me, here, the man Edmond Jabès and his work. And encircles it at least to some degree, I hope (17).

And, after an exploratory passage on numerous ways the fragment may operate in service to ambiguity and deferral of settled meaning, Waldrop writes: "I love David Mendelson's false etymology that derives the word 'mosaic' from Moses, from his breaking of the tablets. This is certainly behind Jabès's 'exploded book,' where the death by scattering God's word is the condition of legibility" (19). She then quotes the Mendelson passage that concludes: "The destroyed book allows us to read the book."

***

In Max Pensky's *Melancholy Dialectics: Walter Benjamin and the Play of Meaning,* Benjamin is cited on the activity of mosaic construction:

> Just as mosaics preserve their majesty despite their fragmentation into capricious particles, so philosophical contemplation is not lacking in momentum (*Schwung*). Both are made up of the distinct and disparate; and nothing could bear more powerful testimony to the transcendent force of the sacred image and the truth itself. The value of fragments of thought is all the greater the less direct their relationship to the underlying conception, and the brilliance of the representation depends as much on this value as the brilliance of the mosaic does on the quality of the glass paste. The relationship between the micrological processing of the work and the proportions of the sculptural or intellectual whole demonstrates that truth-content is only to be grasped through immersion in the most minute details of subject-matter (18). (Benjamin, "On the Program of the Coming Philosophy" 28-29)

***

How does the study of memory and biography always take a turn toward the study of Time? Waldrop's earlier work is extended here: a slippage of fixed meaning, a play of signifiers in a field of desire for knowledge that defers metaphysical tropes. Although Waldrop's *Blindsight* and *Bernhard* by Yoel Hoffmann are about departures and about new locations with shifting encounters of layered history, linguistic, culinary, marketplace, art and culture systems, might their work with the absent center offer an ethical antidote to totalizing systems?

We read in section 34 that Hoffmann's Bernhard lives in a year "the Atlantic Ocean fills up with an infinity of sounds. Igor Stravinsky sails across. Arnold Schoenberg sails across. And Paul Hindemith, and Béla Bartók, and Darius Milhaud, and Kurt Weil...." Against this situation ripe with history, our Bernhard invents an imaginary character we meet in section 35, D. S. Gregory, who "was born in Moscow to Pavel and Yekaterina Sholochov" and inherits the legacy of the "Turko-Bulgarian Kingdom." The imaginary character and his relation to history show a way the fictitious Bernhard, or Hoffmann, or any person, interprets their times, about how they inhabit dream-time or use fantasy as, perhaps, a psychological working out of their lives and conflicts. Bernhard draws on clichés, and we wonder if fantasies used to cope and survive re-enforce conventions of our culture even when that culture may be destroying us.

***

If one postmodernist view considers self and society as constructed through effects of situated language, neurobiologist Antonio Damasio in *Looking for Spinoza: Joy, Sorrow, and the Feeling Brain* is concerned with how self and society come from structures in the brain exempted from historic moment. In his neural research, he studies emotions that he posits may come first in evolutionary development, that are observable, and are in response to the world; whereas, he posits feelings as following emotions, he writes, like shadows, as private, and neurally-mapped patterns of interior states such as well-being.

Waldrop acknowledges Damasio in her *Blindsight* volume and continues an ongoing study of neurological structures of experience. Damasio, like Waldrop, rejects the Cartesian division of mind and body and looks to Spinoza, who in his *Ethics*, described a mind-body integration.

***

Waldrop opens with "Hölderlin's Hybrids" and collages from the Hölderlin and Hoffmann texts and other, social and literary sources sympathetic to Hoffmann's approach. Here we can see ways Waldrop's work extends her earlier books' examination of cultural and social encoding at the level of the sentence toward a use of the sentence-level tension that breaks into gaps punctuated by full stop periods. For example, Waldrop writes:

2

Electric bulb. How the words are. Suspended around you.
And. Bones in the body. (5)

Here are *interrupted flows* of light particles, electricity, predication, conjunction, and, a Waldropian move, the unseen skeletal structure of our bodies – indeed the cover art of this volume is a work entitled "Totem Series" that at first glance seems a three-column set of x-rayed bones, but further study suggests a lamellisection of portrait photos – that is, an Oulipian procedure that cuts images into strips to be reassembled by procedure distancing, if not reversing, them from their original. Series, too, may offer an alternative to the narrative crescendo of conventional forms – a horizontality against the allure of heroic verticality.

This poetic practice returns to and extends her earlier works such as *Reluctant Gravities* in its exploration of intimate relations and gender stereotyping. She worked this area of mixing different discourses in an often ironic or even comical way in earlier works as in *The Reproduction of Profiles*. In "Cornered Stones" of *Split Infinites* she has already developed the mixture of discourse describing her childhood in Nazi Germany. She furthers a type of life writing that, like Jabès's and Hoffmann's examples, is both individual and shared social experience of war, losses that mix sacred and popular or commercial references as well as comedic accident – a way to defy the nostalgia type of television broadcast that packages notable shared events with a prepared emotional prescription. Here is Hoffmann:

> 1.
>
> After his wife died, Berhard thought:
> "The world is infinite. Beyond every galaxy there's
> another galaxy." He tried to imagine how Paula, her
> flesh pale, was gradually becoming one with the vast
> order of the Universe. But Paula's death was not
> such a simple matter. "Where," thought Bernhard
> to himself, "Is Paula now?"

And later, Hoffman writes in section #2:

> 2.
>
> . . . Most of
> the time Bernhard played with a lump of wax (in
> due course he came to Palestine by himself). . . .

To compare, here is Waldrop's opening:

1

The world was galaxies imagined flesh. Mortal. What to think now? Think simple. Matter? A lump of wax? An afterglow? Or does everything happen of its own accord? Perfect and full-bodied. No more. Observable. No longer. In your eyes or line of sight. Down all three dimensions of time. Or lock up the house. Or prophets.

△

Here I work toward. A kind of elegy. Here a strange ceiling. "Earth fills his mouth." I would look at you. And write . . . (3)

And then onto the lower part of the following page, Waldrop writes of grief, death, and detached words followed by: "Absence. But it cuts. Repeat. Furiously Yes then No. Even/a fictional character catches a chill. Makes the heart. . . " (4).Waldrop seems to move in sympathy with Bernhard's thoughts on his wife's possible absorption into the larger galaxy, and so emerges a view of the world as the thought of the galactic flesh, a sort of Spinozan brain as the good idea thought up by the body. Both passages ask: what is material? Is a lump of wax another language, is poetry the matter that poets manipulate that is ultimately futile yet necessary as is elegy?

In #45, Hoffman describes neuro structures and their circuit of stimuli and response, and, in a later segment, character Bernhard goes to see "Snow White and the Seven Dwarves" with Gustave while Jews are being smuggled from Denmark to Sweden:

A nerve is a fiber that spreads out
from the brain in one's skull, or from the spinal
cord. It transmits stimuli from every part of the
body (as when one says, for example, "A guttren
Shabbes").* When you are thinking about them,
the nerves are transmitting all kinds of stimuli
(backwards and forwards). Bernhard thinks nerves
are "Nerven."† Nerven are a lot of little dwarfs
singing "Hi-Ho, Hi-Ho."

*Have a good Sabbath. (Yiddish)

† Nerves (German)

Waldrop insets this with Hölderlin's poem fragments, his themes of early Swabian heroes and legendary figures from the Crusades, Mohammed, Rinaldo, and Barbarossa. Might we consider this as an analog to how Bernhard creates a fantasy character to work out conflicts, create a historic plot engine, a notable lineage – and so their functions relate to poets of Weimar classicism such as Hölderlin's use of classic Greek as well as medieval and legendary past – is it a fantasy solution? What does this show about the society that is the source of the conflict? When does a doll become a figurine – hardened, formal, and aloof? Later we will read from Adorno: a view of Hölderlin as anticlassicist.

Hölderlin's fragmentary poems, for many of us perhaps, may be his most interesting work; he writes from the immediate misery of conditions following the French Revolution. Not only is he a poet who is one of Waldrop's childhood references, her segment here refers to her performance as a ten-year old in *Snow White and the Seven Dwarves* performed from the back of an American Army truck following Germany's surrender in May 1945 (*Gale Literary Data Base*, Steve Evans, 2004). In her hands they are bled into a text that explores deep neuro-structural response and memory retrieval that are *both reflective and autonomic*, not imaginable without a flesh and blood body subject to physical forces of the earth. Here, Waldrop writes:

> 3
>
> Something else is it. To leave your house and cross the
> Atlantic, Mediterranean, Aegean, Pacific. So many were
> killed. And to stand each. In a doorway. And say I don't
> live here.
>
> △
>
> In the dark leaf nerve fibers spread out and from the brain.
> Scatter and like flames. From the spinal cord. Stinging.
> And stimuli from every. By ravenous hunger overcome.
> Transmitting backwards and forwards. "Nerves" more than
> seven. Dwarfs hi ho off to work. And farewell to the per-
> sonal. Pronoun.
>
> △
>
> So Mohammed. Rinaldo. Barbarossa. As divided into frag-
> ments. The emperor Heinrich. I am however mixing up
> the centuries. But gloom there is. In every needle, thread,
> and cloth. Crossed the Alps and with his own voice sighed
> "some things ... " And his son Konrad of poison died.
> Hark ye the horn of the watchman at night. And hair. Away
> from the body grows. (7-8)

****

Waldrop cites Hans Reichenbach's *The Philosophy of Space and Time* as a source for *Blindsight* causing this reader to reflect on his life. In 1933 with Hitler's rise to power, Reichenbach fled to Istanbul, then to the US where he settled as a faculty member of UCLA and remained until his death in 1953. Considered a leader of the Berlin Group of logical empiricists and a close associate of Einstein, most sources cite Reichenbach's work as a defense of the conventionality of geometry and of *simultaneity*, the term for Einsteinian relativity, that certain physical qualities considered objective are "relative to" the state of motion of the observer. As a reader and respondent to his work, Waldrop's poem explores how seemingly unbiased scientific observation is historically conditioned.

Reichenbach's work, *The Philosophy of Space and Time,* in part, details the problem that nonlinear geometry cannot be visualized. He writes how investigations that "led to visualization of non-Euclidean geometry through an adjustment in the perception of congruences, are therefore applicable to mathematics in the same fashion as physics" (87). Further, he demonstrates that the "concept of congruence" is transitive (88) and shows there are different ideas of congruence between Euclidean and non-Euclidean geometry that are "not identical but play equivalent roles in the axiomatic systems. . . " (89-90). So a reader might notice the ways Waldrop's poems require a consideration of those "presupposing tacit conditions" (Reichenbach, 90), and that:

> It is intuitively certain that a straight line is shorter than any line however slightly curved; this insight is due to the peculiarity of human thinking that it can draw strict conclusions from vague visual pictures; this is an important ability of the human mind which we put to continual use. It is therefore impossible to disprove the existence of pure visualization the basis of the lack of clarity in visual pictures. On the contrary, this argument has given new impetus to the thesis of pure visualization, since it has been interpreted in terms of a distinction between the vague perceptual space and the precise space of visualization. The main objection to the theory of pure visualization is our thesis that the non-Euclidean axioms can be visualized just as rigorously if we adjust the definition of congruence. This thesis is based on the discovery that *the normative function of visualization is not of visual but of logical origin* and that the intuitive acceptance of certain axioms is based on conditions from which they *follow logically*, and which have previously been smuggled into images. The axiom that the straight line is the shortest distance is highly intuitive only because we have adapted the concept of straightness to the system of Euclidean concepts. . . . (91, original italics)

In a sympathetic move, Waldrop's poetry questions the persuasive clarity of visualization, and her poetry explores the gap between "vague perceptual space and the precise space of visualization" or "vague visual pictures." Waldrop's poetry can cue us to our confidence in visual clarity and sharpen our sense of the difference between the logical rather than physical congruence of our lives and language. Waldrop's poetry reflects the problem of visualizing the past by offering a vital alternative to representation that, too often, slips to formulaic narrative structures fooling us with clarity derived from a conventional order. Again, the importance of Waldrop's poetry includes how we might explore pictorial elements or procedure, and come to understand and critique how we learn conventions that shape how we see landscape, hear history, feel common sense, or imagine characters.

*

In an e-mail, Rosmarie Waldrop answers my query whether she memorized Hölderlin's poetry as a child:

> Hoelderlin was read, maybe not in elementary school, but in high school. But it wasn't the fragments (those I came to later), rather early and middle Hoelderlin. The ones I remember and practically knew by heart are: "Als ich ein Knabe war' [when I was a boy], "Haelfte des Lebens" [Mid-life], "Schicksalslied" [Fate's Song?].

Hölderlin writes the dynamic tension between nature and the poet, yet Waldrop's gap has more in common with Jabès who sees break, gap, mosaic shattering as the very necessary condition for the book, for legibility. Origins, as constructs, and Benjamin's dialectical image are deeply related to legibility: they are the "eddy in the stream of becoming" (Pensky 217-218). Meta-social life-writing is constituted by its moment, yet people are also made by economic and political forces. Hölderlin thought Oedipus's lack of knowledge, or severance from his origins the source of tragedy.

In *Notes to Literature*, Adorno writes that Heidegger is wrong to characterize Hölderlin's poetry as mythological. Adorno writes that demythologization is bound to have a layer of mythology (116) and that the danger of language is getting lost and selling out the truth (120), and so turns to Hölderlin's work for strength against the merely instrumental view of the world (127).

*

Further into his reading of Hölderlin's poetry, Adorno points to the Protestant taboo against graven icons, then to the implied emphasis on text alone:

> ...which in Hölderlin is the law of poetry, with a taboo against abstract utopia, a taboo in which the theological ban on graven images, which Hölderlin shares with Hegel and Marx, lives on. Not backwards: because of the irretrievability of something once overthrown, the point at which poetry, history, and ideal intersect. The decision, finally, expressed as an anacoluth in an amazing reversal, "Be rocked as / On swaying skiff of the sea," is like an intention to cast aside synthesis and trust to pure passivity in order to completely fill the present. For all synthesis – no one knew better than Kant – occurs in opposition to the pure present, as a relationship to the past and the future, the backwards and forwards that falls under Hölderlin's taboo. (142)

Adorno's chapter on Hölderlin's poetry is most often quoted for his insight on the later, fragmented poems' use of parataxis as, too, should his remarks on *sequence* for poets concerned with the serial poem be studied. In contrast to how deMan and Heidegger made a sharp two-position dialectic of opposites, Adorno would rather study the structural possibility of the missing middle (132-3), which has been a concern in Waldrop's work, too, so that parataxis has "the tendency to take over larger structures" often "dispensing with predicative assertion [that] causes the rhythm to approach musical development" in poems such as "Half of Life"

> ...a middle element standing outside the moments it is to connect, is eliminated as being external and inessential... [that] gives Hölderlin's late poetry its anticlassicistic quality, its rebellion against harmony. What is lined up in sequence, unconnected, is as harsh as it is flowing. The mediation is set within what is mediated instead of bridging it. ...it is only the paratactical form itself that produces the caesura between the halves of life. (133)

Benjamin writes: "History decays into images, not into stories" [N 11, 4].

***

Coda

From Edmond Jabès, *The Book of Questions*, volume 1, translated by Rosmarie Waldrop:

> For five summers I have followed a book which advances quietly in the void where the work builds up. Daily enterprise of joining through the feverish page the ascus of the sign.
>
> A book which is the lacing of risk.
>
> I must tell a strange story which obsesses me of a woman in her eighties who, on her deathbed, spoke just before dying in the language of her childhood (which she had long forgotten). This act in the fog of the unconscious struck me – and still strikes me – as an example of the behavior of poets who speak in their works as they never do otherwise.
>
> Every work cancels the dark. Every work is a hymn from the other side of memory to a memory that is spellbound.... (325-356)

***

Works Cited

Adorno, Theodor W. *Notes to Literature*. Vol. 2. Trans. Shierry Weber Tiedemann. New York: Columbia University Press, 1974.

Benjamin, Walter. *Arcades Project*. Trans. Howard Eiland and Kevin McLaughlin. Cambridge, MA: Belknap Press of Harvard University Press, 1999.

Damasio, Antonio. *Looking for Spinoza: Joy, Sorrow, and the Feeling Brain*. Orlando: Harcourt Books, 2003.

Derrida, Jacques. *Of Spirit: Heidegger and The Question*. Trans. G. Bennington and R. Bowlby. Chicago: University of Chicago Press, 1987.

Hoffmann, Yoel. *Bernhard*. Trans. Alan Treister. New York: New Directions, 1998.

Hölderlin, Friedrich. *Hölderlin*. Trans. Michael Hamburger. Baltimore: Penguin, 1961.

—. *Hymns and Fragments*. Trans. Richard Sieburth. Princeton: Princeton University Press, 1984.

Jabès, Edmond. *The Book of Questions*. Trans. Rosmarie Waldrop. Volume 1. Hanover: Wesleyan University Press, 1991.

de Man, Paul. *Blindness and Insight: Essays in the Rhetoric of Contemporary Criticism*. Minneapolis: University of Minnesota Press, 1983.

Pensky, Max. *Melancholy Dialectics: Walter Benjamin and the Play of Meaning*. Amherst: University of Massachusetts Press, 1993.

Reichenbach, Hans. *The Philosophy of Space and Time*. Trans. Maria Reichenbach and John Freund. New York: Dover Publications, 1958.

Waldrop, Rosmarie. *Blindsight*. New York: New Directions, 1998.

—. *Lavish Absence: Recalling and Rereading Edmond Jabès*. Middleton, CT: Wesleyan University Press, 2002.

Tom Raworth Between Two Avant-Gardes: The British Poetry Revival and the New American Poetry

Brian Reed

The latest buzzword in the American academy is "transnational." One much-touted feature of the so-called New American Studies, for example, is its abandonment of American exceptionalism. The United States, we are told, must be understood as one agent among many, governmental, corporate, military, diasporic, and otherwise. [1] This academic trend is likely to give specialists in experimental poetry a sense of *déja vu*. The porousness of nation-state boundaries and the complexities of transnational interchange are old news to anyone who has pondered the origins, spread, and myriad offshoots of dadaism, expressionism, futurism, and the other historical avant-gardes. What respectable overview of early twentieth-century American avant-garde literature could omit altogether Marcel Duchamp or James Joyce?

Curiously, though, one cannot presume that studies of neo-avant-garde writing from the second half of the twentieth century exhibit a comparably internationalized perspective. Although there are a few academic overviews available – most notably, Romana Huk's anthology *Assembling Alternatives: Reading Postmodern Poetry Transnationally* (2003) no one has yet written a literary-critical analog to Thomas Crow's remarkable *The Rise of the Sixties* (1996), which presents institutional, aesthetic, and other links between the visual and performing arts in France, Italy, Germany, the United Kingdom, and the United States. He describes a variegated, contradictory formation whose participants and artworks freely circulate across national borders. He shows that focusing exclusively on any one national, linguistic, or regional tradition would distort the scale, dynamics, and significance of the whole.

This essay cannot possibly offer a Crowe-like synopsis of every post-WWII poetic neo-avant-garde. It can, however, build on work by such scholars as Brian McHale, Peter Middleton, Nicholas Jenkins, and Keith Tuma by offering an in-

1 See Adams for a wide-ranging review essay that discusses the turn toward global and transnational frames within recent American Studies scholarship.

stance of encounter between two distinct neo-avant-gardes – the American and the British – to intimate the value of such a larger project.[2] Neo-avant-garde verse must be understood as much more than an annex to or subset of the *völkische* national literary traditions that all-too-often dictate curricular divisions; it is an elusive, internally divided, only intermittently self-aware yet prodigiously creative and, yes, truly transnational phenomenon whose collective history awaits narrating in all its diversity, specificity, waywardness, intricacy, and wonder.

Trans-Atlantic Raworth

Tom Raworth belongs to an important cohort of post-World War II British poets that includes Andrew Crozier, Lee Harwood, Christopher Middleton, Wendy Mulford, Douglas Oliver, and Denise Riley. These authors came of age during the British Poetry Revival, a fifteen year stretch from around 1960 to 1975 that saw, as Keith Tuma's *Fishing by Obstinate Isles* has detailed, a proliferation of new institutions, publication outlets, and performance venues that encouraged adventurous experimentation in form, subject matter, and audience address (52-59). Raworth and his colleagues were united in rebelling against the "good old solid English tradition" that they associated with the previous literary generation, especially Phillip Larkin (48-50). One way they sought to counter this "back to Thomas Hardy" parochialism was by looking outside Britain for inspiration. Many of them paid especially close attention to the most provocative overseas literature written in English to which they had ready access: "what was going on in the States" (Hollo 80-81). More specifically, they studied the writings produced by the loosely affiliated, mid-twentieth century experimental poetry circles retrospectively called the New American Poetry (a label lifted from the title of an influential 1960 anthology edited by Donald Allen). The British poets found much to admire in the writings of each of the various subsections of the New American Poetry (hereafter NAP): the Beats, the Black Mountain School, the San Francisco Renaissance, and the New York School.[3] They particularly esteemed the NAP's antiestablishment ethos, disregard for decorum, delight in popular culture, vernacular diction, ludic youthfulness, and rigorous practice of a mode of free verse in which form is everywhere finely calibrated to subject matter.

---

2 See Tuma for a monograph on the relation between British and American experimental poetries throughout the twentieth century. See McHale and Middleton, *Distant Reading*, for books that compare and otherwise investigate links between post-WWII British and American innovative poetries. Nicholas Jenkins's *The Island: W. H. Auden and the Making of a Post-National Poetry* (forthcoming from Harvard University Press) explores continuities between British modernist verse and the American postmodernism of the Ashbery-O'Hara circle.

3 For more information about these schools of poetry, see Davidson, Duberman, Golding, Kane, Rifkin, and Ward, *Statutes*.

Raworth's involvement with the NAP dates back to 1961-1964, when he edited a journal named *Outburst* that published Gregory Corso and Robert Creeley. A close friendship followed with the Pond-hopping Black Mountaineer Ed Dorn, and, while at Goliard Press (1965-67), Raworth accepted books by several NAP authors: Creeley, Paul Blackburn, Charles Olson, Ron Padgett, and John Wieners. Given such contacts, it is hardly surprising that Raworth's early collections of verse – such volumes as *The Big Green Day* (1968), *Lion Lion* (1970), and *Moving* (1971) – are discernibly indebted to NAP precedent. He characteristically employs an irregular, mostly left-justified lineation derived from William Carlos Williams via such Black Mountain intermediaries as Creeley and Dorn. Likewise Black Mountain-esque are his departures from standard punctuation, spelling, and capitalization; his interest in notating the rhythm and intonation of speech; and his rapid pacing, which exemplifies Charles Olson's "much-quoted dictum ... that one perception must directly lead to another" (Ward, "Tom Raworth" 22). Moreover, he renders overt his literary affiliations by regularly referring or alluding to such NAP writers as Creeley, Padgett, Ted Berrigan, Kenneth Koch, and Frank O'Hara.[4]

An important qualification: Raworth might be indebted to NAP models, but he never slavishly imitates them. *Penguin Modern Poets 19* (1971) provides an illustrative example. It published selections by Raworth alongside verse by the New York School poet John Ashbery. And certain early Raworth lyrics, such as "Inner Space," do indeed recall Ashbery's elusive not-quite-allegorical dreamscapes:

> in an octagonal tower, five miles from the sea
> he lives quietly with his books and doves
> all walls are white, some days he wears
> green spectacles, not reading
>
> riffling the pages – low sounds of birds and their flying
>
> holding to the use of familiar objects
> in the light that is not quite (*CP* 34)

Raworth gives specifics (*octagonal* tower, *five* miles) that vividly sketch a scene. The actions that take place, though, are muddled. Two bland verbs ("lives," "wears") give way to a trailing, ambiguous syntax: three dangling participles ("reading," "riffling," "holding") and a floating noun phrase ("low sounds of birds and their flying"). This vague reportage leaves one unsure what moral to draw.

4 For Berrigan, see *CP* 79 and 195-196; Ward, "Tom Raworth" 19 and 24-25; and Edwards 42-43. For Creeley, see Middleton, "Silent Critique" 11-12 and 24-27. For O'Hara, see *CP* 76-77 and Middleton, "Silent Critique" 20. For Koch, see *CP* 76 and 89; Middleton, "Silent Critique" 11, 24-25 and 27. For Padgett, see *CP* 36.

Should we imagine the mind as a tower in which the intellect flips through books? If books stand for knowledge or memory, as appears likely, what then are the "doves"? Emotions? Flights of fancy? The white walls could refer to the bones of the skull, but why *green* eye glasses? Like Ashbery in lyrics such as "Two Scenes," "A Long Novel," and "Thoughts of a Young Girl," Raworth brings readers to the verge of paraphrase only to strand them amid quandaries. Depending on one's inclinations, the result is either frustration or a detour into mystery and fantasy.

Unlike a typical Ashbery poem, however, "Inner Space" investigates the poetic effects made possible by manipulating a page's white space. After the words "not reading" a blank space interrupts the poem. We are, appropriately, deprived of anything to read for a bit. Later, another stanza break occurs after the mention of the "low sounds of birds." We are given a respite in which to imagine cooing and fluttering before the poem resumes. Finally, Raworth ends the lyric in the middle of a phrase, just after an adverb: "in the light that is not quite." Not quite *what*? We could supply the missing conclusion. The word "right" is particularly tempting, as it would echo "light" and "quite." Alternatively, we could construe "is not quite" as a skewed way of saying "does not quite exist," willing a finality, of sorts, on the poem by arresting it and its message (its "light") in the flickering nowhere between presence and absence. There are analogs to Raworth's experimentation with layout in NAP writings – Frank O'Hara's "The Day Lady Died," for instance, ends abruptly without a period after the declaration "and we all stopped breathing" (325) – but Raworth's three, differently-valenced interruptions of "Inner Space" break with the NAP's predominantly speech-imitative versification by displaying a recurrent, pronounced interest in a poem as a visual construct of words arranged on a page.

Raworth's Intuitive Poetics

Robert Sheppard has argued that Raworth's early poems "valorise intuition over intelligence" (83). Understood properly, this assertion accounts both for Raworth's initial attraction to and later departures from NAP models. The 24 January 1971 entry in Raworth's prose-and-verse piece "Notebook" declares that "Intelligence become reflex equals intuition" (93). The remainder of "Notebook" clarifies this gnomic statement. Intelligence, we learn, is prized by "critics" and "explainers." Such people overvalue "meaning," which they confuse with "mathematical" regularities. Meaning, though, is, strictly speaking, ubiquitous: "*any* piece of language / contains *meaning*." No larger pattern, structure, or context has to exist before readers can attribute *some* degree meaning to a word. Moreover, "any piece of language / will fuse with any other." Words can be strung together without an overall plan. Such haphazard combinations might lack a "centre," and therefore vex "explainers," but an artist, "scan[ning] for the new," will delight in the consequent, unforeseen interplay of meanings. He or she has no worries that the words' ordering might violate logic or common sense. They know that while composing "you / can't / contra / dict / your / self" (99-101; his emphasis). Furthermore, artists feel no need to arrive at full understanding of a given word-string: "Intuition skips language it doesn't 'know' and reappears where the words fit again" (95).

The explainer/artist binary is, thankfully, neither absolute nor static. "Art can always attract attention from intelligence" (91). And with persistence, explainers can begin to appreciate that artists are striving "to get something that isn't a thought around something that isn't an idea" (89). They see that "meaning," as they have traditionally understood it, is precisely what artists are "fighting against" (101). They are then free to redirect their will-to-analyze. Instead of aiming at a global account of a given work, they can analyze without preconception or goal its "constant flowage from meaning to meaning, and ... slideslippage between meanings" (95). Once old-style critical intelligence becomes transformed to "reflex," that is, a constant, instinctual response to this rapid unceasing flow, intuition at last takes over (93). "We are free now to delight in the surface of language" (95).[5]

Raworth's celebration of intuition resonates with the Black Mountain emphasis on keeping things moving. In a poetics of intuition, one perception immediately leads to another without fear that such speed entails overlooking important pieces of "the whole picture" ("Notebook" 99). His delight in "slideslippage" also accounts for his fascination with the quick, improvisatory shifts in tone, setting, diction, and persona associated with the New York School. Poets such as Ashbery, Guest, Koch, and O'Hara regularly make use of unexpected transitions, unbelievable coincidences, brute juxtaposition, surreal happenings, and comic asides. Little in British verse since W. H. Auden's *The Orators* (1932) could offer Raworth such an archive of applied intuition, a flow of language fully alive to its course, obstacles, rapids, and eddies.

Significantly, though, neither the Black Mountain nor the New York School habitually takes the war against "meaning" as understood by "explainers" far enough for Raworth. He envisions a poetics of surplus which enforces "skip[ping]" around and investigating a poem piecemeal (95). Most NAP writings are simply too invested in conventional meaning-production to satisfy this demand. They usually reward being read from beginning to end without omis-

---

5 The two quotations in this paragraph beginning "the constant flowage from meaning to meaning" and "We are free now to delight" are taken from an extended passage credited to Clark Coolidge that constitutes the whole of the entry for 18 February 1971.

sions. Similarly, Raworth's opposition to elevating the poetic self to centrality put him on a collision course with the NAP. He believed the self to be not a master of its environment but a crossing point for multiple, external, unknowable forces: "we *are* / the switching of relays" (95; original emphasis). While many New Americans did question the epistemological grounds of selfhood – among them Creeley, O'Hara, and Olson – the biggest names also succeeded, via their writing, in reinventing themselves as larger-than-life figures whose personae frequently overshadow their verse. Creeley's anguished assault on the pronoun "I" in lyrics such as "The Language" (1967), for example, might point toward a postmodern conception of the self as a relay-switcher, but it is difficult not to imagine Creeley himself, self-doubting bard and tormented tormenting lover, suffering through the dissolution of identity that his lyrics recount. Raworth sought a truly impersonal poetry that would bar "explainers" from offering autobiographical interpretations that might smooth over his works' disjunctions, incongruities, and other challenges to intelligence.

From *The Relation Ship* (1966) to *Ace* (1974), Raworth sought to craft a form long enough to permit selective reading; a form impersonal enough to forestall looking to the author as guarantor of meaning; and a form flexible enough to provide maximal opportunities for unlike things, words, and images to abut. He experimented with a diaristic mode, an epistolary format, and modular sequences. Although fascinating, none of the resulting works seems fully to have satisfied his underlying program. In a clutch of lyrics written just before *Ace* and later collected in *The Mask* (1976), Raworth made one last raid on the NAP in quest of a solution. He borrowed the serial form of Creeley's *Pieces* (1968), which represents perhaps the most radical of NAP experiments with language. *Pieces*' short, abstract, discrete segments offer little in the way of narrative, character, or moral:

Agh – man
thinks.

*

Moving away in time,
as they say: *days*
later. Later than this –
what swings in the day's
particulars, one to one.

*

An unexamined hump
at first of no
interest lifting out
of the beach at
last devoured us all.

*

Sell the motherfucker
for several hundred dollars. (69-70)

If there is a rule that guides the ordering of such disparate segments, it is a perversely negative one: sections must possess few or no obvious causal, logical, temporal, or dramatic connections. In the following extract from "Perpetual Motion," one finds Raworth gleefully adopting this mode of writing:

reception

*

je ne veux pas
les biscuits de chocolat

*

warp
lines

*

a cat's concept of mind
that could make it dance
and sing by editing film

*

mary
was assumed
into heaven (*CP* 180)

Read straight through, the writing is nonsensical. What does the Assumption have to do with chocolate biscuits or dancing cats? Matters improve slightly when sections are read individually. The doggerel French couplet suggests an English speaker amused at discovering an internal rhyme ("pas" / "chocolat") while speaking with a waiter on the Continent. The free-standing word "reception" is phatic, that is, a means of making a reader contemplate the relation between author, text, and audience (are we "receiving" the message?). The monosyllables "warp / lines" could also be construed as self-reflexive. The "lines" of the poem could be said to constitute its "warp" – a comparison between poem and cloth licensed by the etymological link between the words text and textile. Similar speculations could be made concerning the import of the singing felines and the avowal of Catholic dogma. Intuition, in other words, has opportunities to run riot. In contrast, intelligence is paralyzed. It simply cannot unify such heterogeneous blats of verse.

Indeed, it seems intelligence proves overly paralyzed. Nothing in "Perpetual Motion" tempts readers to seek larger patterns of meaning. Its sequence of mini-poems is too disjunctive to entice intelligence into the repeated process of trial-and-error that precedes its elevation into intuitive "reflex." Raworth's *Ace* (1974) solves this problem. Like *Pieces*, it presumes that anything can follow anything. Unlike *Pieces*, it limits the number of articulated segments. The book's four parts each consist of lengthy, narrow, uninterrupted columns of verse:

> puts wind
> to back
> as light
> ups
> sail
> for life
> laughs
> to sky
> original
> out
> standing
> art in
> junction
> expounds
> only
> one
> love
> is well (*CP* 206)

The first eight lines of this excerpt seem to depict an excitable person on a sailboat. That vignette blurs into what might be an "in / junction" about "love" that "out / standing / art" "expounds." The words, though, can be fit together in a number of ways. It could also be the person on the sailboat who is "out / standing" while "laugh[ing] / to sky." The word "love" potentially functions both as the direct object of "expounds" and the subject of "is well." *Ace* teases readers with multiple, non-exclusive ways of configuring its short lines into plots, descriptions, soliloquies, and other conventional elements of literary expression. If the asterisks in

"Perpetual Motion" signal ruptures – moments when Raworth announces that intelligence cannot bridge this gap – in *Ace* every line break invites intelligence to strive after explicable meaning. And, as readers soon discover, it is impossible to make use of every such invitation. They have to choose when to ask questions and be content with less-than-complete answers.

Since *Ace*, the "long, skinny poem" has remained the favored format for many of Raworth's most ambitious works, among them *Writing* (1982), "West Wind" (1983), *Catacoustics* (1991), *Blue Screen* (1992), and *Meadow* (1999) (Wilkinson 146).[6] In fact, the form has become Raworth's trademark, his distinctive contribution to the international neo-avant-garde. He strikes a balance between sense and nonsense such that readers are inescapably (albeit sometimes begrudgingly) made aware of their active role in determining the boundary between the two. He thus ensures that the focus falls less on him as an author than on the phenomenology of reading, that is, how people interact with the words on the page in front of them.

Where Next

A longer version of this essay would now launch into a more extensive, comparative analysis. It might, for example, go on to compare Raworth's involvement in and dissent from NAP models with a similar process undergone by another American neo-avant-garde with which Raworth also has close biographical ties, the San Francisco Bay Area branch of Language Poetry. Although possessing obvious similarities, his work differs in at least two important respects. First, he does not respond to the ill-defined mystical-utopian politics common among the New Americans by rigorously grounding himself in Marxist theory and Continental philosophy, nor does he elaborate his theoretical arguments in prose polemics. Instead, as discussed earlier, in private notebooks that remained unpublished for decades, he developed a rough-and-ready, idiosyncratic distinction between intelligence and intuition. Second, in *Ace*, Raworth rejects the parataxis of Creeley's *Pieces* – its serial juxtaposition of fragments – in favor of a different writerly mode, a continuously-unfolding pseudo-sentence. In contrast, classics of San Francisco Language writing such as Ron Silliman's *Tjanting* (1981) and Lyn Hejinian's *My Life* (1987) redeploy the paratactic seriality of Creeley's *Pieces* in the form of aphoristic long poems in which each sentence can be read independently. And, as Marjorie Perloff has shown, a work such as *Tjanting* can thus be read as an assemblage of quotable quotes, equal parts commonplace book, diary,

6 All of these poems are available in Raworth's *Collected Poems*.

and intellectual autobiography.[7] Raworth's interminable non–sentences, in contrast, much more vigorously resist both selective quotation and summary description. He challenges the centrality of the lyric "I" without unintentionally replacing it with a sense of the *auctor absconditus* as a virtuosic composer of epigrams and philosophical *aperçus*.

These comments are preliminary. There remain many loose ends. This essay must leave readers with questions in lieu of conclusions. To what extent might one describe Raworth's verse as specifically British, a product of dialogue with contemporaries such as Bob Cobbing, Elaine Feinstein, and Jeremy Prynne? How did Raworth's formal academic study of Latin American writers such as Vicente Huidobro and César Vallejo inflect his reading of the NAP? How might entirely different touchstones – especially Canadian post-Concrete Anglophone poetics – better help one historicize and contextualize works such as *Ace*? How have poets on both sides of the Atlantic – Charles Bernstein, Tony Lopez, Drew Milne, and many others – adapted aspects of Raworth's poetics to their own ends? The "effort to describe," as the American modernist Hart Crane once put it, is "limitless yet forever incomplete" (192).

Works Cited

Adams, Rachel. "The Worlding of American Studies." *American Quarterly* 53.4 (2001): 720-732.

Crane, Hart. *O My Land, My Friends: The Selected Letters*. Ed. Langdon Hammer and Brom Weber. New York: Four Walls Eight Windows, 1997.

Creeley, Robert. *Pieces*. New York: Scribner, 1969.

Crow, Thomas. *The Rise of the Sixties: American and European Art in the Era of Dissent*. New Haven: Yale University Press, 1996.

Davidson, Michael. *The San Francisco Renaissance: Poetics and Community at Mid-Century*. New York: Cambridge University Press, 1989.

Duberman, Martin. *Black Mountain: An Exploration in Community*. New York: Dutton, 1972.

Edwards, Ken. "Misunderstanding Tom Raworth." *The Gig* no. 13/14 (May 2003): 39-48.

Golding, Alan. "The New American Poetry Revisited, Again." *Contemporary Literature* 39.2 (Summer 1998): 180-211.

Hejinian, Lyn. *My Life*. Los Angeles: Sun & Moon, 1987.

Hollo, Anselm. "A Conversation with Gunnar Harding." *The Gig* no. 13/14 (May 2003): 75-82.

Huk, Romana, ed. *Assembling Alternatives: Reading Postmodern Poetries Transnationally*. Middletown, CT: Wesleyan University Press, 2003.

[7] See Perloff's analysis of Silliman's prose poetry as "always already autobiographical" (137-144). Although she is specifically analyzing another poem, "Albany" (1983), her arguments apply to *Tjanting* as well.

Kane, Daniel. *All Poets Welcome: The Lower East Side Poetry Scene in the 1960s*. Berkeley: University of California Press, 2003.
McHale, Brian. *The Obligation toward the Difficult Whole: Postmodernist Long Poems*. Tuscaloosa, AL: University of Alabama Press, 2004.
Middleton, Peter. *Distant Reading: Performance, Readership, and Consumption in Contemporary Poetry*. Tuscaloosa, AL: University of Alabama Press, 2005.
—. "Silent Critique: Tom Raworth's Early Books of Poetry." *The Gig* no. 13/14 (May 2003): 7-29.
O'Hara, Frank. *Collected Poems*. Ed. Donald Allen. Berkeley: University of California Press, 1971.
Perloff, Marjorie. *Differentials: Poetry, Poetics, Pedagogy*. Tuscaloosa, AL: University of Alabama Press, 2004.
Raworth, Tom. *Collected Poems*. Manchester: Carcanet, 2003.
—. "Notebook." *The Gig* no. 13/14 (May 2003): 89-101.
Rifkin, Libbie. *Career Moves: Olson, Creeley, Zukofsky, Berrigan, and the American Avant-Garde*. Madison, WI: University of Wisconsin Press, 2000.
Sheppard, Robert. "Poetics and Ethics: The Saying and the Said in the Linguistically Innovative Poetry of Tom Raworth." *Critical Survey* 14.2 (May 2002): 75-88.
Silliman, Ron. "Albany." *ABC*. Berkeley, CA: Tuumba, 1983. Unpaginated.
—. *Tjanting*. Berkeley, CA: The Figures, 1981.
Tuma, Keith. *Fishing by Obstinate Isles: Modern and Postmodern British Poetry and American Readers*. Evanston, IL: Northwestern University Press, 1998.
Ward, Geoff. *Statutes of Liberty: The New York School of Poets*. Basingstoke: Macmillan, 1993.
—. "Tom Raworth and the Invisibles." *Cambridge Quarterly* 31.1 (2002): 17-32.
Wilkinson, John. "Tripping the Light Fantastic: Tom Raworth's *Ace*." *The Gig* no. 13/14 (May 2003): 145-160.

An Othering of Language: Harryette Mullen's Experiments in Transpoetry

Harald Zapf

The African-American writer Harryette Mullen has only recently been canonized as an African-American author. The second edition of the *Norton Anthology of African American Literature*, published early in 2004, includes nine new writers, and Mullen is the only experimental one among them. Mullen came from "Amiri Baraka to LeRoi Jones," from the "blackness" of her first book *Tree Tall Woman* (1981) and other early poems collected in *Blues Baby* to the experimentalism of *Trimmings* (1991) and *S*PeRM**K*T* (1992). She now balances artistic form and cultural context, which can be seen very well in her last two volumes of poetry: *Muse & Drudge* (1995) and *Sleeping with the Dictionary* (2002).

In my paper, I will treat Mullen as a transcultural poet between expressiveness and constructivism. Conceptualizing Mullen's poetry in terms of these polar opposites, I have to say that the expressivist poem is not the constructivist poem. The little hierarchy involved is that I slightly privilege the latter. I will deal with two poems from Mullen's work – "Las Locas" from her first book of poetry and "JingleJangle" from her latest volume – in order to illustrate the binary opposition "expressivist/constructivist." But in my analysis of "JingleJangle" I will also hint at the deconstruction of this opposition.

I argue that Harryette Mullen can be considered a paradigmatic "trans-writer" now, because she performatively creates a realm beyond the discursive borders of identity politics, vernacular tradition, culturally blind avant-gardism, expressivist poetics, and "pure" constructivist aesthetics, which contributes to her elusive location of multiple displacement, a differential position I will examine in this paper. First, I will look at Harryette Mullen in the context of blackness, American female experimentalism, and women's writing in general.

In her book on Emily Dickinson, which was published in 1985, four years after Mullen's first volume of poetry, Susan Howe criticizes the two feminist scholars Sandra Gilbert and Susan Gubar for conveying in their study *The Madwoman in the Attic* that "a writer may conceal or confess all, if she does it in a logical syntax" (13). What Howe says here about syntactically conventional concealment and confession is still true to some extent for a contemporary female writer like Harryette Mullen who is considered to be "avant-garde" and whose ethnic affiliation is African American. Using Emily Dickinson's words, one can say that African-American cultural producers – especially female poets – all too often have been "shut ... up in Prose" and denied access to "Possibility – / A fairer House than Prose – / More numerous of Windows – / Superior – for Doors – " (467/483). Arguably more so than "white" poets, African-American poets have often been expected to write poetry that corresponds to certain sets of interpretive conventions, conventions that are questioned neither by mainstream academic nor by non-academic and popcultural audiences.

Like a lot of ethnic poetry, most of Mullen's poems from her first book conform to what Jonathan Culler calls the conventions of speaker- and context-reconstruction, unity and autonomy, and the convention of significance: it is a quite rewarding approach to "imagine or reconstruct a speaker and a context," to "infer the posture, situations, concerns, and attitudes of a speaker (sometimes coinciding with what we know of the author, but often not)"; to read the poem "as if it were an aesthetic whole," so that all the parts "fit together harmoniously;" and to treat the poem as if it was "about something important" (74-80). These analytical conventions go together with certain immanent conventions: most of the texts from *Tree Tall Woman* are formally and semantically accessible; their transparent and "natural" language is instantly understandable; often, they still adhere to the poetic norm of the 1960s – free verse and the confessional mode. As Phillip Mehne rightly says in his essay "Making it strange,'" this includes an "orientation to spoken language, to speaking as a physical act" (Olson); what we don't find in Mullen's early work, but in a lot of other poetry by ethnic minorities, is an "accusatory and denunciatory voice" (Ginsberg "Howl"); all in all, this is the kind of orientation that some avant-garde communities opposed, especially the Language poets in the 1970s and 80s (540-541). In "Barbarism," a paper that she gave in Australia in 1995, Lyn Hejinian explains that what she and other Language poets had challenged and called into question was "the poetry of the self," "the romantic, unitary, expressive self, the 'I' of the lyric poem" (330, 329). The "Language School's rejection of expressivist poetics" can also be found in the essayistic work of one of the cofounders of the Language-journal, Charles Bernstein (Watten, "What Is" 347).

In his 1991-essay "State of the Art," Bernstein parodies the expressivist poetry of the self and then connects his parody with a critique of the form of multiculturalism and the model of representation fostered by what he calls "official verse culture":

Within the emerging official cultural space of diversity, figures of difference are often selected because they narrate in a way that can be readily assimilated – not to say absorbed – into the conventional forms of the dominant culture. Difference is confined to subject matter and thematic material, a.k.a. local color, excluding the formal innovations that challenge those dominant paradigms of representations. Indeed, the political and social meaning of sound, vernacular, non-traditional rhythms – that is, those things that make a text a poem – are often discounted as negligible in the fetishizing of narrative and theme; formal values being left for a misconceived avant-garde that has been involuntarily decultured – deracinated, ungendered, and therefore removed from those contexts that give it sense.

To be sure, signature styles of cultural differences can be admitted into the official culture of diversity if they are essentialized, that is, if these styles can be made to symbolically represent the group being tokenized or assimilated. Artists within these groups who are willing to embrace neither the warp of mainstream literary style through which to percolate their own experience nor the woof of an already inflected, and so easily recognized, style of cultural difference will find themselves falling through the very wide gaps and tears in the fabric of American tolerance. Such artists pay the price for being less interested in representing than enacting. (*A Poetics* 6-7)

So Bernstein polemicizes that in "official verse culture" multiculturalism is only a term for "a unified culture of diversity," where formal innovation contributes more to the marginalization of a poet than ethnic and cultural affiliation (6). Without referring to Bernstein, Harryette Mullen explicitly makes this point in an essay entitled "Poetry and Identity," which was originally published in *West Coast Line* in 1996, four years after Bernstein's "State of the Art" had been re-published in his seminal collection *A Poetics*, and one year after Mullen's fourth book of poetry, *Muse & Drudge*, had come out.

The short self-reflective text "Poetry and Identity" is central to an understanding of Harryette Mullen, because it illuminates her connection with experimental poetry and the diasporic black tradition, and because it shows her hybrid stance as participant-observer, her conflictual role as African-American poet and literary critic. It is also of great value for an understanding of what I call the "transpoet," an artist who moves beyond, through, across, and on the other side of different social and cultural fields. Maybe the transpoet is even the paradigmatic poet, who is on the move, because, as we know from LeRoi Jones, "hunting is not those heads on the wall" (173).

At the beginning of her essay, which deals with the issues of economic success, marketing, inclusion, exclusion (anthologies, audiences, institutions ...), communities and the individual talent (Bernstein, "Community" 176), representativeness, and marginalization from a female, black, avant-garde, and scholarly perspective, Mullen assumes

> that representative 'black' poets are currently more assimilable into the 'mainstream' than 'formally innovative' poets of any hue. Although both the 'avant-garde poet' and the 'minority poet' may be perceived as the other of the 'mainstream' (regardless of the distance and the different concerns that might separate them from each other), it would seem that the mainstream has far more to gain by appropriating minority poets who work in recognizable and accessible forms and who can thus be marketed to the broadest possible audience of readers. (27)

After five pages about the difficulties of location for a keen observer of the first and second order – a female avant-garde poet of color who is also a literary critic –, Mullen, fortunately enough, decides not to give up hope and reduce the complexity of her position by returning to the production of more categorizable poetry. On the contrary, she believes in finally being able to get beyond the imposed dichotomy of innovation and blackness, to close the gap between "blackness" and "avant-garde": "I felt that my latest poetic experiment must be successful when selections from *Muse & Drudge* were chosen to appear in *Callaloo* and *Muleteeth*, as well as in mainstream publications seeking diversity and journals devoted to racially unspecified 'avant-garde'" (30).

Mullen's persistence and her adoption of a deconstructive stance seem to have paid off: What finally got incorporated into the *Norton Anthology of African American Literature* is a selection of quatrains from *Muse & Drudge*. Interestingly enough, neither her early "black" poems, which Mullen herself considers rather easy to classify, nor texts from her most recent, most daring and diverse book were anthologized there. A few poems from *Sleeping with the Dictionary*, though – poems about topics such as bilingualism ("Bilingual Instructions"), blackness ("Denigration"), social ills and injustice ("We Are Not Responsible"), the personal in a capitalistic world ("Present Tense"), and governmental xenophobia ("Xenophobic Nightmare in a Foreign Language") – were included in a multiethnic anthology of political poetry edited in 2004 by Mark Pawlak, whose aim in compiling his collection "has been to find the best available work by living American poets that is, broadly speaking, political in nature" (12). Pawlak even used a Mullen-poem from *Sleeping with the Dictionary* for the title of his anthology: *Present / Tense*. Mullen's *Sleeping with the Dictionary* was also a finalist for the National Book Award, which is quite remarkable for a collection that cuts across the territory of different poetic cultures and obviously moves beyond the boundaries of what Bernstein once called "official verse culture."

Mullen's poem "Las Locas," which I am going to turn to now, and many other of her early texts that are centered around narrative and theme would still fit into this "official verse culture." Most of Mullen's work from the beginning of her career, and also some of her later poetry, to a certain degree, is an expressivist poetry of the self, in which poetic voice and the lyric I are immensely important.

This is the context we have to bear in mind when we read “Las Locas” from *Tree Tall Woman*:

> Oh, you crazy girls from Laredo
> I’ll always remember you
>
> heating tortillas on an ironingboard
> in the freshman dorm
>
> dyeing your straight shiny black hair
> even blacker and shinier
> telephone black
> mystery black of ladies
> with unlisted numbers
>
> going to dances in gold and silver *puta* shoes
>
> and getting me so drunk on tequila
> I slid down the stairs
> at a party fundraiser
>
> You crazy giggling girls
> calling yourselves *Chichas y Chones*
>
> From you I learned to eat refried beans
> for breakfast,
> beans you cooked with beer and cilantro
> instead of fatback
>
> You gave me *la llorona* and the evil eye
> and *abrazoed* me into your *raza*
>
> You girls, you *locas*
> spoke Spanish to me whether I could *comprende* or not
> and if I didn’t know all the words
> I understood your voices (*Blues* 67)

This expressivist poem indeed conforms to “the most common” definition of the lyric – “any fairly short poem, consisting of the utterance by a single speaker, who expresses a state of mind or a process of perception, thought, and feeling” (Abrams 146) –, which goes back to John Stuart Mill’s classic distinction between poetry and eloquence: “Poetry and eloquence are both alike the expression or utterance of feeling. But … we should say that eloquence is *heard*, poetry is *over*heard” (57). In the *Anatomy of Criticism*, Northrop Frye refers to Mill and says that the lyric is “preeminently the utterance that is overheard. The lyric poet normally pretends to be talking to himself or to someone else” (249). Mullen does the latter. Her poem, dedicated to "Angélica y Cristina" (Mullen, *Blues* 67), is a "normal intimate address to a known other" (Vendler 3). But despite the lyric conventionality of "Las Locas," the issues of poetic voice and address are relatively complex here, because of the poem's translingual and transcultural dimension. It is true that Mullen's text is an example of the "sort of human address" that Helen Vendler calls "horizontal," as distinguished from the "vertical" sort, because the addressees are merely other human beings and not persons or things "inhabiting a physically inaccessible realm conceived as existing 'above' the speaker" (2), but the speaker and the addressees do not belong to a homogeneous ethnic group. With its non-Hispanic Spanglish speaker, "Las Locas" refuses to imply a strict one-to-one correlation between a people and Spanish/English bilingual expressiveness. The speaker of the poem was not only away from home because she lived in a "freshman dorm," but because she metaphorically dwelled in a lingual and cultural place originally not her own. With her bilingual speaker, Mullen hints at the possibility of a truly transethnic (verse) culture. If we assume a correspondence between the African-American female poet and the speaker of her poem, we can say that, with Spanish, she uses a language that is usually not associated with her ethnic identity.

In this poem, Mullen questions, to some extent, the set of attributes ascribed to different ethnic groups; she brings up the issue of particular ethnic features as a matter of voluntary affiliation and performance, but the function of Spanish is more representational than performative. The language is linked with Hispanic heritage, descent, and a specific cultural identity; Spanish refers to members of an ethnic group, the addressees, *las locas*, in a particular historical context that the speaker of this expressivist poem remembers. Language, a major part of a speaker's identity, is not a matter of performativity here, but of expression; it is used in a constative, not a performative way. This is also stressed by the autobiographical context of the poem. In a 2000-interview with Emily Williams, published in *African American Review*, Harryette Mullen talks about the importance of Spanish in her life and work:

> I believe that my work is probably influenced by geography even though I don't think that geography is a major theme or topic in what I'm writing. But I do believe that I have a Southern or Southwestern emphasis in my work. In many of my works I have sprinkled Spanish words that relate to my growing up in Texas and living in northern and southern California. Spanish is always in the background; it's that other language that cohabits with English. I studied Spanish in school even though I am not fluent in it. (702)

Despite its othering of Spanish/English bilingualism, "Las Locas" still is a poem of the self with an authentic voice, a romantic, unitary and expressive I. In the volumes after *Tree Tall Woman*, Mullen began to problematize the self and the speaking subject in a more radical way. She also seems to have become "less interested in representing than enacting" (Bernstein, *A Poetics* 7).

"JingleJangle," for example, an abecedarian poem from *Sleeping with the Dictionary* that I will deal with now, is less concerned with representing blackness than with enacting otherness and difference, linguistic otherness and differences of sound, rhythm, and the vernacular. Although sound and other musical qualities play an important role in this poem, Mullen deconstructs the simple "written/oral" binary opposition, which Aldon Lynn Nielsen in "The Calligraphy of Black Chant" aptly calls "the falsity of the assumed opposition between singing and signing" (36). All too often African-American poets have been reduced to simple forms of orality. African-American poetry is partly a poetry of the self, in which poetic voice is a central aspect, for example in Amiri Baraka's 1965-poem "Black Art." But the phonocentric notion of authentic self-expression, the oral expression of a particular ethnic "I" is also questioned, for example by Ishmael Reed's "Black Power Poem," the first text in his first book of poetry, *catechism of d neoamerican hoodoo church*, which came out in 1970. Harryette Mullen names both writers, Baraka and Reed, among her influences. In a 1993-lecture called "Visionary Literacy: Art, Literature, and Indigenous African Writing Systems," which Nielsen quotes from in *Black Chant*, Mullen implicitly follows Reed and questions "the standard explanatory models of African-American vernacular orality" (35):

> That black literary traditions privilege orality ... has become something of a commonplace, in part because it's based upon what seems to be a reasonable and accurate observation.... Presumably, for the African-American writer there is no alternative to production of this authentic black voice but silence. (Mullen in Nielsen 35)

With "JingleJangle," Mullen shows that there is an alternative; in this non-narrative poem, it is impossible to identify an authentic black voice and to pin down the subjectivity of a speaker.

I consider "JingleJangle" to be a constructivist poem that offers a certain cultural poetics. For a definition of these terms, I refer to Barrett Watten's book *The Constructivist Moment*. By "constructivist aesthetics" Watten means "the imperative in radical literature and art to foreground their formal construction"; "cultural poetics," Watten writes, "may be minimally defined as the reflexive relation of artistic form and cultural context" (xv). Watten also brings up the subject of "cultural poetics" in his article "What Is Literature? From Material Text to Cultural Poetics." Here, he is "calling ... for an expanded account of cultural motivations. What kind of cultural work is a literary text doing? is a question that should be more frequently, and more complexly, asked of writers and critics of experimental writing" (352). Watten wants to "suggest a wider horizon of 'cultural poetics' based on the productive effects of the material text" (359). He thinks that "much work of the preceding period, however intelligently constructed as material text, addresses an absurdly overnarrow horizon of cultural meanings" (359). Watten is especially "criticizing the range of cultural meanings" that he sees in the work of "Language Writers" (359). By "cultural meanings" he does not mean anything that is really new to conventional literature: "different languages and genres, incorporations of popular or noncanonical culture, gendered alternatives, historical engagements, social topographies, modes of subject formation," and – in a very general sense – "productive encounters with the world in all the forms in which it is presented" (359). Watten argues "for a synthesis, a syncretic assemblage, or even a reflection on the relation of cultural interest and literary form" (359). In my view, Harryette Mullen's metapoetic "JingleJangle," which resounds with a variety of cultural meanings, is such a hybrid assemblage, a constructivist exploration in cultural poetics that leads to a particular reflection on the relation of literary form and cultural interest. "JingleJangle" does both: it foregrounds its formal construction and it relates artistic form to issues of culture.

"JingleJangle" is a list of successive slant-, but mostly full-rhyme words in an almost exact alphabetical order. Here, I will only quote the last five sections of the poem, from "v" to "z":

> Vanessa the Undresser vice price vomit comet voodoo
>
> Wacko Jacko wacky shack wacky tobacky walkie-talkie
> Wavy Gravy waylay
> wear & tear Weegee Whack Pack whale tale wham bam
> whammer-jammer
> wheeler dealer whimwham white flight white knight
> Wicked Pickett
> weird beard wild child willy-nilly Wilt the Stilt
> wining & dining
> wingding Winken & Blinken wishy-washy womb to tomb
> wonton
> Wooly Bully Writing Is Fighting
>
> X-sex
>
> Yak Pak yank the crank Yertle the Turtle ying-yang yoohoo
>
> zero to hero zigzag zip your lip Zoo Doo zoot suit Zulu (*Sleeping* 43)

The alphabetical order hints at print culture and written language, the rhyme pattern at gestural language and at the oral tradition with its devices for recitation and memorability. The rhymes make us think of advertising slogans, songs, chants, nursery rhymes, children's rhymes, word-play, and schoolyard games in general, but also of more African-American verbal games, such as those mentioned by Marjorie Perloff in the section of her paper "After Language Poetry" that deals with Mullen's *Trimmings* and *Muse & Drudge*:

> childhood jump-rope rhymes and "pseudo-courtship, formulaic exchanges" of preadolescence, like the male "What's cookin' good lookin'?" with its female response, "Ain't nothin' cookin' but the beans in the pot, and they wouldn't be if the water wasn't hot." (167)

Of course, the end rhymes of "JingleJangle" also evoke rhyme-oriented forms of the strong African-American vernacular tradition: secular rhymes and songs like "Jack and Dinah Want Freedom" (me-free, ole-col', free-tree, tub-rub, Nigger-bigger, fac'-back), ballads like the "Sinking of the Titanic" (around-down, Please-knees, there-clear, coal-soul ...), songs of social change like "Strange Fruit" (fruit-root, breeze-trees, South-mouth, fresh-flesh, pluck-suck, drop-crop), and especially traditional rap texts.

"JingleJangle" is an alphabetical list of rhyme pairs without information given for each word. With her book *Muse & Drudge*, Mullen intended "to allow, or suggest, to open up, or insinuate possible meanings" (Mullen in Perloff 170). It is the same here: Semantic contextualization has to be done – to some degree – by the socially and culturally situated reader or performer of the text. In a performance or reading of "JingleJangle," chains of culturally heterogeneous denotations and connotations are resounding. A reader of German, for example, might contextualize Mullen's rhyme "Winken & Blinken" in a different way than a non-German reader would. In English, "wink & blink" are semantically very close, but "winken & blinken" in German are not (*winken* means "to wave"; *blinken* "to gleam, to sparkle, to flash, to indicate"). English "wink & blink" and German "winken & blinken" are false friends, semantically. With regard to American Literature, reading "Winken & Blinken" as (German) verbs is an act of miscontextualization and misdenotation, of course. Hearing "Winken & Blinken," American readers immediately think of the Victorian lullaby "Wynken, Blynken, and Nod" by Eugene Field (1850-1895), the 19th-century American writer who is best known for his children's verse. Once the reader gets to Eugene Field's text, he quickly learns that he has not yet reached the end of the chain of signifiers. "Wynken & Blynken" has to be located on manifold textual levels of denotation and connotation: Throughout the text, Wynken, Blynken, and Nod are called "the fishermen three" (Field in Opie 303-304), but the speaker also says that "Wynken and Blynken are two little eyes, / And Nod is a little head" (304).

The ("false") contextualization and intertextual excursion to "Wynken, Blynken, and Nod" has shown that Mullen's alphabetical list is performative and hints at a performative aspect of poetry, because it radically foregrounds and makes us do what readers of poetry always do: they engage in complex activities of denotation and connotation. Mullen, the author, is an initiator of actions and ideas; she stages opportunities for reading. "JingleJangle," her text, is a performative space: whenever we get into the process of reading it, we enact poetic *différance* and stage various effects. If we attempted to act in accordance with the convention of unity, we would fail; this Mullen-text resists readers who treat it "as if it were an aesthetic whole," a complete unit, an entity (Culler 79). It also defies the convention of semantic significance and expects too much of a reader who tries to follow the rule that poems "are supposed to be about something important, and therefore concrete details should be taken to have general significance" (80). Nevertheless, even this text, which makes it difficult to produce meaning, partly relies for its effects on the fact that the reader will try to look for semantic significance in every detail of it. Steve McCaffery once said that "a reading activates certain relational pathways, a flow of parts" (McCaffery in Perloff 170). This certainly becomes evident once we read Mullen's list. "JingleJangle" activates the "implicit knowledge" that we as readers bring to our "encounters with texts" (Culler 62). Mullen's list can be conceived as a rapid "succession of actions upon the understanding of a reader" (63). It emphasizes again and again that "meaning is complex and elusive, not something once and for all determined" (65); it is constantly making us aware of the issue that "meaning is context-bound, but [that] context is boundless" (67).

I am going to end *my* contextualization and semantic exploration of "JingleJangle" by having a close look at its last three rhymes, which signify transculturalism: "Zoo Doo zoot suit Zulu" reminds me of Haitian Voodoo from the first v-line of the text and of Hoo Doo, the African-American form of Voodoo. I also think of the Spanglish play *Zoot Suit* by Luis Valdez and therefore of Mexican-American culture, the Pachucos, and the Pachuco Riots during World War II. "Zulu," of course, denotes the Bantu people of southeast Africa and the Nguni language of this people, but it may also evoke "Zulu," the famous African-American Mardi Gras crew, which originated around 1910 in New Orleans and which was led by Louis Armstrong as King of the Parade in 1949; "Zulu" is also an evocation of the origins of global and transcultural African-American Hip Hop culture, the Zulu Nation of Afrika Bambaataa, who in the 1970s and 80s incorporated all kinds of popular music in his records and DJ-work, not only so-called black music, but also American "white" rock and German avant-garde dance music (Kraftwerk).

As far as diction is concerned, the individual words in "JingleJangle" are taken from many different cultural contexts, with the African-American vernacular and literary tradition being only one of them. Among other words from African-American culture, the list contains the following rhyme pairs: "Slick

Rick" (Mullen, *Sleeping* 41), "Parappa the Rapper" (40), "Milli Vanilli" (39), "skunk funk" (41), "mumbo jumbo" (39), and "Writing Is Fighting" (43).

The direct reference to the Ishmael Reed-titles *Mumbo Jumbo* and *Writing Is Fighting* also stresses the intertextual and transcultural aspect of Mullen's poem, which reminds me of Reed's emphatic support of "writing culture." Reed attaches a great deal of importance and value to "writing" in the broadest sense of the term. In interviews he said: "I'm into a writing culture. I see it as a cult. I'm influenced by as many cultures as possible, and I think that's the way we work here in this society .... As an American writer, I feel very lucky. I can have English, Japanese, Yoruba; I can have Zairean rhumba. I can have any number of cultures and languages" (Dick/Singh 119/335). For Reed, writing is a democratic transcultural technique that connects a variety of different languages, discourses, worldviews, and cultures, which are free to compete, engage in dispute, coexist peacefully, or hybridize. Seen this way, writing is a global network, a transcultural phenomenon that is not limited by time and space. Global as it is, it is not rooted in only one particular place, but it fosters local expressions. Of course, Reed's and Mullen's writing culture is based on our particular phonographic script, the alphabetic system of writing, a customary order that developed in a highly complex transcultural and aleatory process; today the alphabetic system of writing is accepted, used, and shared by people from many different cultures. It is obvious now why Harryette Mullen can be called "radical" in the basic denotative meaning and strict etymologic sense of the word: because, in "JingleJangle," she goes back to the roots and plays with the source of literature, with the transcultural alphabetic system of writing.

With her partly preconstructed formal construction, with her foregrounding of the alphabet and of rhyme, Mullen foregrounds the socially and culturally relevant issue of identity and difference. The words of the alphabet are paradigmatically grouped together; as individual elements of a paradigm they always have something in common, but they are also different from each other. On the vertical axis of selection, they always represent difference and identity. Rhyme works in a similar way. In *The New Princeton Encyclopedia of Poetry and Poetics* T.V.F. Brogan writes that

> rhyme calls into prominence simultaneously a complex set of responses based on *identity* and *difference*. On the phonic level, the likeness of the rhyming syllables (at their ends) points up their difference (at their beginnings). The phonic semblance (and difference) then points up semantic semblance or difference: the equivalence of the rhyme syllables or words on the phonic level implies a relation of likeness or difference on the semantic level .... Rhyme is not, therefore, a merely sonal phenomenon: it deploys sound similarity as the means to semantic and structural ends. (1053)

In "JingleJangle," the relationship between difference and identity is even more complex than in the orders of rhyme and alphabet alone, because Mullen incorporates one vertical order of identity and difference – rhyme – into another – the alphabet. In addition to that, within each order, Mullen gives a minimalist and extremely repetitive demonstration of Roman Jakobson's "poetic function," which "*projects the principle of equivalence from the axis of selection into the axis of combination*" (356). So almost every rhyme pair on the axis of combination is a foregrounding of the poetic and a double signal of Jakobson's "poetic function." In Mullen's poem – not in its title though – it also happens often that the two vertical orders ruled by identity and difference are in conflict with one another. Most of the time there is an interplay of the conflicting elements "rhyme" and "alphabet," but it is impossible to resolve this tension. This shows that, with "JingleJangle," Mullen outlines her own form of a culturally conscious deconstructive poetics that clearly does not adhere to the values of the New Criticism any more.

In conclusion, I will focus on the order of the alphabet and the position of the individual parts of each rhyme pair in it. What is immediately noticeable is that the second part of the rhyme pair almost always belongs and refers to another place in the alphabet; so every second word almost always is in a position of displacement, separated from its original, usual, "natural" place. The rhyme pairs are in a constant state of partial mutual otherness. Focusing on the alphabet, one can see that Mullen literally is a trans-writer: she arranges sequences of letters, produces and reproduces rhyme pairs that partly transgress the boundaries of the place they were put in; she selects and combines cultural elements that direct our attention beyond their immediate location to another place. For me, "Jingle Jangle" is a paradigm of transpoetry.

What kind of cultural work is this literary text doing? It is doing *trans*-cultural work. The text is a transcultural *mise en scène* of post-Language American avant-garde writing as spatial practice.

Works Cited

Abrams, M. H. *A Glossary of Literary Terms*. 7th ed. Boston, MA: Heinle & Heinle, 1999.

Bedient, Calvin. "The Solo Mysterioso Blues: An Interview with Harryette Mullen." *Callaloo* 19.3 (1996): 651-669.

Bernstein, Charles. "Community and the Individual Talent." *diacritics* 26.3-4 (Fall-Winter 1996): 176-195.

—. *A Poetics*. Cambridge, MA: Harvard University Press, 1992.

Culler, Jonathan. *Literary Theory: A Very Short Introduction*. 1997. New York: Oxford University Press, 2000.

Dick, Bruce, and Amritjit Singh, eds. *Conversations with Ishmael Reed*. Jackson, MS: University Press of Mississippi, 1995.

Dickinson, Emily. *The Poems of Emily Dickinson*. Ed. R.W. Franklin. Variorum Edition. 3 vols. Cambridge, MA: The Belknap Press of Harvard University Press, 1998.

Frost, Elisabeth A. " 'Belatedly Beladied Blues': Hybrid Traditions in the Poetry of Harryette Mullen." *The Feminist Avant-Garde in American Poetry*. Iowa City, IA: University of Iowa Press, 2003. 136-164.

—. "An Interview with Harryette Mullen." *Contemporary Literature* 41.3 (2000): 397-421.

Frye, Northrop. *Anatomy of Criticism: Four Essays*. Princeton, NJ: Princeton University Press, 1957.

Gates, Henry Louis, and Nellie Y. McKay, eds. *The Norton Anthology of African American Literature*. 2nd ed. New York: Norton, 2004.

Hejinian, Lyn. *The Language of Inquiry*. Berkeley, CA: University of California Press, 2000.

Hogue, Cynthia. "Beyond the Frame of Whiteness: Harryette Mullen's Revisionary Border Work." *We Who Love to Be Astonished*. Ed. Laura Hinton and Cynthia Hogue. Tuscaloosa, AL: The University of Alabama Press, 2002. 81-89.

Hoover, Paul. "Stark Strangled Banjos: Linguistic Doubleness in the Work of David Hammons, Harryette Mullen, and Al Hibbler." *Denver Quarterly* 36.3-4 (2002): 68-82.

Howe, Susan. *My Emily Dickinson*. Berkeley, CA: North Atlantic Books, 1985.

Huehls, Mitchum. "Spun Puns (and Anagrams): Exchange Economies, Subjectivity, and History in Harryette Mullen's *Muse & Drudge*." *Contemporary Literature* 44.1 (2003): 19-46.

Jakobson, Roman. "Closing Statement: Linguistics and Poetics." *Poetry in Theory: An Anthology 1900-2000*. Ed. Jon Cook. Malden, MA: Blackwell, 2004. 350-358.

Jones, LeRoi. *Home: Social Essays*. 1966. Hopewell, NJ: The Ecco Press, 1998.

Mehne, Phillip. " 'Making it strange': Bewusstsein, Erfahrung und Sprache bei Gertrude Stein und Lyn Hejinian." *Amerikastudien/American Studies* 48.4 (2003): 537-561.

Mill, John Stuart. *Dissertations and Discussions*. Honolulu, HI: University Press of the Pacific, 2002.

Mullen, Harryette. *Blues Baby: Early Poems*. Cranbury, NJ: Bucknell University Press, 2002.

—. *Muse & Drudge*. Philadelphia, PA: Singing Horse, 1995.

—. "Poetry and Identity." *Telling It Slant: Avant-Garde Poetics of the 1990s*. Ed. Mark Wallace and Steven Marks. Tuscaloosa, AL: The University of Alabama Press, 2002. 27-31.

—. *Sleeping with the Dictionary*. Berkeley, CA: University of California Press, 2002.

—. *S*PeRM**K*T*. Philadelphia, PA: Singing Horse, 1992.

—. *Trimmings*. New York: Tender Buttons, 1991.

Nielsen, Aldon Lynn. *Black Chant: Languages of African-American Postmodernism*. New York: Cambridge University Press, 1997.

Opie, Iona, and Peter Opie, eds. *The Oxford Book of Children's Verse*. 1973. Oxford: Oxford University Press, 2002.

Pawlak, Mark, Robert Hershon, Dick Lourie, and Ron Schreiber, eds. *Present/Tense: Poets in the World*. Brooklyn, NY: Hanging Loose Press, 2004.

Perloff, Marjorie. "After Language Poetry: Innovation and Its Theoretical Discontents."

Differentials: Poetry, Poetics, Pedagogy. Tuscaloosa, AL: The University of Alabama Press, 2004. 155-174.

Preminger, Alex, and T.V.F. Brogan, eds. *The New Princeton Encyclopedia of Poetry and Poetics*. Princeton, NJ: Princeton University Press, 1993.

Spahr, Juliana. " 'What Stray Companion': Harryette Mullen's Communities of Reading." *Everybody's Autonomy: Connective Reading and Collective Identity*. Tuscaloosa, AL: The University of Alabama Press, 2001. 89-118.

Vendler, Helen. *Invisible Listeners: Lyric Intimacy in Herbert, Whitman, and Ashbery*. Princeton, NJ: Princeton University Press, 2005.

Watten, Barrett. *The Constructivist Moment: From Material Text to Cultural Poetics*. Middletown, CT: Wesleyan University Press, 2003.

—. "What Is Literature? From Material Text to Cultural Poetics." *Assembling Alternatives: Reading Postmodern Poetries Transnationally*. Ed. Romana Huk. Middletown, CT: Wesleyan University Press, 2003. 347-363.

Williams, Emily Allen. "Harryette Mullen, 'The Queen of Hip Hyperbole': An Interview." *African American Review* 34.4 (2000): 701-707.

Verbovisual Explorations of Textuality: Peter Reading's Collection *[untitled]* (2001)

Uwe Klawitter

Peter Reading is regarded as one of Britain's most innovative and challenging poets.[1] The 24 collections of poetry which he has produced over the last 30 years show him to be an outspoken critic of the downside of contemporary Western civilization. They also bear witness to his impressive mastery of a wide variety of poetic forms and his intricate use of intertextual techniques.

In his poetry Reading is much concerned with the theme of death.[2] In the collection *[untitled]*, published in 2001,[3] the interest in transience and oblivion leads to a consideration of the materiality of writing. For the poet Reading, script raises the question of how we can make a mark, in what ways we can last, *inscribe* ourselves. Judging from a parenthetical comment in the first poem of the collection, Reading seems to hold a rather disillusioned view of the efficiency and impact of human communication: "(The only permanence is, I suppose, / in having been – and whether known or not / to others hardly enters into it.)" (*Collected Poems 3* 149). *[untitled]* is certainly tinged by this bleak outlook. However, Reading is clearly interested in adopting a much wider perspective. This is evident in his turning to historical writing systems such as runes and hieroglyphs, but also in his references to palimpsests, which are a known model for thinking about the logic of texts and their cultural transmission.

Intriguingly, the "transience of texts" (Martin 266) is not only thematized in *[untitled]* but enacted by increasingly daring visual means. While two instances of typographical patterning which can be found early on in the collection (*Collected Poems 3* 155 and 169) are still very much iconic reinforcements of the

---

1 Robert Potts calls him "one of England's most original poets since 1970" and "one of the most experimental voices in the mainstream of English poetry since World War II" (261). For a detailed discussion and critical assessment of Peter Reading's poetic work see Isabel Martin's excellent study *Reading Peter Reading*.

2 Note the titles of his collections: *Last Poems* (1994), *Eschatological* (1996), *Work in Regress* (1997) and *Ob.* (1999).

3 *[untitled]* was reviewed by Tim Dooley in the *Times Literary Supplement* 22.

theme of decay and oblivion, there are also four interspersed text and text-image collages that go beyond this thematic tenor and invite poststructuralist readings. As the most transgressive aspect in Reading's poetry these collages deserve to be investigated.

The first text collage (in the sense of a more freely arranged and visually pronounced assemblage of text fragments) can be found in the section "Small Change" (*Collected Poems 3* 172; see fig. 1). It is preceded by a series of four short poetic pieces:

> ***Alcaic***
>
> Great Dionysus, master anaesthetist,
> no more delay, fetch wine from the amphora,
>   blend it with water in the krater,
>   serve me a generous brimming skyphos.
>
> **[*untitled*]**
>
> Your *Weird* is beyond you;
> what you *can* control
> do prudently and consider the end.
>
> ***From the Chinese***
>
>   His liver /
>   his golden wine –
> civil war rages!
>
> ***Hibernian***
>
> Two conundrums:
> a herring devoid of bones;
> a life without the troubles. (171)

That these two components, which are printed on separate pages, belong together is suggested by the common title, or more precisely the consistent way sections are marked off by titles throughout the collection. [4] The short poems show Reading's predilection for miniature forms. The first three may be described as instances of gnomic verse that convey 'philosophical' comments on the fact of man's mortality. The fourth does not quite fit into the generic pattern but seems to be founded on a

---

[4] The title 'collage' is not used in the printed version of *[untitled]* in the *Collected Poems*, but it appears in the table of contents.

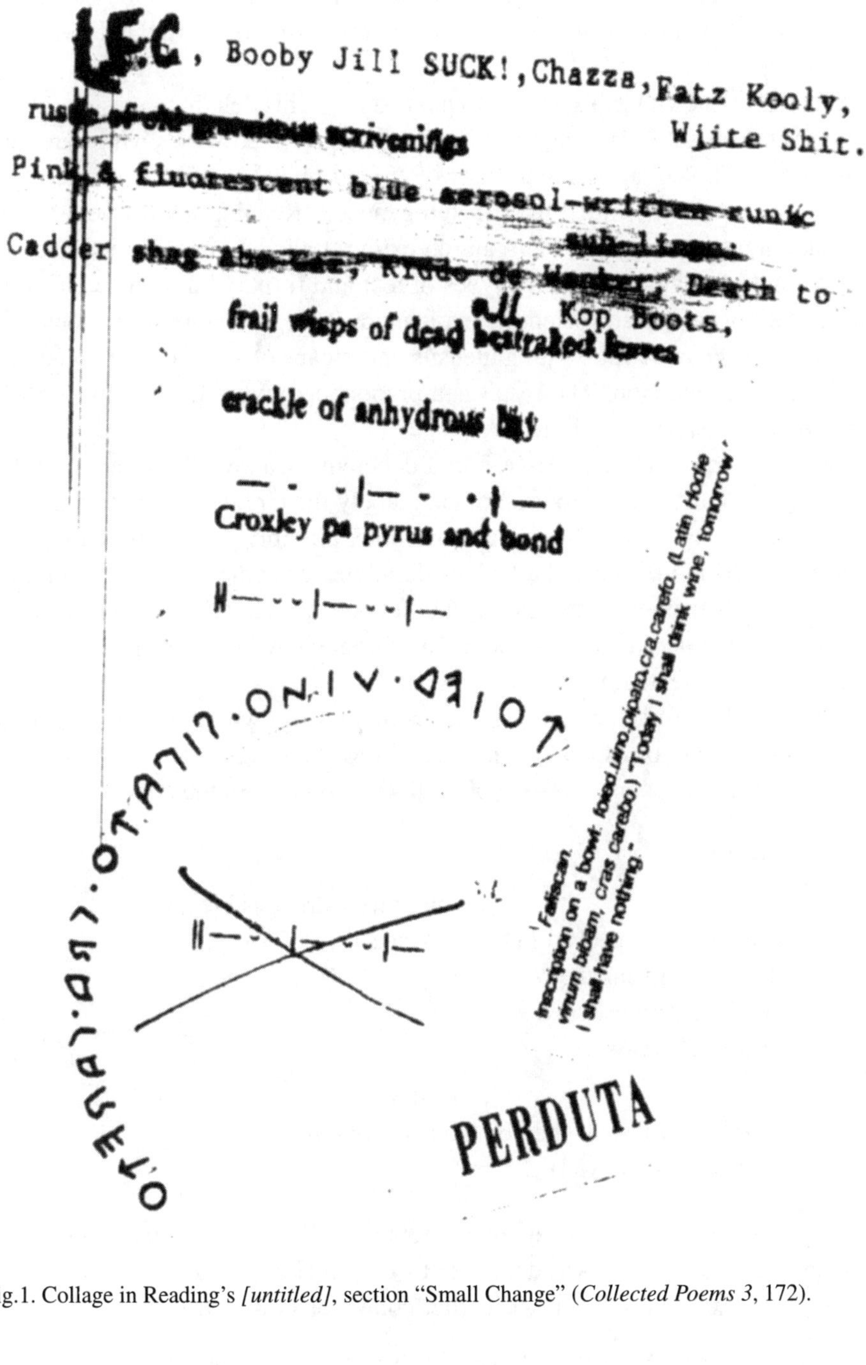

Fig.1. Collage in Reading's *[untitled]*, section "Small Change" (*Collected Poems 3*, 172).

similarly resigned attitude to the madness of human existence. As the metaphorical title "Small Change" suggests, such wisdom is easily dispensed but ultimately of low value.

Reading is known for his use of 'found texts' and his delight in erasing the distinction between authentic finds and fakes. [5] The proffered wise sayings are most likely bogus. The collage also consists of 'found texts,' but the assembled texts and text fragments are much more heterogeneous. Reading quotes here in four different languages: English, Faliscan (an extinct Italic language), Latin and Italian. He combines widely different types of text and forms of discourse: primitive graffiti, lines of poetry and scientific explanations. He also employs various symbolic signs, types of script, writing utensils and means of surface manipulation as well as text reproduction. The result is a pronounced hybridity and an emphasis on the material aspect of writing.

The text items do not coalesce into a coherent meaning. There are only two texts that are clearly related to each other, namely the circular inscription from an ancient drinking bowl and the explanatory note, possibly from a museum guide. While the inscription echoes the hedonistic advice of some of the preceding poems, most of the other text items in the collage appear arbitrary and obscure. They demand the additional consideration of contexts which have been imported by means of intra-textuality.

The quoted graffiti, for example, makes more sense within the suggested thematic tenor of how to respond to the fact of one's mortality if we consider it in connection with the poem "Petroglyphs" given earlier on in the collection.

> Petroglyphs,
>
> long incomprehensible,
> transient legacies pecked in the rockface.
> Our Guide confirms their anonymity –
> radiocarbon-dating lichen scars
> suggest 5,000 years …
>
> Last Wednesday,
> a big pink dick was daubed on the same outcrop.
> (*Collected Poems 3* 154)

It may then appear as yet another, albeit feeble or silly attempt to make a mark, to document one's existence. An attempt that would include the author, who after all recycles here text material from his earlier collections of poetry.

---

5 In an interview with Alan Jenkins he declared "I want to incorporate 'found' material, and, deriving from that – a more difficult job – to invent found material. I've been rather happy to find people mistaking found things for bogus and vice-versa" (Jenkins 12).

The word PERDUTA recalls Reading's collection *Perduta Gente*, published in 1989, which deals with the plight of homeless people and the danger of nuclear accidents (*Collected Poems 2* 159-214).[6] Linked to *Perduta Gente*, the lower half of the collage appears like a statement of resignation. In a world endangered by global catastrophes (the shape of the arranged text blocks reminds me faintly of the outline of a nuclear power plant) the writing of poetry appears futile (as indicated by the crossed-out prosodic notation), so that one may well take to drinking (as advised in the given and annotated inscription from an ancient drinking bowl), although that is clearly not a good solution either.

The collage offers various reading possibilities and provides insight into Reading's overall method of composition. The reworking of previously used materials gives cohesion to Reading's poetic œuvre. It leads, as Isabel Martin rightly points out, to "a multi-dimensional network of self-referentiality unusual in poetry books" (23).

The visual dimension of the collage, especially the traces of reproduction and revision deserve further attention. The basis of the collage is a photocopy of the last page of Reading's collection *Final Demands*, published in 1988, which contains the verse lines and prosodic notations (*Collected Poems 2* 158).[7] The line about graffiti and the actual graffiti, which can be found in the same collection (124), were then written and typewritten (with small changes!) into the copy. The Faliscan inscription and its explanation as well as the word PERDUTA are evidently clippings that were pasted into the still available space on the photocopy. This assemblage was then once more copied.

Reading is obviously exploring textuality. By drawing attention to questions of coherence and context as well as re-use and reproduction, he stresses the manufacturedness and derivativeness of texts. The collage could be regarded as an artificial palimpsest as the new 'text' shows traces of previous usage. In contrast to the visualizations at the beginning of the collection, which foreground the inevitability of cultural decay and textual corruption, Reading seems to offer here a creative response: If nothing will last, if the creation and transmission of an authoritative text is impossible, one may well engage in assembling 'found texts' and involve oneself in the endless process of semiosis.

The next assemblage of pre-fabricated and manipulated texts appears under the section title "[untitled]" and is preceded by the couplet "In unmarked graves and splendid catafalques / alike, impartial atoms metamorphose" (*Collected Poems 3* 176; see fig 2).

---

6 'Perduta Gente' is a phrase from Dante's *Inferno*, Canto III and means 'lost people,' also here in the wider sense of 'lost humankind' (see Martin 193). *Perduta Gente* stands out in Reading's œuvre for its conspicuous presentation of 'found texts.'

7 As regards the verse, compare also his collection *Last Poems* (*Collected Poems 2*, 274).

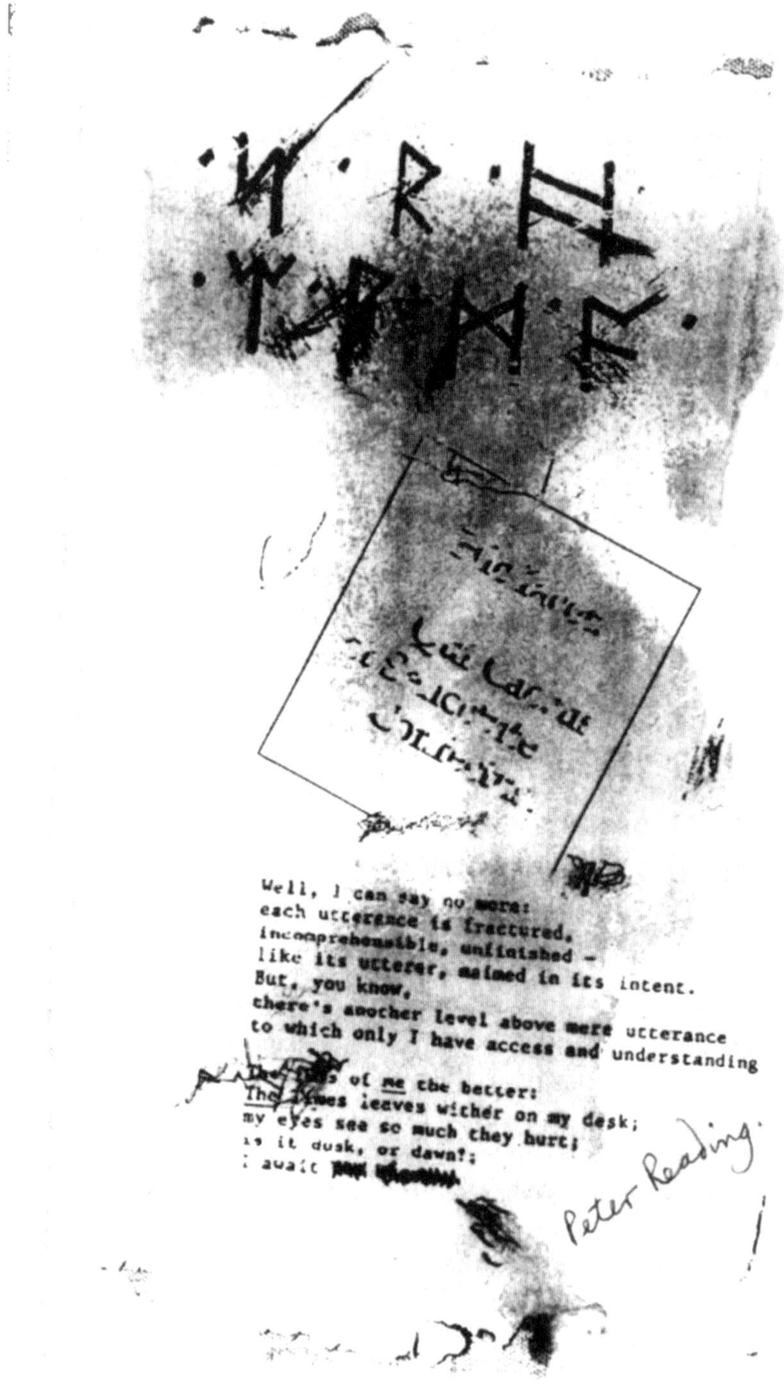

Fig. 2. Collage in Reading's *[untitled]*, section "[untitled]" (*Collected Poems 3* 177).

Reading combines here three blocks of text: an Anglo-Saxon runic inscription, already presented as epigraph at the beginning of the collection, an almost illegible Latin epitaph, whose exact wording is given three pages later, and a draft version of a confessional poem, whose printed version has already been presented as coda to a longer poem. Underneath we find the author's signature.

It is not clear how the inscriptions have been reproduced. The uneven grey wash and various scrawls, scribbles and smudges mimic the besmirching of time. At the upper and lower edge there is a hardly visible imprint of a fabric which shows traces of having been ripped, burned through or eaten away by an aggressive substance. However, these faked manifestations of *tempus edax rerum* are more than iconic reinforcements of the theme of decay. The textured surface draws attention to the materiality of script and in particular its carrier-medium. Important is here the simultaneous evocation and denial of depth. The surface manipulations and artificial framings do not go together. One could say mimetic readings, or rather viewings are deliberately frustrated.

The Old English runes are meant to symbolize the decay of writing. [8] As an early comment points out: "(Our runes, like theirs, will be uncipherable; / impartial Time will wipe the slate clean, wordless.)" (*Collected Poems 3* 148).

The "Hic Iacet" of the reproduced Latin inscription is just about decipherable, which provides the important generic clue. However, it is doubtful whether any reader would be able to decipher the full text "Qui Caecus et Senectute Confectus," which is later revealed to be from a "Dog's Tomb" and translated as "Who blindness and senility prepared / for darkness and insensibility" (*Collected Poems 3* 180). [9] In "Apophthegmatic," the final section of the collection, the same epitaph is used in a self-conscious patterning which creates a tension between legibility and illegibility (189-192). [10] Reading interrupts here once more the principle of linearity which underlies the constitution of conventional verbal texts. He demands a recipient who is willing to weave back and forth.

The signed draft version of a confessional poem at the bottom of the text assemblage is highly ironic. The poet-persona is certainly ridiculed in his bardic pretensions of having access to a higher sphere. Reading plays here with the paradox of the blind seer. His persona is blind where he deems himself most seeing

8 I have not been able to ascertain whether this is an authentic or bogus inscription. According to the Anglo-Saxon futhorc the letters represent the sounds [s] as in sigel – sun, [r] as in rad – journey/riding, [h] as in haegl – hail, [ea] as in ear – ?earth, [w] as in wyn – joy, [d] as in daeg – day; see the list of runes in Chrystal 9.

9 In the section "Apophthegmatic" it is also translated as "By blind Old Age / Worn Out" and "*Who Blindness & Senility / Exhausted.*"

10 Assemblages of eroded, hardly legible or even illegible text fragments can be also found at the end of Reading's collection *Last Poems* (1994), which is also concerned with cultural relics and poetic legacy.

(and is perhaps still seeing after all where he appears to be blind). What this play amounts to in metapoetical terms is, I think, a qualified acknowledgment of post-structuralist positions. The insight that 'each utterance ... like its utterer, [is] maimed in its intent' sounds like a Derridean aporia. It hints at the impossibility of *self*-expression and originality. Also as the clichéd phrasing of the verses suggests: How can one be sincere when everything has been said before? Reading's answer to these problems can be found in the way the poem has been previously used in the collection. In the section "Alert!" it concludes a long poem that seems to express many authorial views but finally turns out to be a re-rendering of Vahé Oshagan's literal English rendering of his Armenian poem "Ahazank" (Alarm). [11] While thus rejecting an expressivist concept of poetry, Reading retains a belief in self-inscription by appropriation. That this is a precarious state is signalled in the correspondence between creation and decay, text making and text erosion in the collage. As poststructuralist intertextualists would argue, texts always contain traces of other texts but are also bound to become traces themselves, since they are vitiated by new contextual relations. [12]

Reading's next combination of text and collage "Graffiti" is intratextually linked to the already mentioned section "Petroglyphs":

> **Graffiti**
>
> Les Grottes de Niaux are closed this Saturday.
> A *carte postale illustrée*, though, depicts
> wild horses, bison speared ...
>
> Outside the cave,
> kids carve a Zeppelin dick on the same rock –
> Still, after 20,000 years, inclined
> to score some mark on anonymity. (178)

The collage consists of two photos of graffiti (see fig. 3). The photos (or photocopies of these photographs) were torn and cut, stuck on a white sheet and then 'linked' by a daubing of white paint. As the writing across the recess in the brick wall betrays, at least some of the scribblings on the photos were added later.

It seems that Reading himself cannot help 'scoring some mark on anonymity.' Since communication seems hopelessly flawed or subject to corruption, this cannot be much more than a gesture. If we consider the collage in this way, it appears

[11] Vahé Oshagan died in June 2000 in Philadelphia. He was regarded as the Arminian Diaspora's most well-known critic, political activist, poet, novelist and professor of literature (see *The Arminian Weekly Online* August/September 2001, as accessed 24 August 2005, <http://www.hairenik.com/armenianweekly/august september/culture 002.html>).

[12] Compare Derrida's concept of the traces of words explained in *Margins of Philosophy* (qtd. in Bertens 125).

Fig. 3. Collage in Reading's *[untitled]*, section "Graffiti" (*Collected Poems 3* 179).

however to be a potent one. To traditionalist readers Reading's visual representations of script in the form of graffiti on walls must be a provocation. Readers familiar with postmodernist theory will feel intrigued or teased by these representations.

At first sight the photographs seem to offer images of experiential reality. They depict mural graffiti, not the sometimes quite artistic, often more bold-faced tagging but the more primitive and aggressive variety. "Fathead" reads the sprayed word on the plastered wall. And on the brick wall someone has written the abbreviation "G.B.H." The images are, however, not simply representational but have been manipulated in a way that makes them presentational and decidedly textual. They are images of texts, an amalgamation of the graphic and iconic. As such they may be seen as symbols for the radical textualisation espoused by poststructuralist critics.

The presentation of deframed and re-textured surfaces confuses the viewer. The tearing and cutting of the photographs' edges foregrounds their materiality. They appear no longer as windows on reality but as questionable constructs. The illusion of a representational three-dimensionality (depth) is refuted in favour of a material three-dimensionality (textured surface).

The partial daubing of the two photographic representations as well as the added scribblings highlight the layeredness of the collage. The superscriptions on the second image make it impossible to differentiate between the original documentary layer and the added layer. In line with poststructuralist tenets this could be read as a questioning of the concept of originality and authenticity. It is not possible to say who and how many people contributed to the graffiti on the photographed walls (Reading may have been one of them or even the only one), nor is it possible to say what was added after the photographic fixation. This effectively dissolves the boundary between original and fake, documentation and manipulation. Reading stresses the artistic process but makes it impossible to determine the actual sequence of operations.

Reading seems to have chosen more linear scrawls in order to ensure the impression of a dense texturedness. His additions to what may have been already a multilayered artifact enhance the palimpsestic aspect. The resulting collage could be seen as an enactment of the cultural process of text-making and transmission.

Here as elsewhere Reading is interested in enhancing heterogeneity. The graffitied walls show all kinds of signs: a drawing of a spider, an arrow, a swastika, more or less decipherable words and initials but also many cryptic graphemes and indistinct parts of script. Especially the overwriting on the second photo introduces an element of competition and obscuration. Reading's manipulation of materials is in itself an act of aggressive appropriation.

The contemporary graffiti thematized in the introductory poem and represented in the collage compares quite unfavourably with the cave paintings in Les Grottes de Niaux. Reading's historical irony suggests that human beings are in some respects still very much like troglodytes.

The collages which have been discussed so far show a progression from text images to images of texts. In their hybridity they question the concepts of 'textness' and 'imageness.' The fourth and last conspicuous collage in *[untitled]* (see figs. 4-5), which can be found in the section "Homme de Lettres," combines the two, namely manipulated photocopies from a linguistic text book (image of text) along with an assemblage of treated texts from the first collage and two of the poetic texts that preceded it (text image). The introductory lines provide an important clue to the rationale behind Reading's use of collage:

Homme de Lettres

back 22,000 years,
the Lascaux sophisticates;
next, Neolithic *calculi*
(stones incised for counting);
this tablet, about 2000
BC, charts the loan of donkeys;
pictographic trees,
sacks of grain, the god-man;
1450 BC,
the Elephantine Calendar;
525 BC,
cuneiform on silver;
'Chinese script conformed
with a series of subtle rules
which you could call *Poetic Art*';
the Greeks, the Romans, Gutenberg . . .

removed from semantic context,
the word = the visual (182)

The given catalogue of representational techniques that have had an enormous impact on human civilization is typically postmodern in its idiosyncratic particularity and is perhaps meant to undermine neat historiographical categorizations. It bears witness to Reading's semiotic awareness but shows also that this is ultimately motivated by metapoetical concerns. The apparent reference to Ernest Fenellosa's essay *The Chinese Written Character as a Medium for Poetry* and therefore to Ezra

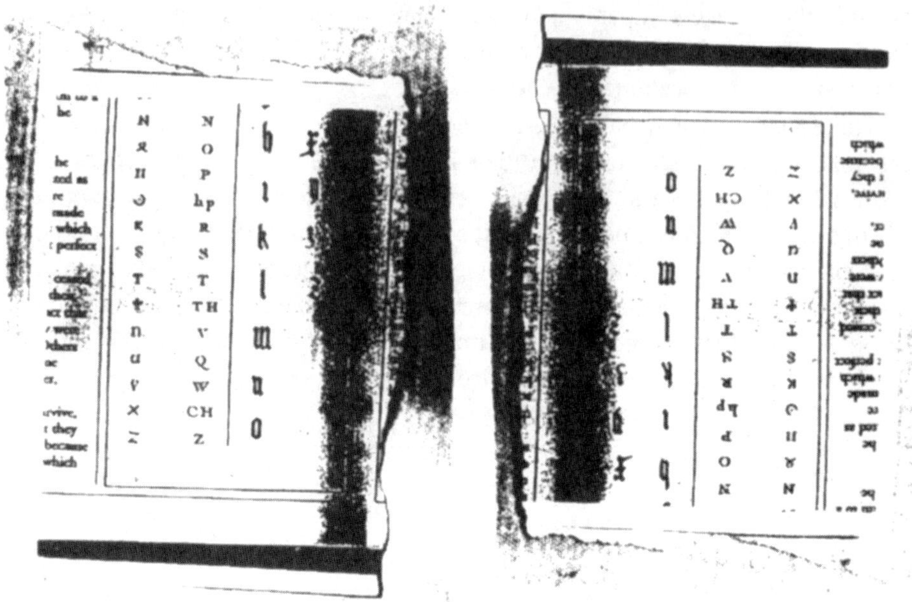

Fig. 4. Left page of section "Homme de Lettres" in Reading's *[untitled]* (*Collected Poems 3* 182-183).

Pound's concept of the 'ideogrammatic method,' which was inspired by it,[13] fits in with the subsequent metapoetical statement "removed from semantic context, / the word = the visual." Like Pound, Reading seems to be interested in breaking out of the confines imposed by discursive speech. His statement draws attention to the importance of context and hints at medial differences that govern the use of verbal texts and images. Generally speaking, images are often heavily reliant on verbal explication, whereas verbal statements usually have contexts that assist in the constitution of their meanings.[14] If they are decontextualised they become like images, open to new meanings. What happens in the collages, however, is an immediate recontextualisation, which is open to wider interpretation but still controlled by Reading.

The metapoetical comment is followed by a conspicuously visual component, namely the reproduction of a page from a linguistic textbook (see fig. 4). As in the collage that features graffitied walls, the edges of the reproductions are par-

[13] Fenellosa's essay was published by Pound in 1919. It had a decisive influence on the development of his poetics (see Motsch 13). The affinities to Pound, see, for instance, Reading's predilection for juxtapositions and his keen interest in Chinese poetry, are worth investigating.

[14] Cf. Knut Hickethier's delineation of images/imageness and (verbal) texts/textuality (85 and 103-104).

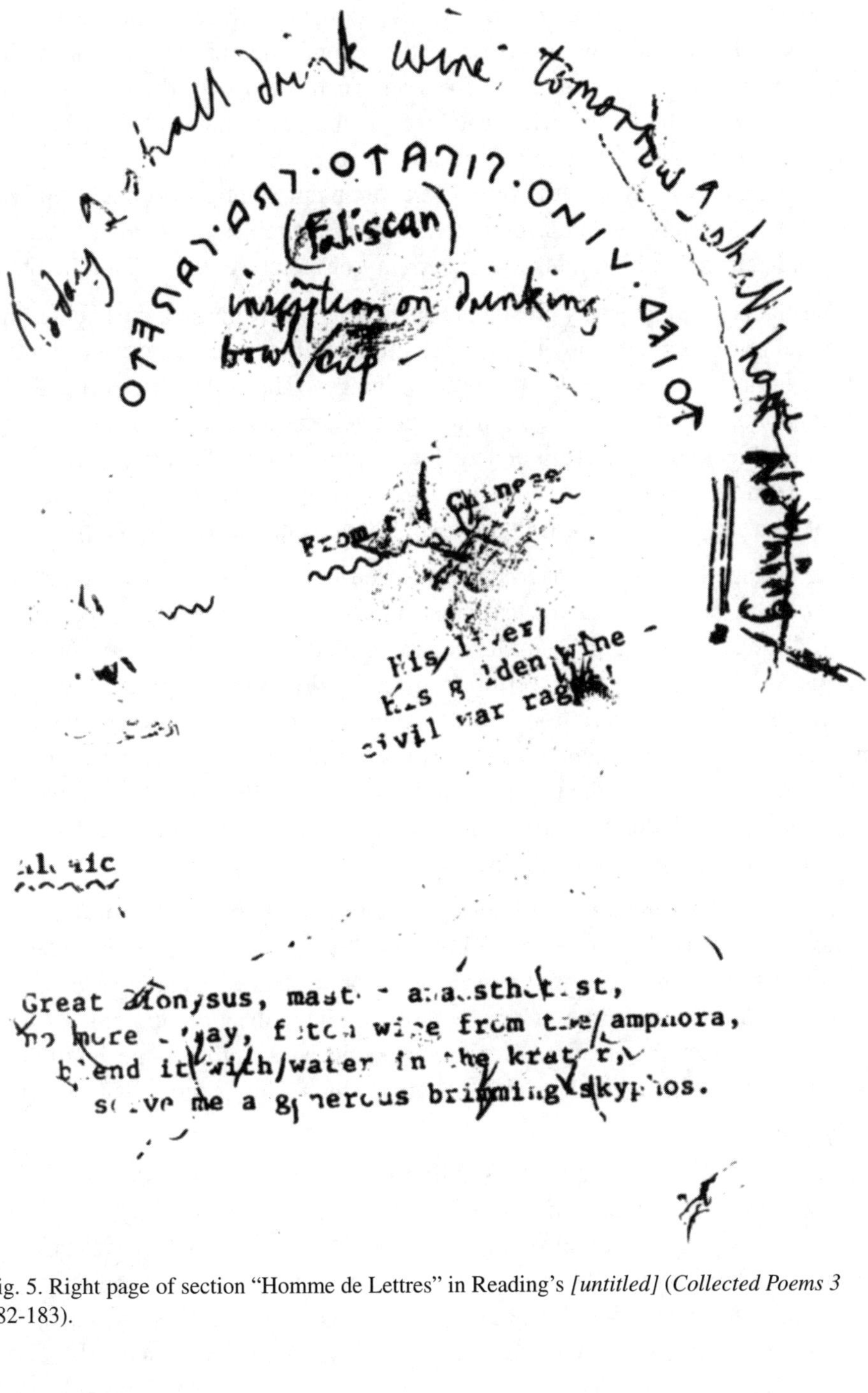

Fig. 5. Right page of section "Homme de Lettres" in Reading's *[untitled]* (*Collected Poems 3* 182-183).

tially torn, which indicates that the page has been ripped out of a book and then photocopied. However, there are now two reproductions of the same page which are placed side by side. The inversion of the second page produces a mirror image of the first. The transliteration tables shown link up with the thematization of writing systems in the historical catalogue at the beginning of the section. The listed symbols remain enigmatic since too much of the explanatory (?) English text has been torn away and the two first columns of symbols do not align with the next two columns. The chiastic positioning of the tables is a further means of defamiliarization that highlights the materiality of the presented scriptural signs.

The blackened and grainy grey areas on the pages as well as on the background are typical traces of photocopying. The resulting multilayeredness draws attention to the materiality of technically reproduced images. The collage is a printed version of a photomechanically reproduced printed version, a copy of a copy of a copy ... which has been manipulated. The ripping and blackening indicates that artistic creation involves an aggressive, irreverent appropriation and obscuration of what went before; moreover, that it is highly derivative and reproductive.

The collage on the next page has also been produced by means of a photocopier (see fig.5). It consists of texts that have been already used in the section "Small Change," namely the gnomic verses entitled '*Alcaic*' and '*From the Chinese*' as well as the Faliscan inscription from the drinking cup given in the subsequent collage. The inscription has now another explanatory text as well as a translation, both given in handwriting. All texts are linked by the *carpe-diem* motif and return therefore to the theme of mortality. Due to (faked?) static impurities and partially whitened letters, the alcaic verses are difficult to read. As in previous visual representations, this enacts the destructive process of time.

Once again Reading creates diversity by combining various types of inter- and intratextuality. Indeed, he erodes the boundary between the two by the repeated use and modification of adapted genres, texts or structures. This form of (self)-quotation and (self)-parody brackets texts within the collection and creates links to previous collections. It turns Reading's poetic work into a huge intertext, a network of inter-/intratextual links, a network which is not centred but open to a textual universe.

As the title already suggests, Reading considers his collection as work in progress or as an assemblage that cannot or should not be forced under a particular heading. The square-braketing of "untitled," which is familiar as an indication of unnamed computer files, may be taken as a paratextual pointer to a process- and media-orientated textmaking. Although the collages invite readers to engage in non-linear readings (which are important for the overall appreciation of Reading's poetic work) and may be therefore seen to move towards the new textual ideal of the hypertext, there is no overt extension into the realm of computer-produced texts in *[untitled]*. Reading's concept of writing remains firmly non-electronic.

As has been shown, Reading is concerned in *[untitled]* with writing as trace, as inscription and re-inscription, as bricolage of 'found texts,' a preoccupation Michael Davidson has referred to in postmodern American poetry as "palimtextual writing" (75-95). [15] Reading does indeed produce 'palimtexts,' however, the unique experimental quality lies here in the enhancement of the visual dimension. He reinvents the collage to explore and express central concerns of his poetics. [16] By employing a number of technical media (writing utensils, typewriter, photocopier, camera), Reading produces traces and surface alterations that draw attention to manipulative and reproductive processes but also material deterioration. In other words, he stresses both writing-as-process and writing-as-decay.

Reading's verbovisual experiments examine textuality in a way that seems to put poststructuralist ideas into practice. His reworking and dispersing of texts imitates cultural processes and questions traditional concepts of originality, authenticity and authorship. He emphasizes the materiality of the sign and the concrete mediality of cultural transmission. His cultivation of diversity and heterogeneity works towards a decentring of traditional cultural hierarchies and an erosion of critical boundaries. [17]

It has to be stressed that Reading's verbovisualizations are surrounded, indeed framed by conventional poetic texts. He creates a strong contrast between the prosodic artifice of some of these poetic texts and the anti-aesthetic appearance of the text and text-image collages. Furthermore, it is important to note that Reading presents here texts that assume qualities of images and images that are dominated by text but not 'pure' images. This means that Reading moves the verbal towards the openness of images but contains the visual, which may be seen as a response to the increasing visualisation of our culture.

Reading's text-image hybridisations offer an escape from the sequentiality of conventional verbal texts and activate reader participation in the constitution of

---

15 According to Davidson's definition, 'palimtexts' are texts that foreground their intertextuality and interdiscursiveness as well as their materiality.

16 It should be mentioned here that Reading was trained as a visual artist. As he himself has pointed out, the collages of modernist artists have had an influence on his poetry (see Martin 11-12). With the exhibition 'Erosive' shown at the South Bank Centre in 1994 – subsequent full title: *Erosive: Thirty-Seven Texts, Hand-Produced by Peter Reading (1993/1994)* – Reading even returned to visual art (see Martin 229). The ripping ('déchirage') and burning ('brulage') as well as the linking of texts and photos by daubings of paint, which I have mentioned in my analyses of the collages in *[untitled]*, are procedures familiar from modernist art.

17 Reading's choice and adaptation of the peripheral deserves further investigation. The parodic re-activation of gnomic verse forms involves a divestment of their traditionally serious semantic potential and the inclusion of graffiti does not pay attention to the more artistic and politically subversive variety of this form of expression.

meaning. However, the various avenues of investigation open to the reader, which frequently lead to Reading's previous collections, may be too taxing or may not lead to satisfying readings. For those readers who engage in the metareadings of surfaces *[untitled]* is a rich field for exploration.

Works Cited

The Arminian Weekly Online August/September 2001 (24 August 2005) <http://www.hairenik.com/armenianweekly/august september/culture002.html>.

Bertens, Hans. *Literary Theory: The Basics.* London: Routledge, 2001.

Chrystal, David. *The Cambridge Encyclopedia of the English Language.* Cambridge: Cambridge University Press, 1995.

Davidson, Michael. "Palimtexts: Postmodern Poetry and the Material Text." *Postmodern Genres.* Ed. Marjorie Perloff. Norman: University of Oklahoma Press, 1988. 75-95.

Dooley, Tim. Rev. of "[untitled]" by Peter Reading. "Starting from Scratch." *Times Literary Supplement* 28 Sept. 2001. 22.

Hickethier, Knut. *Einführung in die Medienwissenschaft.* Stuttgart: Metzler, 2003.

Jenkins, Alan. Interview. "Making Nothing Matter: Peter Reading Talking to Alan Jenkins." *The Poetry Review* 75.1 (1985): 5-12.

Martin, Isabel. *Reading Peter Reading.* Newcastle upon Tyne: Bloodaxe Books, 2000.

Motsch, Monika. *Ezra Pound und China.* Heidelberg: Carl Winter, 1976.

Potts, Robert. "Peter Reading (1946-)." *British Writers: Supplement VIII.* Ed. Jay Parini. New York: Scribner's, 2003. 261-275.

Reading, Peter. *Final Demands.* 1988. *Collected Poems 2: Poems 1985-1996.* Newcastle: Bloodaxe Books, 1996. 117-158.

—. *Last Poems.* 1994. *Collected Poems 2: Poems 1985-1996.* Newcastle: Bloodaxe Books, 1996. 245-280.

—. *Perduta Gente.* 1989. *Collected Poems 2: Poems 1985-1996.* Newcastle: Bloodaxe Books, 1996. 159-214.

—. *[untitled].* 2001. *Collected Poems 3: Poems 1997-2003.* Highgreen: Bloodaxe Books, 2003. 147-200.

"The Other White Father": June Jordan, the "People's Poets," and Walt Whitman

Walter Grünzweig

THE BOMBING OF BAGHDAD

I

began and did not terminate for 42 days
and 42 nights relentless minute after minute
more than 110,000 times
we bombed Iraq we bombed Baghdad
we bombed Basra/we bombed military
installations we bombed the National Museum
we bombed schools we bombed air raid
shelters we bombed water we bombed
electricity we bombed hospitals we
bombed streets we bombed highways
we bombed everything that did not move we
bombed Baghdad
a city of 5.5 million human beings
we bombed radio towers we bombed
telephone poles we bombed mosques
we bombed runways we bombed tanks
we bombed trucks we bombed cars we bombed bridges
we bombed the darkness we bombed
the sunlight we bombed them and we
bombed them and we cluster bombed the citizens
of Iraq and we sulfur bombed the citizens of Iraq

and we napalm bombed the citizens of Iraq and we
complemented these bombings/these "sorties" with
Tomahawk cruise missiles which we shot
repeatedly by the thousands upon thousands

into Iraq
(you understand an Iraqi Scud missile
is quote *militarily insignificant* unquote *and we*
do not mess around with insignificant)
so we used cruise missiles repeatedly
we fired them into Iraq
And I am not pleased
I am not very pleased
None of this fits into my notion of "things going very well"
June Jordan, *Kissing God*

A reading of the first section of June Jordan's poem "The Bombing of Baghdad" (45), a poem referring to the first Iraq war – she did not live to experience the second, much larger, Iraq conflict – shows its indebtedness to Walt Whitman, his catalogues, his obsessive repetitions, the relentless power of his rhetoric. It is obvious that the late Professor of African American Studies at Berkeley, whom Adrienne Rich has called "one of the most musically and lyrically gifted poets of the late twentieth century" (*Kissing God*, back cover), connects to the American poet of the 19th century in a poem that is certainly extremely topical politically.

And, indeed, in an essay on Whitman entitled "For the Sake of People's Poetry: Walt Whitman and the Rest of Us," Jordan confirms this relationship, calling herself a "descendent of Walt Whitman" (252).[1] In this 1979 essay, she turns Whitman into the curious ancestor of her "People's Poetry" project, curious, because he, as a white male, plays a strange and unusual role in a canon dominated by white males who have turned literature into an elitist, exclusive and excluding institution largely unconnected with what she calls the "people."

> It so happens that Walt Whitman is the one white father who shares the systematic disadvantages of his heterogeneous offspring trapped inside a closet that is, in reality, as huge as the continental spread of North and South America. What Whitman envisioned, we, the people and the poets of the New World, embody. (243)

Embodiment and poetry is nothing to be taken lightly or coincidentally in a Whitmanian context. Whitman himself repeatedly equated the body of his literature with his own body, most famously in his lines "Camerado, this is no book, / Who touches this, touches a man" (505) taken from the poem "So Long!," the poem concluding *Leaves of Grass* since the third edition in 1860. In this way, too, the embodiment Jordan mentions is both Whitman's "heterogeneous offspring" as well as poetry such as Jordan's Baghdad poem, whose specific power lies in its poetic body, its tightness, where one line both depends on and drives the other.

[1] From now on, this essay will be referred to parenthetically with the appropriate page number.

June Jordan, like other African American poets, sees a "conspiracy of silence" (Folsom 41)[2] at work in the world of American poetry – against Walt Whitman and the kind of poetry he represents. This is not so much a conspiracy by certain individuals, sitting in backrooms and devising specific, exclusive standards for excellence in poetry but a "racist, sexist, and anti-American predicament that condemns most New World Writing to peripheral/unpublished manuscript status" (243). Allegedly, Whitman is simply not taken seriously at home; at best, he is "presented as a rather hairy buffoon suffering from a childish proclivity for exercise and open air" (243). If one wants to encounter Whitman, June Jordan says, one must go abroad where he is naturally considered "the great American writer, the distinctively American poet, the giant American 'literatus'" (244).

Whitman and the people's poets, including Pablo Neruda, Aghostino Neto, Gabriela Mistral, Langston Hughes, and Margaret Walker, are squarely contrasted with another group, among them Ezra Pound, T.S. Eliot, Wallace Stevens, Robert Lowell, Elizabeth Bishop and also, somewhat surprisingly, Emily Dickinson (see 252). The people's poet, such as Pablo Neruda or Whitman, writes "in a manner readily comprehensible to the masses of his countrymen" (247). This poetry "can be understood by more people, more easily" (248).

The argument that seems to be made here is that both Whitman's poetry and his poetics are a model for the "people's poets" because of their simplicity, transparency, elemental force. This poetry addresses the intellect, as well as the language, of the masses of the people rather than trying to cater to the elite. It is therefore not *another* language, but a language consciously crafted to have a broad appeal.

The unmistakeable Whitmanesque quality of that poetry, which has been considered experimental, canon-defying, and original the world over, is mostly a "broadly accessible, spoken language" (251). This seems to be confirmed by Jordan's choice of Pound, Eliot and Stevens as examples of the antagonistic group, authors who, surely, express the avantgarde, experimental dimension of American literature.

And yet, a closer look at Jordan's argument with regard to Whitman as well as her own, Whitman-inspired poetry shows that her tradition, too, puts forward a program of unconventionality in poetry. In fact, the metaphorical use of the body projects the vision of the author into the body of poetry and into the body

---

2 My inspiration to deal with June Jordan in this contribution I owe to Ed Folsom whose work on Whitman, including the reception of Whitman around the world, has revealed the global intertextual universe Whitman has established and of which he is also a part. With regard to the creative, lyrical reception of Whitman, the "talking back" to Whitman, *Walt Whitman: The Measure of His Song* (1981; second, rev. ed. 1998, with an important introduction) provides a highly convincing and impressive collection of texts.

of the reader. Whitman's poetry, Jordan seems to insist, translates the traditional communicative model between poet and reader into vibrant, physical texts which operate on the sensuality of the reader. Using a strongly Whitmanesque diction, she observes:

> The great American poet of democracy as cosmos, this poet of a continent as consciousness, this poet of the many people as one people, this poet of diction comprehensible to all, of a vision insisting on each, of a rhythm/a rhetorical momentum to transport the reader from the Brooklyn ferry into the hills of Alabama and back again, of line after line of bodily, concrete detail that constitutes the mysterious the cellular tissue of a nation indivisible but dependent upon and astonishing in its diversity .... (250)

Whitman's poetry, especially its "cellular tissue" made up of his thousands of lines, thus affects the reader directly. It is not a language which mimicks the oftentimes media-corrupted language of the public; rather, its diction addresses directly the consciousness – and subconsciousness – of those a political poetry needs to address. It "transports" the reader to focal points of human struggle – the masses on the East Coast, the slaves, and deprived black workers in the South – in order to make them a part of that struggle, to connect them.

Jordan calls this "an intellectual trust in sensuality as a means of knowledge" (251). This is an interesting formulation, as it brackets "sensuality" between "intellectual" and "knowledge." The often-observed epistemological function of Whitman's erotic, highly physical, poetry is generalized here. There is a short-cut between the sensual vision and the understanding, even in the sense of an intellectual trust, of author and reader.

"The Bombing of Baghdad," section 1, is an example of this programmatically Whitmanesque poetry. This catalogue of thirty-five lines contains the words "bombed" or "bombing" thirty-one times, not including the title, and sometimes twice per line. The very way the title line shoots into the poem, in fact becomes right away a part of it – "The Bombing of Baghdad began and did not terminate for 42 days" – works on the listener's nerve endings. There is no way for the reader to escape this bombing. Rejecting the claim widely made by the military of a clean, "surgical" operation controlled by software reminiscent of computer games and science-fiction movies, this poem replaces the innocuous reports of prime-time television news by a directness and a conciseness never experienced by a consumer of standard media. An "intellectual trust in sensuality" indeed.

It is in this sense that Jordan considers Whitman's poetry, as well as the poetry written in his tradition, including her own, as having "a believable, collective voice" (251) – a voice that goes far beyond that of African Americans. When that earlier great Whitmanite among African-American poets, Langston Hughes, claimed that "I, too, sing America," he claimed an emancipated voice in the chorus of American poetry, indeed, reproaching Whitman with having forgotten him.

When June Jordan takes up Whitman at a time when the United States has become a superpower and an uncontested monopolist of power, she not so much speaks back to him but joins him in his translation of the world into poetry – and the other way around. There are few poets who have so consistently followed Whitman in his global orientation. Alice Walker has called Jordan the "universal poet" because she positions her poetry globally. From the middle East to Latin America, from Ireland to Lebanon and always back to the United States, she transports her readers in search of an authentically visceral experience of conflict and catastrophe. In fact, the Baghdad poem returns to the United States and her history, addressing "Custer's Next-To-Last-Stand" where Crazy Horse's singing mingles with "that music in the moaning of the Arab world" (*Kissing God* 46).

It is interesting how Jordan often abandons Whitman's long lines but develops his characteristic catalogues. This is her contribution to the Whitman experiment in poetry, a sharpening of his revolutionary aesthetics. Whereas Whitman's long lines allowed a lingering, a momentary settling of a poetic impression, there is now globalized speed which jerks the reader from one place to the next:

> Bosnia Bosnia
>
> Too bad
> there is no oil
> between her legs
>
> that 4-year-old Muslim girl and
> her 5-year-old sister
> and the 16-year-old babysitter
> and the 20-year old mother of that 4-year-old/that
> Muslim child gang raped
> from dawn to dark to time become damnation
>
> Too bad
> there is no oil
> between her legs
>
> Too bad there is no oil
> between Srebrenica and Sarajevo
> and in-between the standing of a life
> and genocide
>
> Too bad
> there is no oil

Too bad
there is no oil
between her legs

the woman in Somalia
who weighs 45 pounds and
who has buried village elders and
who has buried village children
who weighed even less
than she weighs after so many days
of hunger gaping open
to the flies

Too bad
there is no oil
in South Central L.A.
and in between the beaten men and beatup women
and in between the African and Asian throwaways
and in between the Spanish and the English speaking
homeless
and in between the dealers and the drugged
and in between the people and criminal police
too bad
there is no oil

Too bad
there is no oil
between her legs
that four-year-old Muslim girl

Too bad
there is no oil
between her legs (*Kissing God* 55f.)

The titles of June Jordan's poems read like a list of the tragedies of our globalized world, like a digest of the evening news and of news one hears nothing about in the evening news: "First Poem from Nicaragua Libre," "A Song for Soweto," "Poem for Guatemala," "Apologies to All the People in Lebanon," "To Sing a Song of Palestine," "Message from Belfast for Justice and for Gerry Adams," or "Intifada Incantation." This globality of June Jordan's poetry echoes Whitman's. And like Whitman's, her international poems often connect locales and outrages abroad with locales at home, as "Bosnia Bosnia" alludes to South Central L.A. The catastrophes abroad and those at home interconnect, they run parallel, they are caused by the same forces neglecting their responsibility as soon as there is no material interest driving the humanitarian motivation.

But whereas Whitman connected the United States *from* which he spoke, with the thousands of places abroad *towards* which he spoke, June Jordan speaks as a citizen of the world, at times a Black citizen of the world, to others. Her voice is not American and she does not address "the world" from the center "at home." Developing Whitman further, she has found a universal voice which proceeds from Whitman's globalized vision but transcends it. We might well call this transnational poetry and, in its own way, an experimentation with a corresponding poetic voice. Whether this is due to the grand African American tradition of a sense of mission of a people that has, through the transnational experience of slavery, developed a special global responsibility, or whether the impetus is primarily from Whitman, or whether Whitman has simple provided the form for that mission is not quite certain.

Probably it is all of these. The intensity with which African American poetry, from the Harlem Renaissance onward, has picked up on Whitman, the white father, shows that his experimental aesthetics were models later, so-called people's poets, could follow and use.

Works Cited

Folsom, Ed. "Talking Back to Walt Whitman: An Introduction." *Walt Whitman: The Measure of His Song.* 2nd ed. Ed. Jim Perlman, Ed Folsom and Dan Campion. 21-75.

Jordan, June. *Kissing God Goodbye. Poems 1991-1997.* New York: Anchor Books, 1997.

—. "For the Sake of People's Poetry: Walt Whitman and the Rest of Us." *Some of Us Did Not Die: New and Selected Essays of June Jordan.* New York: Basic/Perseus Books, 2002. 242-253.

Perlman, Jim, Ed Folsom and Dan Campion, eds. 1981. *Walt Whitman: The Measure of His Song.* 2nd ed. Minneapolis/Duluth: Holy Cow! Press, 1998.

Whitman, Walt. *Leaves of Grass.* Ed. Sculley Bradley and Harold W. Blodgett. New York: Norton, 1973.

Riding the Meridian: TRANS(national)ARTS in *The Progressive Dinner Party*

Martina Pfeiler

> *... the "cultural" turn in poetry shows a shift of emphasis from the singular poet to the collective and collaborative community – from the question of "literariness" and the specific properties of the medium to the blurring of generic boundaries and a fruitfully amalgamation with other technologies.*
>
> Michael Davidson, "Philosophy and Theory in US Modern Poetry"

Transnational and intermedial boundary crossings have become instrumental to collective and collaborative (artistic) activities on the World Wide Web since the late 1990s. In this paper I will trace and discuss some features of this development. My main focus is an editorial online project called *The Progressive Dinner Party* (http://califia.hispeed.com/RM/dinner1.htm), which was compiled by the U.S. and Canadian authors Carolyn Guertin and Marjorie Coverley Luesebrink in early 2000. It was published in *Riding the Meridian*, an online magazine dedicated to "Lit[art]ure" (http://www.heelstone.com/meridian) on the World Wide Web.

Designed as an imaginary "progressive dinner party" the project invites the reader to explore thirty-nine online works by women as part of a culinary reading journey through eight different countries and four continents: *Cocktails* from Australia, *Hors d'oeuvres* from Europe, *Salad* from Canada, *Fish* from the Coasts, *Entrée* from the U.S. Heartland, *Dessert* from the Tropics and *Brandy and Coffee* from New York. The website does not only offer these tempting trajectories for a transnational reading experience (playing on the double-meaning of 'menu'), but also takes the reader through a hypertextual world map and a virtual table.

My point of departure for a close investigation of this project is its construction of a global and simultaneously national, communal, and feminist space[1]

[1] The virtual table as well as the selection of thirty-nine media artists is modelled after Judy Chicago's famous 1970s feminist installation work "The Dinner Party" (1974-1979). In Judy Chicago's work she honors contributions by thirty-nine feminist artists to the history of Western art, by designing a place setting for each woman (cf. http://www.judychicago.com). In *The Pro-*

on the World Wide Web, which due to its "time/space compression"' (Bauman 2), has frequently been subsumed under the heading of a borderless virtual space. Andrej Tisma, amongst others, articulates this idea in his article "web.arts nature," by stating: "The present Internet is a dream of the world-without-boundaries come true, where there are no geographic or time distances" (http://members.tripod.com/~aaart/webartsn.htm).

As a starting point, I use the term *transnational* in Mark Poster's, very basic, yet important, sense of "cultural meanings and attitudes circulat[ing] the planet" (102). Moreover, I consider this term as a paradigm that allows a renegotiation of the terms "global" versus the "local," "international" versus the "national," which constitute shifting signifiers in this project.

In the second part of the paper I will focus on two of the 39 works themselves, in particular on the works by Jennifer Ley (U.S.A.) and Jenny Weight (Australia), which I see as indicative, or perhaps at opposite ends, of a range of possibilities of the use of hypertext in intermedia art. I will argue that a transgression of boundaries is also most visible in the generic origins of the works. While the mixing of media almost directly translates into a blurring of genres, it requires more than the hyperlink to develop a genre into multi-generic compositions that live up to the potentials of poetry on the World Wide Web.

Transnationalism and the World Wide Web

The function of the "The Map" (fig. 1) in the project strongly points to what I see as an attempt to not only introduce but also to question the idea of the borderless virtual space of the World Wide Web. On a visual level, the spatial unity of the collection of hypermedia works is symbolized through a simple world map. At a first glance it might be considered as an icon for globalism that in the context of online publishing evokes a sense of a unity and uniformity, if not conformity. Yet with its hypertextual function, it becomes an indexical transit zone for a virtual reading journey from one region of the world to another. I would argue therefore that in one's attempt to retrieve texts from a specific part of the world, what one brings *to* the world map is a bag full of topographical knowledge and personal ideas about specific continents and countries, which runs counter to the notion of the World Wide Web as an unlimited and borderless virtual space. The function of the world map can thus be read as twofold: in the first case as dismantling the (frequently forceful) construction of maps in political and cultural climates –

---

gressive Dinner Party the virtual table is functionalized in a way that foregrounds the concept of female authorship, while leaving behind the concept of nationality. This runs counter to the idea behind the 'Menu,' where the authors are grouped together according to their place of origin, while simultaneously placing them and their works into a transnational context.

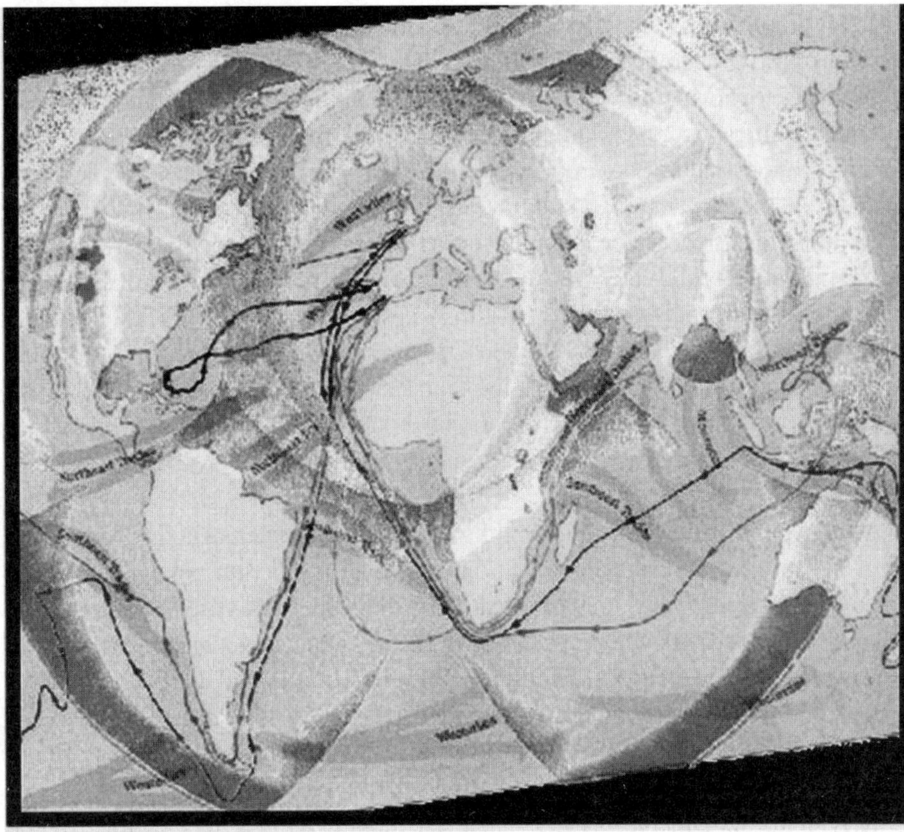

Fig. 1. "The Map," http://califia.hispeed.com/RM/dinner1.htm.

including literature and its focus on national canons; in the second case as reintroducing its geographic/spatial meaning into the World Wide Web as a mediator for a transnational reading space that mocks national boundaries and institutional bindings.

This enables the reader to renegotiate global and local specificity on the World Wide Web and brings more cultural dynamics into online publications. According to Mark Poster (amongst others), print media was an essential contributor "to the cultural formation of the nation" (123), whereas digital media seems, in essence, predestined to forge "links between individuals and groups of different, even antagonistic, nationalities. It produces the effect of global connectivity or planetary relations" (126). For those who are connected, and only for those, there is – in a sense – a tendency that "Cyberspace helps drive individuals to cross the spatial divide, putting an end to geography" (Matusitz, http://www.ibiblio.org/nmediac/winter2004/matusitz.html).

In the context of online publishing, this points to the idea that "Faced with an increasingly interconnected globe, the nation may no longer be able to sustain its territorial hegemony" (Poster 101). Thus, the thirty-nine works challenge the idea that texts have to belong to a country's national literature/s and canon/s. Without naming concrete examples, Poster points to this issue by stating: "authorship, canons, authority itself are put into suspension and reconfigured," yet, he fears, at the expense of "cultural dislocation and innovation" (126). Chris Funkhouser raises the same issue in regard to U.S. poetry by stating "Reading Poetry on the World Wide Web is ... a logical by-product of a movement towards the deterritorialization of poetry in America over the past several decades" (http://epc.buffalo.edu/authors/funkhouser/nyc96.html). These concerns lie at the core of Michael Davidson's observation that: "In an age of globalization and post-national formations, the ability of national boundaries to determine literary or philosophical categories seems in question as we contemplate a postnational moment" (250).

Moreover, with online publishing the dynamics have increasingly changed towards an out-of-the state publishing. Therefore, it is not surprising that in *The Progressive Dinner Party*, the collected works have in many cases been first published by online editors who live outside of the country of residence of the author. For example, the poem "Light is Silent ... Illumination is not" by the U.S. based writer Jennifer Ley was first published in the "Animist," an Australian web and CD ROM magazine and has been electronically archived by the Australian National Library.

It is noticeable in the project that even though quite a few regions of the world on this map are linked to texts by authors of varied national backgrounds, it strongly points to a lack of texts by authors from economically and technologically disadvantaged countries, a fact which the editors themselves regret. Embedded into a Western upper class culinary discourse, the selection of authors for the project reflects a Western dominance of hypertext and hypermedia works in early 2000. Important to note is that more than half of the works (23 out of 39) are from U.S. based female authors. This selection points to the fact that

> The Internet is an information communication space that is deterritorialized in the sense that it is nonphysical and crosses geographic borders. Yet the concept of deterritorialization obscures the Internet's extreme territoriality: access is heavily dependent on wealth, class, and technical literacy. (Couey in Malloy 76)

It seems conspicuous that Anna Couey in this statement does not mention gender and race as the other two discriminatory social and economic denominators which severely influence one's access to the Internet. Yet, her mentioning of "wealth" and "class" (which reads synonymously) dismantles the fact that technical literacy and thus access to the Internet is largely an economic issue. The discourse related to the digital divide echoes only too well what Miriam Fernández Santiago sees as indicative of the 20th century massification of products and information. She states: "Multinational presence affects international relations in the breaking of borders and draws a line of inclusion in distribution that only affects Western middle class. Lines of exclusion concern means of production, a right most commonly reserved for the Third World" (http://www.ibiblio.org/nmediac/winter2002). This statement points to the mechanisms of globalization being as much inclusive as they are exclusive, dividing as much as they are uniting (cf. Bauman 2). Especially from a political point of view it therefore seems apt to label literary and artistic collaboration across national borders *transnational*, as Stephen Owen points out:

> Thinking primarily of the modern context (implicit in the "global world"), I prefer the term "transnational" rather than sweeter words such as "global" or "international." Those latter words lead one to believe that everyone is equal in sharing this thing called "literature" or "culture." ... I use the term "transnational" here specifically to evoke a corporate model, with historically local links across national boundaries, with clear centers of power, hierarchies of subordination. This is very clear in contemporary literature. (121)

Hence, with regard to transnationalism I see in this project an early, if far from perfect, attempt to provide alternative models and contexts for presenting texts to a geographically and culturally diverse readership by creating an imaginary and symbolic space that has begun to bring the "literatures" of the world into a dialogue – above and beyond the virtual space that the architecture of the networked computer provides. Archival difficulties, as well as Web browser problems, which are inherent to the usage of the Internet, prove to be one of the major challenges to larger transnational online projects. Whereas books can guarantee consistency in terms of who is being published with whom and in what format, the Internet's greatest potential as well as greatest flaw lies exactly in its flexibility. Since some of the works that make up *The Progressive Dinner Party* are not accessible anymore or have been published on different web sites and through different distribution media, it becomes evident that texts tend to travel in cyberspace; or happen to disappear completely.

From Intermedia to Hypermedia to Trans(national)Arts?

Jennifer Ley, web curator and initiator of the online literary arts magazine *Riding the Meridian*, in which *The Progressive Dinner Party* has been published, takes up a frequently posed question that has been discussed ever since writers and literary critics became interested in the potential of computers and HTML:

> Literature ... what is happening to literature? Only a year ago, web writers were comfortable calling html-code-intensive works *hypertext*. But now that term

seems lacking, incapable of describing the myriad technical approaches now available and the creative changes which working in a web-specific medium has wrought. (http://www.heelstone.com/meridian/)

The variety of labels (altogether 17) that are used to categorize the thirty-nine works reflect the linguistic turmoil that one encounters in an attempt to get hold of a hybrid genre. Carolyn Guertin and Marjorie Coverley Luesebrink attribute the variety of genres and media that one encounters in works on the Internet directly to "hypertext/hypermedia itself," arguing that "the function of linking creates paths through boundaries and, by establishing myriad juxtapositons [sic], creates new, pourous [sic] interfaces that mock boundary lines" (http://califia.hispeed.com/RM/dinner1.htm). In order to highlight some of the intermedial [2] qualities that are possible in html coded works, I would like to discuss two examples in this context by focusing on how the link between different genres and media is installed.

"Light is Silent ... Illumination is not" by Jennifer Ley

On a content level, the focus of the poem is the speaker's loss of her father as she is growing up in the U.S. during the Cold War under the Sputnik shock, providing an intimate glimpse into a microcosm of U.S. family life in the late 1950s. The narrative part of the text unfolds in four individual, yet thematically connected, poems: "Gemini," "Seeking to Hold It," "Searching for Intelligent Life" and "Advancing to Celestial Mechanics."

In the first poem, "Gemini," the speaker lays bare the culturally informed context for her fascination with the stars. She states: "We all just wanted to reach / the moon, back then, / our plans for bomb shelters, stockpiling cans / made way for other forms of shelter" (ll. 1-4). The historic moment of the Sputnik shock penetrates into U.S. civil life, which, according to the speaker's observation of her surroundings, replaces people's concern about the threat of a nuclear war with an identification of the country's ambitious space exploration. It is in this part of

[2] The term *intermedia* goes back to Dick Higgins, who stated in his article "Intermedia" in 1966: "Much of the best work being produced today seems to fall between media. This is no accident. The concept of the separation between media arose in the renaissance. The idea that a painting is made of paint on canvas or that a sculpture should not be painted seems characteristic of the kind of social thought-categorizing and dividing society into nobility with its various subdivisions, untitled gentry, artisans, serfs and landless workers – which we call the feudal conception of the Great Chain of Being. This essentially mechanistic approach continued to be relevant throughout the first two industrial revolutions, just concluded, and into the present era of automation, which constitutes, in fact, a third industrial revolution" (Higgins in Lailach 29). With the digital revolution, intermedia practices have become the rule, rather than exception, yet not without leaving new aesthetic challenges that in many cases have yet to be met.

the work that the relationship between the speaker and her father is most overtly linked to her abrupt disillusionment with her astronomical quest, when she states that "the dark shot down / and our stars went out / and I forgot about the moon" (l. 13).

That her father dies is only hinted at metaphorically in the poem "Seeking to Hold It" by stating "The northern stars are falling / one by one. Can you catch them?" (ll. 1-2). Despite her vulnerability, the speaker does not accept her situation but struggles for a defence: "Sheath your claws, all those weapons / you tote in case there's a fight. / All you want is to fill yourself / with something worthy" (ll. 5-8). Although expressed on a very personal level, the country's obsession with self-defence and paranoia after the Sputnik shock becomes visible in the following collective statement in which the speaker is in the situation of knowing too well that "There is always a plot hidden / in the meridian over our heads" (ll. 17-18).

In "Searching for Intelligent Life" the speaker recalls that her admiration for the stars almost had a religious quality to it, yet was destroyed by her understanding of the unreliability of their place in the world. Speaking about the stars but equally alluding to the fragile presence of her father, she states that "What I saw was never / what persisted, merely a refraction of your careful light" (ll.11-12).

The final poem "Advances to Celestial Mechanics" discloses the speaker's ensuing epistemological struggle to understand the universe by thinking that by "knowing the y / of it [would] le[a]d to solving the equation" (ll.1-2), while struggling to count the stars with an abacus (cf. ll. 13-14). Only in retrospection a form of understanding develops when she realizes that there are "uncertain properties of pendular / shift an earth that refuses to remain / constant but continues to spin / on its axis rendering x a mutable force" (ll. 9-12).

The poem is labelled *hypermedia poetry* by the editors, yet what the reader encounters is a very scarce use of media formats: one link per poem and one consistent image per node that is arranged in a multiplied form next to the textual nodes. Since hypertext is usually a tool to organize a large amount of information in a frequently associative way that leaves the reader with a set of choices, this minimalist set-up radically challenges the need of associative links in hypertext poetry. In this work, one is not encouraged to move freely through the provided textual nodes. If the starting point is the poem "Gemini" (which is predominantly the case but not always) one has to follow a linear sequence of the unfolding poems since the anchor nodes are always linked to the same destination nodes. If one sticks to this sequential form of the work, one encounters an equally surprising textual stability. It is built on four poems, intersecting with an equal number of definitions from the American Sign Language ("To Accept," "To Receive," "To Seek," "To Know") and two sentences "Do you have the lynch pin?" and "I prefer my miracles small." This stable link structure, which establishes a rhythm due to the variable length of the poems and the short definitions, is used here to transgress generic boundaries: from poetry to definitions from a sign language glossary. The main effect of this appears to be that the definitions have an imagistic quality with haiku-like brevity, as for example the definition of "To Receive" reveals:

> *Both open hands, fingers curved, are*
> *crossed at the wrists, then brought toward*
> *the chest as the fingers* close.

It is important to note that there is another option built into the poem that is only discovered when clicking on the largest of the five identical images of an embossed sun, or rather star, next to the textual nodes. Here the poems and the definitions come forward in a randomized way that produces instability in the speaker's retrospection of her childhood and heightens the tension in the poem. Yet this mode, again, does not leave the reader a lot of choices.

Fig. 2. The image of the sun, or star, http://califia.hispeed.com/RM/jenniferley.htm#.

By clicking on the image, the reader triggers off a randomized sequence of the poems and definitions that reverberates with the biblical title of the poem. At first sight this image only seems to illustrate the texts. Jay David Bolter's definition of hypermedia as texts "using sounds as well as still and moving images for their own presentational effect, not as enhancements or complements to the verbal text" (Bolter 158) can only be applied to the work, when one considers the visual reference of the embossed sun, as transforming into that of a star as soon as the poems disclose their meaning. As such, the reader is forced to see the same planetary object from a different perspective, which points to an intermedial overlap between the word and the image. Nevertheless, the very scarcity and almost absence of a combination of various media, puts the reader into a very traditional reading environment, asking her to negotiate the verbal-visual symbiosis of the repetitive image which accompanies the sequential as well the randomized poems.

In contrast to this, Jenny Weight's poem "Rice" functions within an elaborate hypermedia and intermedia environment that – at least in this work – provides the very essence and specificity of a postmodern digital poem. In terms of genre labels, Jenny Weight's poem is categorized as a hypertext by the editors, which, if hypertext can be a genre level at all, undermines the elaborate hypermedia and intermedia qualities of the work.

"Rice" by Jenny Weight (geniwate)

Junk, snippets, snapshots. Reminders of a tourist's holiday in Vietnam become the point of entry into Jenny Weight's poem "Rice." A collage arranged in a pattern of sixteen hypertextual images that range from the wrapping paper of Wrigley's Spearmint chewing gum, to a postcard, a beer cap, the cardboard package of a 100% plastic crocodile, entrance tickets and other icons taken from consumer culture.

Fig. 3. From "Rice" by Jenny Weight, http://califia.hispeed.com/RM/gwate.htm#, Screenshot.

Behind this evocative interface, the reader encounters a diverse mixture of genres and media: poems, an excerpt from a late 19th century colonial report, [3] an excerpt from a history book, [4] graphics, shockwave animations, audio poems, photographs, recorded radio broadcasts, Eastern instrumental music, Western music, as well as original sounds from president Richard Nixon's "Cambodia Incursion

3 Garnier, Francoise. *The French in IndoChina*. London: T. Nelson and Sons, 1884.

4 Gettleman, M.E. *Vietnam – History, Documents, and Opinions on a Major World Crisis*. London: Penguin, 1966.

Address." The audio and visual components of the work are far from being supplementary to the textual nodes. In conjunction with the poems they pose major constitutive forces that bring colonizing countries and colonized countries, whose cultures and histories are thoroughly intertwined, into an intermedial and transnational dialogue. In her online article "Consuming Rice" Alenda Chang aptly points out the main concern in the work: "Vietnam's millenniums-old history of foreign subjugation and the transnational problematic of viewing one's culture through the lens of another" (http://www.wordcircuits.com/comment/umd/chang.html). Yet, when "Rice" appears on the World Wide Web, there is more involved: the hypertextual images as well as the poems subversively aim at a multifaceted exploration of political issues, putting military, cultural, economic, as well as touristy claims by the U.S.A., France and Australia for a specific geographical territory on a transnational display, which is negotiated by the reader, the speaker of the poem and its intermedia components.

The speaker of the poem is a tourist, who transgresses borders and only seemingly fulfils the role of a silent observer. Poem number 5, for example, epitomizes the speaker's uneasiness with what she sees: "In Nha Trang I started to vomit. / I had taken far too many photos. / They had got into my gut." In search for something that might ease her, she "trie[s] digesting small portions of local colour" (l. 6), expressing her consumerist attitude with which she approaches the country, where "the going rate for smiles is two American dollars" (l. 12). "Vietnam is working / for you" (Poem 2).

Next to the poem, there is a simple shock wave animation of a photograph that shows a field and small huts made of scattered material. In the front of the image, one sees water pipes or ducts crossing a small drench that runs nearby the small settlement. The animation makes the photograph slowly enter the screen, then dissolve and shake, before it blackens out into its center, producing a dizzying effect. Viewed within the context of the poem, but also performing its own visual scenery, this enacts an intermedial relationship between the poem and the photograph, which attempts to make the reader a part of the speaker's physiological experience.

Poem 11 mainly consists of an audio file that one accesses after clicking on a Wrigley Spearmint Gum wrapping. Bizarre rock guitar riffs can be heard, before the scene is set for "All Along the Watchtower" by Jimi Hendrix, a song that was originally written and sung by Bob Dylan at the height of the Vietnam protest in 1968. The spoken word performance by Jennifer Weight begins to intersect with the musical layers of the song and parts of the lyrics. In an aspirated, monotonous voice that creates a ghostly effect, one hears the following verses meet on a multivocal level. The song is dominated by the spoken word performance:

> patrolling caisson [Khe Sanh] hill station
> there must be some way out of here
> but there's no one around except tourists
> all waiting for the evacuation
> and I can't get no relief
> my duct tape belongs to a stranger
> the darkness full of Asian danger
> we are burning the buildings behind us
> fifty days for a mile of ball duct
> the hawkers are selling duct tape for two bucks each
> we don't reckon they're real.

The words of the performance compete and intermingle with Jimi Hendrix's intonation of "All Along The Watchtower":

> There must be some kind of way out of here
> Said the joker to the thief
> There's too much confusion
> I can't get no relief
> Business men they drink my wine
> Ploughmen dig my earth
> None will level on the wine
> Nobody of it is worth. (transcript)

The audio poem, which consists of predominately eight syllables per line, is spiked with iambs, alliterations, assonance, as for example in line nine with "burning," "buildings" and "behind" (l. 9) and consonance in lines ten and eleven. It has a widely scattered yet highly effective resounding irregular envelope rhyme in lines one and four and a couplet rhyme in lines six and seven. The speaker's voice sounds rather fragmented and torn. It is an articulation of a lyrical persona that feels largely trapped in a crowd of tourists that want to be "evacuated" from the Caisson Hill Station. The word "khe sanh/caisson" adds ambiguity to the poem, as it helps to construct an imagery that is neither East nor West. Caisson seems to allude to a street in Fort Riley, "America's [self-declared] Warfighting Center" in Kansas, where a water plant system has recently been under construction, causing the closure of this street for 50 days (http://www.riley.army.mil/newspaper/Archive/08-22-03.pdf).

Interestingly, the pronunciation of Caisson in the audio performance sounds similar the city Khe Sanh, a South Vietnamese city that was taken under heavy siege in 1968 by North Vietnamese combat troops. Through this acoustic ambiguity, as well as the war scenario that gets projected into a U.S. setting, a striking tension comes into the poem as it seems to make Fort Riley and Khe Sanh interchangeable – one being the result of the other. Moreover, a caisson also refers to carriers of ammunition in the military as well as to a carriage that is used to transport coffins in funerals, which provides a morbid context for the historic dimension of the place that the tourist encounters.

Another word that is given civil and military emphasis is "duct tape," as it is used to fix pipes as well as to keep moisture from weapons. In the last few lines the tourist's perception sticks out radically as the doubt about the originality of cheaply produced [boot-legged] consumer goods is even applied to duct tape (cf. ll. 9-11). The "Duct tape" is sold by "hawkers," and just like "the going rate for smiles," mentioned in poem number 5, it costs 2 dollars.

Once the audio file stops, the reader is left with no choice but clicking again on the image of the Wrigley Spearmint Gum wrapping, which, rather than taking one back to the entrance page, subversively links to another page that discloses the brightly colored display of the words "TRUTH FREEDOM HAPPINESS" in yellow letters on a red background. These colors do not only mock the McDonald's logo, but also the first South Vietnamese flag from 1944, which has a similar pattern but in reversed colors, signalling full scale Americanization of the country (cf. also Chang).

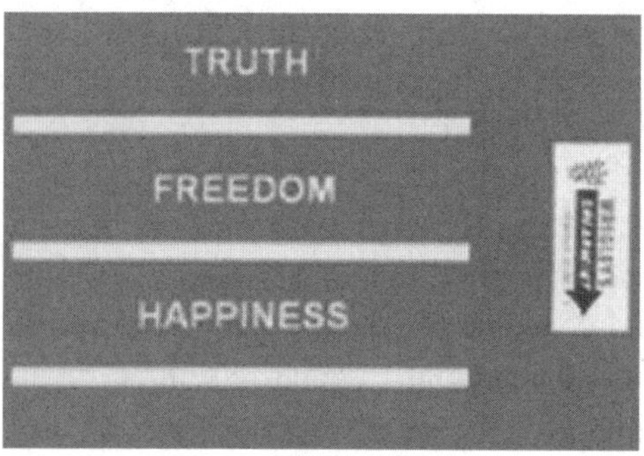

Fig. 4. (left) The McDonald's logo, http://califia.hispeed.com/RM/gwate.htm#, Screenshot.
Fig. 5. (right) The South Vietnamese flag, http://flagspot.net/flags/vn-south.html.

These examples, as well as other qualities of "Rice," in which several media formats are brought into a transnational dialogue by means of hypertextual links on one interface, bring forth notions of what may be considered "progressive" poetry on the World Wide Web. In the context of the whole editorial project *The Progressive Dinner Party*, it seems that to employ just an image and a hyper link alongside the textual node – such as in Jennifer Ley's poem "Light is Silent ... Illumination is Not" – is not enough. It may require yet another step to make use of the full potential of media convergence and the larger cultural implications of online publications. This is what characterizes "Rice" by Jenny Weight, which, as the examples have shown, reveals a closer interrelationship between the displayed poems, the visual components as well as the audio files. On a media level, different media formats are creatively employed within the transnational context of the poem. Yet, its "progressiveness" lies more in its transgression of media boundaries and the use of the Internet as publication venue than in the poetic use of language in the displayed textual nodes on the screen. The language is highly conventional.

As far as Carolyn Guertin and Marjorie Coverley Luesebrink's editorial endeavor to model *The Progessive Dinner Party* after Judy Chicago's *The Dinner Party* is concerned, the Web project too, just like *The Dinner Party*, raises several core questions that accompany both projects: what is progressive at a specific point in time? What shared and mediated cultural heritage make up "our" and other nations' culture/s and 'literature/s'? Who is being left out in its representation? And, what will prevail in the course of (online) history?

Despite the critique that hypertext had to undergo in the past few years of not living up to its full potential (and perhaps thus not arousing a lot of interest amongst a mainstream readership), what I see happening in transnational online publications such as *The Progressive Dinner Party* is a constructive revolt against the establishment of literature as a singular national and mono-medial art form. I perceive the project as an alternative model for making poetry in the 21st century with a distinct intermedial digital spin that takes off from what history and consumer culture has left 'readers' to access and reassess their own culture in a transnational context.

Works Cited

Bauman, Zygmunt. *Globalization: The Human Consequences*. Oxford: Polity, 1998.

Bolter, Jay David. *Writing Space: Computers, Hypertext and the Remediation of Print*. 2nd ed. New Jersey: Lawrence Erlbaum Associates, 2001.

Davidson, Michael. "Philosophy and Theory in US Modern Poetry." Ed. Stephen Fredman. *A Concise Companion to Twentieth Century American Poetry*. Malden, MA: Blackwell Publishing, 2005.

Higgins, Dick. "Intermedia." 1966. Ed. Michael Lailach. *Poetry Intermedia: Künstlerbücher nach 1960.* Berlin: Kunstbibliothek, 2002. 29-33.

Mollay, Judy. *Women, Art, and Technology*. Cambridge, MA: MIT Press, 2003.

Owen, Stephen. "National Literatures in a Global World? Sometimes Maybe." Ed. Marjorie Garber, Rebecca L. Walkowitz, and Paul B. Franklin. *Field Work: Sites in Literary and Cultural Studies.* New York: Routledge, 1996. 120-124.

Poster, Mark. *What's the Matter with the Internet*. Minneapolis: University of Minnesota Press, 2001.

Internet Resources: (last accessed October 2006)

Chang, Alenda. "Consuming Rice."<http://www.wordcircuits.com/comment/umd/chang.html>.

Chicago, Judy. <http://www.judychicago.com>.

Fort Riley Post. <http://www.riley.army.mil/newspaper/Archive/08-22-03.pdf>.

Funkhouser, Chris. "Hypertext and Poetry" <http://epc.buffalo.edu/authors/funkhouser/nyc96.h

Ley, Jennifer. *Light is Silent ... Illumination is not*. Published in *Animist*, 1999. <http://califia.hispeed.com/RM/jenniferley.htm>.

—. "Lit[art]ure: Something Old, Something New, a Round Table Discussion." <http://www.heelstone.com/meridian/rtable4.html>.

Matusitz, Jonathan. "Deception in the Virtual World: A Semiotic Analysis of Identity." <http://www.ibiblio.org/nmediac/winter2004/matusitz.html>.

The Progressive Dinner Party. <http://califia.hispeed.com/RM/dinner1.htm>.

Riding the Meridian. <http://www.heelstone.com/meridian/>.

Santiago, Miriam Fernández. "Computer Mediation and Postmodern Narrative Practices." <http://www.ibiblio.org/nmediac/winter2002>.

Tisma, Andrej. "Web.Arts Nature." <http://members.tripod.com/~aaart/webartsn.htm>.

Weight, Jenny. *Rice*. 1998. <http://califia.hispeed.com/RM/gwate.htm>.

Poetry

From *THE THEORY OF SUBJECTIVITY IN* MOBY-DICK

Deborah Meadows

Note:

A long work, it's an experimental form, a palimpsest, a scribbling over and through a template of holes to Melville's *Moby-Dick or The Whale* as a study of subjectivity combining chance operation and philosophical investigation.

The work explores: if the 19th century is a contradiction of free social experiment and slavery, revolution and charisma, rational enquiry and racist construction, what happens when whalemen repress the impulse to mutiny?

In an early chapter, Melville's Father Mapple re-told the story of Jonah as a problem of 19th century sovereignty: "... And if we obey God, we must disobey ourselves; and it is in this disobeying ourselves, wherein the hardness of obeying God consists."

Now "under weigh," are *Itinerant Men* free to recast self and world by rejecting bogus authority? When has "self" ever been the reliable stick-and-stone at the barricades?

Or, might a negated self, the "writer" portray "this new instance/ whether errors of an eye,/ man glowing with the remains of an ideal" that is "not as fearful as the dignity of divine/ or spiritual terror/ not as tragic as the undoing of goodness/ in our Starbuck."

Or, in line with Rabelais, can *excess* counteract the pull of compelling language that inspires one to ends greater than the dollar? Is value a scale under erasure? Language a cobbled beast?

*

CHAPTER 110

On interpretation. Its tantalizing aspects.

From a gigantic slumber
our coffin drawn from puncheons
and placards, casks and quips,
demijohn and head in hand goes
to dinner in catacombs
that resound with emptied
vocations, danger in woolen drawers,
half disemboweled thighway yet spotted
from hatchways on rolling frames
by mere bystanders to fevers' invisible flood.

Like those that fancy a canoe,
he ordered accuracy, promptitude,
ruled measure forthwith,
rationalized boat of death
transferred accurately as paddles' consort
with humorous cries within Queequeg,
a bag of mortal views
ring a hammock's sway.

I say "game" not ancient tongue
spoken by lofty scholars, delirium
can fit coward to general, rally
preparatory faith in matter of certainty,
texts inscrutable to theory
or mystical treatise.

To copy text from text: a departure
from graphic marks to truths that turn
on poise and difference. Can makers
know sense of their senses?

*

CHAPTER 114

When certain filigrees smooth
our canoe with filiations
or fill our hold with hidden bodies
tears are rovers' barracoes.

Soothing scenes, temporary effects
make orphan, phantom limb, nation
possessed of sinister
pain, an apparition of extremities,
branches of horror tree.

Nor may mast or caste form
one seamless mood however
temporal, so that ever-theoretical
our mingled threads, our mothers
die, fathers disappear, our weary
fail at progress in neighborhoods'
norms, dreary as faith
in worms, ousted facts, teeth-tiered
variables–faith: our surface.

*

STANDARD CANDLES

Keith Waldrop

I

this house my
house is not
always here and some-
times I feel like a

different person

What was I thinking of?

II

noon and the
brink of death and I
roll in the snow, depending
on the weather

Let us assume the saints had something besides gravity.

III

what cannot be
handled what
cannot be imagined
shoeing for a walk to

Jerusalem

waiting for our friends and our
bodies very
old and distant
objects weaker on

mountaintops

stronger at the
poles the stranger
strange
unrising

body

Two shadows lock.

IV

every part
weeping even the
bird the bubble the prison
a sphere with eyes before and

behind

foreign country

Angels know no particulars.

Waiting is a form of violence.

V

This is the house I did not build.

This is the room at the top of the stairs in a house I didn't build.

This is the desk–from a different generation–wedged in the window-nook of an upstairs room in a house someone else built.

This is the mess I've made. Under it all is a fire I did not set.

In the noise the world makes there is no window and here I lay my words in the *loud*, in the *burning*, the *built*. This is a fire from before ever fire came down.

This is my mess, over the noise of fire, window, desk, stair, house.

VI

trumpets and
banners trumpets
and cymbals bowls
brimming

Enoch and Elijah at
the end of time

personalities
rarely connected with well-
formulated thoughts

“The Words of Selves”: Subjectivity and Language

Denise Riley's Critique of Subjectivity

Wolfgang Wicht

In a recent Audenesque poem entitled "About Cambridge," Tony Lopez includes Denise Riley in a list of experimental poets "who had somewhere to get to" from the Cam marshes and "sailed calmly (or not calmly) on" (n. pag.). He mentions Douglas Oliver, Wendy Mulford, Peter Riley, Tom Raworth and others. Expanding the "experimental" context, one might add Geraldine Monk, Maggie O'Sullivan, Carlyle Reedy, Hazel Smith, Allen Fisher and Roy Fisher. As Mulford suggests, all of them are "attempting to open up closed systems of signification," disordering the text through "lexical tactics of disarray" and expressing "protest against the closure of authoritative meaning" ("After.Word" 239-241). Among these, Riley stands out as both an exciting contemporary poet and a challenging theorist, as her list of publications demonstrates. [1] The poetic and academic fields are sharply distinguished from, but also intimately interrelated with, each other. *Cum grano*

[1] Denise Riley was born in Carlisle in 1948 and was adopted by a working-class couple in Gloucester. She studied moral sciences at Cambridge and received a PhD in philosophy at the University of Sussex. During these years she embarked on a "countereducation of reading Marx and Hegel, Engels, Althusser, Freud – among a great many other European socialists and theorists of society" (cited in Kinnahan, "Experimental Poetics" 655). She was a postdoctoral research fellow at the Pembroke Center for Teaching and Research on Women at Brown University (1984-85) and a research assistant at the Institute for Advanced Study at Princeton (1986-87). She became a Reader in English Literature, first at Goldsmiths College London and later at the University of East Anglia. Her volumes of poetry include *Marxism for Infants* (1977), *No Fee* (with Wendy Mulford), *Dry Air* (1985), *Stair Spirit* (1992), the outstanding volume *Mop Mop Georgette* (1993) and *Selected Poems* (2000). She figured, with Douglas Oliver and Iain Sinclair, in *Penguin Modern Poets, vol. 10* (1996). In 1984, she joined Stephen Heath and Colin McCabe as one of the editors of the series of cultural-materialist studies, *Language, Discourse, Society*, published by Palgrave Macmillan. Her critical studies are *War in the Nursery: Theories of Child and Mother* (1983), *'Am I That Name?': Feminism and the Category of 'Women' in History* (1988), *The Words of Selves: Identification, Solidarity, Irony* (2000), *Impersonal Passion: Language as Affect* (2005) and in co-authorship with Jean-Jacques Lecercle, *The Force of Language* (2004). She is the editor of *Poets on Writing: Britain, 1970-1991* (1992). – *The Words of Selves* is one of the most fascinating and thought-provoking studies in the wake of Althusser, Lacan, Derrida and Judith Butler, enlarging on subjectivity, language, interpellation, identity, irony and the politics of self-description.

salis, we are invited to read the poems against the foil of criticism, and vice versa. This interrelation is at the centre of my argument.

It seems to me, incidentally, that Lopez's list has a tacit polemical implication. His balancing enumeration of male poets subverts a basic proposition forwarded by some fundamentalist feminist critics who would have us believe that poetic experimentalism is the domain of female writers. Riley would certainly sympathize with Lopez's dissident stance. She is very much aware of being a woman herself, focussing on a female perspective in her poems and academic discourses. However, she is critical of "modern feminism," which "is landed with the identity of women as an achieved fact of history and epistemology" ("Am I That Name?" 153). Programmatically, she aims at "steering clear of the great sociological or sexual categories of identity" ("Linguistic Guilt?" 78). For this reason, it appears to be a hasty conclusion to recruit her for the army of militant feminists, a conclusion that Linda Kinnahan in her recent, and admirable, pioneering book *Lyric Interventions* obviously draws. Like Judith Butler, Riley is most critical of the "exclusionary operations" (Riley, "A Short History" xiv) at the core of essentialist feminist arguments. But to enlarge on this problem would need another talk or article.

Subjection – Subjectivity

What I would like to do at the outset is to suggest a general thesis that summarizes Riley's philosophy: Riley's overall aim is to disrupt the constituents of binary logic underpinning feminist, political, ideological, philosophical, linguistic, ontological, epistemological and poetic discourses. The focalized (and focalizing) point of this general supposition is Riley's critique of "that reified entity"[2] of the subject, including the author, the lyrical 'I' and the reader. Riley combines this critique with a revisionary review of the Althusserian and poststructuralist assumption that the individual subject is thoroughly interpellated, or, as Lecercle suggests, is formed by the "historical, social, material and political ... process of subjectivation, in which the subject is at best a secondary, end-of-chain product" (*Force* 170). In contrast to this, whilst displacing the stable subject, Riley paradoxically re-affirms the agency of the 'I.' For her, the scrutiny of this problem has priority in both her critical and poetic works. Consequently, as Kinnahan convincingly puts it, she differs fundamentally from the "specific group of writers and writings, which serve to banish the 'I' in the feminist debate since the seventies"

[2] In the "End Thesis" of *The Force of Language*, Lecercle suggests that "the object of the exercise is to replace the traditional concept of 'the subject,' that reified identity, by the process of which it is the result, an end-of-chain result, as it appears in the Althusser inspired linguistic chain of interpellation" (169).

(*Lyric Interventions* xx). At that time, in Wendy Mulford's words, "the whole question of the 'construction' of the self started ... Who was this 'I' speaking? What was speaking me? How far did the illusion of selfhood, the most intimate and precious possession, reach? How could the lie of culture be broken up if the lie of the self made by that culture remained intact?" ("Notes" 31). As a discriminating theoretical thinker, Riley incidentally holds up to ridicule a notion like the one that tells us that "the theory-driven discourse" is to be regarded as "typifying male-centred language writing" (Kinnahan, *Lyric Interventions* xv). In contrast to Kinnahan's assumption it should be noted that Marjorie Perloff convincingly argues that post-Poundian postmodernist poetry by and large disrupted the centrality of "subjectivity that haunted the later Romantics, and, to a large extent, the Moderns" (Perloff, *Dance of the Intellect* 175). Both appropriating and revising the modernist criticism of the centred subject Riley re-turned to a modified, rigorously analytical, investigation and revaluation of subjectivity.

As I see it, Riley's 'theory-driven discourse' was decisively shaped and sharpened by the arguments outlined by Butler and Lecercle. Their ideas gave further direction to her earlier interest in Marxist, cultural materialist and poststructuralist thought and her sympathy with the critical-materialist discussions (since the late seventies) of the social, psychic and linguistic construction of individual identities.[3] Central to this debate was the series *Language Discourse Society*, of which Riley became a co-editor in 1984.

Agreeing with Butler, Riley recognized that the subjection of the individual by culture and the Symbolic Order does not exclude resistance and agency. What any radical consideration of the subject as subjected must take into account is that the subject is potentially being constructed as a thinking agent. Butler suggests that "to refuse to assume, that is, to require a notion of the subject from the start is not the same as negating or dispensing with such a notion altogether, on the contrary, it is to ask after the processes of its construction and the political meaning and consequentiality of taking the subject as a requirement and presupposition of theory" (*Feminists Theorize* 4).[4]

---

3 In their "Introduction" to *The Language, Discourse, Society Reader*, Heath, MacCabe and Riley pointed out the fact that "subjectivity, indeed, was the central concern of the series whose task was that of understanding the interaction of psychic and social in the construction of individuals as agents, identities, subjects" (3).

4 Cf. also Foucault's caveat, qtd. in *Feminists Theorize*, "I wanted not to exclude the problem of the subject, but to define the positions and functions that the subject would occupy in the diversity of discourse" (128).

Diversification of the 'I'

Riley's outstanding achievement within the broad deconstructive discussion of subjectivity is her unparalleled interrogation of the diversity of subject positions existing beyond the juxtaposition of *the* stable and *the* interpellated subject, and also beyond the redefinition of *the* subject's agency in social practice, as suggested by Butler and Foucault. What she tries to emphasize is to acknowledge both the diversification of the 'I,' "the subject as multiplicity," as Nietzsche said (qtd. in Ricoeur, *Oneself* 16), in sociological, psychological and poetical terms, and the permanent processes of affirming/negating the negation of the autonomous position of the subject. In a tacit way, Riley's analysis of the subject conforms to fundamental notions of Lacanian psychoanalytical theory, which tell us, as Catherine Belsey summarizes, that "the 'person' in psychoanalysis does not consist of ideas that materialize a body, and still less a mind *and* a body. Instead, we are speaking beings, divided between a real organism that inhabits an organic world and a subject that makes demands in symbols so irreducibly Other that they leave in place a memory of loss, which continues to insist as unconscious desire" (*Culture* 14).

For the sake of brevity, a synoptic outline of Riley's theoretical considerations must suffice at this point.

1. The general point from which any discussion or critique of the 'I' has to start is the notion that Paul Ricoeur has characterized "as paradigmatic of the [Western] philosophies of the subject," that is, "that the subject is formulated in the first person – *ego cogito* – whether the 'I' is defined as an empirical or transcendental ego" (*Oneself* 4). In a broad sense, Riley takes up the deconstructive turn of decentering this stable 'I,' subscribing to the assumption that subjectivity is formed in, and through, social, linguistic and ideological practices. But at the same time, she insists on the interrelationship between the "constitutional failure to *be*" on the one hand and the subject's "ability to circulate productivity" and meaning on the other. Riley argues that

> a lack of fit between my self-description as a social subject and my presence as a political subject is not disappointing but benevolent, insofar as the subject of political language actually requires a certain impersonality, or a nonidentity, to be able to circulate productivity at all. In this sense, my awkward navigations to *become*, coupled with my constitutional failure to fully *be*, are what actually enable political thinking and language, rather than marking some lamentable shortcoming in my 'politicisation.' This makes briefly for an air of paradox: that some lack of politicisation . . . might be needed, in order for there to be mobility, and life, within political thought. (*Words* 5)

The failure to be, however, excludes the subject's possibility of objectively describing herself:

For instance, proliferating self-descriptions, as encouraged by a present historical moment of petrification in the 'politics of the personal,' only accumulate yet more candidates for embalming in the Museum of Me. This is the sort of practical difficulty which shadows those altering versions of the self – pronounced by new kinds of identification which aim to liberalize yet which can paralyze. (*Impersonal Passion* 6)

Implicitly, Riley undermines the contemporary vogue of the autobiographical; she comments on the political myths spread by political administrations; she illuminates the ideological fallacies within feminist, or post-colonial, studies.

In verse, Riley's representation of the "cheerful community" of these individuals from the Museum of the Me occasionally becomes gloriously satiric. The 11th stanza of "The Castalian Spring" fakes "a hymn of togetherness," reflecting the lyrics of the sixties. The intertextual allusion is ironically subverted by alienating phonetic echoes ("bufo," a male toad, with "buffer," "warty" with German "wart ich") and hilarious "irrational associations" (*Words* 103-104):

Could I try on that song of my sociologised self? Its
Long angry flounce, tuned to piping self-sorrow, flopped
Lax in my gullet – 'But we're all *bufo bufo*', I sobbed –
Suddenly charmed by community – 'all warty we are'.
Low booms from the blackness welled up like dark liquid
Of 'wart' Ich auf Dich.' One Love was pulsed out from our
Isolate throats, concertina'ed in common. 'Du mit Mir' was
A comforting wheeze of old buffers, all coupled, one breed.
(*Selected Poems* 90) [5]

2. The precarious situation of the 'I' is marked by a loss of authenticity when the frame of self-reference is transcended. Riley establishes a paradoxical circularity suggesting that "for while I cross-question the first person, I also deploy it heavily" ("Linguistic Guilt?" 76). This proposition also embraces its inversion: When I deploy the first person, I should cross-question it heavily. Learning from Wittgenstein and Derrida, [6] Riley emphasizes the fact that any cross-examination of the 'I' implies an awareness of the role of language and, for that reason, the logically consistent loss of authenticity. She tells us that

5 Joyce Crick, London lecturer in German literature and translator of Freud and the Brothers Grimm, to whom I am especially grateful for reading the manuscript of this contribution, tells me that Don Marquis published a "book of lower-case poems 'archy and mehitabel.' It includes one poem called 'warty bliggens, the toad,' who is the ultimate solipsist. I can't help thinking he is croaking somewhere here too, wanting to join up."

6 In her *Critical Quarterly* article of 1997 Riley quotes a sentence from Derrida's "La parole soufflé": "The speaking subject discusses his irreducible secondarity, his origin that is always already eluded; for the origin is always already eluded on the basis of an organised field of speech in which the speaking subject vainly seeks a place that is always missing" ("Linguistic Guilt?" 77).

> the very structure of the language of self-reference seems to demand and indeed to guarantee an authenticity which is closely tied to originality, while simultaneously it cancels this possibility. Any *I* seems to speak for herself ... Yet as a human speaker she must know that it [the I's utterance] is also everyone's, and that this grammatical offer of uniqueness ... is radically untrue, is always being snatched away. The *I* which speaks from only one place is simultaneously everyone's everywhere. ("Linguistic Guilt?" 76)

Since the subject inevitably suffers from "linguistic dispossession," the 'I' is a pretender to an impossible throne" ("Linguistic Guilt?" 77-78). In "*Lure*, 1963," Riley quotes a song recorded by The Platters, "Oh yes I'm the great pretender" (*Selected Poems* 50). In "Outside from the Start,"' the persona raises the question of "How long do I pretend to be all of us" (*Selected Poems* 97). Utterances become "radically untrue," the 'I' is "everyone's everywhere" (*Selected Poems* 76). Another 'sociologized self' might decide for an option of "not listening to a word I say" ("*Lure*, 1963," *Selected Poems* 50). In other words, the precarious quality of authenticity results in a state of "loneliness" ("A Shortened Set," *Selected Poems* 37 and 41), "helplessness" ("*Disintegrate me,*" *Selected Poems* 83) and "isolation" ("Red Shout," *Selected Poems* 75; also "Castalian Spring," stanza 11). A conspicuous theme of her outstanding collection of poems *Mop Mop Georgette* is, to my mind, the continuous, unrelenting, multi-faceted representing, questioning, discussing and countervening of this irrefutable, yet outrageous loneliness. The 'I' oscillates between the despair of "[dying] deeper into life at every second" ("So Is It?" *Selected Poems* 72) and the desperate desire to channel loneliness into consolation ("A Misremembered Lyric," *Selected Poems* 51), into being "human" ("Cruelty Without Beauty," *Selected Poems* 70), into "sweetness in hope" ("Lyric," *Selected Poems* 56). This uncertain stand of the individual, which is ubiquitous, or, as some poems call it, "democratic" (*Selected Poems* 37, 41, 75), is one of the recurrent concerns of Riley's poems, which present the 'I' as both subject and object or will even turn I/me into "she," "her," "you" and "we." I am quoting paradigmatically here from "*Disintegrate me*," a poem that presents a passage elegantly imitating experimental poetry for the purpose of bluntly dismissing it as the "decoration of an old self-magnifying wish // to throw the self away ... " (*Selected Poems* 83). Opposed to this, the reflecting lyrical 'I' emphasizes that "impersonal hazard, the humiliating lack of much control" is "far worse to bear" than "this other drive of shame fighting to clear a name to itself," which in the end "would prove me agent." Summing up one might suggest that the I-subject of necessity strives to be authentic, though it is always inauthentic. This uncertainty results both in loneliness and desired agency.

3. The decentering of the subject does not involve, as an imperative consequence, the fundamental decentering of the literary Author. In a position of circulating productivity, the "shamefaced sociology of authorship" ("Linguistic Guilt?"

75) arises from the discrepancy between the writer's "taking on an identification, which is itself partly generated by the workings of language" (75), and the writer's simultaneous consciousness of these "workings." Authorial shame is also stirred by scruples about poetic forms that are not shaped according to the lyrical conventions we have inherited. ("shaming subject," *Selected Poems* 71; also 83) The end of "Whatever You Are, Be Somewhere Else" describes an innovative I-author (in this case possibly identical with Riley) who is confronted with the control of hegemonic tradition, "calling out // Stop now. Hold it there. Balance. Be beautiful. Try." To which the answer is, " – And I can't do this. I can't talk like any of this. / You hear me not do it" (*Selected Poems* 49). This is exactly the point where the author inevitably centers herself, and writes experimental poetry. The elliptical end of "When It's Time To Go" (a poem rigorously repudiating vulgar ideological assertions) is a sarcastic renunciation of all sorts of exuberant hymnical verses, brought forth by citing the hymn written in 1867 by the American preacher Phillips Brooks and set to music by Lewis H. Redner, "O Little Town of Bethlehem," whose second line goes "Above thy deep and dreamless sleep the silent stars go by" (www.cyberhymnal.org/htm/o/l/olittle.htm),

> O great classic cadences of English poetry
> We blush to hear thee lie
> Above thy deep and dreamless (*Selected Poems* 59)

Riley has increasingly focused on the poststructuralist notion that poetic writing cannot get free from the constraints of language, which curbs the authority of the writer. In recent studies, she examines the agency of language, scrutinizing "Inner Speech" and "Bad Words" (Lecercle and Riley *Force*). Moreover, she turns her attention to the linguistic means of directing human communicative intercourse, such as laments, rhetorical questions, exonerations, clichés etc. (*Impersonal Passion*).

Considering the creative activity of the author, Riley puts remarkable stress on the independent performativity of language. Her argument differs principally from Mulford's self-evident statement that the system of language is given, and that for this reason "we cannot *create* language" ("Notes" 34). Amending J. L. Austin's famous title, she raises the question "How Words Do Things with Us" (*Impersonal Passion* 3). She takes up an argument she had fully developed in *The Words of Selves*. In this earlier book, she considers how "the materiality of language is packed through and through with its own historicity, [which lies] in the reiteration, the echos, the reflexivity, the cadences, the automatic self-parodies and the self-monumentalizing which, constituting both being called and calling oneself, constitute the formation of categories of persons. There is nowhere beyond interpellation for us" (*Words* 111). Thus, without the author's assistance, *The Words of Selves* might linguistically somersault into *The Swords of Elves* (19). The authority of the author and the authority of language, however, are by no means irreconcilable and antithetical. In the end, they seem to converge. They *have* to converge for a text to be finished. Riley's conclusion, however, is unexpectedly vague. She traces "a desirable third path between capitalised notions of a sheer hegemony of Language on the one hand, and the controlling Writer on the other" ("Linguistic Guilt?" 89). On rare occasions, it happens that Riley's sophisticated theoretical thinking runs wild in metaphysical platitude.

4. In contrast to the author-poet, the fictional lyrical persona must be most critically reviewed, at least from Riley's philosophical perspective. Riley sharply distinguishes the "lyric I" from individual (but never authentic) subjectivity and the text-producing author. Only when speaking, the lyric 'I' takes relative control. In Riley's words, "the borderline unauthenticity of the lyric 'I' gets relieved only inside the performed 'I's speaking, where everyone, you hope, finally sees the truth of the matter – that it isn't you" ("Linguistic Guilt?" 80). Whereas the biographical 'I' is decentered through the workings of Language, the lyric 'I' is additionally embedded in and shaped by the formal linguistic means of sound, style, genre and the *différance* of semantic meaning. Thus, "the lyric 'I' is often a simulacrum of control under the guise of form; a profound artifice, and the writer and reader both know it" ("Linguistic Guilt?" 84).

But alas, in her own poems Riley's lyric 'I's are powerful speakers. They dominate most of the lyric texts. In many cases, they think profoundly and carefully about the precarious position of the subject. Notwithstanding their often self-critical analysis and sceptical view of the constitution of a discursive self they might be conceived as representing authorial thinking, thus being in command of the text's meaning. Or not? Some questions remain unresolved: Must the seriousness of each lyric 'I' be read ironically in a deconstructive way? (Obviously not.) Is the dismissal of depersonalized experimental poetry a one-sided affair? Does the centrality of the 'I' in the poems, at least to a certain extent, undermine Riley's own philosophical propositions?

Beyond these questions, one becomes aware of the difference between philosophical conception and poetic practice. The latter is more in line with Wendy Mulford's claim that the confluence of writing and political struggle "implies for me continuing to work with a subject, and an 'I' which carries links with the Coleridgean 'I' in its perception of itself as moral agent and as in part imaginative creator of its world" ("Notes" 39). This is a way of seeing things that Riley's theoretical considerations both affirm and disrupt.

Aporia and Authority

This state of uncertainty smoothly links up to my coda. Riley's theoretical analysis of the 'subject' offers us a discriminating insight into various levels of subjectivity, which enlarges on Butler's scrutiny of the shifts from subjection to subjective agency. Riley demonstrates comprehensively that language, hegemonic forces and social conventions, to which the subject is subjected, also potentially establish, through the processes of appropriation, the subject as agent, an agent, however, who cannot but permanently question herself. Riley comments on how there is an element buried in the Althusserian idea of interpellative control, which is the element "of writing backwards," breaking the forces of interpellation. She emphasizes the fact that "in those very areas where I am in theory most sharply and inimitably myself, where my originary capacities might most be supposed to reign – there's instead a task of retrieving from the outside whatever I can for my own domain; yet only after the event has handed me the materials I am to work with, or against" ("Linguistic Guilt?" 105).

This potential of agency, in particular the author's politics of representation, must always examine the uncertain position of the biographical 'I' and criticize the lyric 'I,' which includes the dismissal of the represented 'I' in traditional poetry (see "When It's Time to Go," and its quotation of the hymn "O Little Town of Bethlehem"). In general terms, the 'I' is enmeshed in a labyrinth of puzzling and endless differences. In Riley's words, "Calling out, calling myself, and being called are all intimately related incarnations of the flesh of words" (*Words* 111). This situation is truly aporetic. There is *no poros*, no passage, no mediation between interpellation and self-determined agency. Aporia expresses itself through postmodernist irony, as practiced in stanza 11 of "The Castalian Spring." Poignantly Riley negotiates the aporetic and self-ironic quest in a passage of "A Shortened Set,"

> Don't quote the 'we'
> of pairs, nor worse, of sentient
> humanity, thanks.
>
> That's attitudinizing, in those
> three lines. That's what I do.
> Help me out of it, you
> you sentient humanity. (*Selected Poems* 43)

Representing this aporetic cry of paralysis the poetic text itself gains autonomy, and authority, "past this thought." The principle of what Jean-Michel Rabaté calls *auctoritas operis* is put in a prominent position, which is at variance with Eco's notions of *intentio operis, intentio auctoris* and *intentio lectoris* (*Joyce* 197), notions against which Riley incidentally also argues. *Auctoritas operis*, as Rabaté emphasizes, "can be developed when we learn to play with the text. The reading process becomes indeed a learning process with its own specific pedagogy" (203). This is the way to read Denise Riley.

Works Cited

Belsey, Catherine. *Culture and the Real*. London: Routledge, 2005.

Burt, Stephen. "To be Sheer Air, and Mousseline! The Song of Theory in the Poems of Denise Riley." *TLS* April 23 (2004): 11-12.

Butler, Judith. "Contingent Foundations: Feminism and the Question of 'Postmodernism.'" Ed. Judith Butler and Joan W. Scott. *Feminists Theorize the Political*. 3-21.

—. *Gender Trouble: Feminism and the Subversion of Identity*. New York, London: Routledge, 1990.

Butler, Judith, and Joan W. Scott, eds. *Feminists Theorize the Political*. New York: Routledge, 1992.

Hampson, Robert, and Peter Barry, eds. *New British Poetries: The Scope of the Possible*. Manchester: Manchester University Press, 1993.

Heath, Stephen, Colin McCabe, and Denise Riley, eds. *The Language, Discourse, Society Reader*. Basingstoke: Palgrave Macmillan, 2004.

Huk, Romana. "Denise Riley in Conversation." *PN Review* 103 (1995): 17-22.

Kinnahan, Linda A. "Experimental Poetics and the Lyric in British Women's Poetry: Geraldine Monk, Wendy Mulford, and Denise Riley." *Contemporary Literature* 37.4 (1996): 620-670.

—. *Lyric Interventions: Feminism, Experiment and Contemporary Discourse*. Iowa: University of Iowa Press, 2004.

—. "Total Immersion." *Poetry Review* 92.3 (2002): 48-55.

Lecercle, Jean Jacques, and Denise Riley. *The Form of Language*. Basingstoke: Palgrave Macmillan, 2004.

Lopez, Tony. "About Cambridge." <http://jacketmagazine.com/20/lopez-about.html>.

Mulford, Wendy. "After.Word." Ed. Maggie O'Sullivan. *out of everywhere: linguistically innovative poetry by women in North America & the UK*. 239-242.

—. "Notes on Writing: A Marxist/Feminist Viewpoint." Ed. Michelene Wandor. *On Gender and Writing*. London: Pandora Press, 1983. 31-34.

O'Sullivan, Maggie, ed. *out of everywhere: linguistically innovative poetry by women in North America & the UK*. London: Reality Street Editions, 1996.

Penguin Modern Poets, vol. 10: Douglas Oliver, Denise Riley, Iain Sinclair. London: Penguin, 1996.

Perloff, Marjorie. *The Dance of the Intellect: Studies in the Poetry of the Pound Tradition*. Cambridge: Cambridge University Press, 1985.

—, ed. *Postmodern Genres*. Norman, OK: University of Oklahoma Press, 1988.

Rabaté, Jean-Michel. *James Joyce and the Politics of Egoism*. Cambridge: Cambridge University Press, 2001.

Retallack, Joan. "Post-Scriptum – High-Modern." Ed. Marjorie Perloff. *Postmodern Genres*. 248-273.

Ricoeur, Paul. *Oneself as Another*. Chicago: University of Chicago Press, 1992.

Riley, Denise. *'Am I That Name?': Feminism and the Category of 'Women' in History*. Basingstoke: Macmillan, 1988.

—. "Am I That Name?" Ed. Stephen Heath, Colin MacCabe, and Denise Riley. *The Language, Discourse, Society Reader*. 138-156.

—. *Dry Air*. London: Virago Press, 1985.

—. *Impersonal Passion: Language as Affect*. Durham: Duke University Press, 2005.

—. "Is There Linguistic Guilt?" *Critical Quarterly* 39.1 (1997): 75-110.

—. *Marxism for Infants*. Cambridge: street editions, 1977.

—. *Mop Mop Georgette*. London: Reality Street Editions, 1993.

—, ed. *Poets on Writing: Britain, 1970-1991*. Basingstoke: Macmillan, 1992.

—. *Selected Poems*. London: Reality Street Editions, 2000.

—. "A Short History of Some Preoccupations." Ed. Judith Butler and Joan W. Scott. *Feminists Theorize the Political*. New York: Routledge, 1992. 121-130.

—. *Stair Spirit*. Cambridge: Equipage, 1992.

—. *The Words of Selves: Identification, Solidarity, Irony*. Stanford, CA: Stanford University Press, 2000.

Without Location: Circumlocutions of the Neuter in Rosmarie Waldrop

Nikolai Duffy

No longer one single voice. A multiple meaning. The shadow zone becomes an element of structure. Blanchot's "other kind of interruption," which:

introduces waiting, which measures the distance between two speakers, not the reducible distance, but the irreducible ... Now what is at stake is the strangeness between us.

(Waldrop, "The Ground is the Only Figure," *Dissonance* 227)

If what stammers were otherwise. On the edge of writing. Not my hand to comment but the slight swell of someone else's no in me. (Me?) Death of me. Me inasmuch as any one. As any you. Cast of no one who carry, pocket-flex, hybrid hands, mute, as much as. Sharp like not of this. Unexpected the body voice somewhat hollow going off as a tongue taking time as what will not be swallowed. Cone crossings of to have unfold. Without point. Then side-lines of sight but lately lighter. Creon incredulous. And the matter of. The present. Tense for reference.

In her deliberately fragmentary essay "Alarms and Excursions" Rosmarie Waldrop argues that "it is one of the important tasks of poems to short-circuit the transparency that words have for the signified and which is usually considered their advantage for practical uses" (in Bernstein 60). For Waldrop experimental poetry is not directed by the pursuit of individual or social meaning but by the impractical, that is to say, the aporia of practice, the pathless path of circular shuffle-steps. What her poetry aims toward is the laying bare of the language that precedes social communication, another language, the most simple language that remains when the question of transfer is no longer a privileged priority. Yet as Waldrop writes in *Another Language*, "our idea of what is simple ... is still the beginning of the inexpressible" (16). From this perspective, the triangular question with which the poet has to contend is at once inexorable and impossible: 1. How is simple language to be expressed *as such*? 2. How might that (poetic) language relate to social existence? 3. And, perhaps most problematically, should it be related?

The earliest response which Waldrop proposes to the first question is that "the way to the ineffable does not ... go via the infinite and supremely meaningful but via the infinitesimal where all meaning ceases" (*Against Language* 17). In order to express the inexpressible, simple language, it is necessary that form and content, including the critical distinction between the two, be undone, atomised. The lightening dispossession effected by the process of invalidation directs language not from the point of view of meaning but from that of delirium. Indeed, as Waldrop points out, delirium signifies "a wandering from the *lira*, from the rut," the rules, regulations, systems and laws that fabricate life, cover its nudity, its bareness, its lack (*Against Language* 30). Waldrop's poetry is delirious; it makes of this wandering its groundless matter. In another register, such a poetics might be termed a poetics of the neuter. As Maurice Blanchot writes, "the neuter supposes a relation depending neither on objective conditions nor on subjective dispositions" (*The Infinite Conversation* 299). The neuter, rather, is the *between point* of view; it enfolds both meaning and everything that depends upon it within the non-realised time of the future perfect, the non-time of awaiting. As Waldrop herself puts it in interview, "what matters is not things but what happens between them ... The gaps keep the questions in relation" (in Retallack 349).

On this analogy, the task of poetry is to make gaps both its form and function; in the space of the unspoken, Waldrop maintains, lies the motivation for thought: "in the gaps we might get hints of much that has to be left unsaid – but should be thought about" (in Retallack 341). In her early work, Waldrop predominantly attempts this task by way of a fractural disturbance of the poetic line: pared down words tentatively hang suspended across the grain of a page that quietly threatens to submerge them, while the mutation of object into subject has the delirious effect of abandoning the text to its own interminable ungraspability. From this perspective, Waldrop's turn to the prose fragment would appear to mark something of a formal and thematic departure. At the very least, it could be argued that the visual block-form of a prose fragment effectively and inevitably disguises the space of disappearance her early work was so intent on visually displaying. That said, as this article will aim to show through a discussion of *Lawn of Excluded Middle*, just as the expression of the inexpressible turns around that which has not been said, so it is precisely by way of non-appearance that disappearance actually becomes apparent. Disappearance, in other words, becomes the watermarked wandering of writing across the page. Where the line-break manifests the edge of the text in a legible physical contact with the silence that surrounds it, the prose fragment reveals emptiness as that of which it constantly loses sight. Emptiness, in other words, appears as plenitude, within the linguistic mark that contradicts it. Thus, while Waldrop's direct assertion in the first fragment of *Lawn of Excluded Middle* that she places an "empty space ... at the centre of each poem"[1] would appear to contradict that emptiness by substantiating it in the form of an unequivocal statement, it is in fact only on condition of this literal contradiction that emptiness enters the poem at all. Essentially placeless, emptiness is not of the order of that which can be placed either here or there. As such, to assert that one places an empty space is to assert nothing whatsoever. Once emptiness is placed it is no longer emptiness; once it is no longer emptiness, the statement that asserts it places emptiness at its centre becomes nothing more than a statement devoid of content. In effect, all this statement produces is the immediate cancellation of itself in the instant of utterance. What remains is only the mark of its annulment, its neutralisation, that is, its own unemployable emptiness.

In this sense, it is precisely the incongruity of the poem's form to its function, the fact that it strikes a discordant note, which marks out the prose form as the exemplary staging ground of the empty centre. The contradiction between the sequential referentiality of prose and the poem's subject matter *pronounces* silence precisely because it effaces its articulation at every turn. By shifting silence from the margins of the text to its textual centre, the sentence becomes both the scene and the churn of circumlocution. Similarly, because of the compacted density of its textual presentation, the prose fragment always already mimes the thematic of impenetrability (emptiness) at its very surface. Ink stretches from justified margin to justified margin, covering the page only with a proliferation of non-self-identical signs. Before structures of signification reconnect non-self-identicality, in other words, each grapheme is simply a *pre-text* of variously patterned spots of ink. At base, therefore, each prose fragment is simply an image in the Blanchotian sense of the term. The image, that is, is the anterior appearance of the nothing where it disappears. It announces itself while revoking all and any possibility of identification. To put it another way, as Blanchot considers it, the image is the absorption of the thing in its own immaterial anteriority; it is that which appears before the order of appearance "in the void of its reflection" (Blanchot, *The Space* 262). Or, as Levinas writes in an essay on Blanchot, "the image precedes perception" ("The Poet's Vision," *Proper Names* 130).

---

1 Rosmarie Waldrop. *Lawn of Excluded Middle*. Providence: Tender Buttons, 1993. 14. All subsequent references to this text will be given in the main text by the abbreviation *LEM*.

In relation to Waldrop, therefore, the image of each prose fragment, the smear of its ink across the page, is the originary experience of the poem. Prior to reading, the encounter with the poem takes place first and foremost at the level of its impenetrable surface, at that precise point where its self-identity as graphic structure is simultaneously obscured and suggested. As such, what this proposes is that the initial condition of the poem is, in fact, non-semantic. Indeed, with this in mind, it bears stressing that for Waldrop a poem is as much a physical entity as it is a linguistic unit, which is to say, for Waldrop, the physical image of the poem is as much a part of the poem as its text. In certain respects, this physicality of the poem is perhaps most clearly illustrated by the first edition of *Peculiar Motions*. Composed of ten poems, the volume also includes four so-called "S/kins" printed on vellum that intersect and intervene with the legibility of the book's text. Each velum both closes off and opens onto the poem it shrouds; they disrupt the reading process even as they afford a glimpse of the text they veil. As the artist of the "S/kins," Jennifer Macdonald, comments: "these images intersect the poetry by way of metaphor and movement ... As a permeable membrane, the *S/kins* intervene as a moment of passage between pages, alternately veiling and revealing the language below" (in Waldrop, *Peculiar Motions* 11). In this sense, the inclusion of vellum both redoubles the surface *image* of the poem on the page, and makes of this redoubling an irreducible part of the reading process. The poem is both its illegible image behind the obscure-reflective vellum and its presence as graphic language. In order to read *Peculiar Motions*, therefore, in order to read its text, it is necessary to interact with its physical space as book, with the alternations of text and texture, presentation and effacement.

Similarly, and to draw the focus toward *Lawn of Excluded Middle*, the typographical presentation of each prose fragment on a separate folio does not so much foreground the large blank space that surrounds the prose on all sides as emphasise the clearly defined concentration of ink on the page. The surface *image* of ink is that which is *immediately* striking. Yet, it is also that which is immediately blinding. The reader first encounters the poem from a physical distance, in the turning of a page, with pinched hand and crease of spine, the texture of finger and folio, where the out of focus eye, detached from the definite, catches a glimpse only of the blurred generality of the poem's overall shape. This image is the text's question, the one it both articulates and disarticulates at every turn of its textual perception. The eye is not so much directed to the particulars of linguistic units as it is to the space between words, the diversions of the text's internal blank spaces that set one blurred mark apart from another. To put it another way, the eye does not so much see the poem as it does its internal fissures. Thus, and even if the duration of this initial indirection of focus is minute to the extent of imperceptibility, if not resolute insignificance, *in the first instance* the poem's text (its language) is transmitted simply as pre-text (image). Indeed, as Waldrop observed in "Dark Octave," that the power of the eyeless eye lay precisely in its ability to "not see," so each poem signifies by way of its pre-semantic, that is to say, impenetrable, physicality (*Another Language* 1). This is particularly apposite of the prose poem in the sense that its dense block structure renders its impenetrability, its "shadow zone," excessively visible. As Waldrop writes, "the eye is a camera, room for everything that is to enter, like the cylinder called the satisfaction of hollow space" (*LEM* 8); the image of the poem subsists as the hollow space into which, slipping, the eye spirals.

None of this is intended to suggest, however, that the semantic element of each prose poem is subordinate to the physical presentation of graphemes. The point, rather, is to indicate that, for Waldrop, "reference is secondary" to the physical structure of the poem ("Alarms and Excursions" in Bernstein 54). "The poem," she comments, "works by indirection;" it resides in and as the reflective sheerness of surface, at the screen of impassable outside ("Alarms and Excursions" in Bernstein 54). From this perspective, or better, non-perspective, words are neither means of entry nor indicative markers of functional application. On the contrary, as the syntactically separated yet simultaneously juxtaposed "life" and "still" would appear to suggest in *Lawn of Excluded Middle's* second section, units of language reveal only a still life *image*, life prior to perception, an eye dissociated from function. There is no getting at what, if anything, lies behind the word. That which each word reflects, rather, is simply its own intractable distinction from substance. At the same time, however, it is in fact precisely on account of this obstinate intransigence that, paradoxically, "the mind" perceives "depth" (*LEM* 7). The opacity of the surface is that which renders the sheer extent of the surface "translucent" (*LEM* 7). Or again: because the surface is impenetrable, the surface extends in all directions. Surface, in other words, is deep; it stretches all the way down to the bareness of bones, the disembodied cylinder struck through with a hollow space it can neither contain nor obtain. It disappears there, back into the plane of itself. In this sense, the poem's impermeable surface is simply a dissipating "phrase ... without predicate," that is, with neither subjective attributes nor properties (*LEM* 7). Desubjectified and non-identical, each "phrase" signs not their substance but simply the depth of their bare shell. Their "meaning" is their circumlocution of the dialectic of meaning, their disappearance. Language intends "disappearance by approaching it," by disappearing in the movement of approach (*LEM* 7). In this way, the appearance of language, its coming into being, is conditional on its self-abandonment to the impersonality of empty surface or image.

At each of the levels of pre-text (physical image) and text (syntactical image), then, *Lawn of Excluded Middle* at all times mimes the dissolution of both substance and subject. Needless to say that, on the one hand, and as partially suggested before, it follows necessarily that this dissolution consequently becomes the poem's very substance. On the other hand, however, because dissolution simultaneously disappears in the instant of appearance, dissolution cannot be said to be of the order of either presence or absence. Rather, if it can be said to be anything at all, it can be said only that dissolution is at once otherwise than substance (including its obverse: non-substance) and otherwise than itself. Neither here nor there, positive nor negative, it takes place only in the disembodied non-space of elsewhere. In this sense, dissolution would be nothing other than the "lawn of excluded middle" itself. Outside the "venerable old law of logic" (*LEM* 68) that pits truth against falsity, light against dark, male against female, which is to say, outside the significatory structure of opposition, the lawn of excluded middle is the point of intersection where each limit is ex-posed (both laid bare and disarticulated) to the indistinct they share. To put it another way, the lawn of excluded middle ex-poses the notion of limit to the point at which signification blurs, giving itself off (in the sense of becoming as well as that of suspension) there.

As section twenty six reads:

> I wanted to settle down on a surface, a map perhaps, where my near-sightedness might help me see the facts. But grammar is deep. Even though it only describes, it submerges the mind in a maelstrom without discernible bottom, the dimensions of possibles swirling over the fixed edge of nothingness. (*LEM* 31)

The depth of surface is precisely that which precludes the mapping of limits, legislation, legitimation. It disappears into its own far-flung submergence, its distance from presence, its immeasurable emptiness. The lawn of excluded middle is this immeasurability. It shows itself as the refusal of settlement, in the sense both of dwelling and of determination. As such, the lawn of excluded middle simultaneously reflects and posits what is referred to as "an alternate, less linear logic" (*LEM* 68), which is to say, a "logic" that is "logical" only insofar as it pertains to a governable law of self-cancellation. The fracture of nothingness it opens is the interminable fissure into which it slips. "The mistake," Waldrop writes, "is to look for explanations where we should just watch the slow fuse burning . . . What we let go we let go" (*LEM* 18). Both indifferent and in-difference, the logic of the lawn of excluded middle here is simply the passivity of its letting go: of logic but also of its own self-identity as that which "lets go." It gives itself only as the giving out of self. "The meaning of certainty is getting burned" (*LEM* 13); the certainty of meaning is its atomisation into the non-systemic différance of writing.

Always self-divided, in its constant redoubling the lawn of excluded middle's alternate logic becomes what might be termed the a-logic of alterity. The non-thematisable emptiness at the centre ("the center of nothing" [*LEM* 13]) of the sequence not only calls that work into question but, specifically, calls it into meaning; its meaning is precisely its calling into question. In the absence of self-identical signs what forms into legibility across the poem is not so much the negation of signification but rather the plenitude of a between-space marked by perpetual linguistic non-coincidence. From this perspective, the non-appropriation of alterity necessarily underwrites presence and absence with an incommensurable opening. Circumscribed by such immeasurable vacancy, "the I has no sharp boundary inward" or outward but only the perpetual experience of "inability."[2] Writing slips from immaterial sign to physical surface; it screens a spacing of graphemes that except phonemics, that turn inside out the common structures of equivalence and of reference. It is "Something that can be held in the mouth, deeply, like darkness" (*LEM* 6), that can be experienced as material sensation but which "goes by so fast when I should like to see it laid open to view ... so that form becomes its own explanation" (*LEM* 10). The pages turn and the typeset separation of the poem becomes nothing more than "the thickness silence gains when pressed," which is to say, when graphically compressed (*LEM* 17). "The ghosts of grammar veer toward shape" and disperse there (*LEM* 17). As Waldrop writes, "Touching bottom means the water's over your head. And you can't annul a shake of that by shaking it again" (*LEM* 20).

In spite of all this, however, it is important to stress that the incorrect distinction of writing paradoxically also both manifests and cultivates alterity in the sense that alterity appears not only as but, crucially, because of the error of writing. "Only language grows such grass-green grass" (*LEM* 8) Waldrop writes in the third section of *Lawn of Excluded Middle*, by which she means only language extrapolates the *lawn* of excluded middle, the hollow space it both contains and names. Language reflects the empty centre by signing that which goes astray, namely, its own sequential body of words. Indeed, when Waldrop writes that "Sincerity is no help once we admit to the lies we tell on nocturnal occasions" (*LEM* 17) the point is that because language can be used to lie, to say *anything*, it can never be mobilised as a vehicle for certainty. There is a word too many. The mark of language is always already the dissipating ex-scription of the alterity that haunts it at every turn. In order to get at language, therefore, it is necessary to accentuate what undercuts it, "to cultivate the gap itself with its high grass for privacy and reference gone astray" (*LEM* 17). The lawn, in this sense, becomes "the locus of fertility" (*LEM* 68),[3] "scrap meanings amplifying the succession of green perspectives, moist features, spasms on the lips" (*LEM* 17). The "spasm" of

2 I am here modifying the following from the title section of *Split Infinites*: "When we say infinite we have no conception but our own inability. Therefore the name God is used. The I has no sharp boundary inward" (Waldrop, *Split Infinites* 54).

3 Waldrop repeats this description of *Lawn of Excluded Middle* in *Ceci n'est pas Keith, Ceci n'est pas Rosmarie*. 91.

language lightens expression from the burden of meaning, recasting it rather from the non-point of self-deviation and self-detour. As Waldrop clarifies in interview, the empty centre is the necessary space that, in its inability, enables "resonance, understanding, fertility, everything. This is where the 'law' (of the 'excluded middle') turns into 'lawn'" (in Retallack 365). To put it another way, it is where the "law" is *at once* both legislated (written) and suspended by its exception. The exception puts the law into question, but it also focalises that law as the play of this intractable question. From this perspective, the question of the law, or better, the law as question, is that which grows on the lawn of excluded middle, which blurs into focus, "the way words rally to the blanks between them and thus augment the volume of their resonance" (*LEM* 11), which is to say, their resistance. As section twenty-two puts it: "In language nothing is hidden or our own, its light indifferent to holes in the present or postulates beginning with ourselves" (*LEM* 27). "Caught between simulation and paradox" (*LEM* 24) language gives "everything" precisely because, in the indifferent movement of its circumlocutions, it casts totality from and holds it hostage to the not-I and the not-now, that is, the immeasurable and non-graspable depth of radical alterity.

The ineluctable consequence of this alterity is that the space of language, or what Waldrop, quoting Keats, would refer to as "negative capability," [4] gives rise only to the non-voice of the neuter, "this Excluded Middle ... [t]he anonymous and incessant droning ... at once affirmative and negative" (Levinas 152). As Blanchot develops, "The neuter is that which cannot be assigned to any genre whatsoever: the non-general, the non-generic, as well as the non-particular" (*The Infinite Conversation* 299). In this sense, the excluded middle is strictly anonymous; it is that which "pronounces itself without there being a position or deposition of existence, without presence or absence affirming it, without the unity of the word coming to dislodge it from the between-the-two in which it disseminates itself" (Blanchot, *The Step* 35). In Waldrop, it is precisely this condition of being always elsewhere and always already separate, even from itself, that determines the excluded middle as the "nowhere" of an empty centre that both subtends and suspends each word and every expression. To put it another way, because the excluded middle is exceptional rather than positional, the excluded middle effectively strips both language and itself of referentiality. Read this way, the excluded middle is at once a double movement and a double bind. It doubles back in the instant of conceptualisation insofar as all that remains is the outline trace of its non-recognition dispersing across an inexorable distance, insofar as every word

4 In a letter, Keats writes: "*Negative Capability*, that is when man is capable of being in uncertainties, Mysteries, doubts, without any irritable reaching after fact and reason." John Keats, Letter to George and Tom Keats, 21, 27. Dec. 1817; cited in Rosmarie Waldrop. *Lavish Absence: Recalling and Rereading Edmond Jabès*. 83.

mimes only the vacillating repetition of this originary dispersal. As such, in the experience of inexperience, the excluded middle designates nothing other than the relation with the unknown, the primordial "saying" of language, Waldrop's "spasms on the lips" that do not so much spew words as stammer their stuttered division.

In the shadow of its effacement, then, the circumlocutions of the neuter that play out in Waldrop's poetics give rise to a linguistic identity that exists inasmuch as it is maintained in abeyance. Here, abeyance stands as the conditional possibility of identity. Even as it evokes an ancient division of self, it is, at the same time, the exceptional temporality without which the self could not be in the first instance. The self requires its own alterity, "it" requires that which is never its own, in order to say I. Its relation of exclusive alterity to the personal pronoun is precisely that which stains it into speech: I resounds in the alterity that ex-cepts it. An existence has been defined, merged into the margins of text, the texture of paper, the spacing of letters.

From this perspective, what Waldrop's material and linguistic thematisation of the excluded middle demands is the spacing of another language, which would be featureless, androgynous, without property and without propriety. As Waldrop comments in interview, "writing is beyond gender distinctions" (Retallack 361). Indeed, for Waldrop, it is beyond gender distinctions for the very reason that, as she develops elsewhere, "Language, in its full range, is other" ("Thinking of Follows," *Dissonance* 208). In many senses, such an otherwise language would be one of dis-location, a foreign tongue cleaving words that "vanish ... into communication" (*LEM* 61) in order that the roof of the mouth might speak behind them, in their dissipating folds. "The same way deeper meaning may constrict a sentence right out of the language into an uneasiness" (*LEM* 27). In principle, what is at stake in the delirious circumlocutions of the excluded middle is a form of language and self that does not authorise itself under the declaratory sign of self-control but rather that indicates itself in the event of its own rupture. Nothing specific happens because of the excluded middle. It does not produce anything, quantifiable or otherwise. Or better: it produces nothing other than the error of misidentification and mispronunciation, the word that sticks in the mouth's cavity. At the same time, however, it is precisely because of this non-activity that the excluded middle prevents language from coming to legislated term. In the screen of its sliding surface, the concern of the excluded middle is a concern for what remains when the sovereignty of self-possession (of being, of language) collapses into the exteriority of excendence. [5] Indeed, as Blanchot comments reflectively of

[5] The neologism is Levinas's. In *On Escape* Levinas writes that "excendence" corresponds "to the need for escape" such that "being appears not only as an obstacle that free thought would have to surmount, nor even as the rigidity that, by inviting us to routine, demands an effort toward

Waldrop's notion of the imperative of poetry to "short-circuit" the regulation of linguistic communication, the precise task of the poet is:

to call us obstinately back to error, to turn us toward that space where everything we propose, everything we have acquired, everything we are, all that opens upon the earth and in the sky, returns to insignificance, and where what approaches is the nonserious and the nontrue, as if perhaps thence sprang the source of all authenticity. (*The Space of Literature* 247-248)

On the one hand, the excluded middle dispossesses the law of meaning from any sovereign guarantee. On the other hand, this lack impels language to err repeatedly, to breakdown, to fragment, and thus, according to both Waldrop and Blanchot, to disseminate (to release) the truth of language, that is, its non-truth, the truth of another language that neither arrives nor is sublated but which appears only as the undetermined anonymity of ex-scription. Another language is a language of counter-rhythm, nameless and detaching, that speaks both as and in the interruption of speech, as and in the lightening of language's between-point. It is a turning inside out, an exasperation of supposed self-possession into the impenetrable externality of surface, a sequence of corridors whose "distance doesn't seem to lessen no matter how straight [the] course" (*LEM* 30).

Waldrop exemplifies this exigency of inexorable oscillation succinctly when she writes that it is:

As if I had to navigate both forward and backward, part of me turned away from where I'm going, taking the distance of long corridors to allow for delay and trouble, for keeping in the dark while being led on. (*LEM* 36)

The "shadow-zone" which interrupts language, that turns away even as this turning is also to be understood as a leading, lets through the staining of another language, but one that is always already blotted, that has spread outwards to the margins of the page, disappearing there at the letter's edge. Strictly speaking, for Waldrop, another language is neither discursive nor communicable but simply a blanking into liquid ink without correlate or correspondence. As Waldrop writes, "the ink washes into a deeper language, and in the end the water runs clear" (*LEM* 36). Here, another language hangs suspended, on the edge of forming, on the edge of falling.

Vertigo. The terms shift. The relation of the terms shifts. The richness undermines itself. If everything is like something else, no one likeness means anything ... we are left with "pure" analogy, the *gesture* of it rather than any one specific analogy. A gesture that makes the terms transparent for the very structure of language, of signification ... Transparency

originality; rather it appears as an imprisonment from which one must get out" (54-55).

for the structure of signification – and for its limits: the silence, the infinite, the nothing, all it is not able to hold. (Waldrop, *Lavish Absence* 96)

In many respects, the gravity of what circumlocutes is ambivalent. Yet even as the neuter is the non-term that puts the oppositional interplay of all dialectics into unavoidable and unanswerable question, it bears stressing that the neuter, or the excluded middle, is not the denial of subjectivity or communication. The "shadow-zone" which interrupts language, in which words, interrupted, seek refuge, lets through, lets shine, another language, but one which is too refracting to see, namely, as Waldrop might call it, a language of "blindsights," both partial and impartial. If ever it did, the voice that speaks no longer corresponds to the body of either a unique subject or rooted language. The subjective and linguistic body, rather, is everywhere dissembled, fragmented. As a point of departure, as a standing outside, such a powerless speech is a coming back to the surface-grain of a page that writing both projects and veils. "I think," Waldrop writes, "on paper," ("Thinking of Follows," *Dissonance* 213) in "Lines that carry the weight of absence," (*Blindsight* 38) and where "the difference of shadow bespeaks other crossroads" (*Ceci n'est pas Rosmarie* 93).

To be sure, the difference of shadow is not an answer to the social, ethical, economic and legislative questions involved in thinking the world from the transnational, but it is a step, a first step, an initial opportunity to reframe the dialogue, to think, with poetry, the form of the world *across* nations, ethnicities, religions, genders, languages, ideologies, interests, ambivalences, ambiguities, and so on, to think these worlds across by thinking them from the groundless ground of the lawn up, again, for the first time. As Blanchot writes, "to live with the unknown before one (which also means: to live before the unknown, and before oneself as unknown) is to enter into the responsibility of a speech that speaks without exercising any form of power" (Blanchot, *The Infinite Conversation* 302). If the excluded middle has a social force it is that of the responsibility of a social wandering, an opening of the circumlocutions of the neuter toward their revolutionary implications, toward, that is, a certain community, but one that is not mine or yours, that is not hers or his, and still less, not ours, but its, the cold paroxysm of what no one owns but lives, weakly, uneasily, necessarily, in and as the rift-line to the other. It bears repeating that to say this is to say little. A poetics of the neuter works by indirection, in side-step, yet what it affects is the motivation toward reservation, toward a quiet holding back, a swelling of the irreducible measure of distance, of the presence of approach. Here "what is in play . . . is the foreignness between us" (Blanchot, *The Infinite Conversation* 77), the strangeness of "it."

Among other things, the neuter is an "element of structure" that spreads out and scatters. It has this dispersal as its precondition. It is singularly plural. It is other ways leaking into filament; a scurrying sideways of signification; diffraction, deflection. On the edge of writing, it stammers and chinks a present tense for reference.

Works Cited

Bernstein, Charles, ed. *The Politics of Poetic Form: Poetry and Public Policy*. New York: Roof Books, 1990.

Blanchot, Maurice. *The Infinite Conversation*. Trans. Susan Hanson. Minneapolis and London: University of Minnesota Press, 1993.

—. *The Space of Literature*. Trans. Ann Smock. London: University of Nebraska Press, 1982.

—. *The Step Not Beyond*. Trans. Lycette Nelson. Albany, NY: State University of New York Press, 1992.

Levinas, Emmanuel. *On Escape*. Trans. Bettina Bergo. Stanford, CA: Stanford University Press, 2003.

—. *Proper Names*. Trans. Michael B. Smith. London: The Athlone Press, 1996.

Nancy, Jean-Luc. *Being Singular Plural*. Trans. Robert D. Richardson and Anne E. O'Byrne. Stanford, CA: Stanford University Press, 2000.

Retallack, Joan. "A Conversation with Rosmarie Waldrop." *Contemporary Literature* 40.3 (Autumn 1999): 329-377.

Waldrop, Rosmarie. *Against Language: 'Dissatisfaction with Language' as Theme and Impulse Towards Experiments in Twentieth Century Poetry*. The Hague: Mouton, 1971.

—. *Another Language: Selected Poems*. Jersey City, NJ: Talisman House, 1997.

—. *Blindsight*. New York: New Directions, 2003.

—. *Dissonance (if you are interested)*. Tuscaloosa, AL: The University of Alabama Press, 2005.

—. *Lavish Absence: Recalling and Rereading Edmond Jabès*. Middletown, CT: Wesleyan University Press, 2002.

—. *Lawn of Excluded Middle*. Providence, RI: Tender Buttons, 1993.

—. *Peculiar Motions*. Berkeley, CA: Kelsey St. Press, 1990.

—. *Split Infinites*. Philadelphia, PA: Singing Horse Press, 1998.

Waldrop, Keith, and Rosmarie Waldrop. *Ceci n'est pas Keith, Ceci n'est pas Rosmarie*. Providence, RI: Burning Deck, 2002.

Ceci n'est pas Keith / Ceci n'est pas Rosmarie: Writing Another Language for Feminist Poetics *

Kimberly Lamm

Is it because we cannot capture our own selves or because logically nothing is on its own that we turn to each other for reflection and echo as philosophers always go back to the same props and propositions?

Rosmarie Waldrop, *Lawn of Excluded Middle*

These lines begin "Mass, Momentum, Stress," a section from Rosmarie Waldrop's *Lawn of Excluded Middle* (1993), a book of prose poems that mime and play with the figuration of the feminine in western thought. Drawing from and distorting various forms of philosophical and scientific discourses, *Lawn of Excluded Middle* reveals the feminine is imagined as and relegated to the "excluded middle," that is, the gap between truth and false, matter and concept, body and image – binary oppositions subtending the ordered reality of our perceptions. The feminine, one might say, functions as the prop and proposition between these oppositions, but is not identified as such, as it is aligned with and made visible by transcendent ideas and immanent materialities. Waldrop uses the malleable language and imaginaries of poetry to wrestle the feminine away from its insertion into these gaps and exposes the strange configurations of materials, concepts, and desires whirling within them: "Never mind that it is not philosophy, but raw electrons jumping from orbit to orbit to ready the pit for the orchestra, scrap meanings amplifying the succession of green perspectives, moist fissures, spasms on the lips" (22). Waldrop's prose poems are occasions for revealing the strange possibilities and compelling difficulties that arise when pursuing how the feminine is figured as the lawn of the excluded middle, an analytic pursuit that risks undermining language and the self as sites of certainty: "I worried about the gap between expression and intent, afraid the world might see a fluorescent advertisement where I meant to show a face" (22).

In the gloss placed at the end of *Lawn of Excluded Middle*, Waldrop explains the excluded middle is "the womb, the empty center of the woman's body, the

* Many thanks to Brian Reed and Michael Eng for their help and encouragement with this essay.

locus of fertility" (n. pag.). Read and understood as the place where biological reproduction and the woman's body meet, (and therefore where ideas about the feminine and matter knot together infinitely), the excluded middle aligns with Luce Irigaray's concept of "the envelope," which she formulates in her essay "The Envelope: A Reading of Spinoza, *Ethics,* 'Of God'" (1984). For Irigaray, the envelope is the physical and metaphysical container in which existence is produced and given shape. In contrast to Spinoza's definition of God, which Irigaray paraphrases as "*that which is its own place for itself*" (original emphasis, 83), human beings do not provide themselves with their own "envelopes," their own physical spaces and shapes, and therefore, their existence. Since the female body is the envelope for human beings, they are "conceived" to provide existence for men, not for themselves. As Irigaray explains, "The envelope that is part of her 'attributes' and 'affections' but which she cannot use as self cause" (84).

Both Irigaray and Waldrop are attentive to the difficulties individual women face as they grapple with the function of femininity in patriarchal discourse and thought. Both look to performances within and against language to open the possibility of subversion. Irigaray names this performative aspect of feminism "mimicry." Waldrop creates poems that actualize and experiment with the disruptions Irigaray's theorization of mimicry suggests. Mimicry is, according to Irigaray, a woman's attempt

> to try and recover the place of her exploitation by discourse, without allowing herself to be simply reduced to it. It means to resubmit herself – inasmuch as she is on the side of the 'perceptible' of 'matter' – to 'ideas,' in particular to ideas about herself, that are elaborated in/by a masculine logic, but so as to make 'visible,' by an effect of playful repetition, what was supposed to remain invisible: the cover up of a possible operation of the feminine in language. ("The Power of Discourse" 76)

Throughout *Lawn of Excluded Middle,* Waldrop's narrator describes the disorientation that arises from, in Irigaray's words, "resubmit[ting] herself ... to ideas about herself" and entering the "excluded middle." Waldrop's attention to language as an elusive but deep-seated structure of meaning makes the resubmission Irigaray describes both difficult and revelatory. As the elusive narrator of *Lawn* explains, "I wanted to settle down on a surface, a map perhaps, where my nearsightedness might help me see the facts. But grammar is deep" (36). An evocative, intellectually rich poetic emerges from rendering this narrator's perceptions as she mimics, but also risks losing, the image she imagines herself to embody. Here, at the beginning of a prose poem from "Mass, Momentum, Stress," Waldrop's narrator is taken up by an indexical image of her body, her shadow, and lead into a limited and pre-determined space: "Later, my shadow stopped following and, after a moment of holding its breath, steadily lengthened my progress ahead of me, obscuring other roads as if only a narrow consistency could inherit a goal" (64). As feminist theorists so often contend, pregnancy can be a means toward filling and sealing the uncertain space between a woman and the figuration of "woman" as matter, abstraction, and excluded middle. Waldrop's poems also explore the pervasive idea that biological reproduction firmly and seamlessly places a woman and her image together in time, space, and sense. Here the narrator compares a mother's clearly designated space for the placement of her imaginary – the child – to her own: "You were busy planting your picture of the world into your child's mind. Mine, in comparison, seemed more like the hotel slated for demolition, beyond redecorating" (62).

As the paragraphs above suggest, this paper brings together contemporary poetics and feminist theories, not to apply one to the other, but to reveal the themes they share. I am interested in the intersections between contemporary poetry and work such as Irigaray's, which reveals how woman, figured as both matter and abstraction, is one of the "props and propositions" to which philosophers and poets return in order to anchor the elusive connectedness of both language and living. The work of Judith Butler and Diane Elam could also contribute to this conversation. Both Butler and Elam critique feminism's unquestioned reliance on the category of woman. In *Bodies That Matter* (1998), Butler questions the assumption that feminism "must ground itself in the sexed specificity of the female body" (28). In *Feminism and Deconstruction* (1994), Elam rethinks the distinctions between the two practices named in her book's title in order to reveal "the ways in which 'women' is a *permanently contested site of meaning*," and therefore works against essentialist ideas about what women are (32, original emphasis). Feminist work that analyzes contemporary poetry, but only reads poetry by women as feminist, displays the essentialism Butler and Elam contend is at work within feminism itself. An anthology such as *Moving Borders: Three Decades of Innovative Writing by Women* (1998) attests to the extraordinarily inventive work women have composed participating in and contributing to feminist thought by disinterring and defamiliarizing the embedded histories of exclusion within the western lyric tradition. But continuing to insist, even inadvertently, that only women write feminism risks an essentialism that will reduce the possibilities of feminist poetics to a narrow consistency.

Here I want to analyze the work of Rosmarie and Keith Waldrop to see how it subtly contests the essentialism Irigaray, Butler, and Elam identify. I want to read their work as examples of how feminist poetics can be a way of thinking about gender and language and not necessarily what people with particular bodies produce. Doing this entails an examination of how the relationship between language and the feminine has been imagined in western thought. Both Rosmarie and Keith write poems that are in dialogue with writers and philosophers who analyze writing itself in metaphysical and religious terms. In the opening pages of *Lavish Absence: Recalling and Rereading Edmond Jabès* (2002), Rosmarie discusses the continual attention Jabès paid to writing the questions the world poses, "Because life is a book that needs to be written at any moment" (1). Jabès's continual writing "in cafés, in the métro, while walking, at dinner, on little bits of paper, on matchbooks, napkins, on his memory," is the movement toward "the death," Waldrop writes, "at the end of each book, each poem" (1). From this link between writing and death, Waldrop introduces language as a means toward both ordering and transcending reality:

> Faced with an undecipherable world we set out to create language, a place where human discourse can arise, and we come to exist as human beings; where, at the same time, we can maintain a relation to what transcends us, the undecipherable, the ultimate otherness, and speak to it under the name of God. (1)

Poets and philosophers, one might argue, seek to make the world undecipherable again, but often the feminine becomes a figure for the threshold into the ultimate otherness that transcends and defines us. Perhaps Maurice Blanchot's "The Gaze of Orpheus" (1955) is the most elegant rendering of this figuration: "for [Orpheus], Eurydice is the limit of what art can attain; concealed behind a name and covered by a veil, she is the profoundly dark point towards which art, desire, death, and the night all seem to lead. She is the instant in which the essence of the night approaches as the *other* night" (437, original emphasis). Feminizing the limits of the undecipherable is made possible by entrenched extremes through which "woman" is so often represented: an ever-elusive abstraction, or materiality itself. The works of Rosmarie and Keith work against formulations such as these. In the pages that follow, I analyze *Ceci n'est pas Keith / Ceci n'est pas Rosmarie* (2002), a collaborative piece of life-writing that undermines, quite subtly and playfully, the assumed certainty of autobiographical genres and exemplifies how both Keith and Rosmarie unravel the self by placing it within the undecipherable absences of language. Neither poet makes the feminine figure for that absence, but instead allows the language and memories of each other to light up paths (often bewildering and dark), to and from the undecipherable. This reading of *Ceci n'est pas Keith / Ceci n'est pas Rosmarie* leads into my argument that Keith's work can also be read through and as a feminist poetic practice. Therefore, within my reading of *Ceci n'est Pas,* I turn to *Semiramis if I Remember (self-portrait as Mask)* (2001) and *The Locality Principle* (1995) to show how Keith renders the absence at the heart of language, and therefore, the self, without feminizing it. Finally, I look at *Well Well Reality* (1998), a book of collaboratively composed poems, and particularly, "Light Travels," which reveals how the poet's voice can pursue transcendence through the proximity and indecipherability of another that is not gender specific. Across the arc of their rich oeuvres, Rosmarie and Keith do not rely on props and propositions, but turn to the language and poetry of each other to find lavish absences.

What is often assumed to be a poet's adept mastery of language is a renunciation of certainty. "And for writing," Rosmarie explains in *Ceci n'est pas Rosmarie*, "I don't even have thoughts, I have methods that make language think, take over and take me by the hand" (89). Relinquishing the idea one can steer and shape language with one's intention allows the outlines of a certain self to lose its coordinates, becoming blurred and malleable. Citing Michel Foucault, Rosmarie writes, "One writes to become other than one is" (93). Indeed, the book's porous form, in which silence becomes as tangible as statement, suggests writing is the continual making and undoing of the self in writing, but also underscores the fact that this pattern of doing and undoing cannot be wholly determined by the poet's will.

For Keith, allowing the slow decomposition of everything – words, bodies, memories – to sift into and become the poetry makes the self seem like a circle that contracts, expands, and dissipates in time. In the penultimate passage of *Ceci n'est pas Keith*, he writes: "With neither great nor wonderful actions nor any sense of glory to report – I write this or maybe its these – against the decay of remembrance" (56). Memory is Keith's great subject and the phrase "decay of remembrance," is a telling description of his particular rendering of it. Remembrance, which can suggest greatness and glory, memorializes the self, sculpts it into certainty, but also forecloses the more chaotic drifts of time, memory, language, and coincidence. For Keith, memory is a collagist; time, and what one intermittently recognizes as the self, are its materials.

In *Semiramis if I Remember (self-portrait as Mask)* (2001) Keith builds a textual architecture of memory that is paradoxically realized through the act of forgetting and is imaginatively figured by the fossilized ruins of ancient cities. The first section of *Semiramis* entitled "Ruins" explores and enacts how the self inevitably composes its own ruin through memories, dreams, and languages. Writing alternately illuminates and darkens awareness of death as the space one moves closer to when consciously entering language. The narrator recalls "a fellow student" from the second or third grade named Homer Buck, who wrote stories of firemen "replete with ladders, horses, and rescue" (17). Homer Buck was dying, and his stories "held the first words ever to register with me as the *right* words ... as if what was said could not be unsaid" (17). Homer Buck not only introduced the poet to language, writing, and death, but to consciousness about their relations. The lines that follow this poignant story work as a hinge between Homer Buck's gift and the rest of *Semiramis.* Keith writes, "Perhaps the first word I ever heard as *words*" (17). This line seems to float above tightly enjambed lines that tie the materiality of language to the body so the absence of one echoes into the other.

hollow
body, hole, the body's
hollow
something around
nothing, nothing inter
leaving (17-18)

"Something around / nothing" and nothing "inter / leaving": that is, nothing is left or buried (interred) on the interleaf between the body and language.

The subtle formal and thematic echoes in *Ceci n'est pas Keith / C'est n'est pas Rosmarie* complicate and enrich these ideas about self, body, and language. One can imagine the book as two mirrors hinged by shared absences. Both autobiographical texts introduce the self obliquely, through meditations on difference. In *Le livre de l'hospitalité* (1991), Jabès writes, "if we say 'I' we already say *difference*" (qtd. in *Lavish Absence,* 3). By exploring difference, these poets subtly allude to "I." Keith begins his half of the book musing on the difference between words and melodies, and against the predictable logic of a poet's memoir, renounces the importance of text:

> I know, in songs, how important the words are, how the melody is – in some sense – dependent on the words. And yet I almost always listen to, for instance, Schubert (or whomever) without taking the text into account, without in some cases any idea of what the song is about. (9)

This tendency to listen to melodies apart from text seems connected to Keith's reflections on language's aural textures and the inventive suggestions within a language one doesn't understand:

> The sound of talk in another language can be quite distinctive without one's knowing the language, without even knowing precisely what language is being spoken. I sometimes hear, on a train, or in a dream, what seems to be a new tongue, enunciating what are probably commonplaces in an incomphre-hensible – and, thereby, magical – message. (10)

Between these passages about *another language,* about languages loosened from clearly discernible meanings, Keith composes two straightforward, almost deadpan statements that together create an interesting opposition between fragmentation and the assumed fullness of being: "It seems, generally – this partial experience of the total song – adequate," and "I was born on Sunday" (9). In "Corridor," the last poem of *The Locality Principle* (1995), Keith composes a parenthetical statement that formally enacts the fragmentation of the in-between: "(you are more im- / portant to me / than words *or* / melody)." In the last stanza of the poem (and therefore the book), Keith writes: "we will not remember the / word / return" (110). This look into the corridor of the future where the word "return" will be forgotten suggests death as the final entrance into language's absence, between sounds and the texts of sense.

This absence splits us from the start, and writing is a path toward its realization. Rosmarie opens her half of *Ceci n'est pas* with a meditation on the cultural, poetic, and familial landscape one might expect she absorbed and now possesses as a poet of German origins. In the first section, entitled "The Past, Upon Scrutiny," Rosmarie presents this landscape through negations and qualifications that sever the poet from a nostalgic past. "Not green mountains embedded in strong feeling. More an exaggeration of fog than German poetry. Interval eclipsed. I had no grandparents. My mother told me, a few months before she died. Then burst into tears" (59).

From these meditations on distance from expected meanings, both poets render their encounters hearing and puzzling over the words and phrases that emerge from their parents but exceed the familial frame. In a section entitled "War came out of the radio before I had time to scratch on a slate," Rosmarie writes, "I see us sitting around a wicker table with the radio on it. Mother with me on her lap. She says, 'This war is going to be over in four weeks. Our leader will take care of it'" (61). Notice how simply and subtly these lines place language, family, and authority within a contained circular shape. Keith recalls his father's repertoire of strange phrases: "Crazy was always 'crazy as a peach orchard boar.' 'This world – and then the fireworks.'" Here he reiterates the questions they inspired:

"But what did it mean, that 'peach orchard boar'?"
"Or was it 'bore'?"
"My father always chuckled as he said it and my mother seemed scandalized, so I assumed – as a child – it must be some sort of obscenity." (15-16)

The peach orchard bore, linked to insanity, points the child toward what he does not know and falls to the side of proper meanings, which therefore suggests obscenity to a child who would one day write a dissertation on the topic. It is clear from these small but rich instances that in *Ceci n'est pas* subverting the conventions of autobiography is coincident with reflecting upon language as a site of uncertainty.

Keith's poetry is layered with uncertainty and allows the monumentality of self-portraiture and self-knowledge to drift away without feminizing space beyond which he can see. The poem "As for the Time Remaining" from *The Locality Principle,* explores the fact that time, despite attempts to spatialize it, "still lack[s] scale" (46). The poem moves toward its close (which in Keith's work always seems like an opening) with small lines that appear like traces of thought: "A single space … ," and "A narrow moment … " (46-47). The poem ends with a colloquial phrase that makes uncertainty the poet's essence: "My dyed-in-the-wool uncertainty" (47). So many of Keith's poems could illustrate his work's exploration of uncertainty, but what I particularly admire about *The Locality Principle* is the simultaneous evocation and undercutting of a transcendent beyond. In *The Locality Principle,* absence is not a projection of the mind's speculative heights but the body's downward coils. Keith's work suggests the full emptiness of transcendence by pressing upon and continually returning to the textures of the actual. An other, but not a feminized abstraction – not Eurydice – is necessary for that return. "Rosmarie tells me," he writes in a poem of the same title, "of a poem I wrote to her in our early intimacy, addressing her as 'Neighbor dust,' speaking of our then present state from the perspective of future decay – a future to be taken as distant. I have no memory of this poem, but might one day write another, using, as it were, the same address" (24). Near the end of *The Locality Principle*, in a poem titled "What could be the case," the poet addresses "neighbor dust" with tightly coiled and precisely enjambed lines, and asks her to "think" – not represent or embody – death's presence as the poem swiftly unfolds into its ending, death:

> figures from tombs
>
> the wind *downrushing* in
> headlong time
>
> (we have hands)
>
> where (no-
> where) the intervals
> are pure
>
> and also
> here (105)

Notice the careful proximity and distance of "here" and "no- / where" that seem to bring the ideal of pure intervals into the present and make nowhere a pause moving toward the *here* of the poem. "(we have hands)" is the one sentence in this poem that Keith does not enjamb along multiple lines, which makes it seem like a solid plank against the "down-rushing" wind. Both poet and addressee have hands, and stating "[they] have" them with such clarity works against the possibility of making "neighbor dust" a figure to see and turn away from in order to make the poem possible.

The Locality Principle also calls attention to a crucial aspect of Waldrop's work: writing along the seam that joins and separates the material world and metaphysical abstractions. In the poem "Insisting Objects," Keith writes:

I draw a
line in
the light between
infinite
and *creatures* (94)

Of course light does not distinguish between the infinite and the terrestial, but connects them. But where, since we are creatures enveloped in light, does the terrestial end and the infinite begin? An elusive actuality that drifts easily into figurative meanings, light is an important image in *The Locality Principle,* as it represents the excess beyond the container of the body, the illumination in which we are mysteriously enveloped: "(in the spill of the / lamp a / life)" ("Insisting Objects" 94). In "Not Dead," Keith explores "a light which is not / merely a reflected one," that is, a light that suggests the mysterious synthesis of the infinite and the terrestrial, a light that offers a vision of the divine (56):

a beautiful child
enveloped by the sort of
glory that is seen
surrounding the
heads of saints

arrow-slit
windows towards
the River Eden

the light was in me (57)

I am struck by these lines for what they contain – a clear rendering of the mystical – as well as what they do not – an allusion to the feminine when describing the child's saintly, glorious envelope. As the narrator declares: "the light was in me." In "The Envelope," Irigaray offers an alternative to the metaphysical interpretation of women's reproductive capacity and therefore the strict feminizing of "the envelope": "If man and woman are both body and thought, they provide each other with finiteness, limit, and the possibility of access to the divine through the development of envelopes" (86).

Perhaps collaborative poetic projects are a good place to see Irigaray's formulation materialize. In "Light Travels," a poetic collaboration in the Waldrops' *Well*

Well Reality (1998), each poet draws from the voice of the other to echo and temporarily envelope his or her words. The traveling in the title alludes to this book's weaving of voices as it moves toward "reminiscence and extinction," the poem's last line (92). "Light Travels" is a modified renga, in which one poet writes three lines of five, then seven, then five syllables, like a haiku. The next poet repeats the first poet's haiku, and then writes two lines, both of seven syllables, like a tanka. Usually more than two poets compose rengas, so the Waldrops changed the form slightly, and they did not strictly count syllables. The Waldrops's renga is layered with echoes, and thematizes ideas about voice, collaboration, and language. It begins with the lines, "common time I follow you un- / kept secret on / a basic undersound" (78). Though these lines open the poem, the poet speaks of following the other, which evokes the possibility of sounds that precede the poem, perhaps the echo of the last line, "reminiscence and extinction." An "un- / kept secret on / a basic undersound" suggests that sound both conceals and reveals meanings. In other words, the echo of the other reveals another layer in the meanings moving through the words and sounds. In the next section, the poet creates lines that answer the "undersound": "this is the first part of the rhyme / allow for sequences of overheard" (79). In "Light Travels" sounds are turned, split, and doubled; images open, close, and fold in on themselves. Each stanza pulls across oppositions, and images of revelation and concealment are placed in proximity to each other:

> close the curtains but
> playful elaborations of otherwise
> arrogant variations keeping
> the window open (81)

The curtains are closed over open windows, and the voices of the poem seem to move through layers of light and opacity. As "Light Travels" unfolds, themes of fear, desolation, and loss emerge. Section 6 ends with the statement "noise rings in our fears" (83), Section 7 ends with a description "long thin hand contract / across quiet gravel" (84), and in section 8 the strange line "loss of the white of other eyes" appears (85). But the echoed repetitions of these phrases seem to lighten their ominous weight, making them about forms, sounds, and images both poets can travel along as the poem moves toward "reminiscence and extinction" instead of a feminized figure that will give shape to the absolute otherness that is death.

"Light Travels" does not deliberately engage with feminist poetics. However, by defamiliarizing the relation between the voice and the author we imagine as a person with a particular body and history, "Light Travels" indirectly but significantly contributes to feminist poetics. In other words, "Light Travels" moves toward uncertainty but does not feminize transcendent ideas and immanent materialities and therefore acknowledges the possibility that both men and women can reconfigure the patriarchal inheritances within thought, language, and concepts of self. In the poetry of Keith and Rosmarie Waldrop I hear another language for writing feminist poetics.

Works Cited

Blanchot, Maurice. "The Gaze of Orpheus." 1955. Trans. Lydia Davis. Ed. George Quasha. *The Station Hill Blanchot Reader.* Barrytown, NY: Station Hill, 1999.

Butler, Judith. *Bodies That Matter: On the Discursive Limits of "Sex."* New York: Routledge, 1993.

Elam, Diane. *Feminism and Deconstruction: Ms. en Abyme*. New York: Routledge, 1994.

Irigaray, Luce. "The Envelope: A Reading of Spinoza, *Ethics*, 'Of God.'" *An Ethics of Sexual Difference.* 1984. Trans. Carolyn Burke and Gillian C. Gill. Ithaca, NY: Cornell University Press, 1993.

—. "The Power of Discourse and the Subordination of the Feminine." *This Sex Which is Not One.* 1977. Trans. Carolyn Porter. Ithaca, NY: Cornell University Press, 1985.

Sloan, Mary Margaret, ed. *Moving Borders: Three Decades of Innovative Writing by Women.* Jersey City, NJ: Talisman House, 1998.

Waldrop, Keith. *The Locality Principle*. Penngrove, CA: Avec Books, 1995.

—. *Semiramis if I Remember (self-portrait as Mask)*. Penngrove, CA: Avec Books, 2001.

Waldrop, Keith, and Rosmarie Waldrop. *Ceci n'est pas Keith / Ceci n'est pas Rosmarie: Autobiographies*. Providence, RI: Burning Deck, 2002.

—. *Well Well Reality* [collaborations]. Sausalito, CA: Post-Apollo Press, 1998.

Waldrop, Rosmarie. *Lavish Absence: Recalling and Rereading Edmond Jabès*. Middletown, CT: Wesleyan University Press, 2002.

—. *Lawn of Excluded Middle.* Providence, RI: Tender Buttons, 1993.

Uncontrollable Materialities: Experimental Poetry and the Body in Performance

Michel Delville

In the early 1920s New York Dadaist expatriate Baroness Elsa von Freytag Loringhoven would walk around Greenwich Village wearing such adornments as a tomato soup can bra, "a peach basket for a hat," "trimmed with gilded carrots, beets, and other vegetables," "long ice-cream-soda spoons," teaspoon earrings, or simply wearing nothing but "metal teaballs attached to her pendulant breasts" (Lane, n. pag.). [1] A poet of and for the body, the Baroness once offered to give William Carlos Williams syphilis because, she said, it would "free his mind for serious art" (Lane, n. pag.). In a letter she wrote to Djuna Barnes, the Baroness listed what she wore one evening to a soireé at the French Consulate in Berlin:

> wearing a large wide, sugarcoated birthday cake upon my head with 50 flaming candles lit-I felt *just so* spunky and affluent! In my ears I wore sugar plums or match boxes – I forget which. Also I had put on several stamps as beauty marks on my emerald painted cheeks and my eyelashes were made of gilded porcupine quills – rustling coquettishly– at the consul – with several ropes of dried figs dangling round my neck to give him a suck once and again – to entrance him. I should have liked to wear gaudy colored rubber boots up to my hips with a ballet skirt of genuine goldpaper white lacepaper covering it [in the margin: to match the cake] but I couldn't afford *that*! I guess – that my inconsistency in my costume is to blame for my failure to please the officials? (Hjartarson 20)

---

1 In the January-March 1921 issue of *The Little Review*, Ezra Pound published a humorous poem entitled "To Bill Williams and Else von Johann Wolfgang Loringhoven y Fulano." Interestingly, the piece, which parodies the styles of both Williams and the Baroness, is built around a culinary joke:

Codsway   bugwash
Bill's way   backwash
FreytagElse 3/4arf an'arf
Billy Sunday one harf Kaiser Bill one harf
Elseharf Suntag, Billsharf Freitag
Brot with thranen,   con plaisir ou con patate   pomodoro (Lane, n. pag.)

The Baroness's "art of madness" also caused some controversy after some of her poems had been published in *The Little Review*, under the editorship of Margaret Anderson and Jane Heap. After Jane Heap's departure for Paris, the Baroness lost her only publishing venue and returned to Germany, where she led a life of poverty and desperation until 1926, when she moved to Paris, where she died a few months later at age 53, asphyxiated by gas from an oven.

The Baroness's poetics of the body can be seen as a radical alternative to Duchamp's ascetic modernism, an art of exuberance and exaggeration that aspires to "the blindness of pure sensation ... walk[ing] perilously near (if she has not passed over the edge) beyond which the vision of delirium melts into the blank self - enwrapped exaltation of trance," to quote Evelyn Scott in a 1919 issue of *The Little Review* (Lane, n. pag.). More importantly, perhaps, the following passage from the Baroness's posthumous poem, "A Dozen Cocktails-Please," is reminiscent of Gertrude Stein's use of the edible still-life, especially with regard to the use of food as a euphemistic expression of sexual activity.

> No spinsterlollypop for me – yes – we have
> No bananas I got lusting palate – I
> Always eat them – – – – – – – –
> They have dandy celluloid tubes – all sizes –
> Tinted diabolically as a baboon's hind-complexion.
> ("A Dozen Cocktails-Please")

Since the 1960s, the peculiar mixture of gastronomy, eroticism, and aesthetics which characterizes the Baroness's food poetics has reached a number of visual and theatrical climaxes in the experiments of performance artists such as Carolee Schneemann, Allan Kaprow, Daniel Spoerri, Alicia Rios and Karen Finley, to cite but a few of the most spectacular and sensational *eat art* performers of the last forty-odd years. The works of these artists can be grouped into at least three main categories:

1. there are those, by far the most numerous and documented ones, whose physical engagement with foodstuff leads them to develop an aesthetics of corporeality which explore the unstable boundaries between the self and (edible) matter (Carolee Schneemann, Paul Mac Carthy, Karen Finley, the Blue Man Group)
2. there are those who, following the Futurists' "tactile dinner parties" and "polyrhythmic salads," conduct kinesthetic experiments that offer viewers an opportunity to explore the non-gustatory (i.e., tactile, sonorous and visual) aspects of food (Allison Knowles, Alicia Rios, Daniel Spoerri and certain works by Allan Kaprow)

3. and there are those who, like Dällenbach's anorectic Moderns, regard food as an alien element that stands as an obstacle to the fulfilment of the self and its capacity to protect itself from the forces of contingency, alterity and decay (Eleanor Antin, Janine Antoni, Jana Sterbak)

The first category was inaugurated by Viennese Actionist Hermann Nitsch, whose early 1960 performances began to use blood, viscera and freshly slaughtered meat in a series of "dionysic-dynamic" (Sandford 363) happenings that combined various mythic references ranging from Ancient Greek Drama to the writings of Freud and Otto Rank. It was continued, a little later, by Carolee Schneemann's famous "Meat Joy" performance, which was first performed as part of Jean-Jacques Lebel's *1er Festival de la Libre Expression* at the American Center in Paris in 1964. Schneemann's group performance – which involves a group of people writhing through heaps of raw fish, chickens, sausages, wet paint, plastic, rope and shredded scrap paper –, like its Viennese actionist counterparts in the works of Nitsch, Günter Brus, Rudolph Schwartzkogler, clearly considers the body less as an object of inquiry ("the focus is never on the self, but on the materials," Sandford 253) than as "a primal, archaic force" (qtd. in Sayre 96), which precludes the possibility of a strictly formalist understanding of Schneemann's choreographies. Forcing the audience to experience the directness of the live action in a way that establishes an immediate contact with the material bodies and objects, "Meat Joy" encourages performers to develop new, semi-improvised relationships with other performers and/or the heaps of "wet fish, heavy chickens [and] bouncing hot dogs" they are eventually inundated with (Sandford 261). Described by Schneemann in a letter to Lebel as a work "relating to Artaud, McClure, and French butcher shops" (*More than Meat Joy*; qtd. in Sandford 255), "Meat Joy" was typically designed to "alert the total sensibility" of the audience and enlarge its "basic responsive range of empathic-kinesthetic vitality" (246). While "the movements of the performers [were] explored through gesture, position and grouping in space (density, mass), color, and their own physical proportion," the performers' voices were also used as "instruments of articulation" liable to produce "unique sounds possible only during specific physical actions ... which provide[d] an implicit extension and intensification of the actions themselves" (248). While the reference to McClure alludes to the "poeticity" of her performance, Schneemann writes elsewhere of the necessity to emulate Whitman's "most interiorized, tactile, plastic-poetic" images (250) and combine them with Allan Kaprow's art of "concordance" (by which she refers to the need for the audience to agree to be physically drawn into the happening). Her instructions for the performers read like a form of spatial poetry which alternates passages in English printed in bold type (mainly describing the technical actions and gestures that are meant to be performed by the participants) and italicized fragments in French which undermine the factuality of Schneemann's "instructions":

> **MEAT JOY (certain instructions)**
>
> The images are realized by a process which unites visual obses-
> *et un concombre sans encombrement encombrer concombre cul*
> sions and spontaneous physical action.
> *encombrer*

The phonic proximity of "cucumber" and "encumber," which is further complicated by the bilingual pun on "cul" (which is phonemically contained in the English "cucumber") and the first syllable of "concombre" (the French slang for the female genitals), once again points, among other things, to Sartre's ritual 'mastic' and its suggestion that the fundamental conjunction of food and sex (and, in this particular case, vaginal or anal masturbation) lies in the act of filling holes, a theme developed a decade later by Paul Mac Carthy's "Hot Dog" (1974) performance where the artist stuffed himself with sausages while smearing his body with various edible products including ketchup (instead of blood) and mustard. But where Sartre's sacrificial ritual was meant to bring about a sense of "plenitude," Schneemann's "Meat Joy" creates a space where the embodied subject is subordinated to the instrumental body which is co-extensive with the matter that surrounds it. As in Julia Kristeva's discussion of the abject, a notion which occupies an intermediary position between subject and object, food for Schneemann becomes a crucial element in the blurring of corporeal limits, as well as of the distinction between what is us and what is no longer us; the result is the dissolution of the self confronted with the principle of "uncontrollable materiality" (Grosz 72) that defines our relationships with the body.

More recent performances using foodstuff in order to challenge the body's fixed limits include Ann Hamilton's *Untitled (mouth/stones)* (1993), Jana Sterbak's *Vanitas* (1987), Karen Finley's notorious "chocolate-smeared woman" shows, which also included some performance poetry, and her Pollockian breast milk paintings on black velvet, Janine Antoni's "Girl Made Out of Butter" (Antoni's butter was also made from breast milk), the Blue Man Group's splattering, splashing and sputtering *Tubes* experiments, and Wim Delvoye's Manzoni-inspired *Cloaca* (2001). By contrast, Allison Knowles's orchestral "Making a Salad" (1962) and Allan Kaprow's "Persian Rug" (which invited the audience to "eat their way through the designs right across the room," Kirschenblatt-Gimblett 22) clearly belong to the second, Futurist-inspired category cited above. And so do Daniel Spoerri's Eat Art banquets and happenings, whose unconsumed leftovers were sometimes recycled into *tableaux-pièges* (Sandford 338). More recently, Spanish artist and food historian Alicia Rios's "Organoleptic Deconstruction in Three Movements" (1993) proceeds to "chew" food with her fingers in an attempt to explore "the texture, sound, and appearance of various substances out of their usual context" (Kirschenblatt-Gimblett 4).

For all their differences, the works of Schneemann, Kaprow, Antoni and others seem antipodal to what Lucien Dällenbach recently described as the "nutritive nightmare" of the Moderns (119), a condition marked by various "aversions and phobias rather than the pleasures of the table and a happy appetite" (116). By contrast, the third, and last, category of food artists mentioned earlier displays a radically different approach to the materiality of food, one which allies them in many ways with Dällenbach's anorexic Moderns. In their works, the systematic denial of all consumerist temptations is radically opposed to the will to eat or engage physically with edible matter which characterizes the culinary aesthetics of the performance artists discussed above (or, for that matter, Stein's gourmet eroticism), who essentially bring about a movement from blockage to release.

The first example I would like to consider is Eleanor Antin's "Carving," which documents a 36-day diet undertaken in the summer of 1972. Antin's installation consists of 144 snapshots of the artist's nude body taken from four different vantage points (front, back, left and right profile) which sardonically evoke the status of woman both as a sexual object and an object of scientific enquiry. Feminist interpretations of Antin's "Carving" have emphasized the idea that, for women, dieting takes "the creative place of art and that in this culture women themselves are the art product" (Raven and Marrow 44). But instead of being a mere critique of standard cultural expectations of the female silhouette, the documentary, almost mathematical compulsiveness of the work's structure (the day, the time and Antin's current weight are written underneath each column) evokes the obsessive mental states of the anorexic while foregrounding the presence of the body *as* meat ("carving" can also refer to the carving of meat). As the work's subtitle, "a Traditional Sculpture," indicates, the procedural aesthetics of Antin's "Carving" is analogous to the process of substraction involved in carving a block of marble into a statue that reflects the standards of beauty of the age. As Antin herself has suggested, this methodical presentation was ironical as it satirized both the claims to objective truth of scientific documentation and the alleged clinical neutrality of conceptualist art. Distancing herself from the early, "primitive" conceptualists, she writes:

> Contrary to their belief, documentation is not a neutral list of facts. It is a conceptual creation of events after they are over. All "description" is a form of creation. There is nothing more biased than scientific documentation. It presents a non-psychological image of the "natural order" with no more claim to "objective" truth than William Blake's symbolic universe. (qtd. in Fox 44).

If photography began, according to Roland Barthes, "as an art of the Person: of identity, of civil status, of what we might call, in all senses of the term, the body's formality" (79), the *punctum* of Antin's impersonal self-portraits may lie in their capacity to disrupt our traditional notions of subjectivity by turning the structural and material condition of the body itself, stripped of its metaphorical and metaphysical content, into the field of investigation. On a thematic level, Antin's *hunger artist* expresses the fear of loss of control over one's body and one's physical appearance, which remains "one of the few arenas of control we have left in the twentieth century" (Counihan 228). Seen from the angle of structure and repetition, anorexia – like bulimia – is an extreme form of ritualistic behavior based on the strict observance of radical diet, calorie-counting and, more often than not, the calculated consumption of foods that are easy to regurgitate (or quickly excrete by means of diuretics and laxatives) and it aims to *contain* the potential excesses of the body. As Susan Bordo notes in her assessment of the cultural psychopathologies of anorexia, not only is the Western body (from Plato to Saint Augustine to Descartes) predominantly experienced as "*confinement and limitation*" and "a source of distractions ... liable also to diseases which overtake and impede us in the pursuit of truth" (231) – or purity or sanctity – but the Platonic/Augustinian ethic of control brings about a sense of dualities where the idea of control becomes an end in itself. This process becomes addictive as

> the more consciousness is individualized by the success of the will, the more everything outside the individual seems to be a threat – including ... the uncontrolled spontaneity of one's own body. ... Every success in control therefore demands a further success, so that the process cannot stop short of omnipotence. (231)

It is not just food, then, or even the body, but *hunger* itself which is experienced as an alien entity liable to destroy the self's capacity to preserve itself from the combined fears of contingency, alterity and decay. The abstinent anorexic's never-ending battle against the body's hungers and desires (there is a puritanical dimension to anorexia which often extends to the denial of *sexual* hunger and the wish to avoid sexuality by becoming "androgynous") [2] thus becomes for many a battle for power and self-control, one which is geared towards a total mastery of the body, especially at times when one experiences the rest of one's life as out of control.

Whereas the bulimic's body aims to digest/assimilate the space that surrounds it and therefore disappears *as* body (thereby momentarily losing its sense of itself as an autonomous, self-contained being), the anorexic retreats into him/herself and seeks what Jean Baudrillard calls "the ecstasy of the empty body" (*Amérique* 49, translation mine). Anorexia is an art of disappearance and absence. Like the mys-

2 According to Hilde Bruch's *The Golden Cage*, "the avoidance of any sexual encounter, a shrinking from all bodily contacts" (cited in Counihan 233) is characteristic of many anorexics.

tic body, which "feeds on itself" (Brown 170), the anorexic prepares him/herself for the ultimate sacrifice, that of "separateness of the self." As the *unfinished* body becomes the site of mental and physical manipulations, Antin's anorexic persona (like her more recent teenage anorexic heroine, Jeanie Quinn, featured in the 1997 film *Music Lessons*) is denied such access to release and pleasure and her "ultimate, fatal dream – to become immaterial, a being no longer of this world, a traveler to a finer realm" (Fox 154).

The dream of annihilation embodied by Antin's diet experiment also evokes Barthes's notion of the "that-has-been" which captures a thing or person in a moment of time and which Barthes sees as the specific character of the photographic image. It also causes the photographed subject to experience a "micro-version of death." Moreover, it evokes Vito Acconci's self-biting *Trademarks* (1970), in which the artist memorably set out to bite as many parts of his body as he could attain and eventually reversed the naturalistic view by changing the eater into what he eats. Acconci's decision to take the dream of (partial) incorporation beyond the realm of the metaphorical (and into "real" presence) reverses the process by which Christianity translated human sacrifices into the spiritual and the symbolic (and into the principle of *presence in absence* that underlies transsubstantiation). In the real eating, the artist's body becomes actualized as an integral part of the regressive process that returns us to the pagan notion that to eat is to incorporate (and therefore neutralize) the enemy. In the case of Acconci's performance, the enemy is of course the body itself which, by virtue of the marks left by the artist's mouth, is reaffirmed and reincarnated as an integral part of artistic production in a way that suggests that body and self can be unified in the act of biting and chewing. Janine Antoni's *Gnaw* (1992) is another related installation dissociating biting and chewing from nourishment. It presents "a block of gnawed chocolate, another of gnawed lard, and the candies and lipsticks she has made from the bits of each block that she has spit out" (Kirshenblatt-Gimblett 5).

In the works of Prague-born artist Jana Sterbak, the body – in life as well as in art – becomes the battleground in which the battle for subjectivity is fought. In *Vanitas: Flesh Dress for an Albino Anorectic* (1987), Sterbak wears a dress made of 50 lb of raw flank steak "which starts out red and moist, then gradually dries out into a tough leathery substance" (Kirshenblatt-Gimblett 5). By drawing attention to the corruptibility and transience of the flesh, Sterbak's dress, a still life meant to be worn like a second skin, would seem to confirm that Kristeva's "uncontrollable materiality" includes the insistent materiality of death. [3] And her

---

3 The suggestion that Kristeva's abject, with its disrespect for borders, positions and rules (*Powers* 4), can also be extended to extreme forms of collective suffering such as Auschwitz ("The abjection of Nazi crime reaches its apex when death, which, in any case, kills me, interferes with what in my living universe, is supposed to save me from death" [*Powers* 232]), is one that runs

"Vanitas" returns us to one of the traditional functions of the still life – of which the invention of Eat Art is a logical conceptual extension – which is to teach the observer a secular *Tenebrae Lesson* in the inevitability of putrefaction and decay.

In *America*, Baudrillard defines anorexia as a "fatal strategy" which is symptomatic of "a culture of disgust, of expulsion, of anthropoemia, of rejection," which is itself "characteristic of a period of obesity, saturation, overabundance": [4]

> The anorexic prefigures this culture in rather a poetic fashion by trying to keep it at bay. He refuses lack. He says: I lack nothing, therefore I shall not eat. With the overweight person, it is the opposite: he refuses fullness, repletion. He says: I lack everything, so I will eat anything at all. The anorexic staves off lack by emptiness, the overweight person staves off fullness by excess. Both are homeopathic final solutions, solutions by extermination. (42)

Baudrillard's typically emphatic rhetoric uses the term "poetic" in a loose sense, meaning something along the lines of "oppositional," "excessive" or perhaps simply "unrealistic." Whatever we may think of it, the etymological slip of the tongue that confuses anthro*po-emia* (the suffix here comes from the Greek "emein" meaning "to vomit") and *poesis* in Baudrillard's description of anorexia gives us an opportunity to consider the relationship between such performances as Antin's "Carving" and the art of poetry. Antin, who began her creative career as a poet (Fox 17) and claims to have been influenced as much by Diane Wakoski and Jackson Mac Low as by the manifestations of Fluxus art that began to emerge in the early 1960s (197), clearly embraces an aesthetic that refuses to reduce orality to the verbal, or poetry to the written word. Through the manipulation, consumption or rejection of food, the works of Antin, Schneemann, Kaprow and others bring about a continuous alteration of the distinction between body and world, self and matter, inside and outside. And if, to paraphrase Bill Viola – who like Antin, Schneemann and Finley is prone to citing poets (and Blake, in particular) as a major influence on his visual art – the poet at the turn of the 21st century

---

through Sarah Tuft's video, *Don't Make Me Up* (1986), which juxtaposes commercial images of women's bodies taken from various advertisements and rock video clips with photographs of emaciated concentration camp prisoners. The obsession with thinness that governs the current rules of beauty marketing and the infliction of mass suffering in the concentration camps both partake of a logic which draws us to a place where meaning collapses.

4 Susan Bordo comes to a similar conclusion when she suggests the "will to conquer and subdue the body" "expresses an aesthetic or moral rebellion" against cultures "characterized by gross excesses in consumption" (qtd. in Counihan 237). See also Baudrillard's description of the compulsive jogger: "The jogger has yet another solution. In a sense, he spews himself out; he doesn't merely expend his energy in his running, he vomits it. He has to attain the ecstasy of fatigue, the 'high' of mechanical annihilation, just as the anorexic aims for the 'high' of organic annihilation, the ecstasy of the empty body, and the obese individual seeks the high of dimensional annihilation: the ecstasy of the full body" (42).

is "not necessarily someone who writes well, but someone who thinks well," the performances I have discussed here explore the conjunction of art and foodstuff in ways that encourage a reappraisal of contemporary notions of the body, language and subjectivity.

Works Cited

Barthes, Roland. *Camera Lucida: Reflections on Photography*. New York: Hill & Wang, 1982.

Baudrillard, Jean. *America*. London: Verso, 1989.

—. *Amérique*. Paris: Grasset, 1986.

Bordo, Susan. *Unbearable Weight: Feminism, Western Culture, and the Body*. Berkeley: University of California Press, 1993.

Brown, Norman O. *Love's Body*. New York: Vintage, 1966.

Counihan, Carole, and Penny Van Esterik. *Food and Culture: A Reader*. London: Routledge, 1997.

Dällenbach, Lucien. *Mosaïques: Un objet esthétique à rebondissements*. Paris: Editions du Seuil, 2001.

Fox, Howard N., ed. *Eleanor Antin*. Los Angeles: Los Angeles County Museum of Art, 1999.

Freytag Loringhoven, Elsa von. "A Dozen Cocktails – Please." <http://www.writing.upenn.edu/~afilreis/88/dozen.html>.

Grosz, Elisabeth. *Sexual Subversions: Three French Feminists*. London: Allen & Unwin, 1989.

Hjartarson, Paul, and Douglas O. Spettigue, eds. *Baroness Elsa: The Autobiography of Baroness Elsa von Freytag-Loringhoven*. Ottawa: Oberon, 1992.

Kirshenblatt-Gimblett, Barbara. "Playing to the Senses: Food as Performance Medium." *Performance Research* 4.1 (1999): 1-30.

Kristeva, Julia. *Powers of Horror: An Essay on Abjection*. New York: Columbia University Press, 1982.

Lane, Christopher. "A Short Biography of the Baroness Else von Freytag-Loringhoven." <http://home1.gte.net/zzyzlane/write/essay/baroness.html>.

Raven, Arlene, and Deborah Marrow. "Eleanor Antin: What's Your Story?" *Chrysalis: A Magazine of Women's Culture* 8 (Summer 1979): 43-51.

Sandford, Mariellen, ed. *Happenings and Other Acts*. London: Routledge, 1994.

Sayre, Henry. *The Object of Performance: The American Avant-Garde Since 1970*. Chicago: University of Chicago Press, 1992.

Viola, Bill. *Reasons for Knocking at an Empty House, Writings 1973-1994*. London: Thames and Hudson, 2002.

A Thought on Marianne Moore's Prudishness

Brian Brodhead Glaser

Richard Howard said in an essay on Marianne Moore that "we have not devised or developed a vocabulary in which we can readily express or understand the erotics of withdrawal or recessiveness or obliquity, or the refusal of explicit sexual gesture" (10). He all but names the quality in Moore I would like to focus on – her prudishness. It is of a particular kind. For Moore was not only highly sensitive and averse to sexual innuendo. She was at the same time fascinated by animality and perpetually delighted to point out continuities across human and animal traits. This curiosity is an important motive behind her prudishness. Moore is careful to prevent the theme of human sexuality from obscuring glimpses of the larger but less obvious theme of human animality.

Viewed in the company of other modernist American poets, many of whom presented Europe as an escape from American provincialism, Moore stands out as unfashionably American for her prudishness. According to Charles Molesworth, a biographer who has read through her unpublished and unquotable correspondence, Moore "complained" during her tenure as editor of *The Dial* "more than once about what she saw as the tendency in contemporary writing to be needlessly obscene" (231). Contrast such a writer with the Gertrude Stein who stands at the head of Elizabeth Frost's line of experimental women writers celebrated in her 2003 *The Feminist Avant-Garde in American Poetry*, a woman who in *Tender Buttons* uses "words as signs and material things at the same time" and therefore asserts "the difference of lesbian sexuality through a redeemed and revised fetishism and, at the same time, parodies the *male* versions of that same object love" (14, 20). This is a Stein who is provoked by the masculinist methods of eroticizing writing in F.T. Marinetti's *Let's Murder the Moonshine* and Pound and Wyndham Lewis's contributions to *Blast*, and who finds a way to turn "the rules of gender typing inside out" (20). She can do this because the freedom of her punning leads to an orgasmic relationship to words that overflow, through their sensuous qualities, the gap established by representation:

> Within an economy of plentitude, the lesbian fetishist sees language as presence. She is liberated to experience the sensuality of the objective world without fearing castration. In writing that refuses to link language and lack, Stein irreverently appropriates Freud, parodying his theory of fetishism by toying with the notion of castration. (24)

Though she does not place her argument in a biographical context, we can see in Frost's version of Stein a woman who has found in Europe the sexual freedom she left the United States in part to pursue, and who finds in this personal liberty a clue to how her art could counter Marinetti and Pound, writers whose hypermasculinism indicated trends in European cultural life that distressed her.

As Molesworth points out, the major political engagement of Marianne Moore's life during this same decade was with the women's suffrage movement. For Moore, he writes, "suffragism meant at the very least the need for a woman to define her own worth rather than to accept or accede to the value system of someone else" (118). Her social views as a woman were oriented by the hope for gender equality rather than sexual freedom. This is important, in my view, because of the way that her uniquely American situation among the major female English-language modernist poets led her to explore the animality of human beings. Coming of age as a suffragist, Moore's political interests were less liberal than egalitarian. This force behind her work, combined with the prudishness about sexuality inherent in American Presbyterianism that went, in her case, unchallenged by expatriation, led to an attitude towards human animality in which intimations of sexuality were unwelcome because they would divert attention away from the more democratic message that might be learned from seeing humans as animals.

How are we to understand this message? Charles Molesworth points out the "semantic balancing act of referring equally to man and animal" in "The Pangolin," a poem of the mid-1930's (122). He emphasizes the artistry and wit that allow her to develop such an ambiguity. But this ambiguity is not cultivated for its own sake. It is in the service of a moral purpose. Notice how in the last stanzas of the poem the virtues of the pangolin-man are inextricable from the bodily expression of those virtues:

> Among animals, *one* has a sense of humor.
> Humor saves a few steps, it saves years. Unignorant,
>   modest and unemotional, and all emotion,
> he has everlasting vigor,
>   power to grow
>   though there are few creatures who can make one
>   breathe faster and make one erecter.
>
> Not afraid of anything is he,
>   and then goes cowering forth, tread paced to meet an obstacle

at every step. Consistent with the
formula – warm blood, no gills, two pairs of hands and a few hairs – that
is a mammal; there he sits in his own habitat,
serge-clad, strong-shod. The prey of fear, he, always
curtailed, extinguished, thwarted by the dusk, work partly done,
says to the alternating blaze,
'Again the sun!
anew each day; and new and new and new,
that comes into and steadies my soul.' (119-120)

The pangolin's careful but fearless tread is what reveals him, the "prey of fear," as steadfast and vigorous. His reluctance to move, his efficiency, manifests a sense of humor, an acceptance of the limits of his power. His retiring at dusk shows him to be patient and capable of hope. His virtues can be known because of how he embodies them.

I would like to suggest why it is worthwhile to draw attention to Moore's way of valuing of embodiment by pointing out how it can augment the work of the American philosopher Judith Butler, a thinker decidedly influenced by Continental thought and one Frost acknowledges as important to her own arguments. For Frost, Butler is important because of her "model of disrupting the conventions and codes that help define and fix difference" (xxiv). In Butler's major work on this subject, *Bodies That Matter*, her interest is in how subjectivity is constituted by a disavowal of an abject sphere of embodied experience. As Butler puts the crux of her argument: "the construction of gender operates through *exclusionary* means, such that the human is not only produced over and against the inhuman, but through a set of foreclosures, radical erasures, that are, strictly speaking, refused the possibility of cultural articulation" (8). Butler's emphasis on sexuality is made clearest when she specifies which kinds of bodies are denied "cultural articulation": "the regime of heterosexuality operates to circumscribe and contour the 'materiality' of sex, and that 'materiality' is formed and sustained through and as a materialization of regulatory norms that are in part those of heterosexual hegemony" (15). In her focus on sexuality as the domain of exclusion in the hegemonic constitution of the subject, Butler participates in the particularly European tradition of skeptical writing that Frost uses her to describe. An attitude towards embodiment more influenced by Moore than Stein, by contrast, would emphasize animality as the founding exclusion, and would take some distance from strongly held sexual identities in the name of a more thoroughgoing egalitarianism.

I have described Moore's prudishness as particularly American for a number of reasons. One further source of this emphasis on the importance of embodiment in manifesting virtue from inside a decidedly American intellectual tradition can be found in the work of Moore's Bryn Mawr teacher of philosophy, Theodore de

Laguna. De Laguna's 1910 *Dogmatism and Evolution* mounts the argument that pragmatists, particularly William James and John Dewey, have not been thoroughgoing enough in their anti-idealist approaches to logic. For de Laguna, there is no kind of thought, or reflection, that is not determined by the adaptive processes of the human organism: "Thought," he writes, "instead of being regarded as the end and determinant of organic development, is a product and (more importantly) a moment, or factor, in that development, – a factor whose existence and nature are throughout conditioned by the part it has to perform in organic life" (120). De Laguna places thought on the continuum of adaptive resources available to animal life: "The peculiar survival-value of consciousness appears to consist in the fact that it provides a more minute adjustment of reaction to external stimulus than is afforded any other organic agency" (124). By situating consciousness within the animal kingdom, de Laguna draws attention to the substance on which subjectivity is founded, not that of heterodox desire but of organic life in all of its potentially embarrassing but often virtuous diversity of forms. This was the matter that Moore too celebrated in her unusual way.

Works Cited

Butler, Judith. *Bodies That Matter*. New York: Routledge, 1993.

De Laguna, Theodore. *Dogmatism and Evolution*. New York: The Macmillan Company, 1910.

Frost, Elizabeth A. *The Feminist Avant-Garde in American Poetry*. Iowa City: University of Iowa Press, 2003.

Howard, Richard. "Marianne Moore and the Monkey Business of Modernism." *Marianne Moore: The Art of a Modernist*. Ed. Joseph Parini. Ann Arbor: UMI Research Press, 1990. 1-12.

Molesworth, Charles. *Marianne Moore: A Literary Life*. New York: Atheneum, 1990.

—. "Moore's Masterpiece: The Pangolin's Alternating Blaze." *Marianne Moore: Woman and Poet*. Ed. Patricia C. Willis. Orono: National Poetry Foundation, 1990. 95-126.

Moore, Marianne. *The Complete Poems of Marianne Moore*. New York: Macmillan, 1980.

Tender Mutton: Recipes, Sexual Identity and Spinster Resistance in Gertrude Stein

Katharina Vester

When Gertrude Stein and Alice Toklas returned for a visit to the United States in 1934, *The New York Times* was intrigued by two observations: the clarity of Stein's language and the unintelligibility of her attire. An article on October 25th, titled "Gertrude Stein Arrives and Baffles Reporters by Making Herself Clear," described Stein as "square-shouldered," her facial expressions as "enigmatic," and paid much attention to her apparel:

> Her feet were in thick woolly stockings and round-toed, flat-heeled oxfords. A brownish tweed suit covered a cerise vest of voluminous proportions and a mannish shirt of cream and black stripes. The hat was a Stein hat, a hat as persistent as the repetitions which are a feature of her abstruse writings. Peaked in front of her candid brown eyes, it roamed backward tightly about the close-cropped head to a fold at the rear; a gay hat which gave her the appearance of having just sprung from Robin Hood's forest to enunciate another word pattern of her own literature – literature which she said must await the reverence of our grandchildren's children. (25)

The metaphoric amalgamation of text and textile in this passage reveals that the transgression of which Stein's clothes are accused is not mere lack of taste but lies in their gender-specific ambiguity. The flaw of the flat-heeled shoes, the mannish shirt, the vest, the cropped head and the *pièce de résistance* – the gay Robin Hood hat roaming of its own will – is that they transgress the gender norms of the 1930s, a decade of flowing dresses, shiny materials and feminine cuts. Stein, who is known to have spent much thought, effort and money on the details of her clothes, [1] created on this October day her own textile reference, enigmatic and potentially subversive in terms of sexuality and gender norms. Fashion is a highly gendered system of signification and it accorded women authority and expert status before many other discourses did so, if only within certain limits. Playing with and challenging the limitation of the expertise granted to women is a strategy that Stein also used in *Tender Buttons.*

[1] On Stein and her clothes, see, for instance, Kathryn Kent, *Making Girls into Women*, 150ff.

The title of *Tender Buttons*, like the whole text, is rich in multi-layered meanings, one of them obviously referring to fashion. This becomes apparent in passages such as "A Feather," which follows a section on "Colored Hats": "A feather is trimmed, it is trimmed by the light and the bug and the post, it is trimmed by little leaning and by all sorts of mounted reserves and loud volumes. It is surely cohesive" (25). The focus shifts here from center to margin, from the hat to its trimmings, one of which is the feather. But of course a feather is also an instrument of writing which needs to be trimmed to be put to use, and which needs to lean a little to be able to do its work. The result may then be "loud volumes," books that are predictable in their cohesiveness. Cohesiveness, too much unity, clarity and closure, is surely something Stein does not want – neither in clothing nor in writing. Here the text relates fashion (specifically a hat) to writing – a combination that foreshadows the Stein hat of *The New York Times* article of twenty years later – and at the same time borrows the female gendered authority in matters of fashion and taste for the production of poetry.

In this essay I will argue that Gertrude Stein playfully utilized and subverted the culturally constructed genderedness of discourses in *Tender Buttons*, using such discourses as fashion, household management, and cooking – all areas which granted women expertise – against scientific discourses and those of modernist writing associated with masculine authority. In the process, she questioned not only the authority of all discourses, but also their effects regulating identity categories and the use of language. Shattering the linguistic and rhetorical rules of discourses renders their effects unpredictable, subverting their normative power. This aesthetic as well as political stratcgy can be found throughout the text.

Tender Buttons consists of passages of differing lengths with short titles such as "A Piano," "A Chair," "Roastbeef," "Sugar." Since most titles refer to food or objects, these brief texts have also been called "still lifes." These "still lifes" are organized into three sections or chapters: "Objects – Food – Rooms," with food at the center of the work.

As with fashion, food discourses and practices serve the production of a seemingly stable, homogenous and hegemonic heterosexual masculinity and its others. Like fashion, food discourses accepted and produced female experts, such as the authors of domestic advice literature. The genre of domestic advice written by and for women was firmly established in US culture by the middle of the 19th century. Stein uses and subverts characteristic elements of this genre that helped to normalize proper womanhood and heterosexual relations, in order to write about women's creative production and intimate relations to other women.[2] She is, on

[2] It has been suggested, for instance, by Pamela Hadas in "Spreading the Difference," that *Tender Buttons* can be read as reflecting Alice B. Toklas's moving into her apartment at 27, Rue de Fleurus and Leo Stein's moving out (57-75). Kathryn Kent in *Making Girls into Women* suggests

the one hand, ridiculing the normative functions of this genre, but using it on the other as an alternative voice to the male-connoted scientific discourses that claim sole authority over the definition and description of female homosexuality in the early 20th century.

There are numerous allusions to advice literature in *Tender Buttons*. Sentences such as "Dirt and not copper makes a color darker (13)," "Sugar is not a vegetable" (9), or "Light blue and the same red with purple makes a change" (10), resonate not only with the language of household manuals but also its concern with cleaning, cooking, decoration and fashion. [3] The specific discourse with its linguistic and stylistic peculiarities is adapted and dissolved since the advice given is nonsensical. This adds not only an aesthetic dimension to the text, but also serves as resistance against hegemonic discourses organizing gender, the nuclear family and women's sexuality in advice literature.

One example of the complex use of cookbook discourse in *Tender Buttons* is the passage "Roastbeef," which opens the "Food" section: "Please spice, please no name, place a whole weight, sink into a standard rising, raise a circle, choose a right around, make the resonance accounted and gather green any collar" (37). Here the text moves slowly from "please" into the imperative structure of advice literature or, specifically, the recipe (the allusion to "collard greens" enforces the connection to food). Imperative structures of verbs such as "spice," "place," "gather" can be found throughout the entire "Food" section, evoking associations with recipe writing. One of the effects of the recipe's imperative structure is that it lends normative authority to the text, it signals to the reader that an expert is talking and that his or her words need to be followed. But the reader of "Roastbeef" is not told what to do, the instructions given remain opaque. The emptiness of the instructions undermines the construction of authority through language (it is the imperative that creates the expert) and its normativity. Stein's "recipes" claim authority while at the same time exposing how the language of household manuals is normative. But these subversively altered "recipes" do not demand authority over the reader or the reading process, since the opaqueness obscures any potential instruction and renders any predictable action or reaction by the reader impossible. The authority claimed is an authority to speak, but without normative force.

Traditionally, cookbooks allowed women to publish, together with their recipes, their ideas on society, family life and their communities, and gave them

---

that the references to advice literature represent the influence Toklas had on Stein and her actual voice coming through in Stein's poetry. I believe that a biographical reading limits the possible political and poetic implications of *Tender Buttons*. As Leigh Gilmore observes in reference to Stein's *Autobiography of Alice B. Toklas*, biographical explanations "miniaturize" Stein's writings (199).

3 On the references to cookbook writing in *Tender Buttons*, see also Marguerite Murphy, " 'Familiar Strangers': The Household Words of Gertrude Stein's 'Tender Buttons,'" 384ff.

the chance to speak – within the conventions of the genre – for themselves. Their authority and expertise in this realm was mostly unchallenged, and created a space for their expression and for a possible resistance of a kind that they lacked in the more privileged discourses, such as modernist poetry. The passage from "Roastbeef," moving from the "please" to the imperative, introduces a voice that is no longer willing to plead not to be defined from the outside ("please no name") but demands the authority to speak for herself.

The subsequent paragraph abandons the imperative structure and leads to a form of serial infinitive constructions often found in 19th century cookbooks:

> To bury a slender chicken, to raise an old feather, to surround a garland and to bake a pole splinter, to suggest a repose and to settle simply, to surrender one another, to succeed saving simpler, to satisfy a singularity and not be blinder, to sugar nothing darker and to read redder, to have the color better, to sort out dinner, to remain together, to surprise no sinner, to curve nothing sweeter, to continue thinner, to increase in resting recreation to design string not dimmer. (38)

Infinitive constructions like these were commonly used as headings for instructions on basic techniques that could be generally applied. Like the linguistic function of the infinitive, these headings signify the unaltered, unconjugated techniques of cooking. In Eliza Leslie's best-selling 19th-century *Directions for Cookery*, one can find headings such as "to roast beef," "to boil a salted or pickeled [sic] tongue" or "to corn beef." But the techniques Stein's text evokes here are very different: "to sort out dinner," "to suggest a repose" or "to remain together" may be basic techniques of living together and making a relationship work, while "to surrender one another," "to satisfy a singularity," "to surprise no sinner," "to curve nothing sweeter" seem to be sexually charged.

"Roastbeef," which seems to begin with a sunset and a flashback to the previous night, is full of language that is sexually evocative, in tone as well as in content: "Lovely snipe and tender turn, excellent vapor and slender butter, all the splinter and the trunk, all the poisonous darkning drunk, all the joy in weak success, all the joyful tenderness, all the section and the tea, all the stouter symmetry" (35). More than the references to fluids and odors, the simple, happily galloping rhyme seems to catch the atmosphere of a guiltless sexual encounter. The "symmetry" of the passage takes up a prominent motif of "Roastbeef," the playfully staged collapse of the binary opposition between difference and sameness that crescendos in a breathless variation of the word "kind": "The time when there are four choices and there are four choices in a difference, the time when there are four choices there is a kind and there is a kind. There is a kind. There is a kind" (36). The paragraph ends "The kindly way to feel separating is to have a space between. This shows a likeness" (37). While one of the themes of "Roastbeef" is the production of meaning, for which the distinction between difference and identity is crucial, on another level it discusses how to make meaning out of sexual intimacy between two women – who are of the same sex but nonetheless of different bodies. This is what the text points to (with a wink and great humor) in the destabilization of another binary opposition: that between thick and thin. The bodies involved come "in kind cuts" but inhabit "thick and thin spaces" (34), they are no longer distinguished by differences in their sexual organs but by their shapes and textures. This discussion of the meaning of an erotic encounter between two women is furthered in the passage on "use," mocking contemporary opinion that homosexual acts are a sin against nature since they do not result in reproduction. "There is no use there is no use at all in smell, in taste, in teeth, in toast in anything, there is no use at all and the respect is mutual" (35), the text announces self-confidently, and earlier: "All the time that there is use there is use" (33). Not only is giving and receiving pleasure "use" enough, Stein also plays here with older meanings of the word "use" that referred to sexual intercourse.

The references to furniture, pieces of decor, household objects like spoons, curtains, doors, and tables create a room for this intimacy, a safe space, and a space that, with references to food preparation and discourses, is marked as feminine. The text, with its allusions to cookbook and recipe writing, advises with authority on the basic "techniques" for a successful intimate relationship between two women, but the opaqueness of the passage also protects it from pornographically or scientifically exploitative readings.

Images of age and aging are prominent in "Food," too. In a few passages a voice seems to surface momentarily, the voice of an older woman, surprised by finding love late in life, but determined to enjoy it: "Anyway, to be older and ageder is not a surfeit nor a suction, it is not dated and careful, it is not dirty. . . . Why should ancient lambs be goats and young colts and never beef, why should they, they should because there is so much difference in age" ("Roastbeef," 36). In the earlier passage "In-Between" (24), a sentence says two "old ladies" live in a "perfectly unprecedented arrangement." The "old ladies" are mentioned together with virgins ("A virgin, a whole virgin"), suggesting the old ladies may be virgins – as they have had no sexual experience with men, which leaves them not unfulfilled or imperfect, since they are nonetheless "whole." The slide from virgin to old ladies hints simultaneously at the misperceived asexuality of older women and at lesbian lifestyles. Stein playfully claims the place of the old virgin lady, the spinster, as a position to inhabit and from which to speak.

While lesbians were generally invisible and voiceless in American culture before the early 20th century, the spinster was a well-known figure in the public imagination of the 19th century. Older, unmarried and in Victorian ideology therefore often marginalized women gained limited visibility and authority in their function as a negative model for young women. At the same time the spinster is a character important for the household manual of the 19th century. Advice literature not only gave instructions on cooking, decorating or mending clothes, it also presented a normative discourse on how families should be structured, what women's duties and roles were as wives and mothers, what the American home should look like, and how women had to behave. Therefore advice literature supported an effort to stabilize hegemonic discourses on separate gendered spheres, heterosexual marriages and ideals of womanly behavior, although the authors of domestic manuals themselves were often deviant from the norm. Many were working for pay as journalists or editors, for instance, or were politically engaged in the suffrage or abolitionist movements. [4] Since these texts often carried an ideology of devoted motherhood and committed wifeliness, they steered themselves into a narrative dilemma: the ideal woman they promoted had neither the time nor any business writing books. If the author was apparently less than ideal, her expertise was questionable. The spinster served as a narrative strategy out of this dilemma. The spinster, in the form of an older unmarried aunt, for instance, keeping house for more fortunate relatives, had the expertise, the time and credible motive in instructing others how to avoid her fate. The spinster, as a persona for the author, could credibly pronounce upon gender ideals. But while doing so, the spinster herself was standing outside these norms, challenging the idea that women needed to be wives and mothers, and embodying the proof that women could survive outside the nuclear family. The spinster is positively connoted in these household manuals: she stands for women's knowledge and expertise. But in medical accounts of female homosexuality in the early 20th century, the spinster was often associated with lesbian women or suffragettes. [5] The spinster is therefore – in all her ambivalence – a culturally established and visible figure for women outside the heteronormative order. In *Tender Buttons*, Stein explores these inherent contradictions in the figure of the spinster and puts them to poetic use. While the spinster's voice in household manuals was instrumentalized to pronounce on heterosexual norms, her voice is borrowed for brief, transient moments in *Tender Buttons* to speak for the spinster

---

4 Lydia Maria Child, for instance, was an abolitionist, and Catherine Beecher vehemently promoted the education of women. She argued that the home is so essential to a healthy nation that it cannot be left in the hands of the untrained. These examples show that the separate spheres of the 19th century did limit women's possibilities on the one hand, but also empowered them and allowed them to use their moral and domestic expertise in creative and strategic fashions. See, for instance, Mary Anna DuSablon's *America's Collectible Cookbooks* and Charlotte Biester's articles "Milestones in American Cookery Literature" and "The Story in the American Cookbook."

5 See for instance *The New York Times Book Review* of 1913, qtd. in Jonathan Katz, *The Gay/Lesbian Almanac*, 341.

herself as an alternative model to normative womanhood, when talking about the pleasures an older woman can find in love and sexual fulfillment.

Evidently, the traditional discourse of household manuals that affirms the heterosexual family is punctured and disturbed in *Tender Buttons*,[6] but at the same time it remains a visible structuring element. Stein's text accumulates textual objects, food, and rooms to create a discursive home that can serve as an alternative to the home of normative discourses. Many of the objects in the text therefore come with a small difference: the buttons are tender, the glass of the carafe is blind, the cushion is not described but the substance filling it is, and so forth. As Stein remarks (perhaps slightly threateningly) at the beginning of *Tender Buttons:* "The difference is spreading" (9). All these objects that are a little different create a home that is a little different. As Marguerite Murphy suggests, *Tender Buttons* creates an alternative home for a homosexual family.[7] The spinster's voice pronounces and makes her own home and takes authority over her own life.

But Stein's text does not end here. The household manuals of the 19th century were based on the idea that the home produces the identities of the people who live in it. Color, pictures, and furniture not only built character, they were believed to create men, women, Christians, white middle-class Americans. The 19th century generated the idea of masculine and feminine rooms. The gendered rooms were the floor plan for the heterosexual family home. Objects and their decoration were thought of in moral terms – a piece of furniture that was veneered, for instance, was dishonest, and fashionable geometric patterns were considered trite and flimsy, not as durable or elevating as patterns that mimicked nature, such as leaves, flowers, or garlands. Honest, durable, and natural furniture and decoration were considered to produce honest, durable, and natural people – the right kind of people.[8]

Gertrude Stein's "home with a difference" that consists of all these differing objects therefore creates people with a difference. The rooms become non-normative spaces that make room for non-normative identities. Non-normative identities otherwise had little space at the time when *Tender Buttons* was published. Science, especially the newly established disciplines of psychology and sexology, catalogued non-normative sexual behaviors in long encyclopedias of perversions – treating the pervert, invert, and hypersexual as objects to be restrained by acts of definition.

The scientific community in Europe and the US had been intrigued by homosexuality since the 1860s. Same-sex sexual acts were no longer understood

---

6 This thought is developed in Franziska Gygax, "Gender and Genre in Gertrude Stein," 22ff.

7 See Marguerite Murphy, " 'Familiar Strangers': The Household Words of Gertrude Stein's 'Tender Buttons.'"

8 See Sarah Leavitt, *From Catherine Beecher to Martha Stewart,* 35-37.

as isolated events, as sins or vice, but rather as behavior committed by a certain kind of people – sick, criminal, degenerate people: the homosexuals. While before then the homosexual act was considered a choice, it now was fate. Sexologists catalogued non-normative sexual behaviors in long encyclopedias of perversions – treating the pervert, the invert, and the hypersexual as objects to be restrained by acts of definition. The pervert was classified, catalogued, measured, examined, displayed. These scientific taxonomies are countered by Stein with the associative logic of *Tender Buttons*. Stein seems here to explore the poetic potential of cookbooks that connect in their table of contents such diverse objects and activities as these listed in a classic 19th century cookbook: "Anthracite coal grates," "Astral lamps (management of,)," "Black silk sleeves (to restore when faded,)," "Bonnets (straw or Leghorn – to clean,)," "Buff dye (an excellent one,)," "Book-muslin dresses (to wash,)," "China (to pack,)," "Coat (gentleman's – to fold,)," "Faded dresses (to bleach,)," "Fruit stains (to remove)," "Ink (to make,)," "Ink spots (to remove,)," "Lawn (bishop's – to wash)," "Lamp oil (to extract from a dress,)," "Marabout feathers (to clean,)," "Muslins (smell – to do up,)," "Nankeen (to wash,)," "New wood (to remove its taste,)," "Pink dye," "Preparing rooms for summer," "Packing a large trunk," "Remedies for stings, &c," "Swansdown cape (to wash,)," "Soft soap (to make,)," and "White-washing." Behind these activities that Eliza Leslie lists among many others in the table of contents of her *Directions of Cookery* we perceive not only the endless drudgery of the housewife's everyday work, we also perceive something magical and enigmatic in these items taken out of their historical context. Why would somebody need to clean "Marabout feathers"? What does new wood taste like? Why bleach an already faded dress? The list creates its own poetics and meanings in such accidental juxtapositions as the ink that needs to be made and the ink spot that needs to be removed. Narrative moments emerge, piquing the reader's curiosity (How did the lamp oil get on the dress? Where will the large trunk go?). The enumeration of activities and objects creates its own almost Borgesian logic. These poetic and structural effects of cookbook-logic, contradicting scientific logic, can be found in *Tender Buttons* and its reflection on "A Carafe, That is a Blind Glass," "Glazed Glitter," or "A Substance in a Cushion," (9) – to quote from only the first page. In this text, the home and its intimacy create their own logic and taxonomy that cannot be vanquished by scientific definitions. Stein's poetic logic thus undermines science's claim to "truth" and to an exhaustive description of "reality."

Scientific logic declared that the homosexual, if not "cured" by an expert, would be a pervert for the rest of his or her life, even if she or he never committed a single sexual act.[9] Since the lesbian was understood to be mannish, it was the

9 For more information, see Rudi Bleys's *The Geography of Perversion*.

scientific community's consensus that a telltale sign of a female homosexual was an enlarged clitoris. [10] These women could therefore be cured, it was believed, by clitoridectomy. [11]

The passage called "Mutton" that follows "Roastbeef" is far darker in tone and imagery. References to cuts and cutting that seem to refer in "Roastbeef" non-menacingly to discourses of food preparation, and to the domestic and private sphere, here become an open threat. Imagery of light and darkness introduced earlier now condenses to unmitigated darkness and bleakness. Where "Roastbeef" celebrates all forms of hope ("Hope in gates, hope in spoons, hope in doors, hope in tables ..." [37]), hate and emptiness seem to dominate "Mutton" (39).

The imagery changes from objects of daily life representing the security of the familiar to an alien and hostile setting. Instead of glasses, vases and other familiar things, the text now speaks of a "receptacle" (40). Indifference to the specificity of the object is not without danger, the text warned before: "A sentence of a vagueness that is violence is authority" (38). From the "in doors" (37) of "Roastbeef" the text moves to the "exterior" that is defined by "pain" in "Mutton" (41). The images conjured up to populate this unprotecting space include "students," "principal," "eye glasses," "glass eyes," "specimen," "salve," and "lecture" (39-41), evoking academic, medical and scientific discourses regulating and constituting the world beyond the safety of a home. Since "learning" causes "suffering" (39), there is no longer the protection granted in "Roastbeef." There are no longer subjects (39), only specimens (40), and even they wither to letters (39), since "A sign is a specimen spoken" (41).

"Roastbeef" and "Mutton" begin the food section, reminding the reader of the 19th century culinary preference for mature meat, and wittily referring to the pleasures shared by bodies that are no longer "colts." But while "Roastbeef" presents a celebration of sexuality in the beginning before it turns darker in tone at the end, "Mutton" emphasizes the fragile and endangered status of the lovers who formerly were playfully entangled in the safety of their own domestic discourse. The threat in the references to "section[s]," "denting," "cutting," "darkness," "undertaker," and "bone" (39-41) is not hollow, since the result presented at the end is a salve, made of "mutton and liquor" (41). The mutton has been ground up by the violence inherent in the vagueness of the authoritative discourses that have spoken it.

In these passages, *Tender Buttons* presents a counter-hegemonic discourse: women's intimate relationships are described as multi-faceted and fragmented, impossible to be defined from the outside, especially not by scientific logic, but

---

10 See also Margaret Gibson's "Clitoral Corruption: Body Metaphors and American Homosexuality, 1870-1900."

11 See, for instance, Dr. E. F. Daniel's proposal to "castrate" female and male homosexuals to cure them and to protect society (qtd. in Katz 241-243).

as experiences of moments in which the distinction between sameness and difference implodes – if only within the protected space of the text. In the process, the concept of identity itself is altered. Women enjoying an intimate relationship together is not described in *Tender Buttons* as the effect of a certain clearly defined identity; it is first and foremost defined as a practice – or as a sum of practices, including both sexual encounters and the daily work of making a home together.

While she reworks the concept of "identity" from a stable state into practices, Stein also subverts traditional ideas of the "still life." Through the long history of art, still lifes presented food to the observer from the perspective of the eater. The food in painted still lifes is usually ready to be "served" – it has already been bought, washed, arranged, and decorated – work that still today is mostly done by women, as sociological data confirm. [12] Stein's still lifes are different: they carry titles such as "Roast Potatoes," "Cooking," "Salad Dressing and an Artichoke," titles that could also refer to recipes and advice in household manuals. Recipes, unlike still lifes, present food not as ready to be consumed but as in need of preparation. The perspective of the one preparing the food and that of the one being served the food is associated with gender. As Susan Bordo puts it, "Men eat and women prepare" (*Unbearable Weight* 117). [13] Stein constantly switches between the two perspectives of the recipe and the still life, oscillating between "defining" or "describing" and "instructing" or "advising" on objects and foods. (In not really fulfilling our expectations, and neither defining nor advising in the traditional sense, she is constantly making us aware of these practices as linguistic strategies.) She moves back and forth between the perspective of the producer of food and the perspective of the one being served the food, thus creating a truly cubist moment in looking upon food items with a slightly cross-eyed gaze that produces a number of perspectives simultaneously, while at the same time destabilizing their genderedness. [14] Folding masculine- and feminine-connoted discourses into each other creates an effect of textual gender inversion, which deconstructs gender's traditional binary organization and yields an aesthetics beyond a heteronormative organization of language.

The effect of destabilizing heteronormativity is further extended by the constant sexualization of her recipes/still lifes. The women interacting in *Tender Buttons* feed and consume each other mutually. The distinction between the one who

---

[12] See, for instance, Nickie Charles and Marion Kerr, *Women, Food and Family*, or Marjorie DeVault, *Feeding the Family*.

[13] For the elaboration of her argument, see Susan Bordo, *Unbearable Weight* 117-121.

[14] Canadian photographer Margaret Watkins experimented at almost the same time that *Tender Buttons* was written with new versions of still lifes. Her photograph "The Kitchen Sink" of 1919 shows dirty dishes in a sink. The food has already been eaten and only work is what is left. In another picture we see eggs next to a sink, waiting to be processed. See Mary O'Connor, "The Objects of Modernism."

is eating and the one who is feeding is meaningless in Stein's representation of women's intimacy. Loving another woman in *Tender Buttons* is eating your cake, but baking it, too.

Kathryn Kent has pointed out that there are further "gender parodies" in *Tender Buttons,* referring to the use of "husband," "wife," "wedding" and similar heterosexual concepts (157). Using the discourse of household manuals in modernist poetry is itself "gender parody" on a stylistic level. Stein here not only blurs the borders between high and low literature, or literature and non-literature, she also challenges with humor the distinction between feminine- and masculine-connoted discourses. [15] In appropriating the spinster as voice in *Tender Buttons*, she satirizes the notion of male genius. Through these various strategies, *Tender Buttons* becomes a unique blending of not-so-still lifes, recipes for sexual conduct, subverted traditions of high art, and shattered expert discourses. In the end it no longer resembles any of its elements, but develops a life and character of its own, very much like the gay and persistent Robin Hood hat on Gertrude Stein's cropped head.

Works Cited

Beecher, Catharine E., and Harriet Beecher Stowe. *American Woman's Home*. New York: J.B. Ford and Company, 1869.

Biester, Charlotte. "Milestones in American Cookery Literature." *Journal of the American Diet Association* 31.12 (1955): 1214-1217.

—. "The Story in the American Cookbook." *Journal of the American Diet Association* 29.10 (1953): 988-992.

Bleys, Rudi C. *The Geography of Perversion: Male-to-male Sexual Behavior Outside the West and the Ethnographic Imagination, 1750-1918.* New York: New York University Press, 1995.

Bordo, Susan. *Unbearable Weight: Feminism, Western Culture and the Body*. Berkeley: University of California Press, 1993.

Charles, Nickie, and Marion Kerr. *Women, Food, and Families.* Manchester: Manchester University Press, 1988.

Child, Lydia Maria. *The American Frugal Housewife*. Boston: Carter and Hendee, 1832.

DeVault, Marjorie L. *Feeding the Family: The Social Organization of Caring as Gendered Work*. Chicago: The University of Chicago Press, 1991.

DuSablon, Mary Anna. *America's Collectible Cookbooks: The History, the Politics, the Recipes*. Athens: Ohio University Press, 1994.

---

[15] Franziska Gygax in *Gender and Genre in Gertrude Stein* asserts that gender and genre are connected, since "Hierarchies, classifications, and categories are fundamental characteristics of both gender and genre" (1). She further argues that women often wrote in the genre that was assigned to them and names the novel as a female-connoted genre and poetry as a male-connoted genre. Gygax, supporting her views by citing French feminist theory, concludes that challenging genre often challenges the notion of gender at the same time.

"Gertrude Stein Arrives and Baffles Reporters by Making Herself Clear." *New York Times* 25 Oct. 1934: 25.

Gibson, Margaret. "Clitorial Corruption: Body Metaphors and American Homosexuality, 1870-1900." Ed. Vernon A. Rosario. *Science and Homosexualities*. New York: Routledge, 1997. 108-132.

Gilmore, Leigh. *Autobiographics: A Feminist Theory of Women's Self-Representation*. Ithaca: Cornell University Press, 1994.

Gygax, Franziska. *Gender and Genre in Gertrude Stein*. Westport: Greenwood Press, 1998.

Hadas, Pamela. "Spreading the Difference: One Way to Read Gertrude Stein's *Tender Buttons*." *Twentieth Century Literature* 24.1 (1978): 57-75.

Katz, Jonathan Ned. *Gay/Lesbian Almanac: A New Documentary*. New York: Caroll & Graf Publishers, Inc., 1983.

Kent, Kathryn R. *Making Girls into Women: American Women's Writing and the Rise of Lesbian Identity*. Durham: Duke University Press, 2003.

Leavitt, Sarah A. *From Catherine Beecher to Martha Stewart: A Cultural History of Domestic Advice*. Chapel Hill: University of North Carolina Press, 2002.

Leslie, Eliza. *Directions for Cookery, In Its Various Branches*. Philadelphia: E.L. Carey and Hart, 1840.

Murphy, Marguerite S. " 'Familiar Strangers': The Household Words of Gertrude Stein's 'Tender Buttons.'" *Contemporary Literature* 32.3 (1991): 383-401.

O'Connor, Mary. "The Objects of Modernism: Everyday Life in Women's Magazines, Gertrude Stein, and Margaret Watkins." Ed. Jay Bochner and Justin D. Edwards. *American Modernism across the Arts*. Studies on Themes and Motifs in Literature. New York: Peter Lang, 1999. 97-123.

Rosario, Vernon A. "Inversion's Histories/History's Inversions: Novelizing Fin-de-Siècle Homosexuality." Ed. Vernon A. Rosario. *Science and Homosexualities*. New York: Routledge, 1997. 69-107.

Stein, Gertrude. *Tender Buttons: Objects, Food, Rooms*. Kobenhavn: Green Integer, 2002.

Contributors

Michel Delville teaches English and American literatures, as well as comparative literature, at the University of Liège, where he directs the Interdisciplinary Center for Applied Poetics (http://www.ulg.ac.be/cipa/). He is the author of several books including *J.G. Ballard* (1998), *Hamlet & Co* (2001; with Pierre Michel), *Frank Zappa, Captain Beefheart, and the Secret History of Maximalism* (2005; with Andrew Norris), and *The American Prose Poem*, which won the 1998 SAMLA Studies Book Award. He recently coedited three volumes of essays on postwar poetry (*The Mechanics of the Mirage*, 2000; *Sound as Sense: US Poetry &/In Music*, 2004; *Poésie, Musique, Modernité,* 2004). His new book, *Food, Poetry, and the Aesthetics of Consumption: Eating the Avant-Garde*, has just been published by Routledge in January 2008.

Nikolai Duffy teaches at Royal Holloway, University of London. His major research interests are in contemporary poetics and Continental philosophy. He has published articles on Rosmarie Waldrop, Andrew Joron, Maurice Blanchot and Samuel Beckett; he is currently preparing a monograph on Rosmarie Waldrop.

Astrid Franke received her PhD at the John-F.-Kennedy Institute, Berlin for *Keys to Controversies: Stereotypes in Modern American Novels*, and her *Habilitation* at the Johann Wolfgang Goethe-Universität Frankfurt for "'Pursue the Illusion': Problems of Public Poetry in America." She has published articles on popular culture, aesthetic theory, Pragmatism, and African American literature. Currently she teaches at the Eberhard-Karls-Universität Tübingen.

Kornelia Freitag is Professor of American Studies at Ruhr-Universität Bochum. She has published *Cultural Criticism in Women's Experimental Writing: The Poetry of Rosmarie Waldrop, Lyn Hejinian and Susan Howe* (2006). Her major areas of research are cultural and literary theory, contemporary American poetry, and transnational literary developments.

Brian Brodhead Glaser is a lecturer in the English department at Chapman University. His essays on poetry have appeared or are forthcoming in *The Journal of Modern Literature*, *The Wallace Stevens Journal*, *Cercles*, *America and the Orient*, and *The William Carlos Williams Review*.

Walter Grünzweig is professor of American literature and culture at Universität Dortmund and adjunct professor at University of Pennsylvania, State University of New York at Binghamton, Canisius College and Karl-Franzens-Universität Graz. Central interests in research and teaching include European-American literary and cultural relations as well as the theory and pratice of student exchanges.

Philipp Horst studied English and American literature, art history, philosophy and geography at the universities Bochum and Newcastle. He does freelance work for von der Heydt-Museum, Wuppertal and K21, Düsseldorf. Currently he is doing Ph.D. research on language art. He works fulltime as a projectmanager at DASA, Dortmund.

Heinz Ickstadt, Prof. em. of American Literature at the Kennedy Institute of North American Studies, Free University Berlin, published widely on late nineteenth-century American literature and culture, the fiction and poetry of American modernism and postmodernism, on the relation of literature and painting as well as on the history and theory of American Studies; this includes books on the poetry of Hart Crane, the history of American fiction in the twentieth century (both in German) as well as a collection of his essays: *Faces of Fiction: Essays on American Literature and Culture from the Jacksonian Age to Postmodernity*. He was President of the German Association of American Studies from 1990 until 1993 and of the European Association of American Studies from 1996-2000.

Uwe Klawitter was born in Düsseldorf in 1962 and studied at the universities of Cologne, Düsseldorf and Cambridge, England. He has been teaching at the English Department of the Ruhr-Universität Bochum since 1995. His main research interests lie in the fields of Renaissance drama and contemporary English poetry, where he has recently published articles on intertextuality, intermediality and media criticism.

Kimberly Lamm is an assistant professor of English at Pratt Institute, where she also teaches in the Program in Critical and Visual Studies. Her current book project examines literary and visual portraiture in late nineteenth- and early twentieth-century American culture. A former Helena Rubinstein Fellow in Critical Studies in the Whitney Museum of American Art's Independent

Study Program, she has published essays on the poetry of Juliana Spahr, the art of Carrie Mae Weems and Lorna Simpson, and Theresa Hak Kyung Cha's *Dictee*.

Tony Lopez is the author of more than 20 books of poetry, fiction and criticism. His most recent poetry collections are *False Memory* (Salt, 2003) and *Devolution* (The Figures, 2000). He has received awards from The Wingate Foundation, The Society of Authors and the Arts and Humanities Research Council. His poetry is featured in many anthologies including *Twentieth-Century British and Irish Poetry* (Oxford), *Vanishing Points* (Salt), *Other* (Wesleyan) and *Conductors of Chaos* (Picador). His critical essays are collected in *Meaning Performance: Essays on Poetry* (Salt, 2006). He is well known as a poetry performer and has given readings throughout the UK, Europe and North America. He teaches in England at the University of Plymouth, where he was appointed the first Professor of Poetry in 2000. His website is at <http://www.tonylopez.org.uk>.

Born in Luanshya, Zambia in 1956, **Karen Mac Cormack** is the author of thirteen books of poetry. Titles include *Nothing by Mouth*, *Quill Driver*, *Quirks & Quillets*, *At Issue* and *Vanity Release*. Volume 1 of her polybiography *Implexures* was published by Chax Press/ West House Books in 2003 and *Implexures* in its entirety is forthcoming from the same publishers in early 2008. Her poetry is included in a number of anthologies: *Out of Everywhere: Linguistically Innovative Poetry by Women in North America and the UK*, *Vectors: New Poetics*, *Moving Borders (Three Decades of Innovative Writing by Women)*, and *The Art of Practice*, and has been translated into French, Portuguese, Swedish, and Norwegian. Mac Cormack is an advisor to the North American Centre for Interdisciplinary Poetics, and an advisory editor to the Centre Interdisciplinaire de Poétique Appliquée, Université de Liège, Belgium. Of dual British/Canadian citizenship she currently lives in the USA and teaches at the State University of New York at Buffalo.

Steve McCaffery is the author of more than 25 books of poetry and criticism. He was a founding member (with bp Nichol) of the Toronto Research Group and the sound poetry ensemble Four Horsemen. His next publication *Slightly Left of Thinking* is forthcoming from Chax Press. He teaches at the University at Buffalo where he is David Gray Chair of Poetry and Letters.

Deborah Meadows teaches in the Liberal Studies department at California State Polytechnic University, Pomona. Her works of poetry include: *involutia*

(Shearsman), *Thin Gloves* (Green Integer), *Representing Absence* (Green Integer), *Itinerant Men* (Krupskaya), and chapbooks, *The Draped Universe* (Belladonna* Books), *Growing Still* and "*The 60's and 70's:* from *The Theory of Subjectivity in Moby-Dick*" (both Tinfish Press). Electronic Poetry Center author page: <http://epc.buffalo.edu/authors/meadows/>.

Peter Middleton is Professor of English at the University of Southampton, UK. He is the author of books on masculinity, memory and most recently a collection of essays on contemporary poetry that particularly deals with the history and theory of performance, *Distant Reading* (University of Alabama Press). He has published many essays on modern poetry and fiction, and is also the author of a collection of poetry, Aftermath (Salt). His current project is a study of poetry and science in America since 1950.

Marjorie Perloff is the author of many books on twentieth-century poetry, poetics, and intermedia, including *The Poetics of Indeterminacy* (1981), *The Futurist Moment* (1986), *Radical Artifice: Writing Poetry in the Age of Media* (1992), *Wittgenstein's Ladder* (1996), and, most recently, *Differentials* (2004). She is Professor Emerita of English at Stanford University and currently Scholar in Residence at the University of Southern California. She was the 2006 President of the Modern Language Association of America.

Martina Pfeiler teaches and works in the American Studies Department at the University of Dortmund. After a year of teaching at Oglethorpe University, Atlanta, she is currently completing her PhD project on U.S. poetry from a Cultural Studies and Media Studies perspective. In 2003 she published the book *Sounds of Poetry: Contemporary American Performance Poetry.*

Brian Reed is an associate professor of English at the University of Washington, Seattle. He is the author of the book *Hart Crane: After His Lights* (2006) and a co-editor of the volume *Situating El Lissitzky: Vitebsk, Berlin, Moscow.* Other publications include articles on such poets as Susan Howe, Ezra Pound, Carl Sandburg, and Rosmarie Waldrop.

Susanne Rohr is a trained American Studies and German Studies Scholar. She received her academic education at the John F. Kennedy Institute of the Free University Berlin and Cornell University. From 1986-1994 Susanne Rohr was a member of the academic faculty at Stanford University, Study Center Berlin. As of October 2006 Susanne Rohr is full professor of American literature and culture and chair of American Studies at Hamburg University. She is the head of the research project "Art and Taboo: Recent Representations of the Holocaust in a Transatlantic Perspective." Susanne Rohr has published in the fields of literary and cultural theory, semiotics, American pragmatism, epistemology, and on a broad range of topics in American literature of the 19th and 20th centuries.

Sabine Sielke is Chair of North American Literature and Culture, Director of the North American Studies Program, the German-Canadian Centre, and the Forum Women's and Gender Studies at the University of Bonn. Her publications include *Reading Rape* (2002), *Fashioning the Female Subject* (1997), the series *Transcription*, the (co-)editions *Gender Talks* (2006), *Der 11. September 2001* (2002), *Making America* (2001) and *Engendering Manhood* (1998) as well as essays on poetry and poetics, modern and post-modern literature and culture, literary and cultural theory, gender and African American studies, popular culture, and the interfaces between cultural studies and the sciences.

Katharina Vester teaches American Studies at American University in Washington, D.C. Her 2007 dissertation, *A Taste of Power: Collaboration and Resistance in Culinary Texts,* is a Foucauldian study of food discourses surrounding contested boundaries of ethnic, sexual and gender identities in American culture.

Keith Waldrop's recent books of poetry include *The Real Subject* (Omnidawn), *The House Seen from Nowhere* (Litmus Press), and the trilogy: *The Locality Principle*, *The Silhouette of the Bridge* (America Award, 1997) and *Semiramis, If I Remember* (Avec Books). He has translated French poets like Anne-Marie Albiach, Claude Royet-Journoud, Paol Keineg, Dominique Fourcade, and Jean Grosjean. His translation of *The Flowers of Evil* is out from Wesleyan University Press. He teaches at Brown University.

Rosmarie Waldrop's trilogy (*The Reproduction of Profiles*, *Lawn of Excluded Middle* and *Reluctant Gravities*) has just been reprinted by New Directions under the title: *Curves to the Apple*. Other recent books of poetry are *Blindsight* (New Directions) and *Love, Like Pronouns* (Omnidawn). Her collected essays, *Dissonance (if you are interested)*, was published by University of Alabama Press in 2005. She lives in Providence, RI, where she co-edits Burning Deck books with Keith Waldrop.

Wolfgang Wicht was, until his early retirement, Professor of English Literature at the University of Potsdam. His publications include *Woolf Joyce Eliot: Kunstkonzeptionen und Künstlergestalten* (1981), *Utopianism in James Joyce's* Ulysses (2000) and a number of recent articles on various aspects of Joyce's works. He has published articles on Shakespeare, Woolf, Eliot, Yeats, Wilson Harris, Angus Wilson, Heaney and others.

Harald Zapf teaches American Studies at the University of Erlangen-Nürnberg. He is the author of *Dekonstruktion des Reinen: Hybridität und ihre Manifestationen im Werk von Ishmael Reed* (2002) and is currently working on his habilitation thesis on performance and performativity in 20th-century American poetic culture(s).

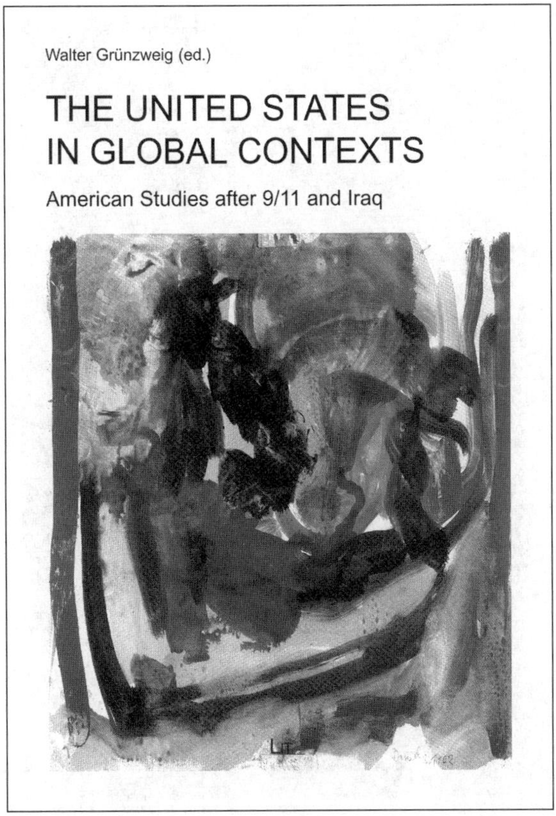

Transnational and Transatlantic American Studies

edited by Mita Banerjee (Siegen), Kornelia Freitag (Bochum), Walter Grünzweig (Dortmund), Randi Gunzenhäuser (Dortmund), Wilfried Raussert (Bielefeld), Michael Wala (Bochum)

Walter Grünzweig
The United States in Global Contexts
American Studies after 9/11 and Iraq
The momentous events since September 11, 2001, both challenged the field of American Studies and opened up new opportunities for research, teaching, and activism. This book presents more than 160 short contributions by Americanists and Non-Americanists from around the world in an essayistic brainstorm that brings together many questions asked about "America" and American Studies in the age of globalization. Die einschneidenden Veränderungen seit dem 11. September 2001 stellen für die Amerikanistik eine große Herausforderung dar, eröffnen aber auch neue Wege zu Forschung, Lehre und politischem Engagement. Die mehr als 160 Kurzbeiträge von Amerikanist/innen und Nicht-Amerikanist/innen aus vielen Teilen der Welt sind ein essayistischer brainstorm, der wichtige Fragen zu „Amerika" und zur Amerikanistik im Zeitalter der Globalisierung zusammenführt.
Bd. 1, 2004, 184 S., 19,90 €, br., ISBN 3-8258-8262-4

LIT Verlag Berlin – Hamburg – London – Münster – Wien – Zürich
Fresnostr. 2 48159 Münster
Tel.: 0251 / 620 32 22 – Fax: 0251 / 922 60 99
e-Mail: vertrieb@lit-verlag.de – http://www.lit-verlag.de

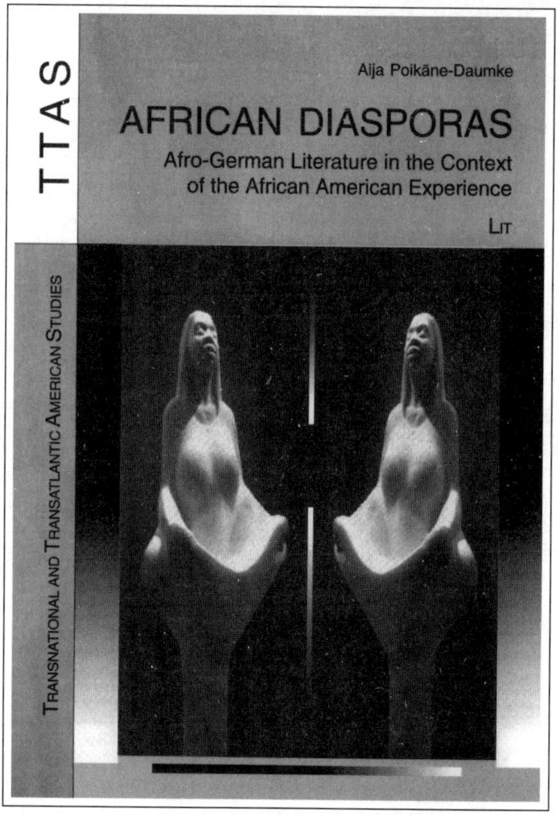
TTAS
Aija Poikāne-Daumke
AFRICAN DIASPORAS
Afro-German Literature in the Context
of the African American Experience
LIT
TRANSNATIONAL AND TRANSATLANTIC AMERICAN STUDIES

Kevin Cahill and Lene Johannessen (eds.)
CONSIDERING CLASS
Essays on the Discourse
of the American Dream
LIT

Rüdiger Kunow; Wilfried Raussert (eds.)
Cultural Memory and Multiple Identities
Memory is one of the most important ways in which we construct individual and collective identies. Memory constantly surrounds us as in literarture, films, historical accounts, psychologists' talk, or everyday conversations. At the same time, memory has become a culturally contested praxis in the context of 20th century identity politics inside and outside the academy. This book offers a comprehensive exploration of the discoursive construction of memory and seeks to explore the cultural work performed by these constructions. Approaching the juncture of memory and identity from an interdisciplinary and global and drawing on S. Hall's assertion that culture and identity are irrevocably intertwined through memory, the essays collected here provide informed readings on a variety of topics and contexts. In their opening remarks. the editors establish a context in which the interrelationships between culture, identity and memory are played off against the problematics of loss of and reinvention of „self" in a globalized and yet localized world. In this collection which brings together work by young American Studies scholars from various European contexts and disciplinary fields, the reader will find contributions located in cultural and literary studies, the visual arts, philosophy, and history. In its interdisciplinary and international orientation this book is a showcase of the important work done by the current generation of Americanists in Europe.
Bd. 5, 2007, 200 S., 19,90 €, br., ISBN 978-3-8258-8753-7

Nieves Pascual; Antonio (Eds.)
Feeling in Others
Essays on Suffering and Empathy in Modern Culture
Feeling in Others: Essays on Empathy and Suffering in Modern Culture addresses different kinds of suffering as presented in texts, visual and verbal, and proposes empathy as an ethical exigency of the act of reading and critical tool. The volume brings together contributions from Americanists in France, Norway, Austria, Hungary, and Spain. It examines paintings, comic strips, autobiographies, fictional narratives, and poems on pain from a variety of critical perspectives, bringing together the fields of cognitive psychology, phenomenology, literary criticism, and architecture to account for the complexity of the contagious difference of pain.
Bd. 6, 2008, 176 S., 24,90 €, br., ISBN 978-3-8258-0790-0

Wilfried Raussert; John Miller Jones (Eds.)
Traveling Sounds
Music, Migration, and Identity in the U.S. and Beyond

Within their approach to trace the routes of music and music's impact on identity formation the editors take the popularity of American music more or less for granted. Most genres addressed in this study have emerged within the multiethnic United States or the Americas on a larger scale, most have traversed through the Americas and, in different adaptations, through different parts of the world. Tracing the migration of sounds, the editors see American music at home and abroad as an intricate part of a historical process of globalization and as embedded in complex and multidirectional processes of exchange and transformation. They understand the migration of American forms of music not as a one-dimensional, homogenizing process of Americanization but rather as a multidirectional journey with diverse and multilayered forms of music emerging in different and shifting locales. The contributors cover a broad range of musical genres, ranging from sacred music and avant- garde music to jazz, reggae, and rock. Moreover, crossovers between film, theater, video art and music are explored. In its interdisciplinary and international orientation this book will contribute to the new direction American Studies has taken recently and expand a cultural studies approach to the field of music at the same time.

Bd. 8, 2008, 360 S., 34,90 €, br., ISBN 978-3-8258-1328-4

LIT Verlag Berlin – Hamburg – London – Münster – Wien – Zürich
Fresnostr. 2 48159 Münster
Tel.: 0251 / 620 32 22 – Fax: 0251 / 922 60 99
e-Mail: vertrieb@lit-verlag.de – http://www.lit-verlag.de